Library Mascot Cage Match

Library Mascot Cage Match

an Unshelved® collection
by Bill Barnes and Gene Ambaum

**OVERDUE
MEDIA**
Seattle

"Unshelved" is a registered trademark of Overdue Media LLC.

Library Mascot Cage Match copyright ©2005 Overdue Media LLC. All rights reserved. No part of this book may be used or reproduced in any manner whatsoever without written permission except in the case of reprints in the context of reviews. For information visit http://www.overduemedia.com.

Reprinting *Unshelved* comic strips originally published on the Overdue Media LLC website from February 16, 2004 to February 15, 2005, the American Library Association website, and *ALA CogNotes* newspapers in June 2004 and January 2005. Comic strips copyright © 2004 and 2005.

The stories, characters, and incidents portrayed in this book are entirely fictional. Any resemblance to persons living or dead is entirely coincidental.

ISBN: 0-9740353-2-7

First printing: May 2005

Printed in Canada.

Introduction

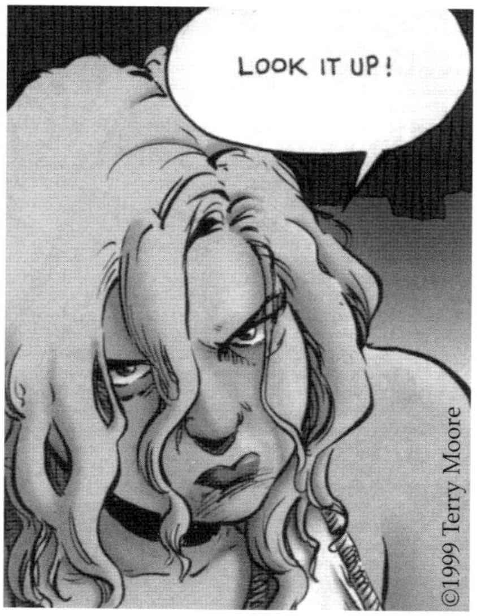
LOOK IT UP!
©1999 Terry Moore

Terry Moore is the Eisner Award-winning creator of **Strangers in Paradise**, one of the best-selling and most beloved graphic novels of our time.

Unshelved is a chronicle of the Mallville Public Library and the people who give it life, but in a very real sense it is your local library. Dewey, Mel, Tamara, Colleen… you've seen them working behind the counter or out on the floor. You've seen a 12-year old Merv haunt the computer area. You've smiled at Buddy the Book Beaver handing out flyers in the parking lot. You've avoided Ned the nudist in the civil liberties section. Well, maybe your library doesn't have a resident nudist but nevertheless, *Unshelved* is good stuff.

Unshelved is the brainchild of writer/librarian Gene Ambaum (a pen name) and cartoonist Bill Barnes. Strips are posted daily at their extremely popular website. Merchandise and apparel from the strip sell like hotcakes at the web store and conventions where the two creators meet their legion of fans and sign autographs. Despite Ambaum's well-known fear of flying, he and Barnes travel extensively to libraries and trade meetings all over the country, delivering key-note speeches and, again, meeting more fans and signing more autographs.

Why is *Unshelved* so popular? Because Ambaum writes about the life of librarians with affection and humor. He likes people, and it shows, but he also thinks they're funny. Reading *Unshelved*, we're compelled to agree. Colleen's hopeless struggle with technology, Tamara's vegan tranquility, Mel's reluctant mother-figure role as head librarian and Dewey, the twenty-something prince of intellectual irony who seems determined to put off maturity as long as possible… all of these characters are unique to *Unshelved* yet familiar to us as people.

What does Dewey look like? How does Mel dress and walk? Ambaum leaves that to Barnes. Barnes is a wonderful cartoonist who instills a sense of place to the citizens of Mallville. He fills *Unshelved* with characters that take on a life of their own through the deft line of his pen. He shows us the indignant befuddlement on Colleen's face, the embraceable optimism of Tamara and the chaos of the aisles during children's hour. It is through Barnes that Dewey and the gang come alive on paper and register in our brains as friends and co-workers, and that's all any cartoonist could hope to achieve.

Together, Barnes and Ambaum are producing a humorous, charming and heart-warming story about the life of a library and the people who work there. They work in a comic strip medium — six inch vignettes — and post them on their website, but the end result is a great book you can find in any library. Very few creators can make that claim and, as a result, Barnes and Ambaum are in a league of their own. *Library Mascot Cage Match* is just the latest collection from this inspired team. Let's hope there will be many, many more.

Terry Moore
Houston
March 2005

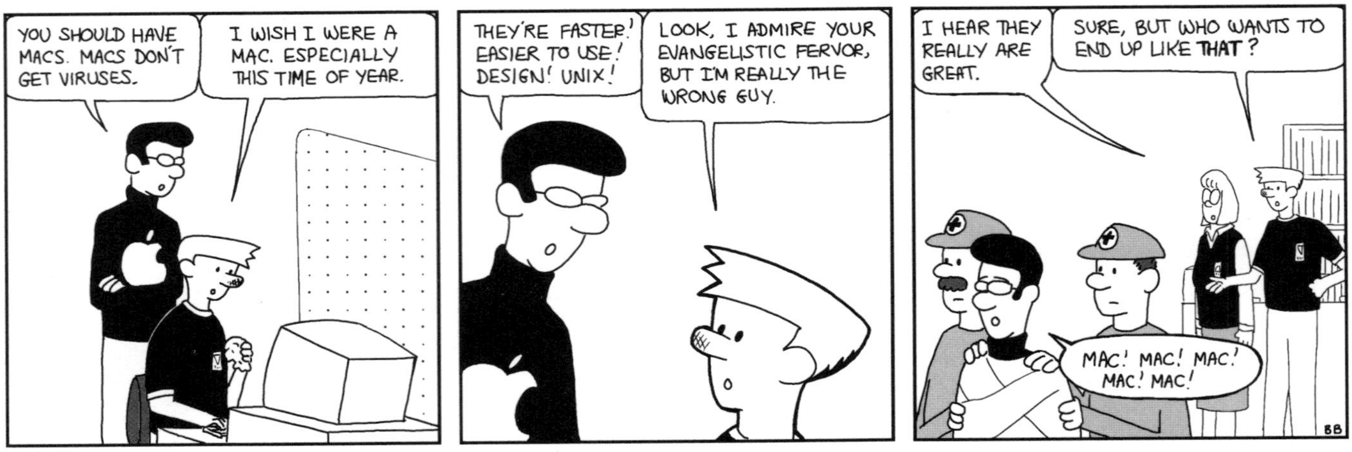
YOU SHOULD HAVE MACS. MACS DON'T GET VIRUSES.
I WISH I WERE A MAC. ESPECIALLY THIS TIME OF YEAR.
THEY'RE FASTER! EASIER TO USE! DESIGN! UNIX!
LOOK, I ADMIRE YOUR EVANGELISTIC FERVOR, BUT I'M REALLY THE WRONG GUY.
I HEAR THEY REALLY ARE GREAT.
SURE, BUT WHO WANTS TO END UP LIKE **THAT**?
MAC! MAC! MAC! MAC! MAC!

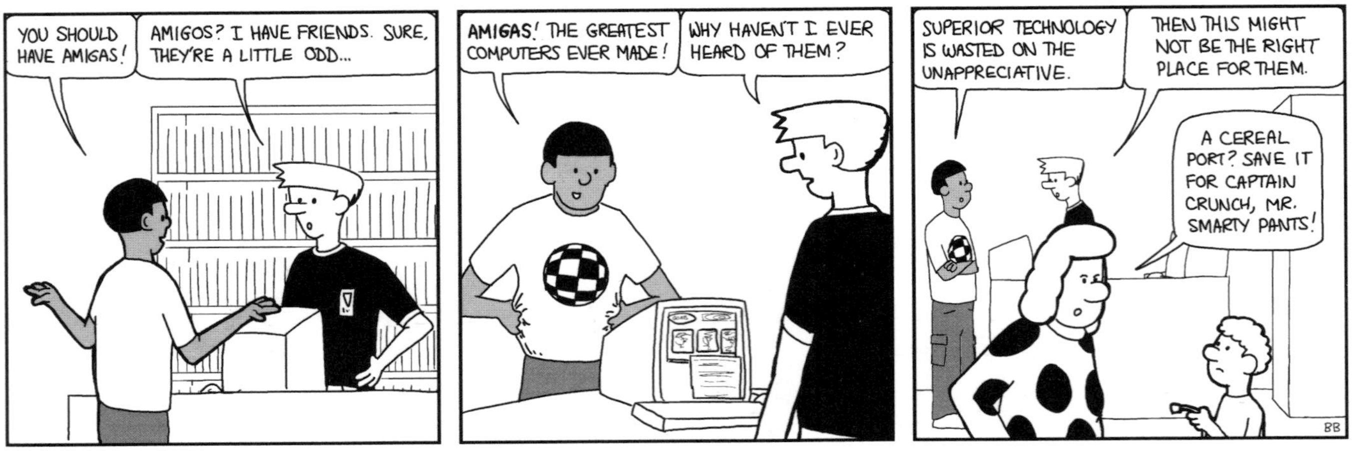
YOU SHOULD HAVE AMIGAS!
AMIGOS? I HAVE FRIENDS. SURE, THEY'RE A LITTLE ODD...
AMIGAS! THE GREATEST COMPUTERS EVER MADE!
WHY HAVEN'T I EVER HEARD OF THEM?
SUPERIOR TECHNOLOGY IS WASTED ON THE UNAPPRECIATIVE.
THEN THIS MIGHT NOT BE THE RIGHT PLACE FOR THEM.
A CEREAL PORT? SAVE IT FOR CAPTAIN CRUNCH, MR. SMARTY PANTS!

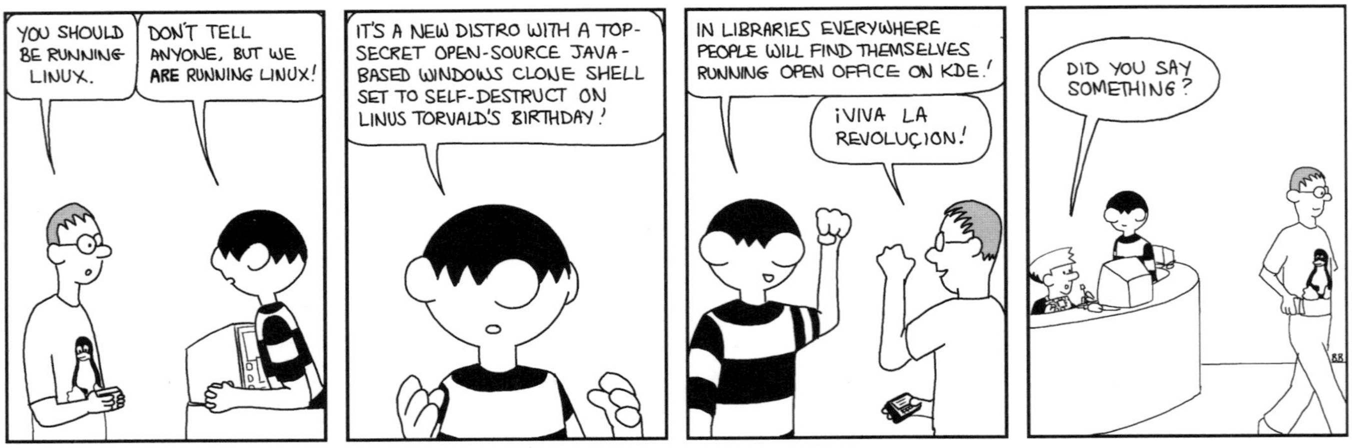
YOU SHOULD BE RUNNING LINUX.
DON'T TELL ANYONE, BUT WE **ARE** RUNNING LINUX!
IT'S A NEW DISTRO WITH A TOP-SECRET OPEN-SOURCE JAVA-BASED WINDOWS CLONE SHELL SET TO SELF-DESTRUCT ON LINUS TORVALD'S BIRTHDAY!
IN LIBRARIES EVERYWHERE PEOPLE WILL FIND THEMSELVES RUNNING OPEN OFFICE ON KDE!
¡VIVA LA REVOLUÇION!
DID YOU SAY SOMETHING?

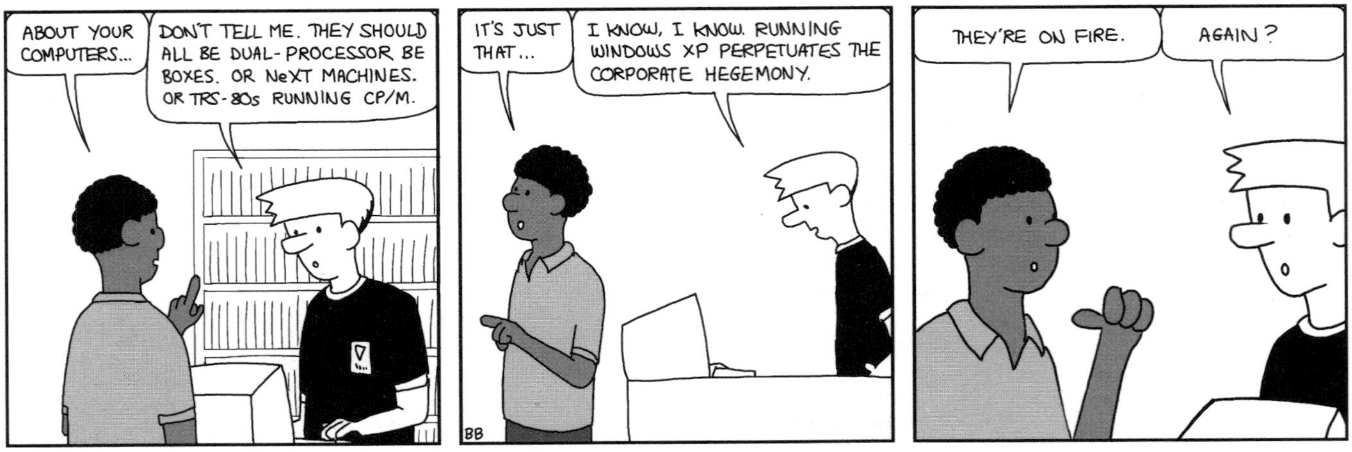
ABOUT YOUR COMPUTERS...
DON'T TELL ME. THEY SHOULD ALL BE DUAL-PROCESSOR BE BOXES. OR NeXT MACHINES. OR TRS-80s RUNNING CP/M.
IT'S JUST THAT...
I KNOW, I KNOW. RUNNING WINDOWS XP PERPETUATES THE CORPORATE HEGEMONY.
THEY'RE ON FIRE.
AGAIN?

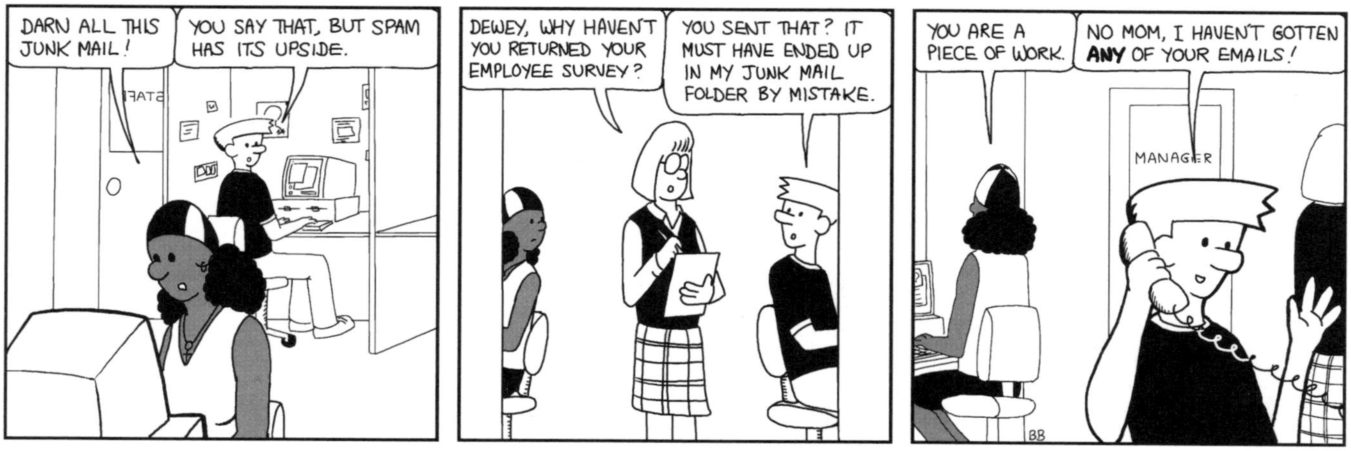
DARN ALL THIS JUNK MAIL!
YOU SAY THAT, BUT SPAM HAS ITS UPSIDE.
DEWEY, WHY HAVEN'T YOU RETURNED YOUR EMPLOYEE SURVEY?
YOU SENT THAT? IT MUST HAVE ENDED UP IN MY JUNK MAIL FOLDER BY MISTAKE.
YOU ARE A PIECE OF WORK.
NO MOM, I HAVEN'T GOTTEN **ANY** OF YOUR EMAILS!
MANAGER
BB

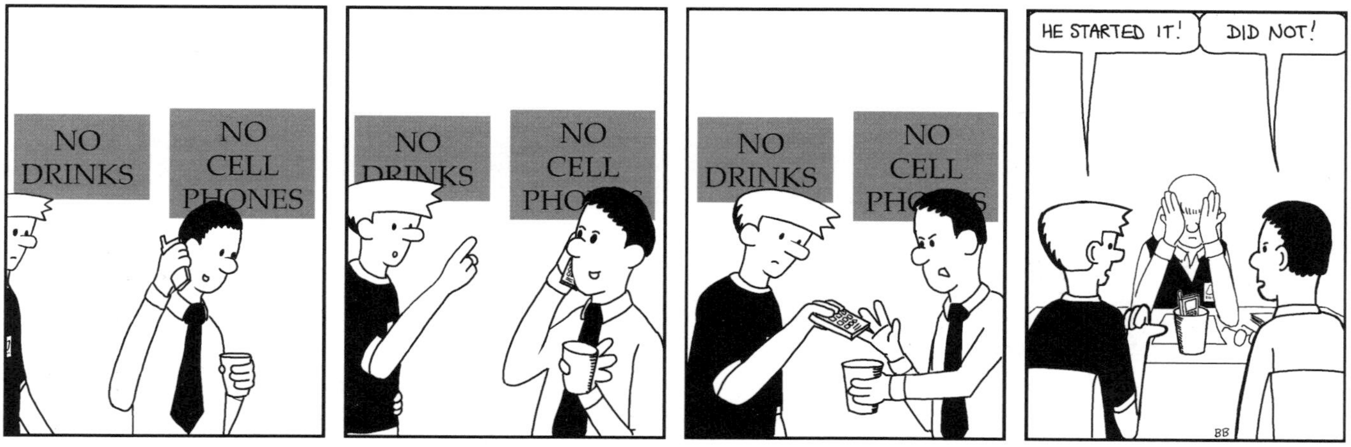
NO DRINKS
NO CELL PHONES
HE STARTED IT!
DID NOT!
BB

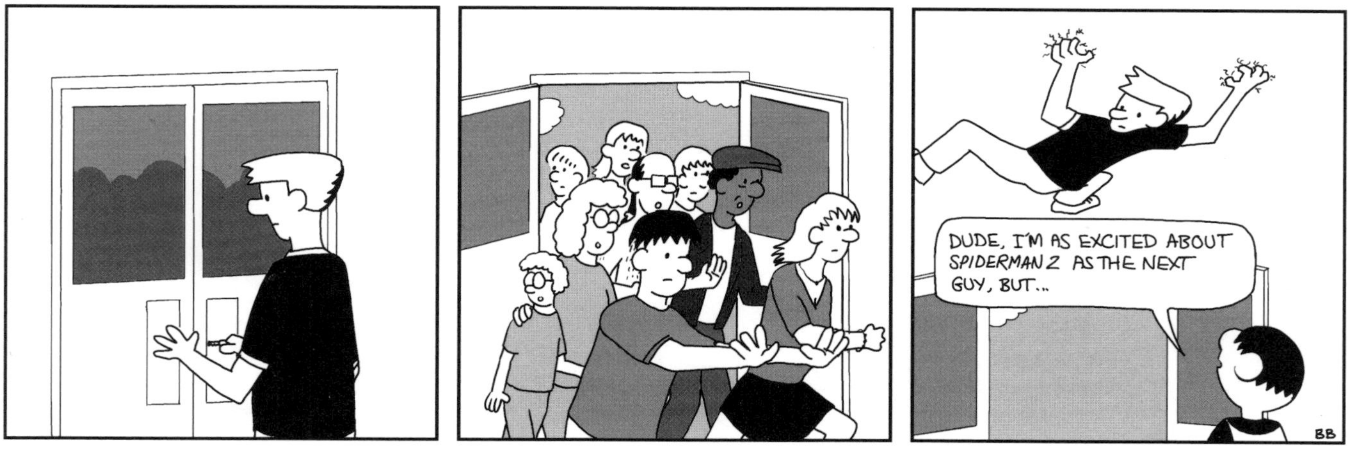
DUDE, I'M AS EXCITED ABOUT *SPIDERMAN 2* AS THE NEXT GUY, BUT...
BB

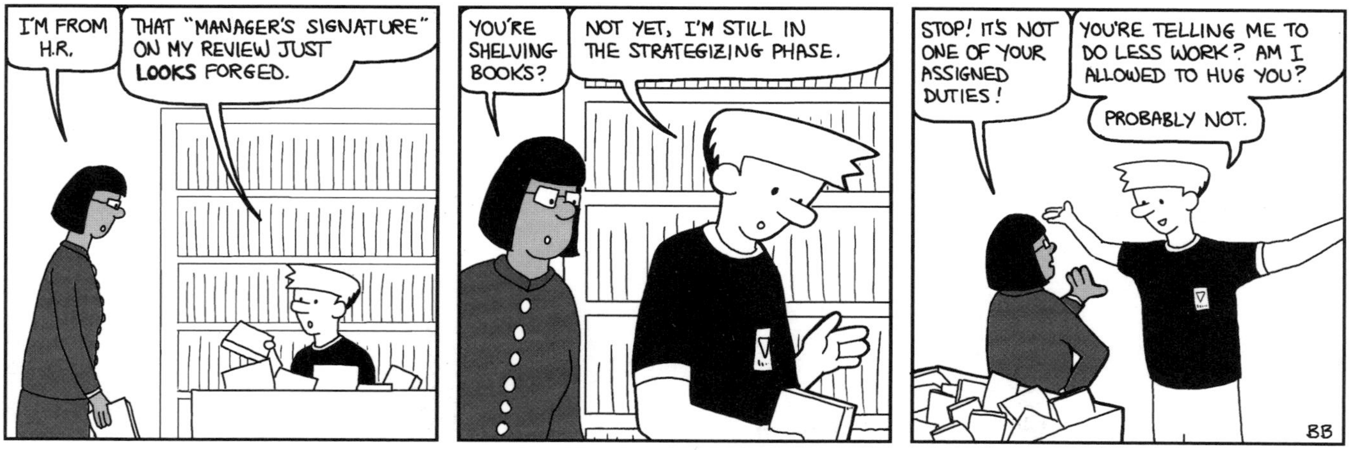
I'M FROM H.R.
THAT "MANAGER'S SIGNATURE" ON MY REVIEW JUST **LOOKS** FORGED.
YOU'RE SHELVING BOOKS?
NOT YET, I'M STILL IN THE STRATEGIZING PHASE.
STOP! IT'S NOT ONE OF YOUR ASSIGNED DUTIES!
YOU'RE TELLING ME TO DO LESS WORK? AM I ALLOWED TO HUG YOU?
PROBABLY NOT.
BB

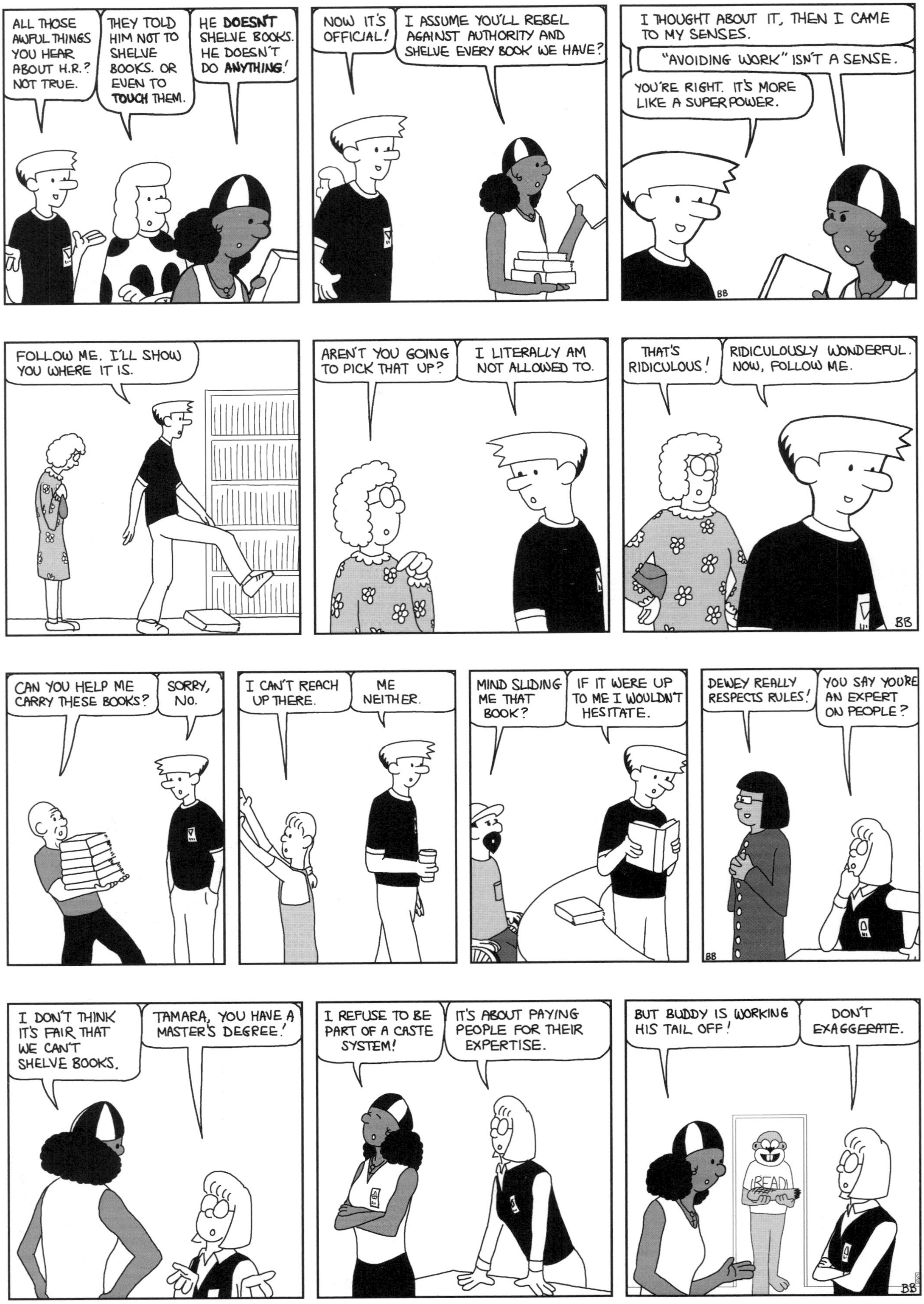
ALL THOSE AWFUL THINGS YOU HEAR ABOUT H.R.? NOT TRUE.
THEY TOLD HIM NOT TO SHELVE BOOKS. OR EVEN TO TOUCH THEM.
HE DOESN'T SHELVE BOOKS. HE DOESN'T DO ANYTHING!
NOW IT'S OFFICIAL!
I ASSUME YOU'LL REBEL AGAINST AUTHORITY AND SHELVE EVERY BOOK WE HAVE?
I THOUGHT ABOUT IT, THEN I CAME TO MY SENSES.
"AVOIDING WORK" ISN'T A SENSE.
YOU'RE RIGHT. IT'S MORE LIKE A SUPERPOWER.
BB
FOLLOW ME. I'LL SHOW YOU WHERE IT IS.
AREN'T YOU GOING TO PICK THAT UP?
I LITERALLY AM NOT ALLOWED TO.
THAT'S RIDICULOUS!
RIDICULOUSLY WONDERFUL. NOW, FOLLOW ME.
BB
CAN YOU HELP ME CARRY THESE BOOKS?
SORRY, NO.
I CAN'T REACH UP THERE.
ME NEITHER.
MIND SLIDING ME THAT BOOK?
IF IT WERE UP TO ME I WOULDN'T HESITATE.
DEWEY REALLY RESPECTS RULES!
YOU SAY YOU'RE AN EXPERT ON PEOPLE?
BB
I DON'T THINK IT'S FAIR THAT WE CAN'T SHELVE BOOKS.
TAMARA, YOU HAVE A MASTER'S DEGREE!
I REFUSE TO BE PART OF A CASTE SYSTEM!
IT'S ABOUT PAYING PEOPLE FOR THEIR EXPERTISE.
BUT BUDDY IS WORKING HIS TAIL OFF!
DON'T EXAGGERATE.
READ
BB

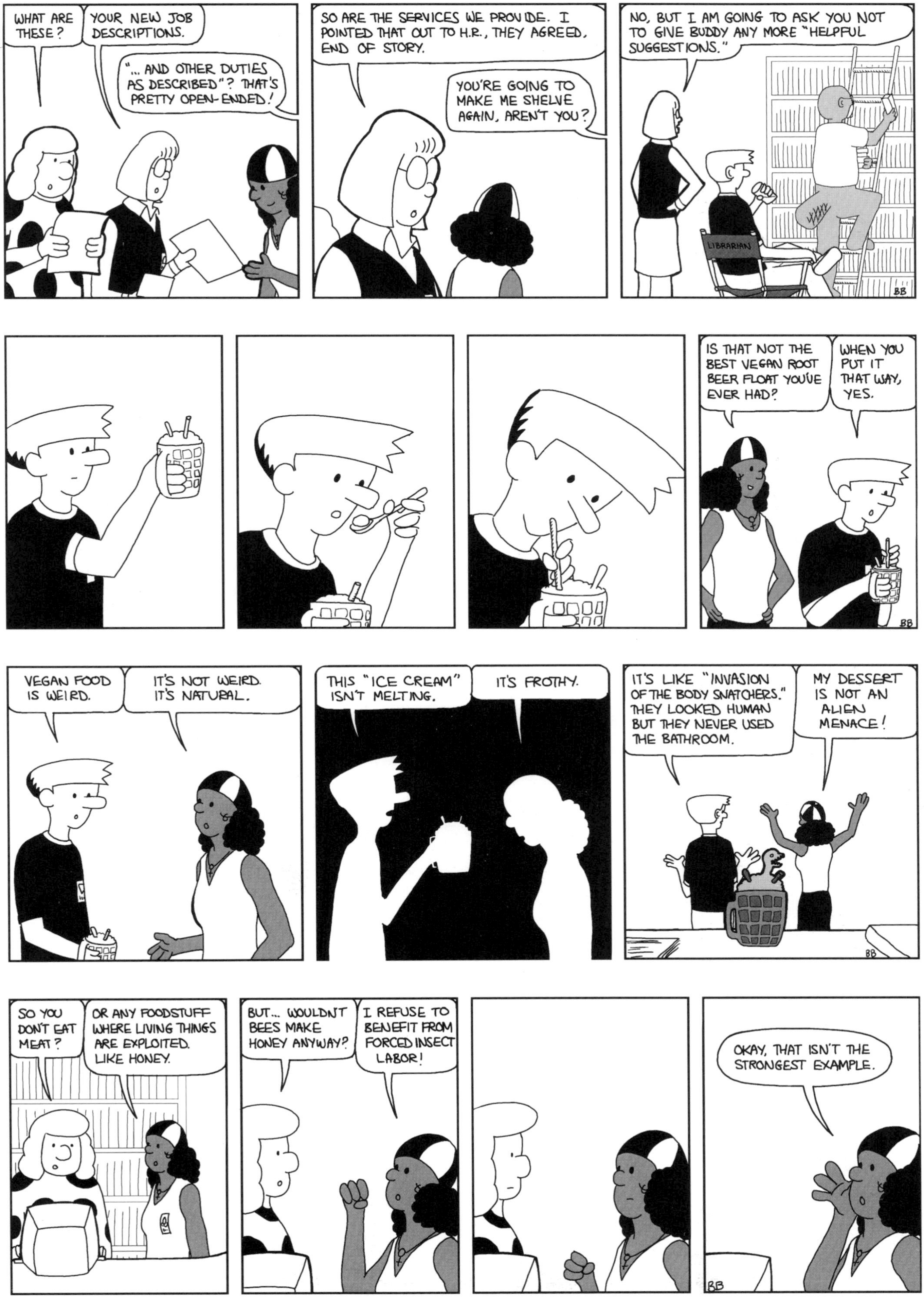
WHAT ARE THESE?
YOUR NEW JOB DESCRIPTIONS.
"... AND OTHER DUTIES AS DESCRIBED"? THAT'S PRETTY OPEN-ENDED!
SO ARE THE SERVICES WE PROVIDE. I POINTED THAT OUT TO H.R., THEY AGREED, END OF STORY.
YOU'RE GOING TO MAKE ME SHELVE AGAIN, AREN'T YOU?
NO, BUT I AM GOING TO ASK YOU NOT TO GIVE BUDDY ANY MORE "HELPFUL SUGGESTIONS."
LIBRARIAN
BB
IS THAT NOT THE BEST VEGAN ROOT BEER FLOAT YOU'VE EVER HAD?
WHEN YOU PUT IT THAT WAY, YES.
BB
VEGAN FOOD IS WEIRD.
IT'S NOT WEIRD. IT'S NATURAL.
THIS "ICE CREAM" ISN'T MELTING.
IT'S FROTHY.
IT'S LIKE "INVASION OF THE BODY SNATCHERS." THEY LOOKED HUMAN BUT THEY NEVER USED THE BATHROOM.
MY DESSERT IS NOT AN ALIEN MENACE!
BB
SO YOU DON'T EAT MEAT?
OR ANY FOODSTUFF WHERE LIVING THINGS ARE EXPLOITED. LIKE HONEY.
BUT... WOULDN'T BEES MAKE HONEY ANYWAY?
I REFUSE TO BENEFIT FROM FORCED INSECT LABOR!
OKAY, THAT ISN'T THE STRONGEST EXAMPLE.
BB

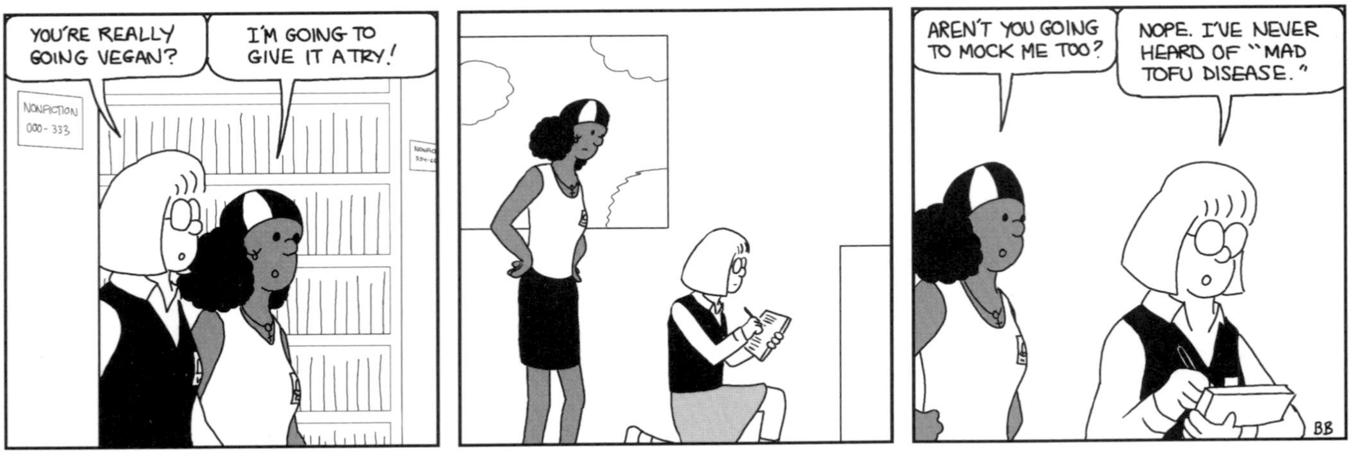
YOU'RE REALLY GOING VEGAN?
I'M GOING TO GIVE IT A TRY!
NONFICTION 000-333
AREN'T YOU GOING TO MOCK ME TOO?
NOPE. I'VE NEVER HEARD OF "MAD TOFU DISEASE."
BB

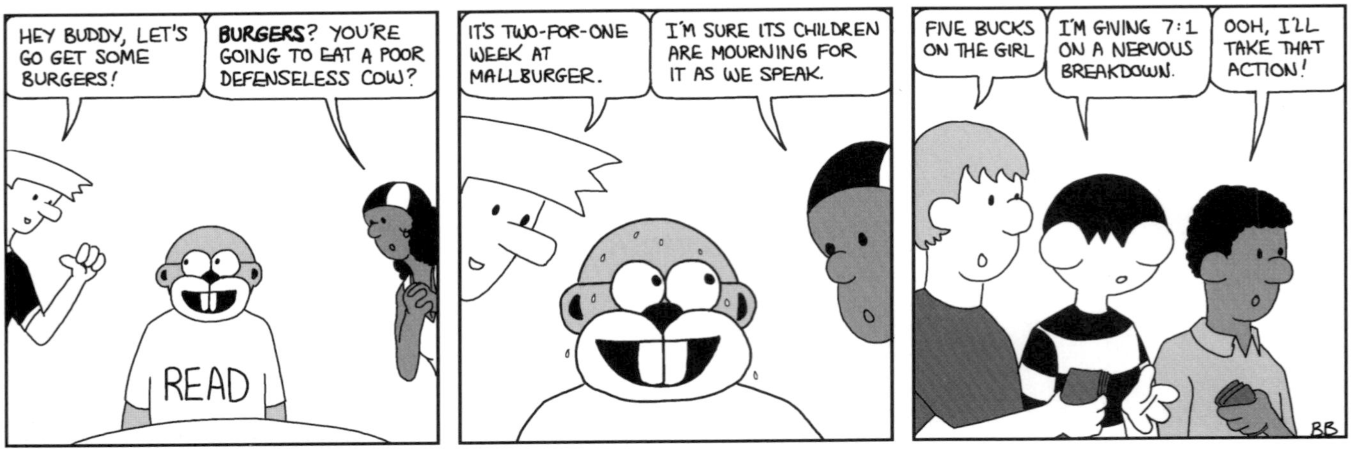
HEY BUDDY, LET'S GO GET SOME BURGERS!
BURGERS? YOU'RE GOING TO EAT A POOR DEFENSELESS COW?
READ
IT'S TWO-FOR-ONE WEEK AT MALLBURGER.
I'M SURE ITS CHILDREN ARE MOURNING FOR IT AS WE SPEAK.
FIVE BUCKS ON THE GIRL
I'M GIVING 7:1 ON A NERVOUS BREAKDOWN.
OOH, I'LL TAKE THAT ACTION!
BB

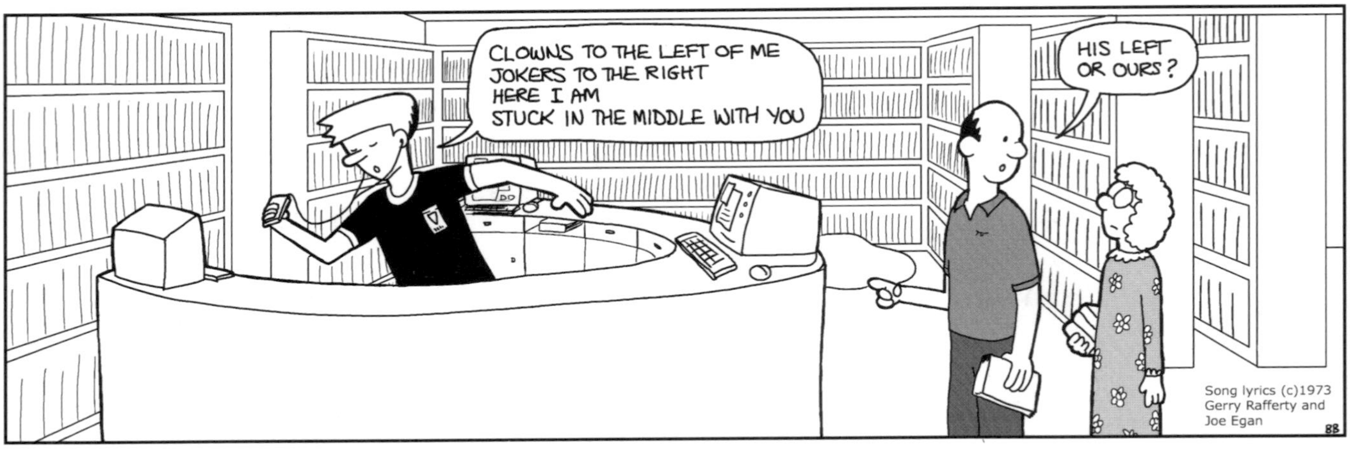
CLOWNS TO THE LEFT OF ME
JOKERS TO THE RIGHT
HERE I AM
STUCK IN THE MIDDLE WITH YOU
HIS LEFT OR OURS?
Song lyrics (c)1973 Gerry Rafferty and Joe Egan
BB

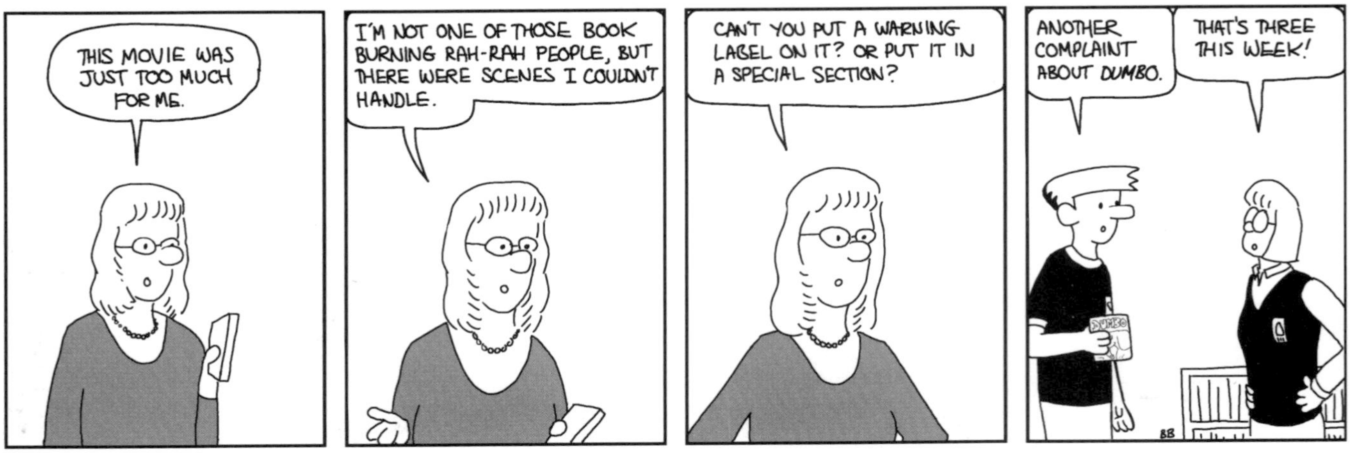
THIS MOVIE WAS JUST TOO MUCH FOR ME.
I'M NOT ONE OF THOSE BOOK BURNING RAH-RAH PEOPLE, BUT THERE WERE SCENES I COULDN'T HANDLE.
CAN'T YOU PUT A WARNING LABEL ON IT? OR PUT IT IN A SPECIAL SECTION?
ANOTHER COMPLAINT ABOUT DUMBO.
THAT'S THREE THIS WEEK!
BB

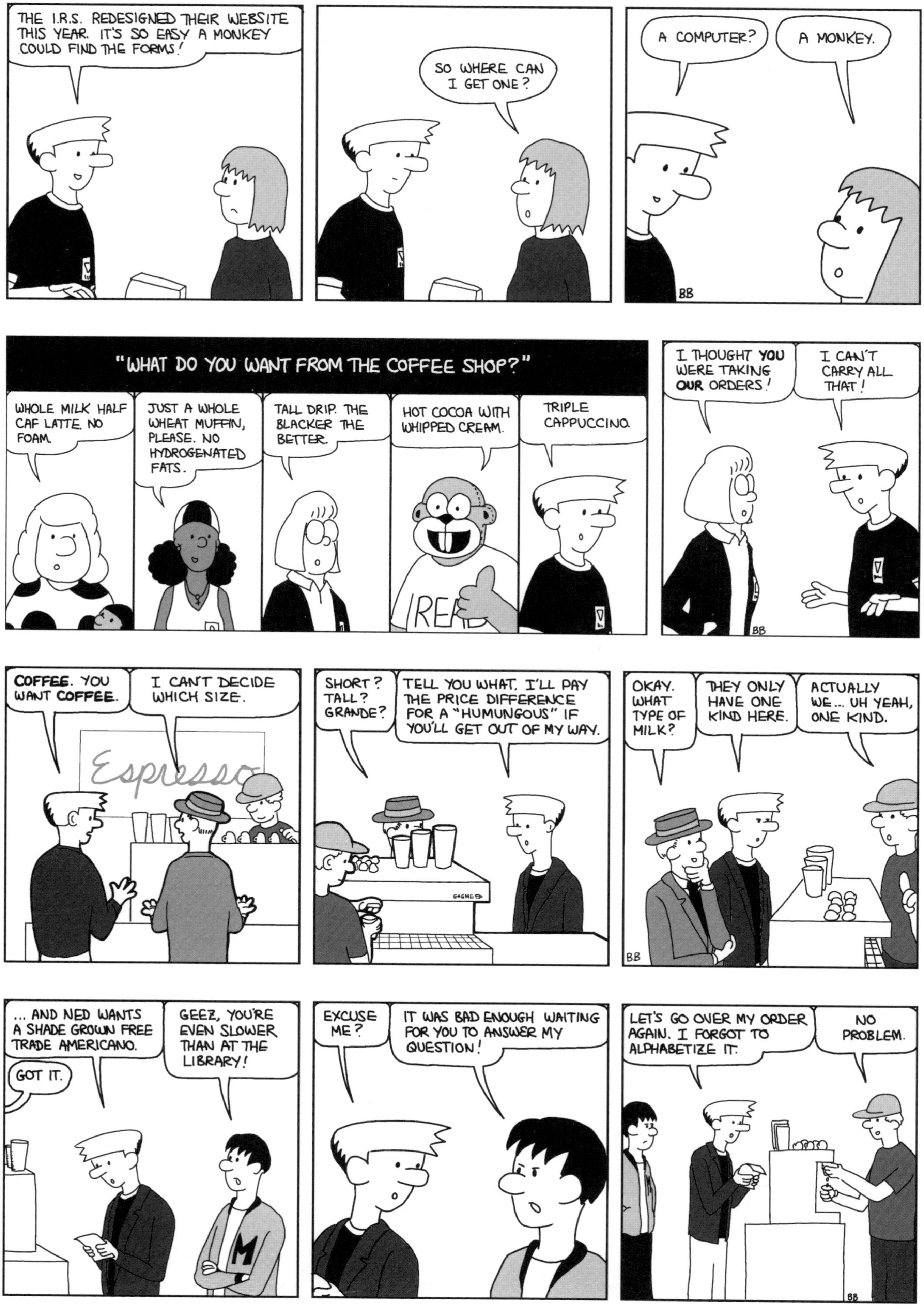
THE I.R.S. REDESIGNED THEIR WEBSITE THIS YEAR. IT'S SO EASY A MONKEY COULD FIND THE FORMS!
SO WHERE CAN I GET ONE?
A COMPUTER?
A MONKEY.
"WHAT DO YOU WANT FROM THE COFFEE SHOP?"
WHOLE MILK HALF CAF LATTE. NO FOAM.
JUST A WHOLE WHEAT MUFFIN, PLEASE. NO HYDROGENATED FATS.
TALL DRIP. THE BLACKER THE BETTER.
HOT COCOA WITH WHIPPED CREAM.
TRIPLE CAPPUCCINO.
I THOUGHT **YOU** WERE TAKING **OUR** ORDERS!
I CAN'T CARRY ALL THAT!
COFFEE. YOU WANT **COFFEE**.
I CAN'T DECIDE WHICH SIZE.
Espresso
SHORT? TALL? GRANDE?
TELL YOU WHAT. I'LL PAY THE PRICE DIFFERENCE FOR A "HUMUNGOUS" IF YOU'LL GET OUT OF MY WAY.
OKAY. WHAT TYPE OF MILK?
THEY ONLY HAVE ONE KIND HERE.
ACTUALLY WE... UH YEAH, ONE KIND.
... AND NED WANTS A SHADE GROWN FREE TRADE AMERICANO.
GOT IT.
GEEZ, YOU'RE EVEN SLOWER THAN AT THE LIBRARY!
EXCUSE ME?
IT WAS BAD ENOUGH WAITING FOR YOU TO ANSWER MY QUESTION!
LET'S GO OVER MY ORDER AGAIN. I FORGOT TO ALPHABETIZE IT.
NO PROBLEM.

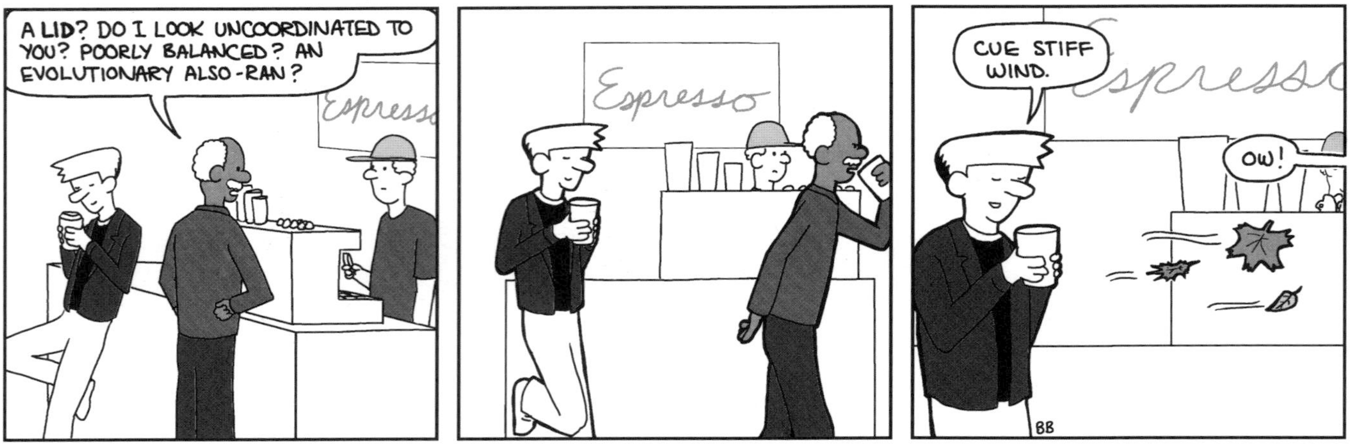
A LID? DO I LOOK UNCOORDINATED TO YOU? POORLY BALANCED? AN EVOLUTIONARY ALSO-RAN?
Espresso
CUE STIFF WIND.
OW!
BB

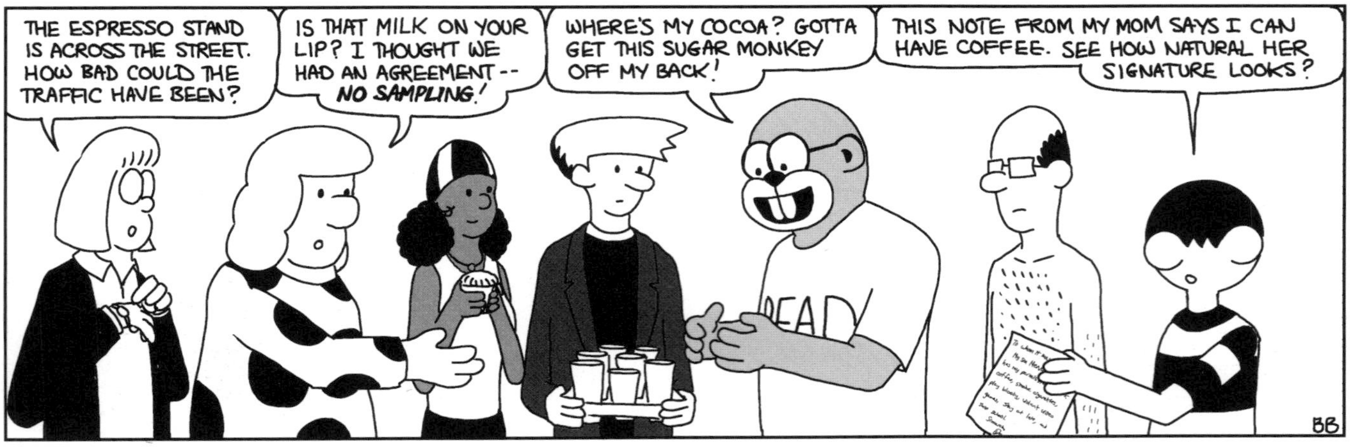
THE ESPRESSO STAND IS ACROSS THE STREET. HOW BAD COULD THE TRAFFIC HAVE BEEN?
IS THAT MILK ON YOUR LIP? I THOUGHT WE HAD AN AGREEMENT -- NO SAMPLING!
WHERE'S MY COCOA? GOTTA GET THIS SUGAR MONKEY OFF MY BACK!
THIS NOTE FROM MY MOM SAYS I CAN HAVE COFFEE. SEE HOW NATURAL HER SIGNATURE LOOKS?
BB

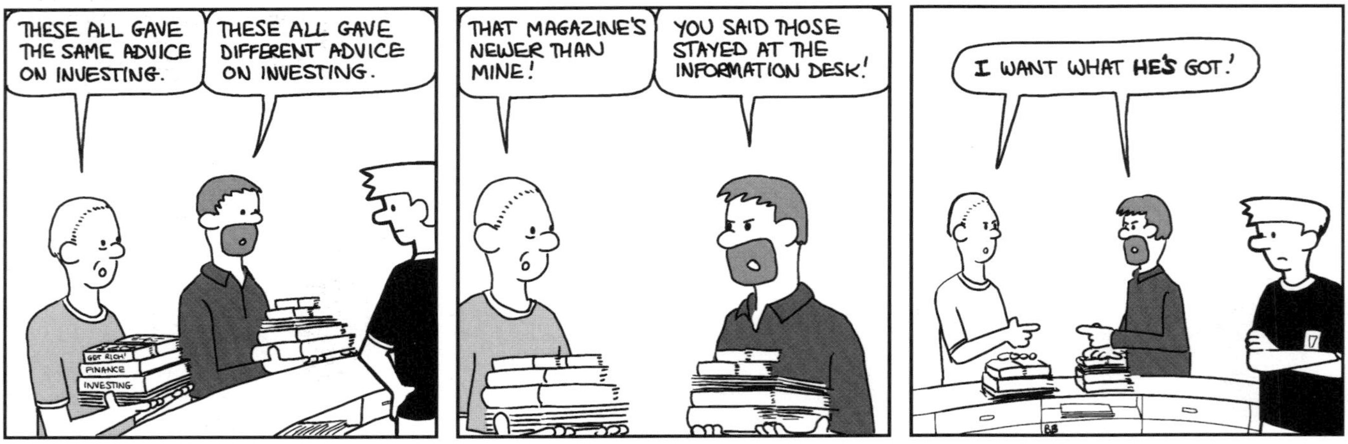
THESE ALL GAVE THE SAME ADVICE ON INVESTING.
THESE ALL GAVE DIFFERENT ADVICE ON INVESTING.
GET RICH!
FINANCE
INVESTING
THAT MAGAZINE'S NEWER THAN MINE!
YOU SAID THOSE STAYED AT THE INFORMATION DESK!
I WANT WHAT HE'S GOT!
BB

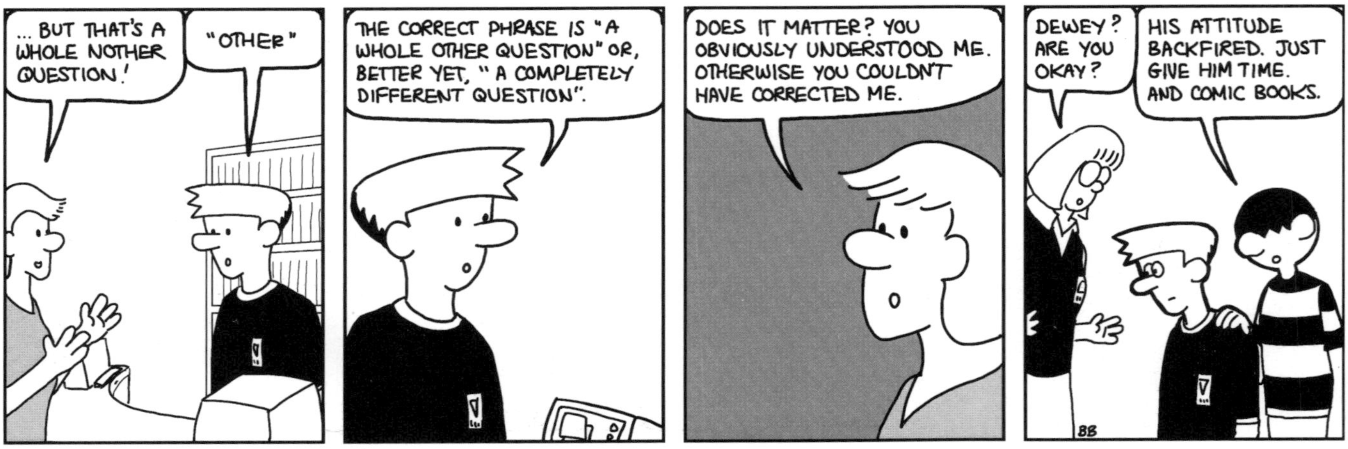
... BUT THAT'S A WHOLE NOTHER QUESTION!
"OTHER"
THE CORRECT PHRASE IS "A WHOLE OTHER QUESTION" OR, BETTER YET, "A COMPLETELY DIFFERENT QUESTION".
DOES IT MATTER? YOU OBVIOUSLY UNDERSTOOD ME. OTHERWISE YOU COULDN'T HAVE CORRECTED ME.
DEWEY? ARE YOU OKAY?
HIS ATTITUDE BACKFIRED. JUST GIVE HIM TIME. AND COMIC BOOKS.
BB

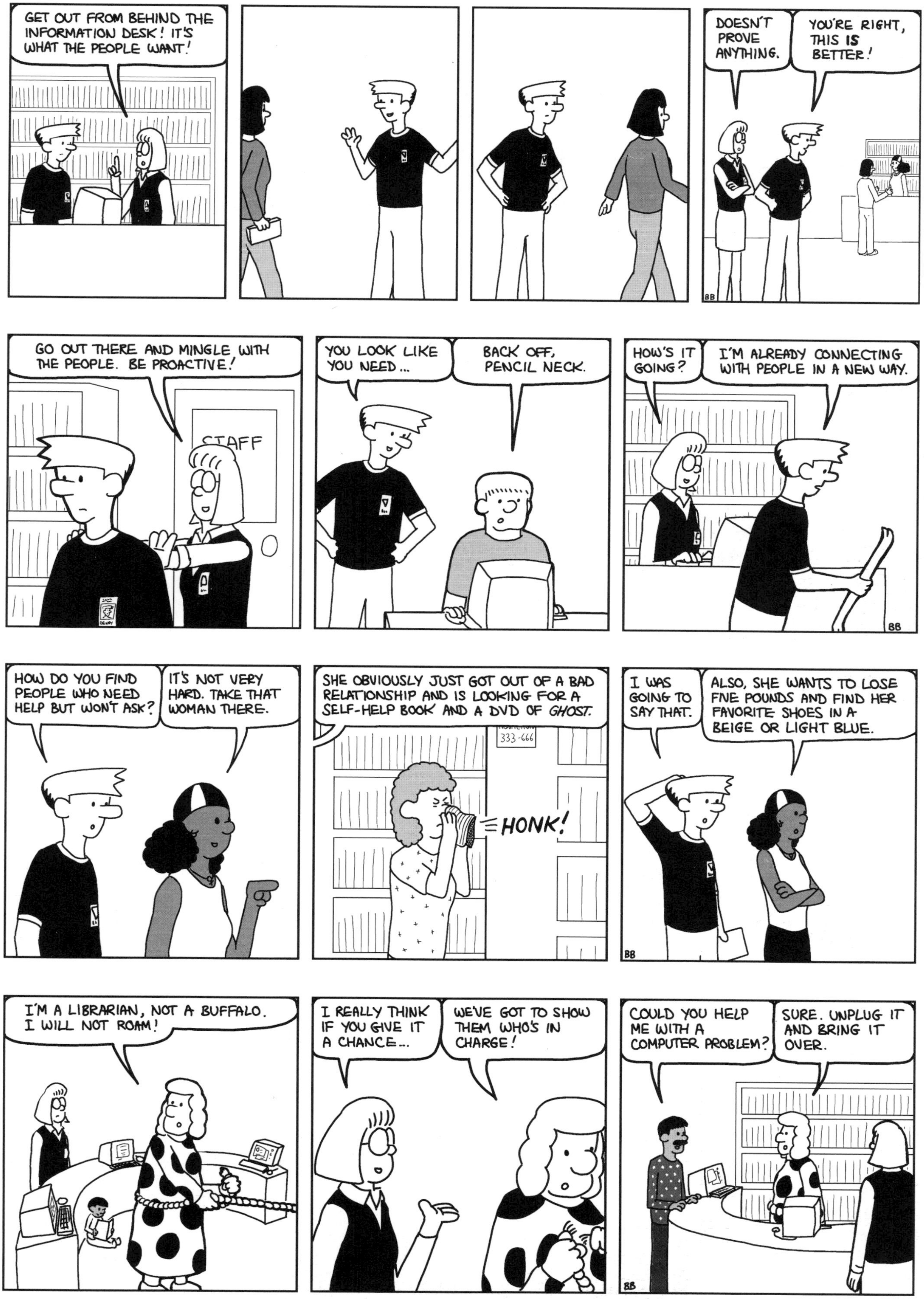
GET OUT FROM BEHIND THE INFORMATION DESK! IT'S WHAT THE PEOPLE WANT!
DOESN'T PROVE ANYTHING.
YOU'RE RIGHT, THIS **IS** BETTER!
GO OUT THERE AND MINGLE WITH THE PEOPLE. BE PROACTIVE!
STAFF
YOU LOOK LIKE YOU NEED...
BACK OFF, PENCIL NECK.
HOW'S IT GOING?
I'M ALREADY CONNECTING WITH PEOPLE IN A NEW WAY.
HOW DO YOU FIND PEOPLE WHO NEED HELP BUT WON'T ASK?
IT'S NOT VERY HARD. TAKE THAT WOMAN THERE.
SHE OBVIOUSLY JUST GOT OUT OF A BAD RELATIONSHIP AND IS LOOKING FOR A SELF-HELP BOOK AND A DVD OF *GHOST.*
HONK!
I WAS GOING TO SAY THAT.
ALSO, SHE WANTS TO LOSE FIVE POUNDS AND FIND HER FAVORITE SHOES IN A BEIGE OR LIGHT BLUE.
I'M A LIBRARIAN, NOT A BUFFALO. I WILL NOT ROAM!
I REALLY THINK IF YOU GIVE IT A CHANCE...
WE'VE GOT TO SHOW THEM WHO'S IN CHARGE!
COULD YOU HELP ME WITH A COMPUTER PROBLEM?
SURE. UNPLUG IT AND BRING IT OVER.

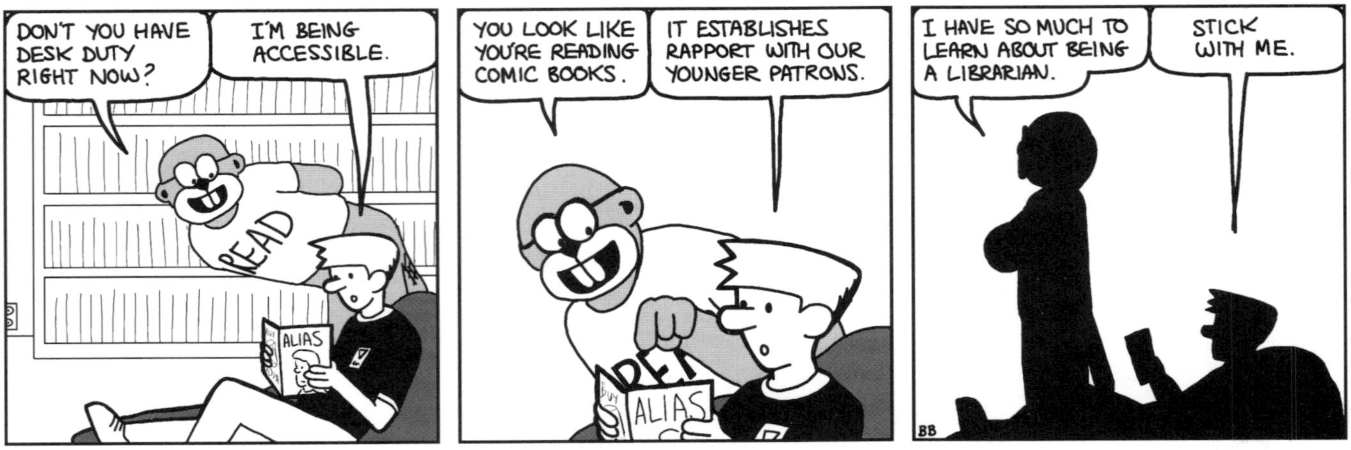
DON'T YOU HAVE DESK DUTY RIGHT NOW?
I'M BEING ACCESSIBLE.
READ
ALIAS
YOU LOOK LIKE YOU'RE READING COMIC BOOKS.
IT ESTABLISHES RAPPORT WITH OUR YOUNGER PATRONS.
ALIAS
I HAVE SO MUCH TO LEARN ABOUT BEING A LIBRARIAN.
STICK WITH ME.
BB

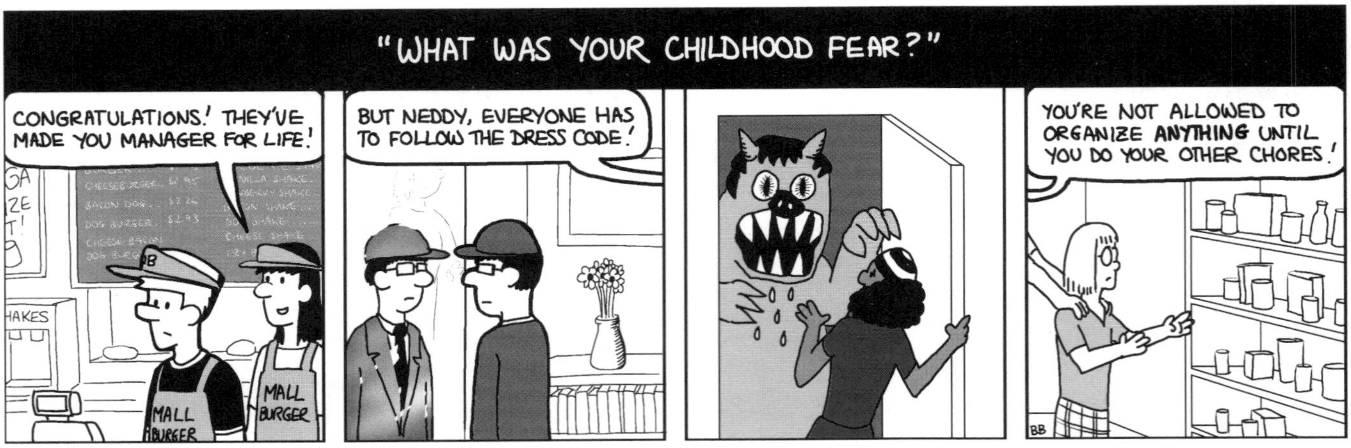
"WHAT WAS YOUR CHILDHOOD FEAR?"
CONGRATULATIONS! THEY'VE MADE YOU MANAGER FOR LIFE!
MALL BURGER
MALL BURGER
BUT NEDDY, EVERYONE HAS TO FOLLOW THE DRESS CODE!
YOU'RE NOT ALLOWED TO ORGANIZE **ANYTHING** UNTIL YOU DO YOUR OTHER CHORES!
BB

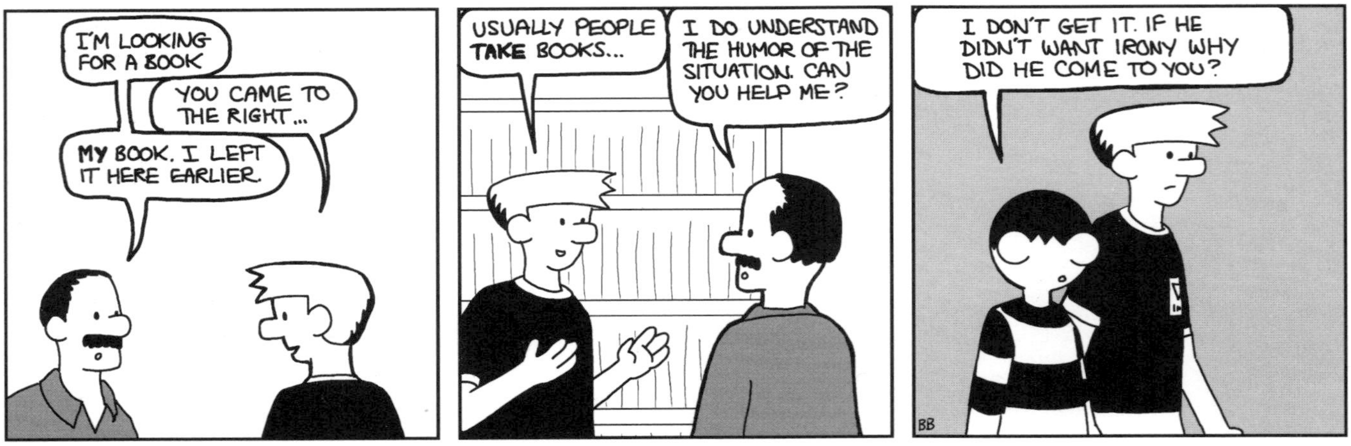
I'M LOOKING FOR A BOOK
YOU CAME TO THE RIGHT...
MY BOOK. I LEFT IT HERE EARLIER.
USUALLY PEOPLE **TAKE** BOOKS...
I DO UNDERSTAND THE HUMOR OF THE SITUATION. CAN YOU HELP ME?
I DON'T GET IT. IF HE DIDN'T WANT IRONY WHY DID HE COME TO YOU?
BB

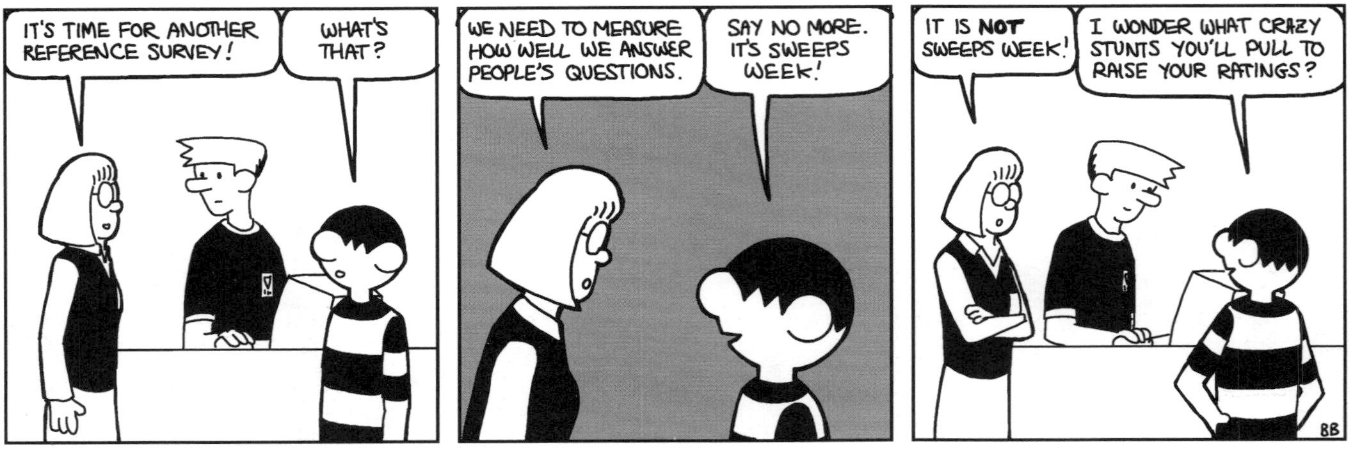
IT'S TIME FOR ANOTHER REFERENCE SURVEY!
WHAT'S THAT?
WE NEED TO MEASURE HOW WELL WE ANSWER PEOPLE'S QUESTIONS.
SAY NO MORE. IT'S SWEEPS WEEK!
IT IS **NOT** SWEEPS WEEK!
I WONDER WHAT CRAZY STUNTS YOU'LL PULL TO RAISE YOUR RATINGS?
BB

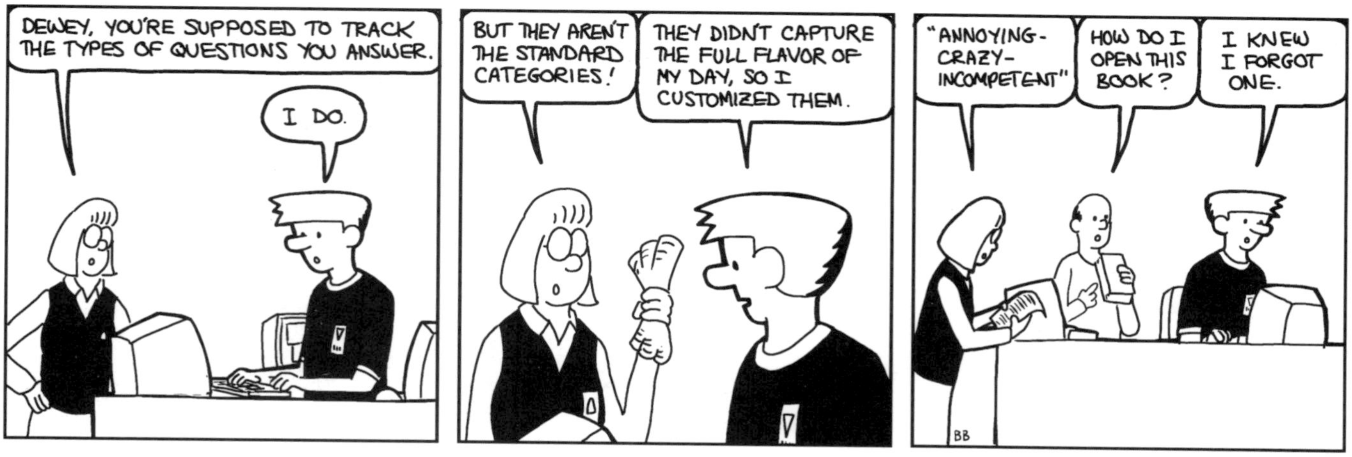
DEWEY, YOU'RE SUPPOSED TO TRACK THE TYPES OF QUESTIONS YOU ANSWER.
I DO.
BUT THEY AREN'T THE STANDARD CATEGORIES!
THEY DIDN'T CAPTURE THE FULL FLAVOR OF MY DAY, SO I CUSTOMIZED THEM.
"ANNOYING-CRAZY-INCOMPETENT"
HOW DO I OPEN THIS BOOK?
I KNEW I FORGOT ONE.
BB

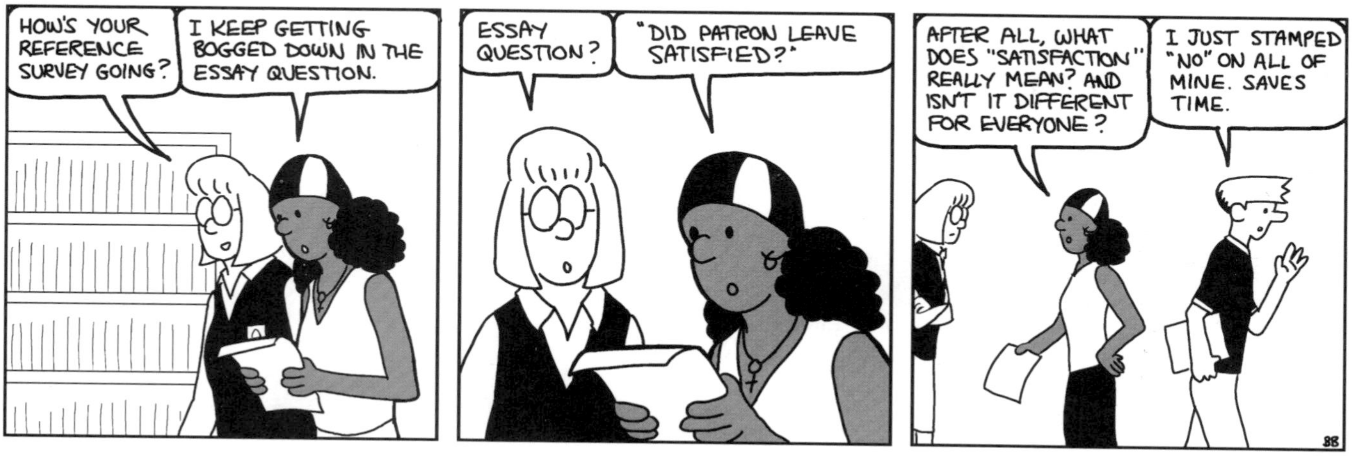
HOW'S YOUR REFERENCE SURVEY GOING?
I KEEP GETTING BOGGED DOWN IN THE ESSAY QUESTION.
ESSAY QUESTION?
"DID PATRON LEAVE SATISFIED?"
AFTER ALL, WHAT DOES "SATISFACTION" REALLY MEAN? AND ISN'T IT DIFFERENT FOR EVERYONE?
I JUST STAMPED "NO" ON ALL OF MINE. SAVES TIME.
BB

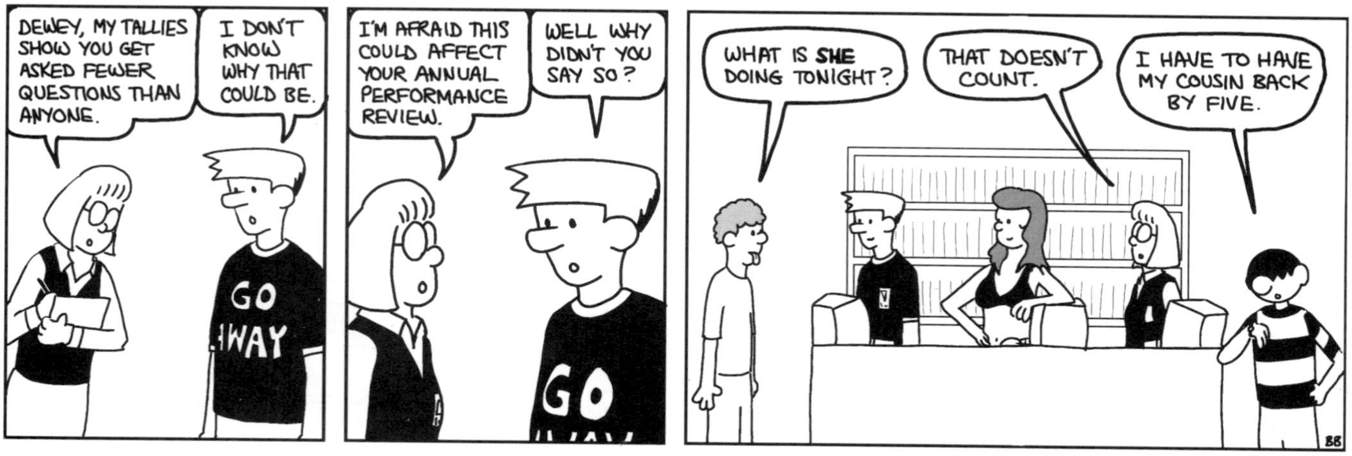
DEWEY, MY TALLIES SHOW YOU GET ASKED FEWER QUESTIONS THAN ANYONE.
I DON'T KNOW WHY THAT COULD BE.
GO AWAY
I'M AFRAID THIS COULD AFFECT YOUR ANNUAL PERFORMANCE REVIEW.
WELL WHY DIDN'T YOU SAY SO?
GO
WHAT IS **SHE** DOING TONIGHT?
THAT DOESN'T COUNT.
I HAVE TO HAVE MY COUSIN BACK BY FIVE.
BB

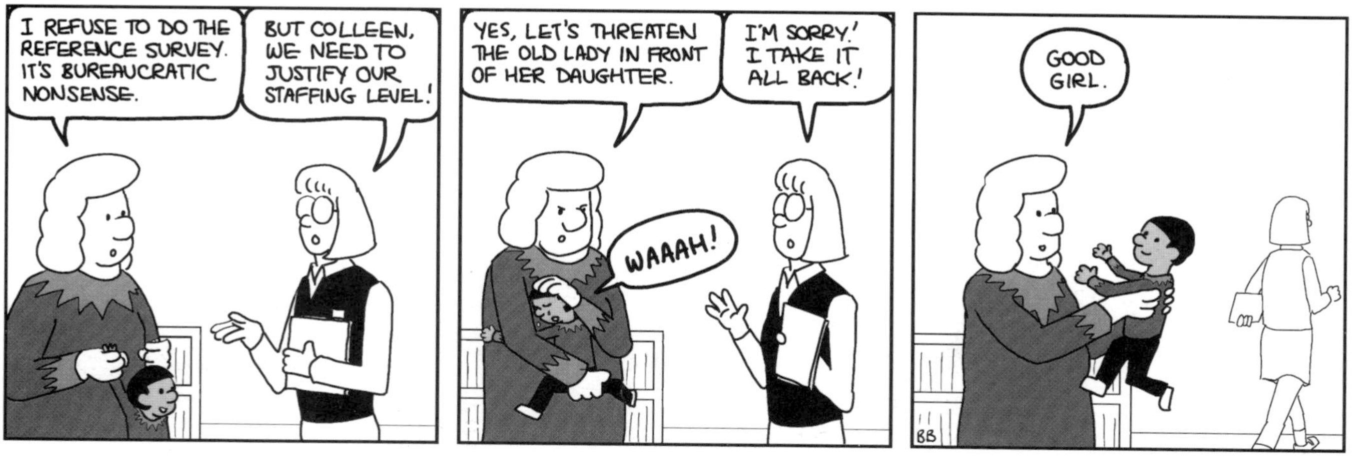
I REFUSE TO DO THE REFERENCE SURVEY. IT'S BUREAUCRATIC NONSENSE.
BUT COLLEEN, WE NEED TO JUSTIFY OUR STAFFING LEVEL!
YES, LET'S THREATEN THE OLD LADY IN FRONT OF HER DAUGHTER.
WAAAH!
I'M SORRY! I TAKE IT ALL BACK!
GOOD GIRL.
BB

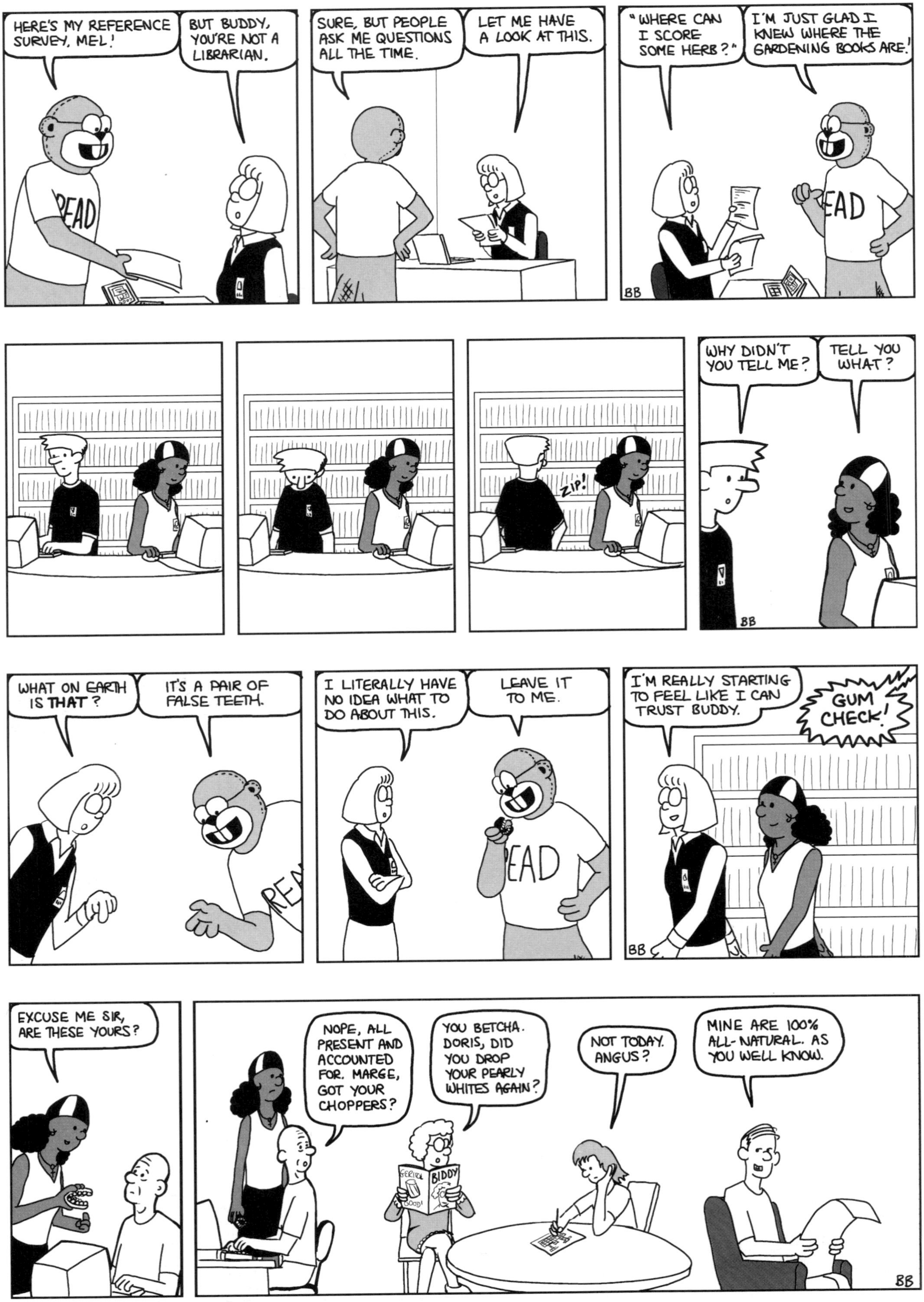
HERE'S MY REFERENCE SURVEY, MEL!
BUT BUDDY, YOU'RE NOT A LIBRARIAN.
SURE, BUT PEOPLE ASK ME QUESTIONS ALL THE TIME.
LET ME HAVE A LOOK AT THIS.
"WHERE CAN I SCORE SOME HERB?"
I'M JUST GLAD I KNEW WHERE THE GARDENING BOOKS ARE!
BB
ZIP!
WHY DIDN'T YOU TELL ME?
TELL YOU WHAT?
BB
WHAT ON EARTH IS **THAT**?
IT'S A PAIR OF FALSE TEETH.
I LITERALLY HAVE NO IDEA WHAT TO DO ABOUT THIS.
LEAVE IT TO ME.
I'M REALLY STARTING TO FEEL LIKE I CAN TRUST BUDDY.
GUM CHECK!
BB
EXCUSE ME SIR, ARE THESE YOURS?
NOPE, ALL PRESENT AND ACCOUNTED FOR. MARGE, GOT YOUR CHOPPERS?
YOU BETCHA. DORIS, DID YOU DROP YOUR PEARLY WHITES AGAIN?
BIDDY
NOT TODAY. ANGUS?
MINE ARE 100% ALL-NATURAL. AS YOU WELL KNOW.
BB

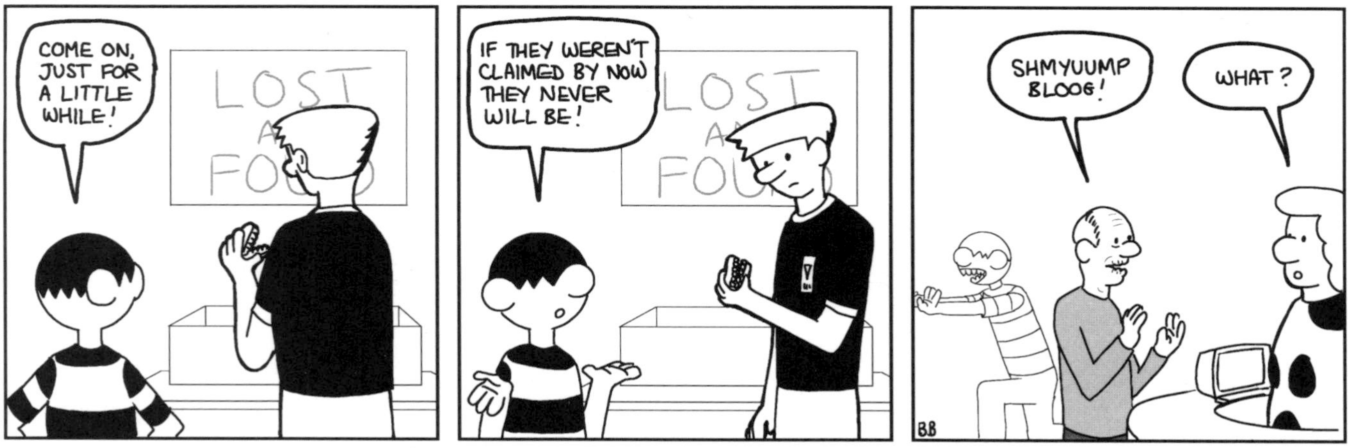
COME ON, JUST FOR A LITTLE WHILE!
IF THEY WEREN'T CLAIMED BY NOW THEY NEVER WILL BE!
SHMYUUMP BLOOG!
WHAT?
BB

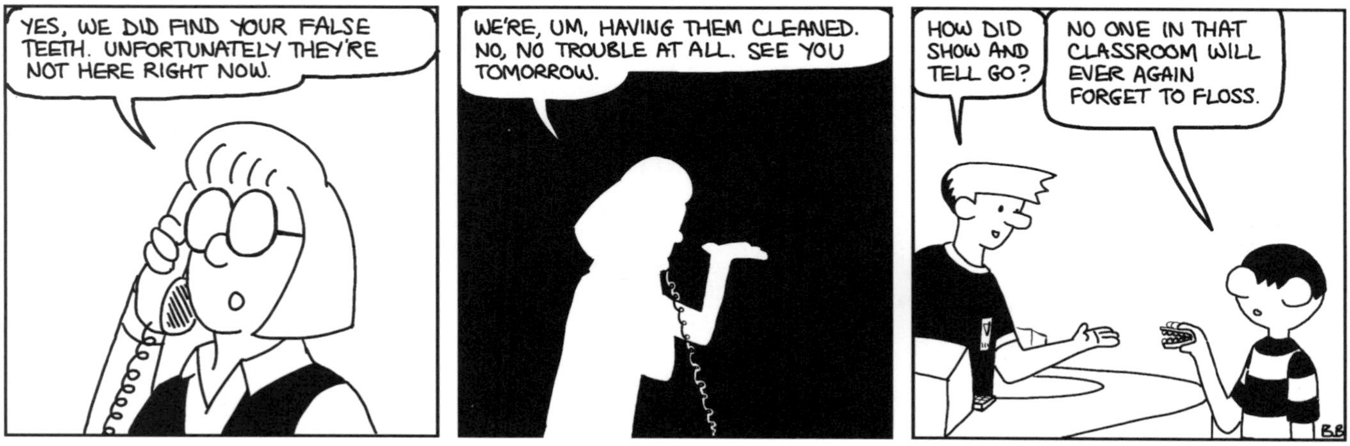
YES, WE DID FIND YOUR FALSE TEETH. UNFORTUNATELY THEY'RE NOT HERE RIGHT NOW.
WE'RE, UM, HAVING THEM CLEANED. NO, NO TROUBLE AT ALL. SEE YOU TOMORROW.
HOW DID SHOW AND TELL GO?
NO ONE IN THAT CLASSROOM WILL EVER AGAIN FORGET TO FLOSS.
BB

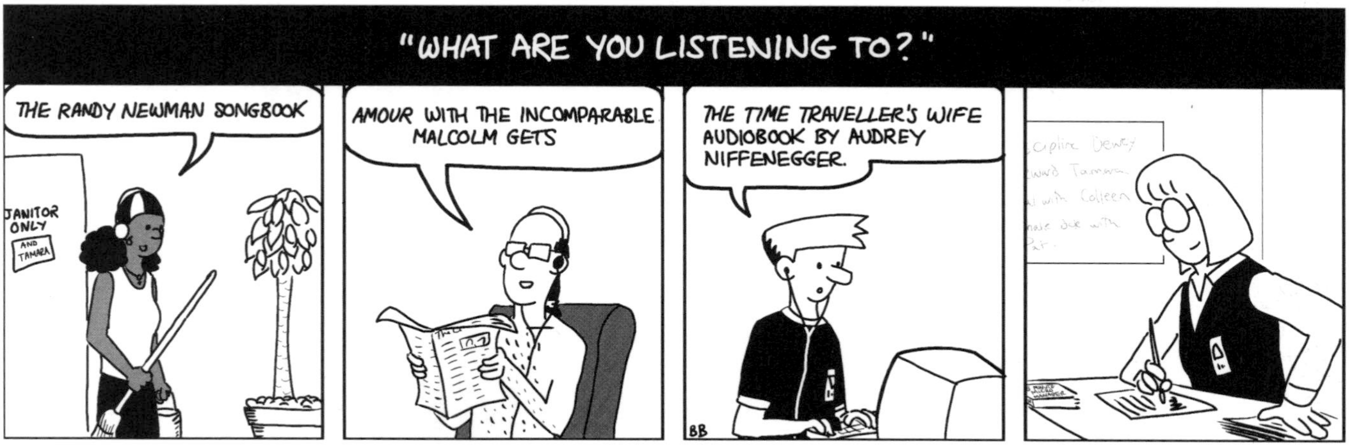
"WHAT ARE YOU LISTENING TO?"
THE RANDY NEWMAN SONGBOOK
JANITOR ONLY
AND TAMARA
AMOUR WITH THE INCOMPARABLE MALCOLM GETS
THE TIME TRAVELLER'S WIFE AUDIOBOOK BY AUDREY NIFFENEGGER.
BB

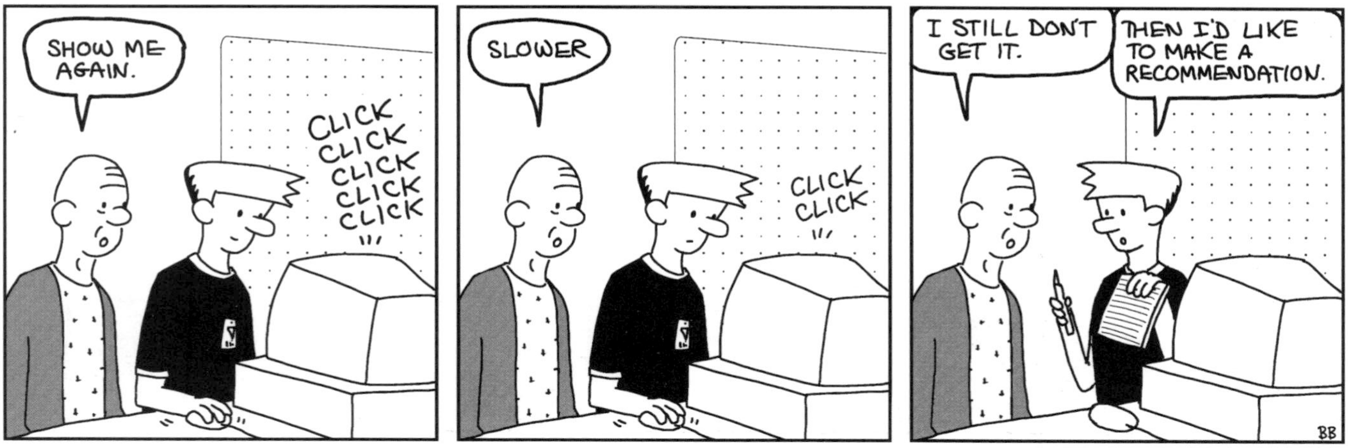
SHOW ME AGAIN.
CLICK CLICK CLICK CLICK CLICK
SLOWER
CLICK CLICK
I STILL DON'T GET IT.
THEN I'D LIKE TO MAKE A RECOMMENDATION.
BB

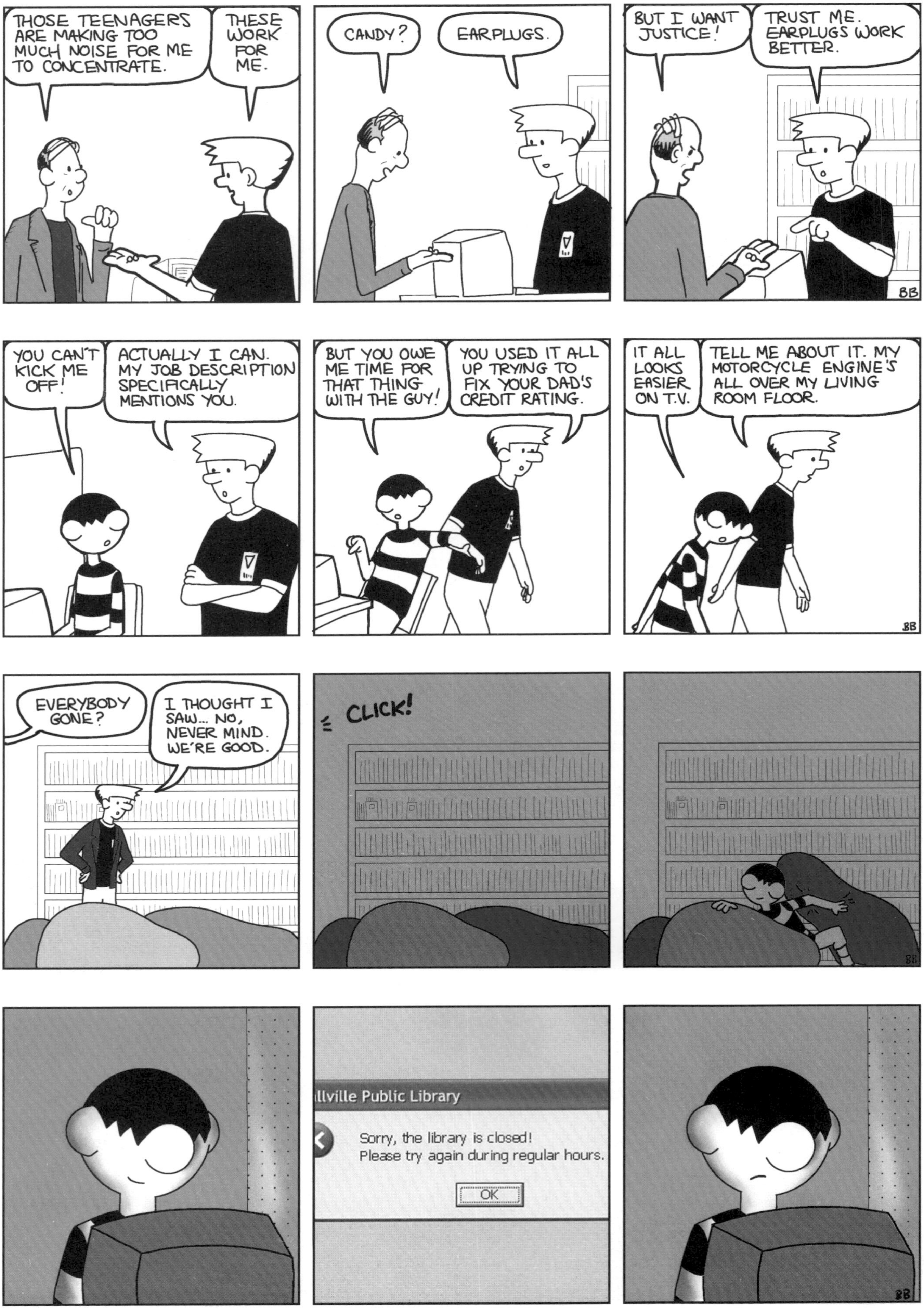
THOSE TEENAGERS ARE MAKING TOO MUCH NOISE FOR ME TO CONCENTRATE.
THESE WORK FOR ME.
CANDY?
EARPLUGS.
BUT I WANT JUSTICE!
TRUST ME. EARPLUGS WORK BETTER.
BB
YOU CAN'T KICK ME OFF!
ACTUALLY I CAN. MY JOB DESCRIPTION SPECIFICALLY MENTIONS YOU.
BUT YOU OWE ME TIME FOR THAT THING WITH THE GUY!
YOU USED IT ALL UP TRYING TO FIX YOUR DAD'S CREDIT RATING.
IT ALL LOOKS EASIER ON T.V.
TELL ME ABOUT IT. MY MOTORCYCLE ENGINE'S ALL OVER MY LIVING ROOM FLOOR.
BB
EVERYBODY GONE?
I THOUGHT I SAW... NO, NEVER MIND. WE'RE GOOD.
CLICK!
BB
llville Public Library
Sorry, the library is closed!
Please try again during regular hours.
OK
BB

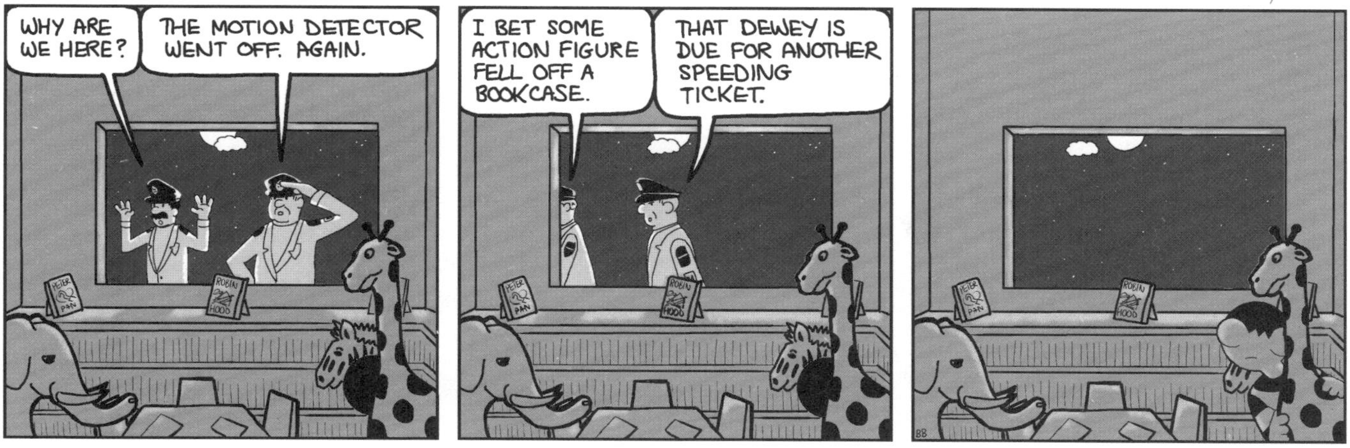
WHY ARE WE HERE?
THE MOTION DETECTOR WENT OFF. AGAIN.
I BET SOME ACTION FIGURE FELL OFF A BOOKCASE.
THAT DEWEY IS DUE FOR ANOTHER SPEEDING TICKET.

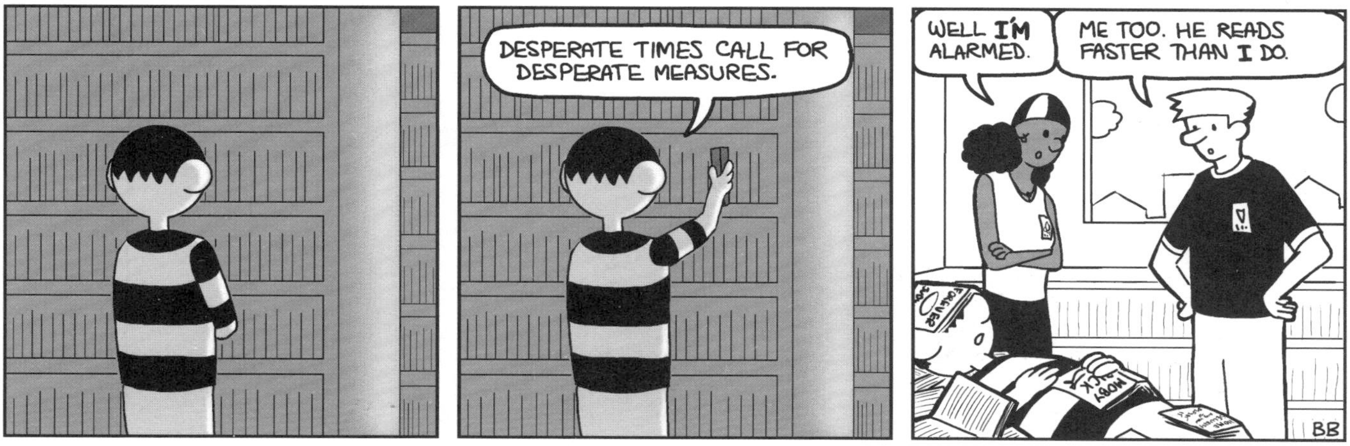
DESPERATE TIMES CALL FOR DESPERATE MEASURES.
WELL **I'M** ALARMED.
ME TOO. HE READS FASTER THAN **I** DO.

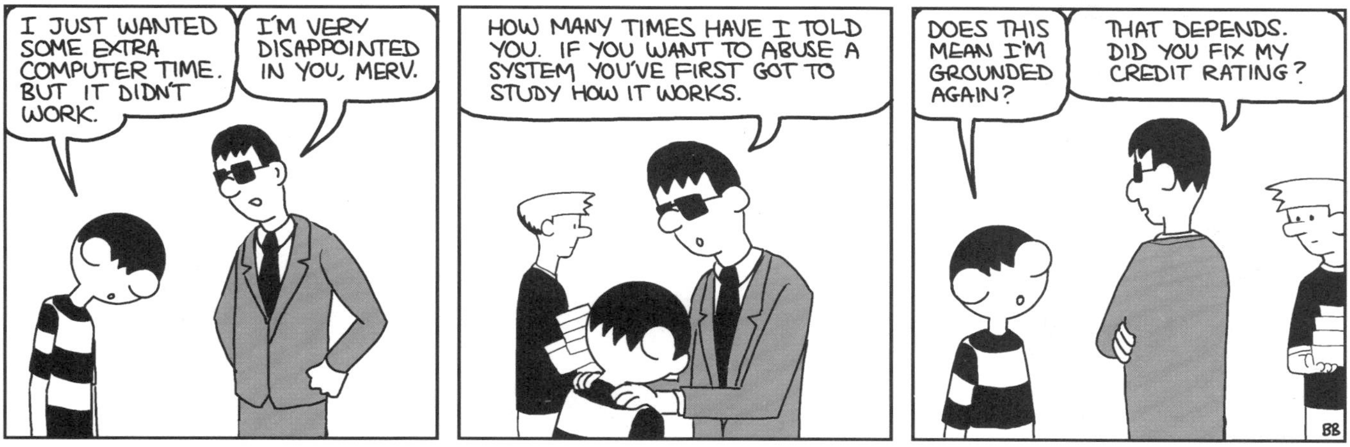
I JUST WANTED SOME EXTRA COMPUTER TIME. BUT IT DIDN'T WORK.
I'M VERY DISAPPOINTED IN YOU, MERV.
HOW MANY TIMES HAVE I TOLD YOU. IF YOU WANT TO ABUSE A SYSTEM YOU'VE FIRST GOT TO STUDY HOW IT WORKS.
DOES THIS MEAN I'M GROUNDED AGAIN?
THAT DEPENDS. DID YOU FIX MY CREDIT RATING?

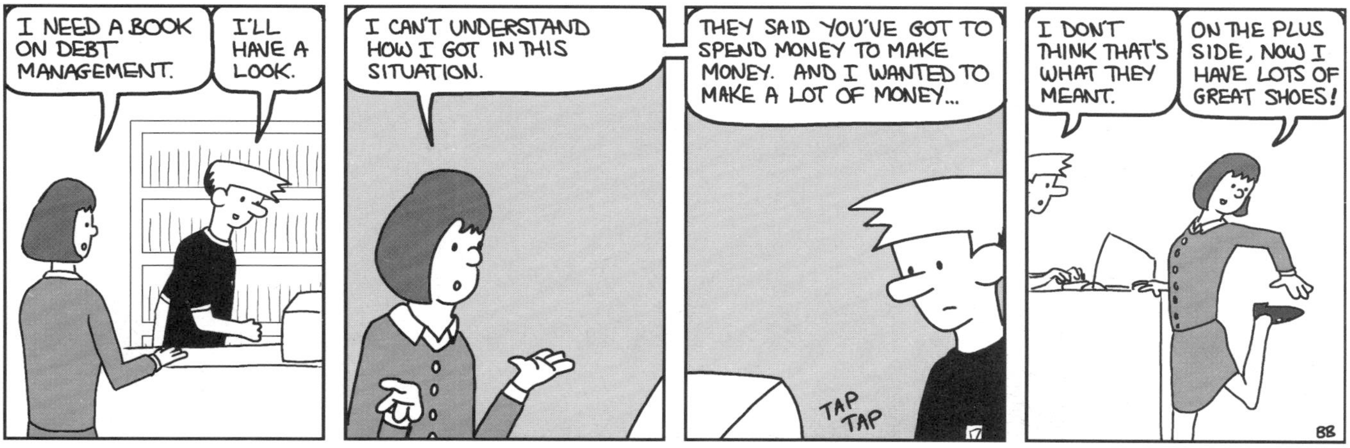
I NEED A BOOK ON DEBT MANAGEMENT.
I'LL HAVE A LOOK.
I CAN'T UNDERSTAND HOW I GOT IN THIS SITUATION.
THEY SAID YOU'VE GOT TO SPEND MONEY TO MAKE MONEY. AND I WANTED TO MAKE A LOT OF MONEY...
TAP TAP
I DON'T THINK THAT'S WHAT THEY MEANT.
ON THE PLUS SIDE, NOW I HAVE LOTS OF GREAT SHOES!

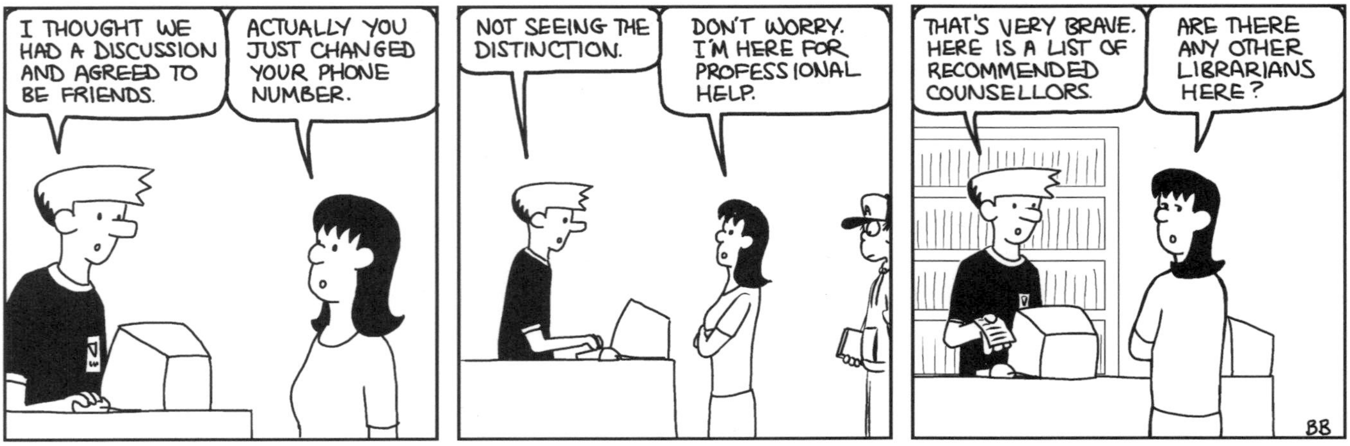
I THOUGHT WE HAD A DISCUSSION AND AGREED TO BE FRIENDS.
ACTUALLY YOU JUST CHANGED YOUR PHONE NUMBER.
NOT SEEING THE DISTINCTION.
DON'T WORRY. I'M HERE FOR PROFESSIONAL HELP.
THAT'S VERY BRAVE. HERE IS A LIST OF RECOMMENDED COUNSELLORS.
ARE THERE ANY OTHER LIBRARIANS HERE?
BB

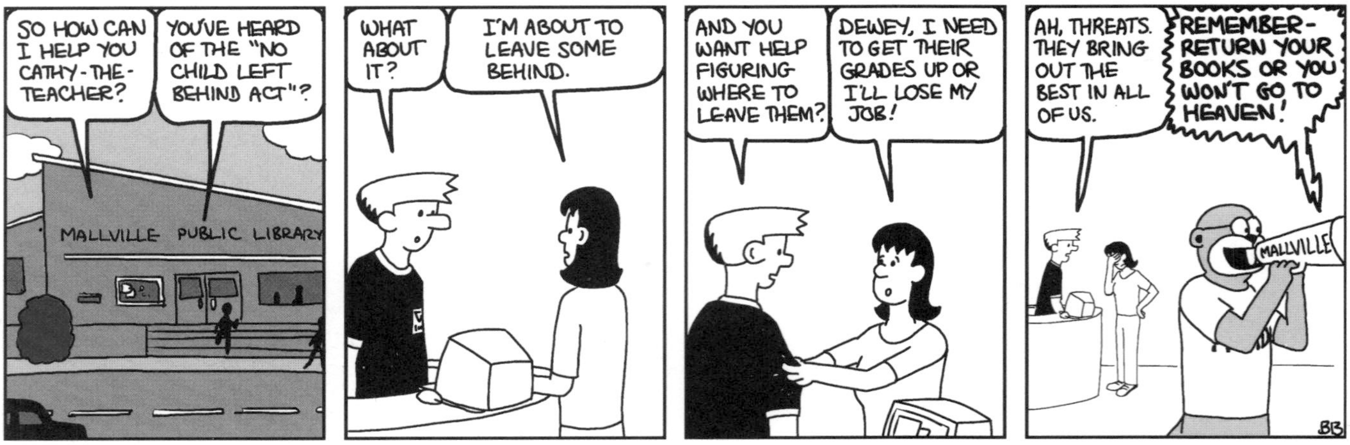
SO HOW CAN I HELP YOU CATHY-THE-TEACHER?
YOU'VE HEARD OF THE "NO CHILD LEFT BEHIND ACT"?
MALLVILLE PUBLIC LIBRARY
WHAT ABOUT IT?
I'M ABOUT TO LEAVE SOME BEHIND.
AND YOU WANT HELP FIGURING WHERE TO LEAVE THEM?
DEWEY, I NEED TO GET THEIR GRADES UP OR I'LL LOSE MY JOB!
AH, THREATS. THEY BRING OUT THE BEST IN ALL OF US.
REMEMBER- RETURN YOUR BOOKS OR YOU WON'T GO TO HEAVEN!
MALLVILLE
BB

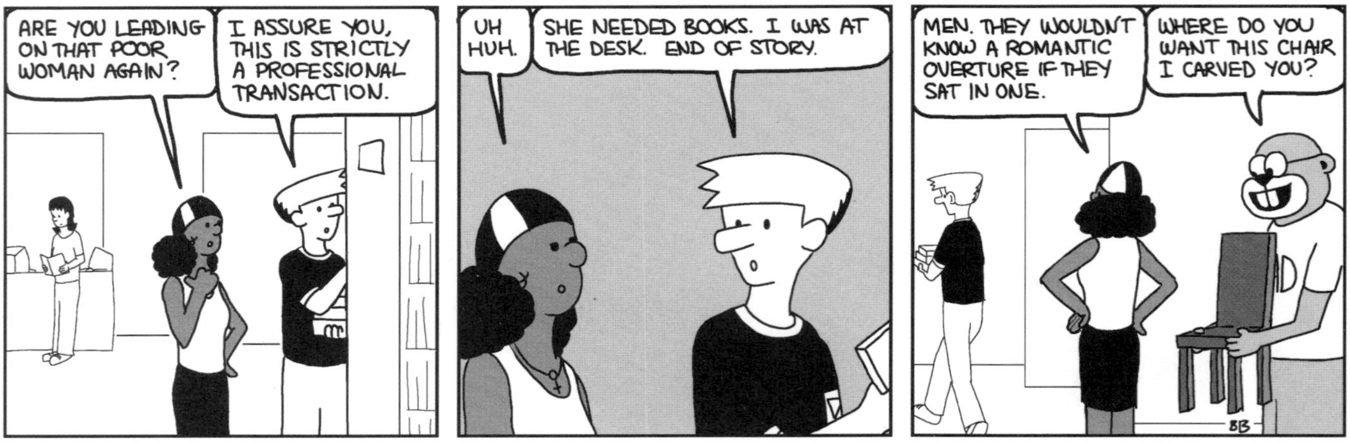
ARE YOU LEADING ON THAT POOR WOMAN AGAIN?
I ASSURE YOU, THIS IS STRICTLY A PROFESSIONAL TRANSACTION.
UH HUH.
SHE NEEDED BOOKS. I WAS AT THE DESK. END OF STORY.
MEN. THEY WOULDN'T KNOW A ROMANTIC OVERTURE IF THEY SAT IN ONE.
WHERE DO YOU WANT THIS CHAIR I CARVED YOU?
BB

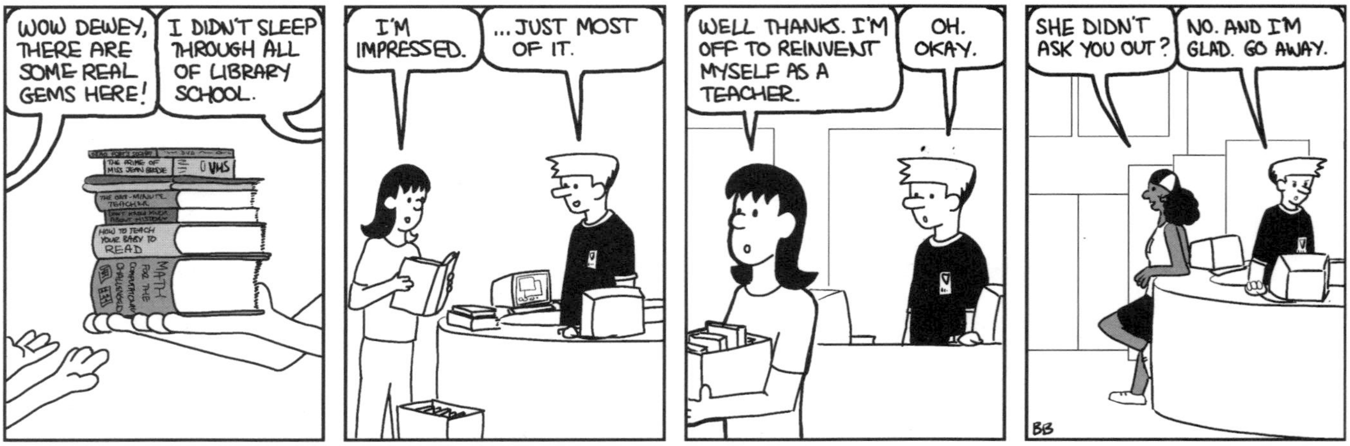
WOW DEWEY, THERE ARE SOME REAL GEMS HERE!
I DIDN'T SLEEP THROUGH ALL OF LIBRARY SCHOOL.
THE PRIME OF MISS JEAN BRODIE
VHS
THE ONE-MINUTE TEACHER
HOW TO TEACH YOUR BABY TO READ
MATH FOR THE
I'M IMPRESSED.
...JUST MOST OF IT.
WELL THANKS. I'M OFF TO REINVENT MYSELF AS A TEACHER.
OH. OKAY.
SHE DIDN'T ASK YOU OUT?
NO. AND I'M GLAD. GO AWAY.
BB

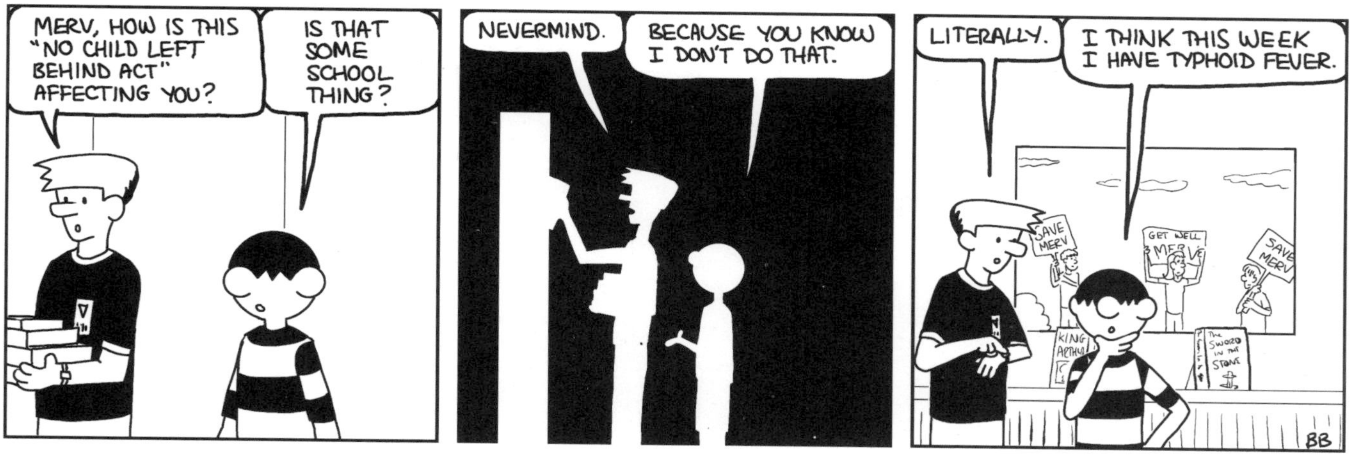
MERV, HOW IS THIS "NO CHILD LEFT BEHIND ACT" AFFECTING YOU?
IS THAT SOME SCHOOL THING?
NEVERMIND.
BECAUSE YOU KNOW I DON'T DO THAT.
LITERALLY.
I THINK THIS WEEK I HAVE TYPHOID FEVER.
BB

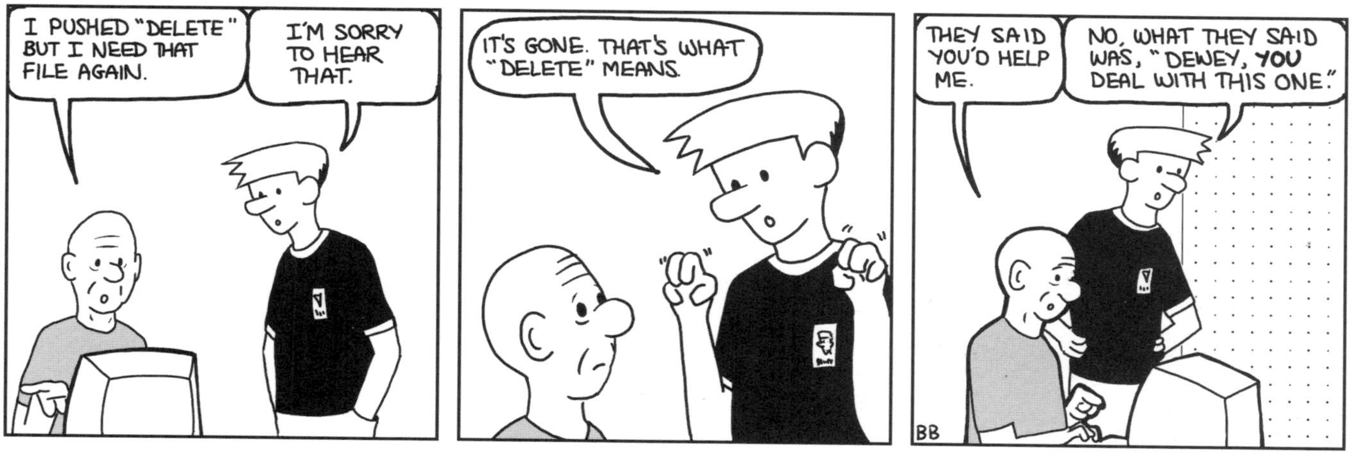
I PUSHED "DELETE" BUT I NEED THAT FILE AGAIN.
I'M SORRY TO HEAR THAT.
IT'S GONE. THAT'S WHAT "DELETE" MEANS.
THEY SAID YOU'D HELP ME.
NO, WHAT THEY SAID WAS, "DEWEY, **YOU** DEAL WITH THIS ONE."
BB

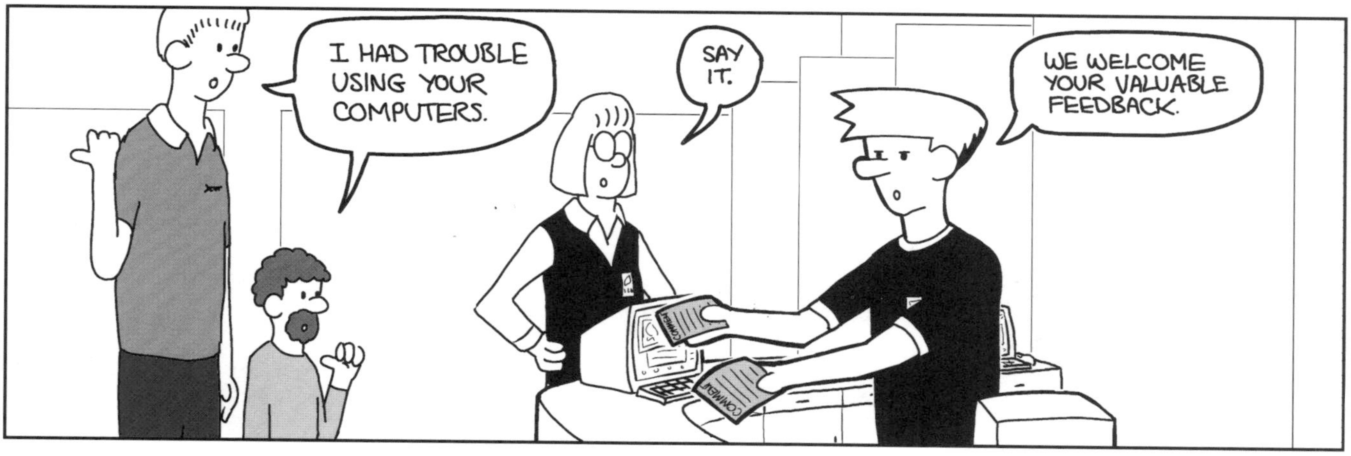
I HAD TROUBLE USING YOUR COMPUTERS.
SAY IT.
WE WELCOME YOUR VALUABLE FEEDBACK.

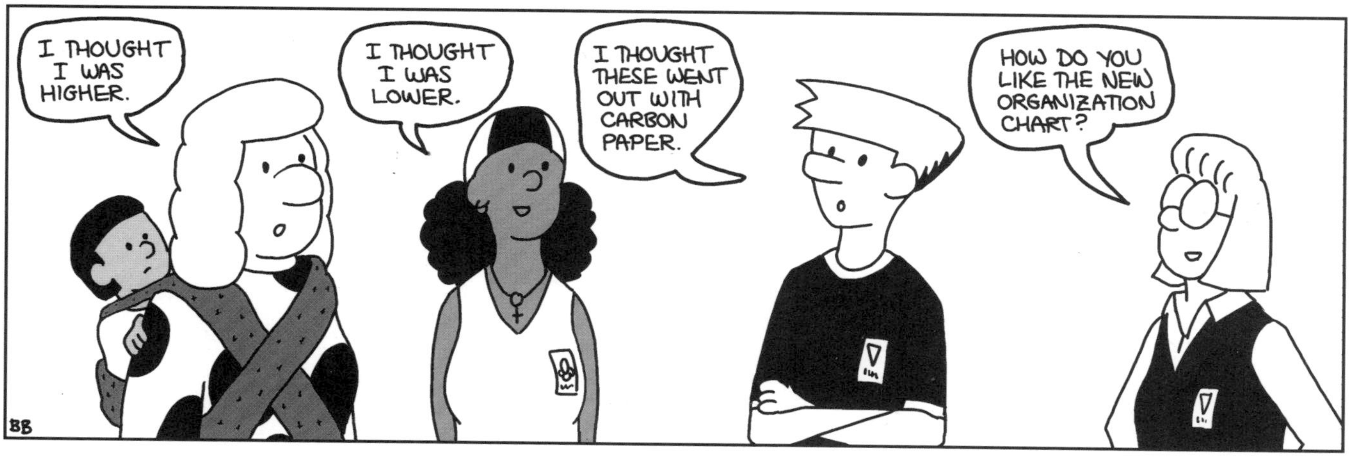
I THOUGHT I WAS HIGHER.
I THOUGHT I WAS LOWER.
I THOUGHT THESE WENT OUT WITH CARBON PAPER.
HOW DO YOU LIKE THE NEW ORGANIZATION CHART?
BB

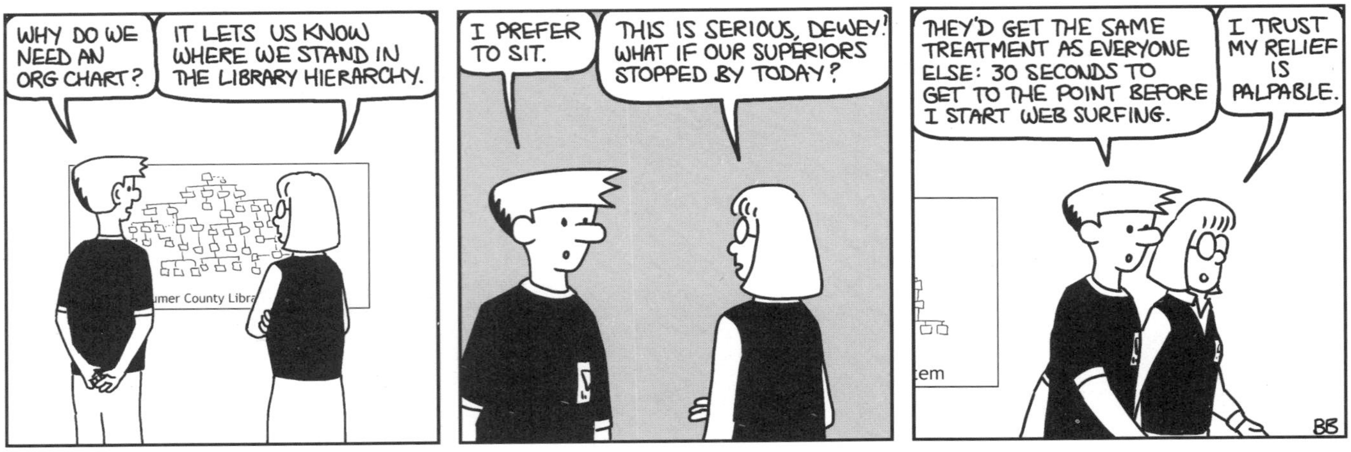
WHY DO WE NEED AN ORG CHART?
IT LETS US KNOW WHERE WE STAND IN THE LIBRARY HIERARCHY.
I PREFER TO SIT.
THIS IS SERIOUS, DEWEY! WHAT IF OUR SUPERIORS STOPPED BY TODAY?
THEY'D GET THE SAME TREATMENT AS EVERYONE ELSE: 30 SECONDS TO GET TO THE POINT BEFORE I START WEB SURFING.
I TRUST MY RELIEF IS PALPABLE.
BB

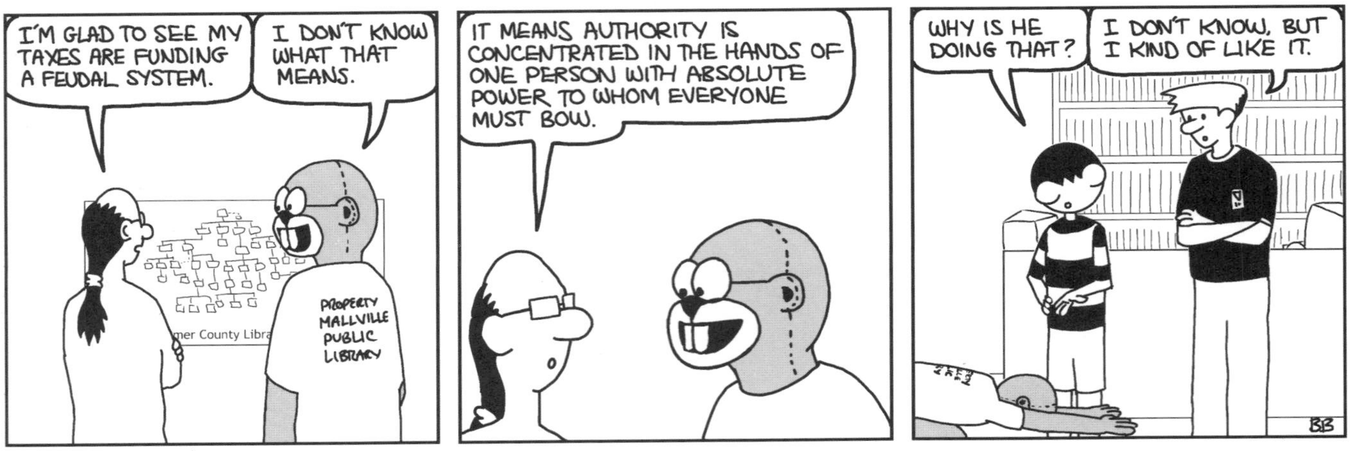
I'M GLAD TO SEE MY TAXES ARE FUNDING A FEUDAL SYSTEM.
I DON'T KNOW WHAT THAT MEANS.
PROPERTY MALLVILLE PUBLIC LIBRARY
IT MEANS AUTHORITY IS CONCENTRATED IN THE HANDS OF ONE PERSON WITH ABSOLUTE POWER TO WHOM EVERYONE MUST BOW.
WHY IS HE DOING THAT?
I DON'T KNOW, BUT I KIND OF LIKE IT.
BB

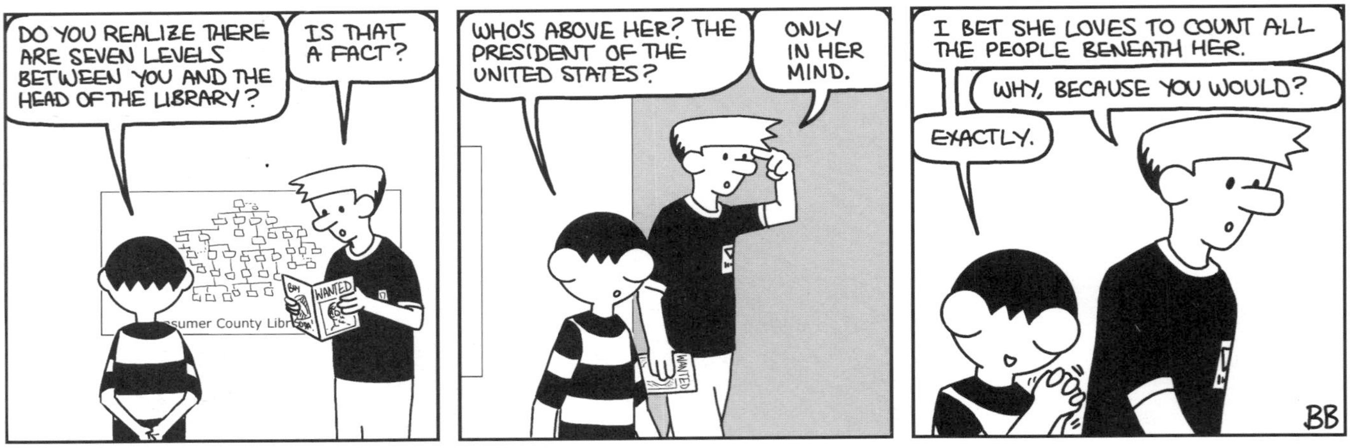
DO YOU REALIZE THERE ARE SEVEN LEVELS BETWEEN YOU AND THE HEAD OF THE LIBRARY?
IS THAT A FACT?
WANTED
WHO'S ABOVE HER? THE PRESIDENT OF THE UNITED STATES?
ONLY IN HER MIND.
I BET SHE LOVES TO COUNT ALL THE PEOPLE BENEATH HER.
WHY, BECAUSE YOU WOULD?
EXACTLY.
BB

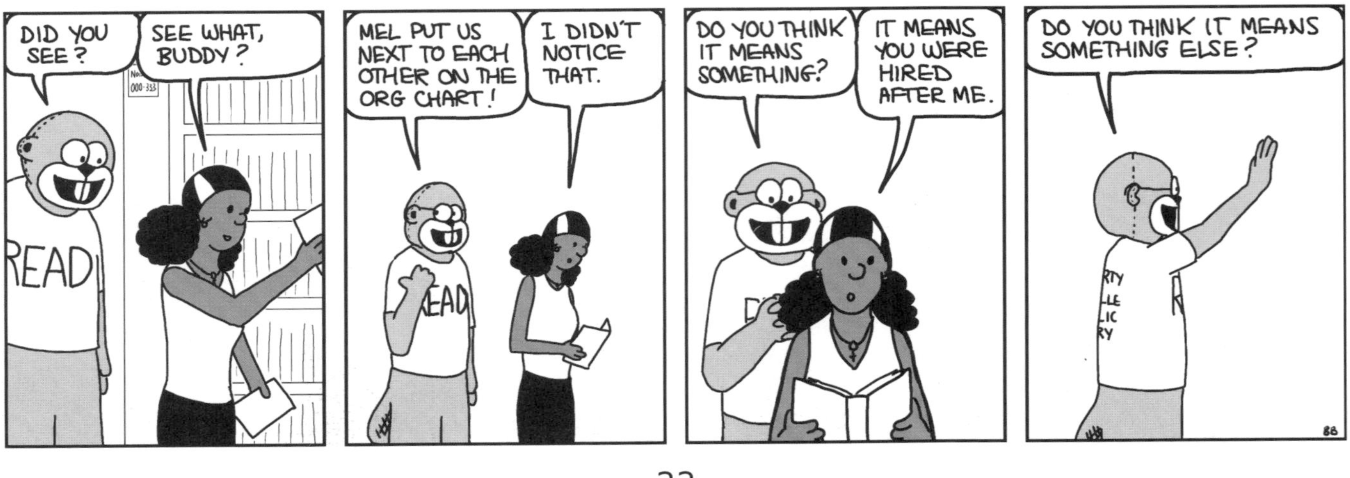
DID YOU SEE?
SEE WHAT, BUDDY?
READ
MEL PUT US NEXT TO EACH OTHER ON THE ORG CHART!
I DIDN'T NOTICE THAT.
DO YOU THINK IT MEANS SOMETHING?
IT MEANS YOU WERE HIRED AFTER ME.
DO YOU THINK IT MEANS SOMETHING ELSE?
BB

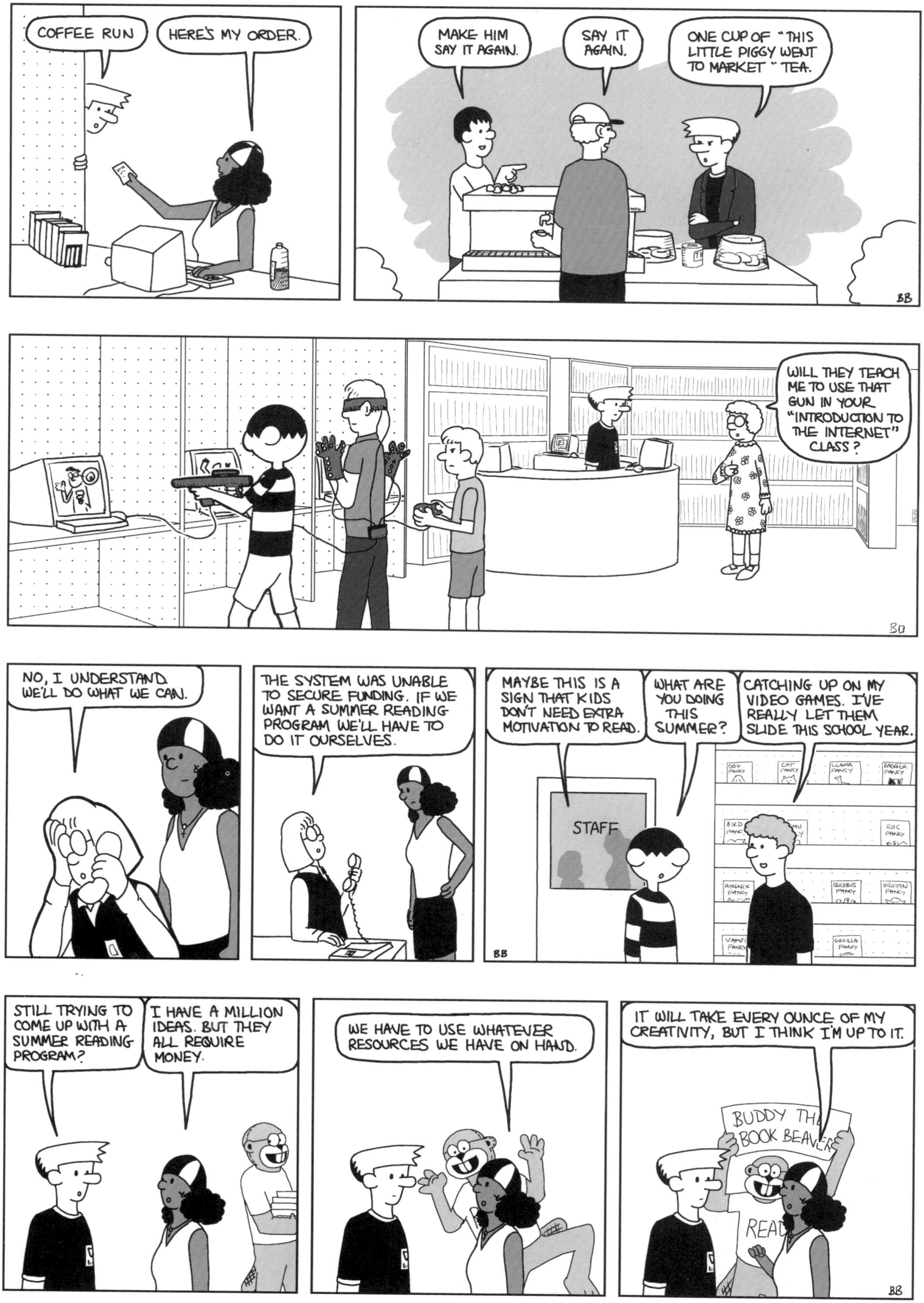
COFFEE RUN
HERE'S MY ORDER.
MAKE HIM SAY IT AGAIN.
SAY IT AGAIN.
ONE CUP OF "THIS LITTLE PIGGY WENT TO MARKET" TEA.
WILL THEY TEACH ME TO USE THAT GUN IN YOUR "INTRODUCTION TO THE INTERNET" CLASS?
NO, I UNDERSTAND. WE'LL DO WHAT WE CAN.
THE SYSTEM WAS UNABLE TO SECURE FUNDING. IF WE WANT A SUMMER READING PROGRAM WE'LL HAVE TO DO IT OURSELVES.
MAYBE THIS IS A SIGN THAT KIDS DON'T NEED EXTRA MOTIVATION TO READ.
WHAT ARE YOU DOING THIS SUMMER?
CATCHING UP ON MY VIDEO GAMES. I'VE REALLY LET THEM SLIDE THIS SCHOOL YEAR.
STAFF
STILL TRYING TO COME UP WITH A SUMMER READING PROGRAM?
I HAVE A MILLION IDEAS. BUT THEY ALL REQUIRE MONEY.
WE HAVE TO USE WHATEVER RESOURCES WE HAVE ON HAND.
IT WILL TAKE EVERY OUNCE OF MY CREATIVITY, BUT I THINK I'M UP TO IT.

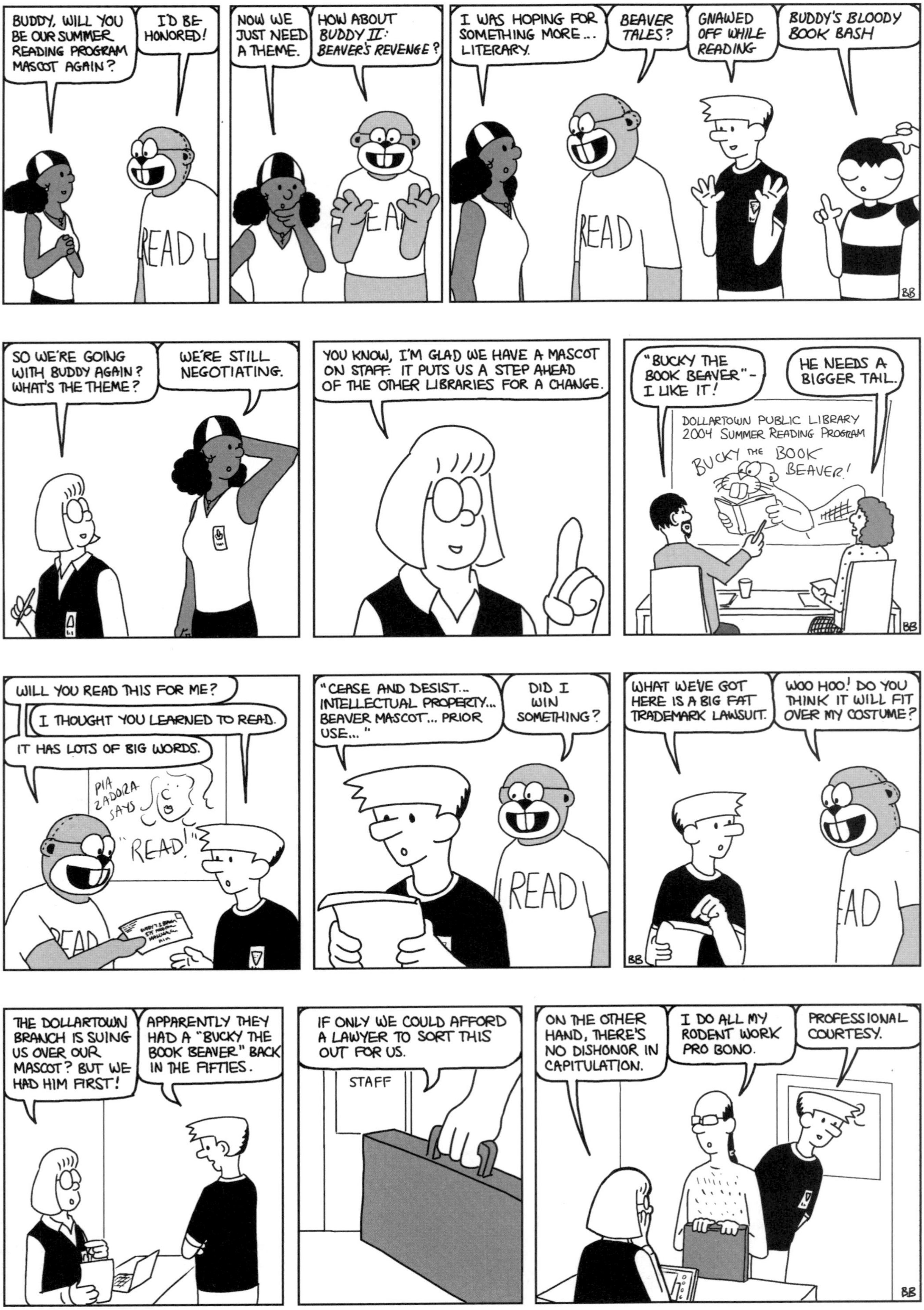
BUDDY, WILL YOU BE OUR SUMMER READING PROGRAM MASCOT AGAIN?
I'D BE HONORED!
READ
NOW WE JUST NEED A THEME.
HOW ABOUT BUDDY II: BEAVER'S REVENGE?
I WAS HOPING FOR SOMETHING MORE... LITERARY.
BEAVER TALES?
GNAWED OFF WHILE READING
BUDDY'S BLOODY BOOK BASH
READ
BB
SO WE'RE GOING WITH BUDDY AGAIN? WHAT'S THE THEME?
WE'RE STILL NEGOTIATING.
YOU KNOW, I'M GLAD WE HAVE A MASCOT ON STAFF. IT PUTS US A STEP AHEAD OF THE OTHER LIBRARIES FOR A CHANGE.
"BUCKY THE BOOK BEAVER" – I LIKE IT!
HE NEEDS A BIGGER TAIL.
DOLLARTOWN PUBLIC LIBRARY 2004 SUMMER READING PROGRAM
BUCKY THE BOOK BEAVER!
BB
WILL YOU READ THIS FOR ME?
I THOUGHT YOU LEARNED TO READ.
IT HAS LOTS OF BIG WORDS.
PIA ZADORA SAYS "READ!"
"CEASE AND DESIST... INTELLECTUAL PROPERTY... BEAVER MASCOT... PRIOR USE..."
DID I WIN SOMETHING?
READ
WHAT WE'VE GOT HERE IS A BIG FAT TRADEMARK LAWSUIT.
WOO HOO! DO YOU THINK IT WILL FIT OVER MY COSTUME?
BB
THE DOLLARTOWN BRANCH IS SUING US OVER OUR MASCOT? BUT WE HAD HIM FIRST!
APPARENTLY THEY HAD A "BUCKY THE BOOK BEAVER" BACK IN THE FIFTIES.
IF ONLY WE COULD AFFORD A LAWYER TO SORT THIS OUT FOR US.
STAFF
ON THE OTHER HAND, THERE'S NO DISHONOR IN CAPITULATION.
I DO ALL MY RODENT WORK PRO BONO.
PROFESSIONAL COURTESY.
BB

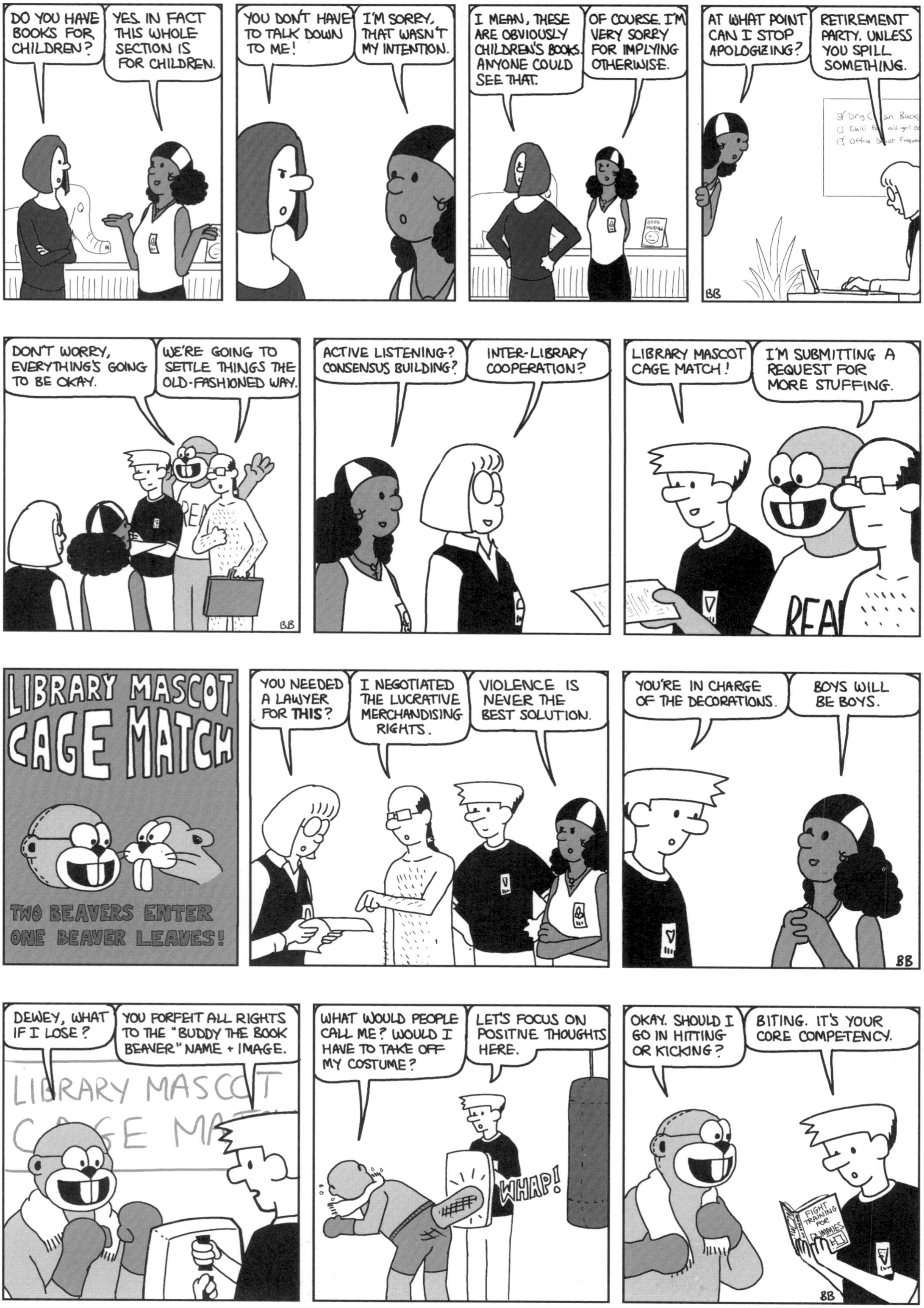
DO YOU HAVE BOOKS FOR CHILDREN?
YES. IN FACT THIS WHOLE SECTION IS FOR CHILDREN.
YOU DON'T HAVE TO TALK DOWN TO ME!
I'M SORRY, THAT WASN'T MY INTENTION.
I MEAN, THESE ARE OBVIOUSLY CHILDREN'S BOOKS. ANYONE COULD SEE THAT.
OF COURSE. I'M VERY SORRY FOR IMPLYING OTHERWISE.
GOOD MORNING
AT WHAT POINT CAN I STOP APOLOGIZING?
RETIREMENT PARTY. UNLESS YOU SPILL SOMETHING.
BB
DON'T WORRY, EVERYTHING'S GOING TO BE OKAY.
WE'RE GOING TO SETTLE THINGS THE OLD-FASHIONED WAY.
BB
ACTIVE LISTENING? CONSENSUS BUILDING?
INTER-LIBRARY COOPERATION?
LIBRARY MASCOT CAGE MATCH!
I'M SUBMITTING A REQUEST FOR MORE STUFFING.
LIBRARY MASCOT CAGE MATCH
TWO BEAVERS ENTER ONE BEAVER LEAVES!
YOU NEEDED A LAWYER FOR THIS?
I NEGOTIATED THE LUCRATIVE MERCHANDISING RIGHTS.
VIOLENCE IS NEVER THE BEST SOLUTION.
YOU'RE IN CHARGE OF THE DECORATIONS.
BOYS WILL BE BOYS.
BB
DEWEY, WHAT IF I LOSE?
YOU FORFEIT ALL RIGHTS TO THE "BUDDY THE BOOK BEAVER" NAME + IMAGE.
WHAT WOULD PEOPLE CALL ME? WOULD I HAVE TO TAKE OFF MY COSTUME?
LET'S FOCUS ON POSITIVE THOUGHTS HERE.
WHAP!
OKAY. SHOULD I GO IN HITTING OR KICKING?
BITING. IT'S YOUR CORE COMPETENCY.
FIGHT TRAINING FOR DUMMIES
BB

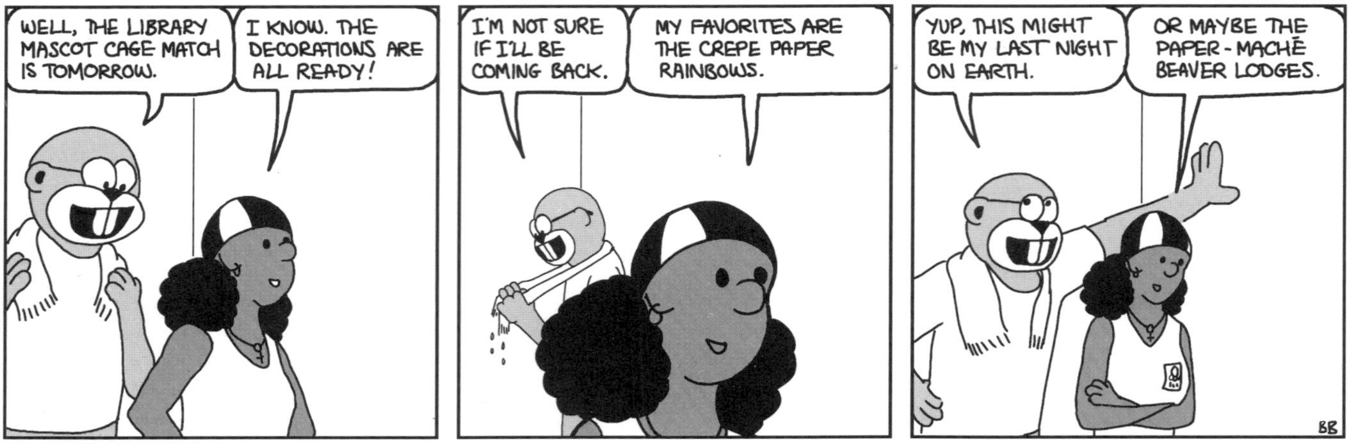
WELL, THE LIBRARY MASCOT CAGE MATCH IS TOMORROW.
I KNOW. THE DECORATIONS ARE ALL READY!
I'M NOT SURE IF I'LL BE COMING BACK.
MY FAVORITES ARE THE CREPE PAPER RAINBOWS.
YUP, THIS MIGHT BE MY LAST NIGHT ON EARTH.
OR MAYBE THE PAPER-MACHÉ BEAVER LODGES.
BB

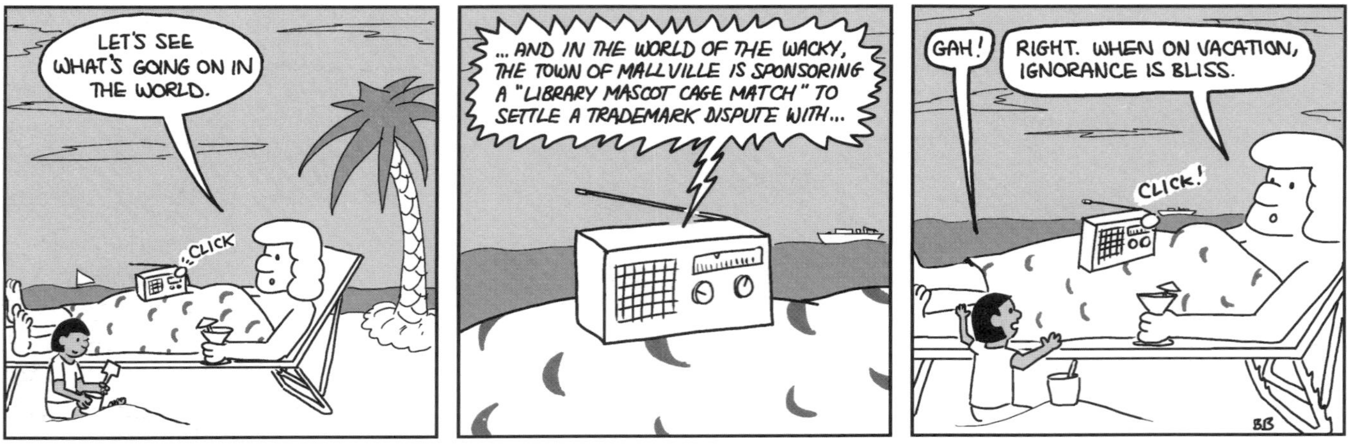
LET'S SEE WHAT'S GOING ON IN THE WORLD.
CLICK
... AND IN THE WORLD OF THE WACKY, THE TOWN OF MALLVILLE IS SPONSORING A "LIBRARY MASCOT CAGE MATCH" TO SETTLE A TRADEMARK DISPUTE WITH...
GAH!
RIGHT. WHEN ON VACATION, IGNORANCE IS BLISS.
CLICK!
BB

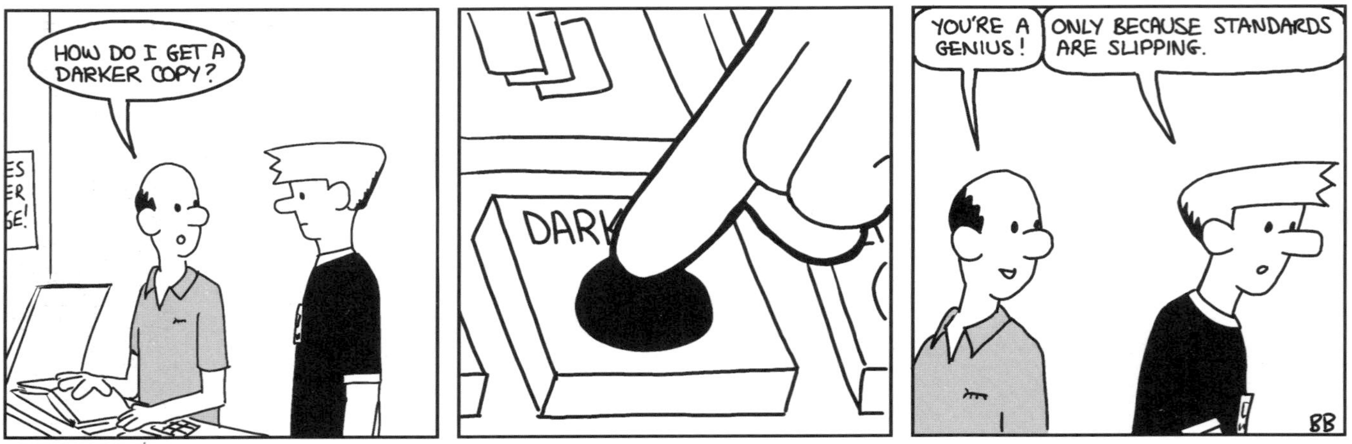
HOW DO I GET A DARKER COPY?
DARK
YOU'RE A GENIUS!
ONLY BECAUSE STANDARDS ARE SLIPPING.
BB

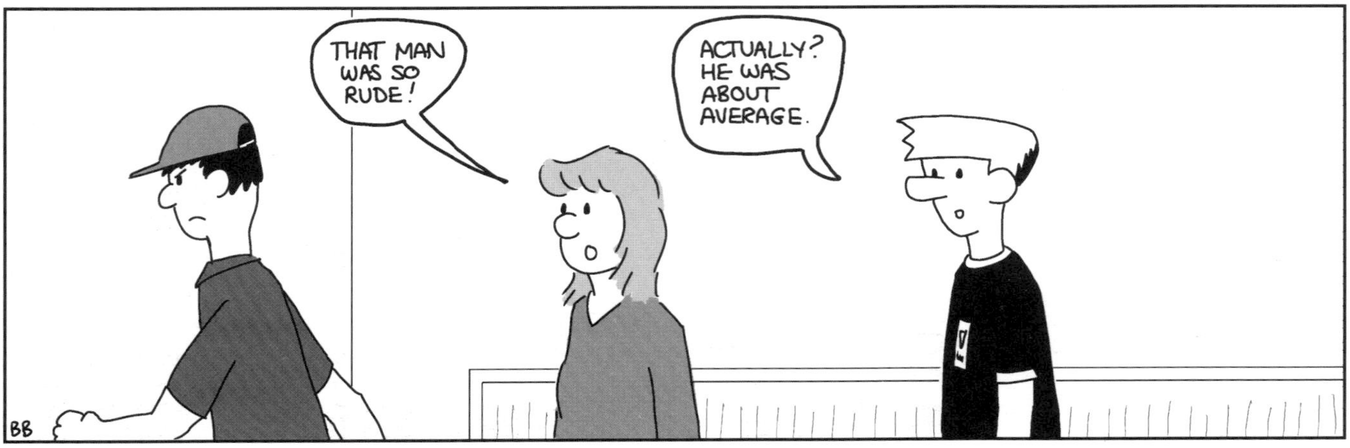
THAT MAN WAS SO RUDE!
ACTUALLY? HE WAS ABOUT AVERAGE.
BB

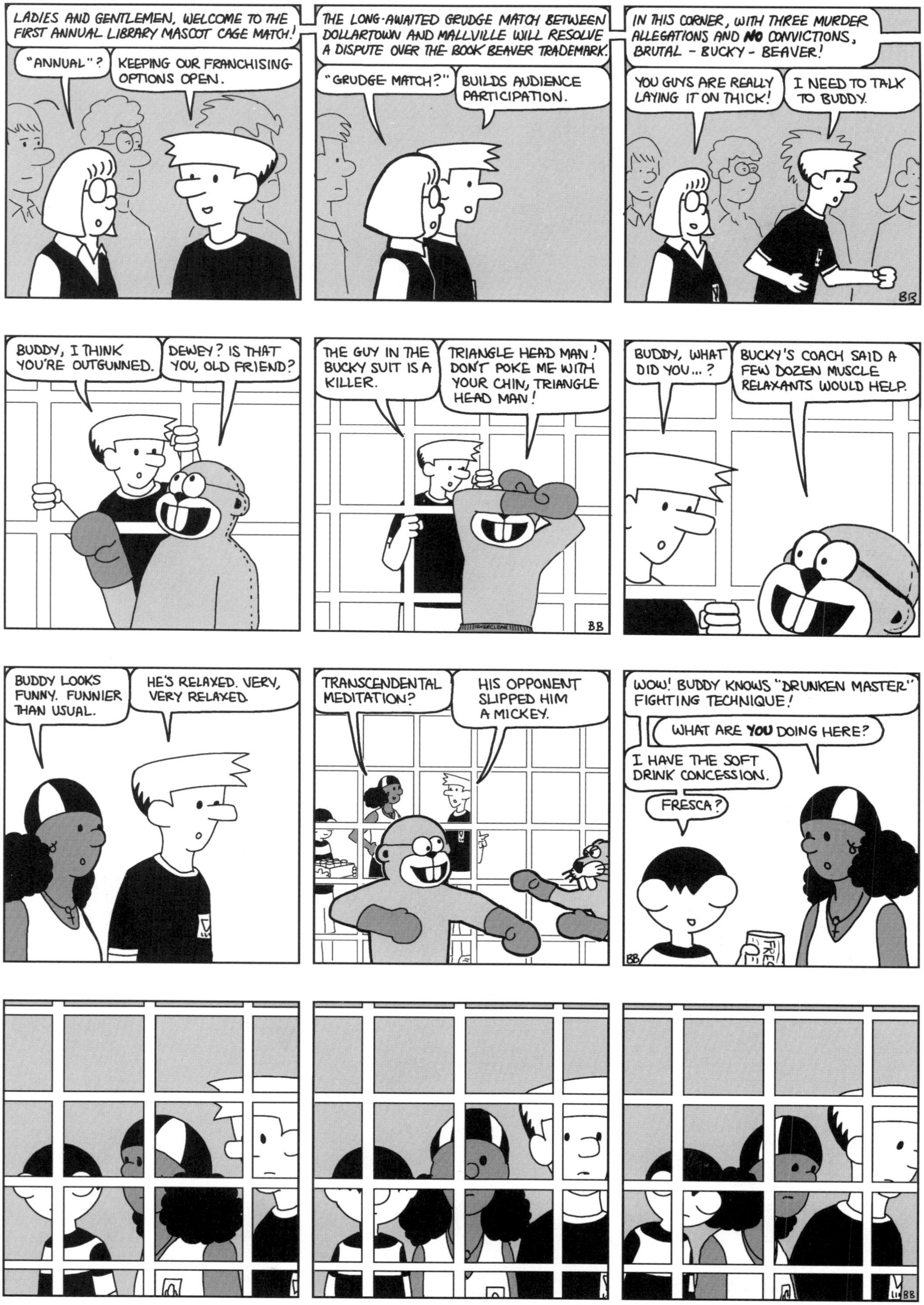
LADIES AND GENTLEMEN, WELCOME TO THE FIRST ANNUAL LIBRARY MASCOT CAGE MATCH!
"ANNUAL"?
KEEPING OUR FRANCHISING OPTIONS OPEN.
THE LONG-AWAITED GRUDGE MATCH BETWEEN DOLLARTOWN AND MALLVILLE WILL RESOLVE A DISPUTE OVER THE BOOK BEAVER TRADEMARK.
"GRUDGE MATCH?"
BUILDS AUDIENCE PARTICIPATION.
IN THIS CORNER, WITH THREE MURDER ALLEGATIONS AND NO CONVICTIONS, BRUTAL - BUCKY - BEAVER!
YOU GUYS ARE REALLY LAYING IT ON THICK!
I NEED TO TALK TO BUDDY.
BUDDY, I THINK YOU'RE OUTGUNNED.
DEWEY? IS THAT YOU, OLD FRIEND?
THE GUY IN THE BUCKY SUIT IS A KILLER.
TRIANGLE HEAD MAN! DON'T POKE ME WITH YOUR CHIN, TRIANGLE HEAD MAN!
BUDDY, WHAT DID YOU...?
BUCKY'S COACH SAID A FEW DOZEN MUSCLE RELAXANTS WOULD HELP.
BUDDY LOOKS FUNNY. FUNNIER THAN USUAL.
HE'S RELAXED. VERY, VERY RELAXED.
TRANSCENDENTAL MEDITATION?
HIS OPPONENT SLIPPED HIM A MICKEY.
WOW! BUDDY KNOWS "DRUNKEN MASTER" FIGHTING TECHNIQUE!
WHAT ARE YOU DOING HERE?
I HAVE THE SOFT DRINK CONCESSION.
FRESCA?

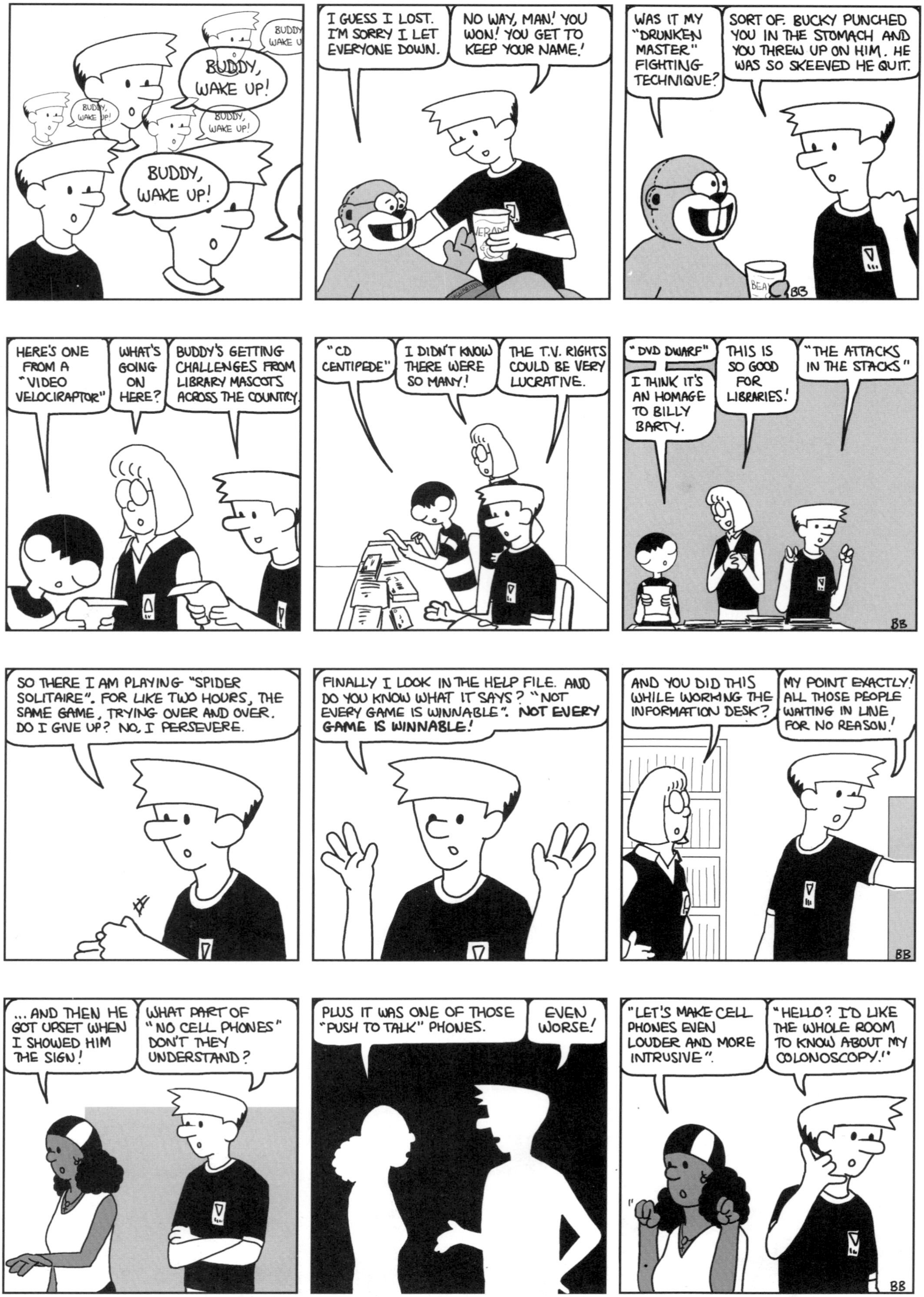
BUDDY, WAKE UP!
BUDDY, WAKE UP!
BUDDY, WAKE UP!
BUDDY, WAKE UP!
I GUESS I LOST. I'M SORRY I LET EVERYONE DOWN.
NO WAY, MAN! YOU WON! YOU GET TO KEEP YOUR NAME!
WAS IT MY "DRUNKEN MASTER" FIGHTING TECHNIQUE?
SORT OF. BUCKY PUNCHED YOU IN THE STOMACH AND YOU THREW UP ON HIM. HE WAS SO SKEEVED HE QUIT.
BB
HERE'S ONE FROM A "VIDEO VELOCIRAPTOR"
WHAT'S GOING ON HERE?
BUDDY'S GETTING CHALLENGES FROM LIBRARY MASCOTS ACROSS THE COUNTRY.
"CD CENTIPEDE"
I DIDN'T KNOW THERE WERE SO MANY!
THE T.V. RIGHTS COULD BE VERY LUCRATIVE.
"DVD DWARF"
I THINK IT'S AN HOMAGE TO BILLY BARTY.
THIS IS SO GOOD FOR LIBRARIES!
"THE ATTACKS IN THE STACKS"
BB
SO THERE I AM PLAYING "SPIDER SOLITAIRE". FOR LIKE TWO HOURS, THE SAME GAME, TRYING OVER AND OVER. DO I GIVE UP? NO, I PERSEVERE.
FINALLY I LOOK IN THE HELP FILE. AND DO YOU KNOW WHAT IT SAYS? "NOT EVERY GAME IS WINNABLE". NOT EVERY GAME IS WINNABLE!
AND YOU DID THIS WHILE WORKING THE INFORMATION DESK?
MY POINT EXACTLY! ALL THOSE PEOPLE WAITING IN LINE FOR NO REASON!
BB
...AND THEN HE GOT UPSET WHEN I SHOWED HIM THE SIGN!
WHAT PART OF "NO CELL PHONES" DON'T THEY UNDERSTAND?
PLUS IT WAS ONE OF THOSE "PUSH TO TALK" PHONES.
EVEN WORSE!
"LET'S MAKE CELL PHONES EVEN LOUDER AND MORE INTRUSIVE".
"HELLO? I'D LIKE THE WHOLE ROOM TO KNOW ABOUT MY COLONOSCOPY!"
BB

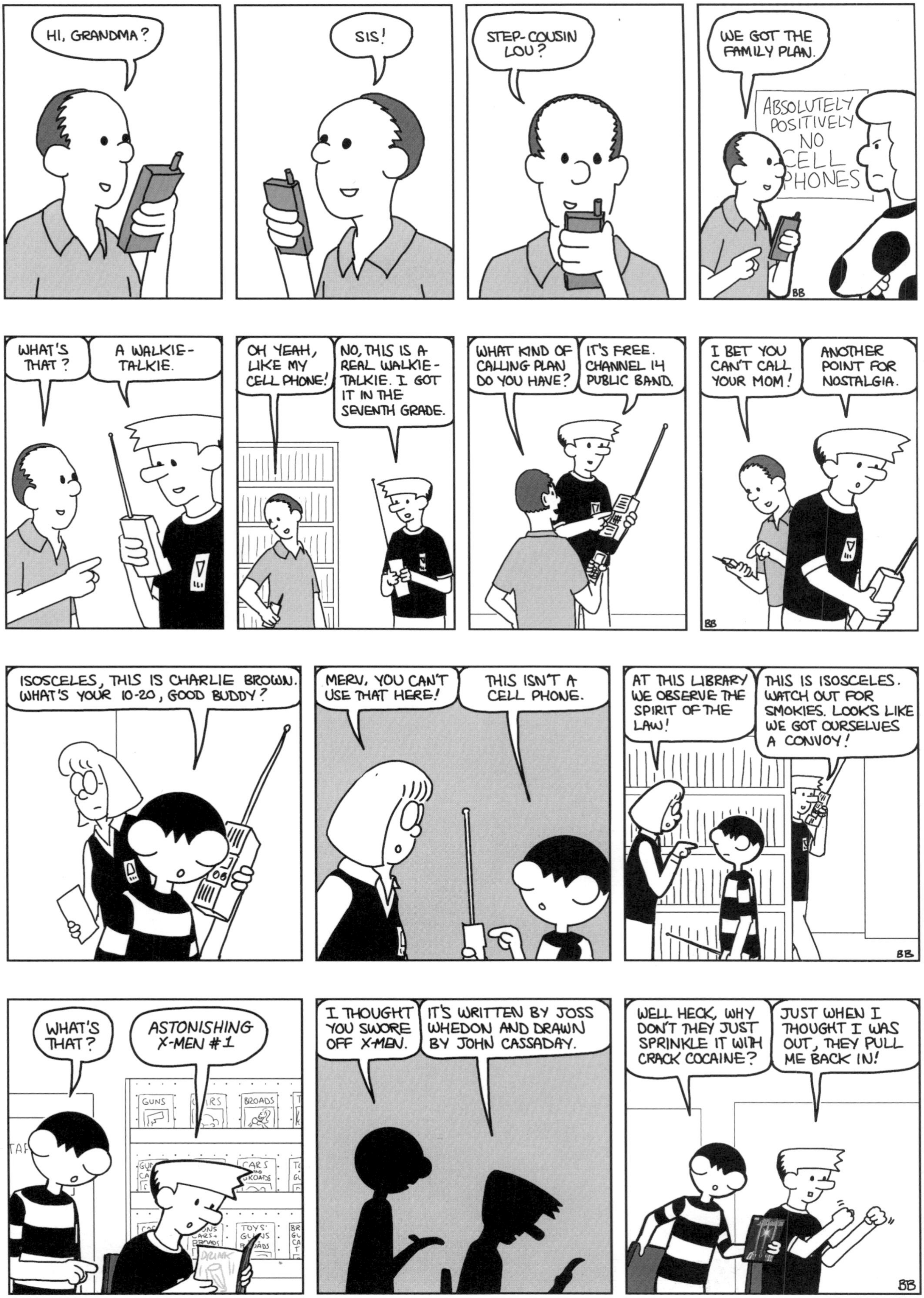
HI, GRANDMA?
SIS!
STEP-COUSIN LOU?
WE GOT THE FAMILY PLAN.
ABSOLUTELY POSITIVELY NO CELL PHONES
BB
WHAT'S THAT?
A WALKIE-TALKIE.
OH YEAH, LIKE MY CELL PHONE!
NO, THIS IS A REAL WALKIE-TALKIE. I GOT IT IN THE SEVENTH GRADE.
WHAT KIND OF CALLING PLAN DO YOU HAVE?
IT'S FREE. CHANNEL 14 PUBLIC BAND.
I BET YOU CAN'T CALL YOUR MOM!
ANOTHER POINT FOR NOSTALGIA.
BB
ISOSCELES, THIS IS CHARLIE BROWN. WHAT'S YOUR 10-20, GOOD BUDDY?
MERV, YOU CAN'T USE THAT HERE!
THIS ISN'T A CELL PHONE.
AT THIS LIBRARY WE OBSERVE THE SPIRIT OF THE LAW!
THIS IS ISOSCELES. WATCH OUT FOR SMOKIES. LOOKS LIKE WE GOT OURSELVES A CONVOY!
BB
WHAT'S THAT?
ASTONISHING X-MEN #1
GUNS
BROADS
I THOUGHT YOU SWORE OFF X-MEN.
IT'S WRITTEN BY JOSS WHEDON AND DRAWN BY JOHN CASSADAY.
WELL HECK, WHY DON'T THEY JUST SPRINKLE IT WITH CRACK COCAINE?
JUST WHEN I THOUGHT I WAS OUT, THEY PULL ME BACK IN!
BB

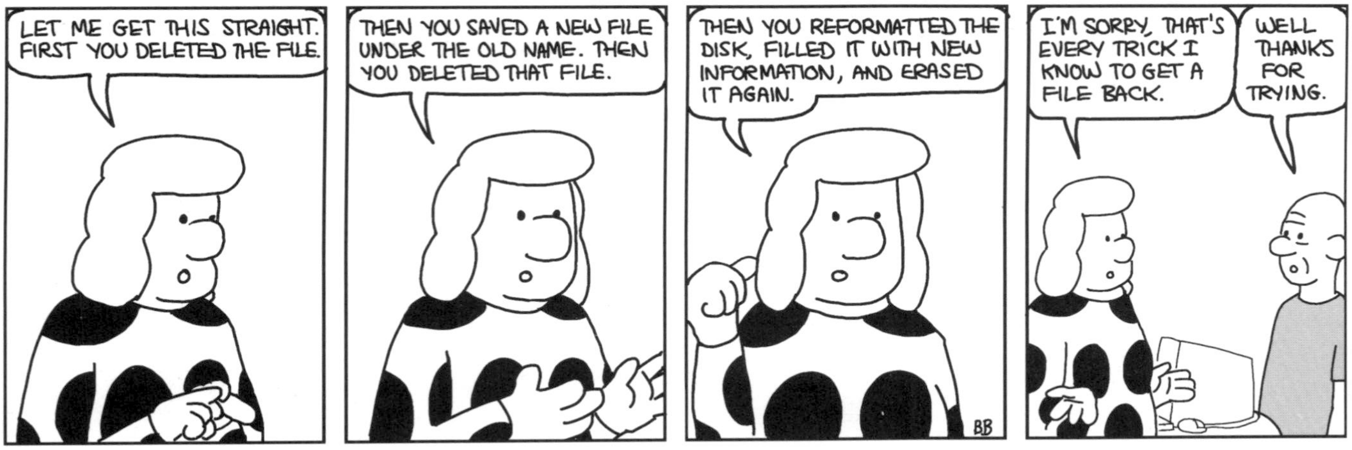
LET ME GET THIS STRAIGHT. FIRST YOU DELETED THE FILE.
THEN YOU SAVED A NEW FILE UNDER THE OLD NAME. THEN YOU DELETED THAT FILE.
THEN YOU REFORMATTED THE DISK, FILLED IT WITH NEW INFORMATION, AND ERASED IT AGAIN.
I'M SORRY, THAT'S EVERY TRICK I KNOW TO GET A FILE BACK.
WELL THANKS FOR TRYING.
BB

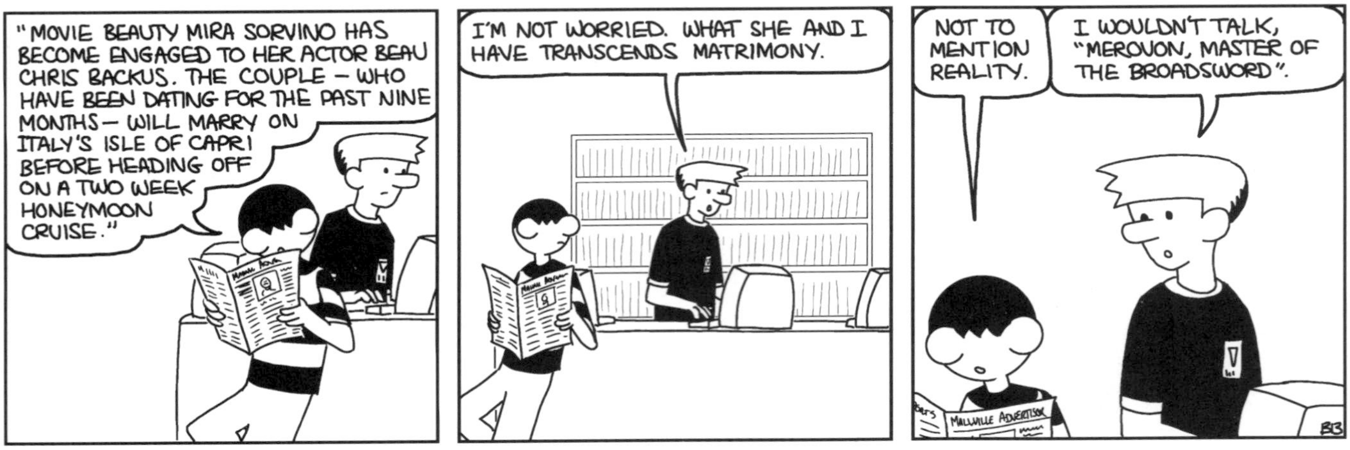
"MOVIE BEAUTY MIRA SORVINO HAS BECOME ENGAGED TO HER ACTOR BEAU CHRIS BACKUS. THE COUPLE – WHO HAVE BEEN DATING FOR THE PAST NINE MONTHS – WILL MARRY ON ITALY'S ISLE OF CAPRI BEFORE HEADING OFF ON A TWO WEEK HONEYMOON CRUISE."
I'M NOT WORRIED. WHAT SHE AND I HAVE TRANSCENDS MATRIMONY.
NOT TO MENTION REALITY.
I WOULDN'T TALK, "MEROVON, MASTER OF THE BROADSWORD".
BB

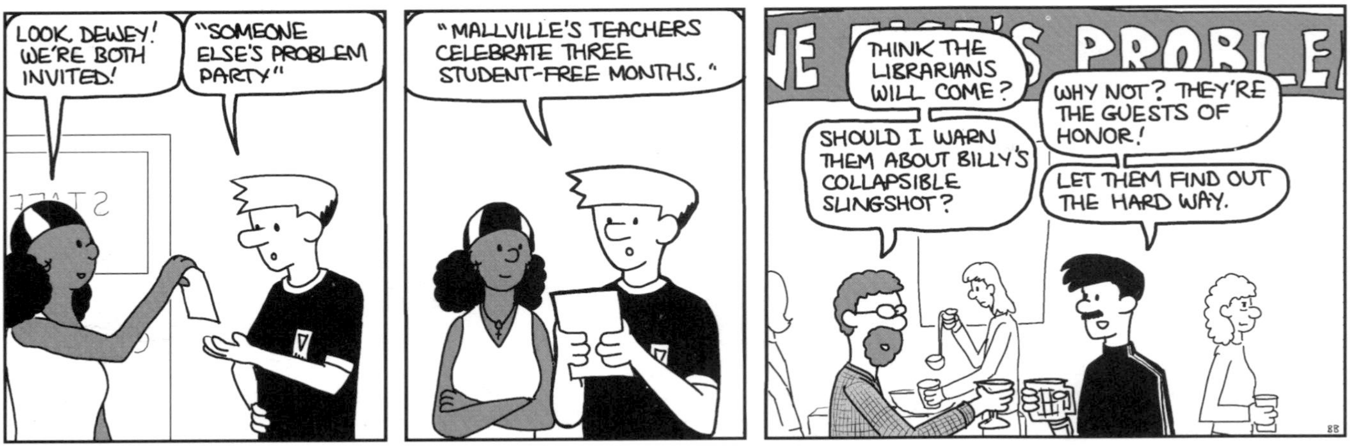
LOOK, DEWEY! WE'RE BOTH INVITED!
"SOMEONE ELSE'S PROBLEM PARTY"
"MALLVILLE'S TEACHERS CELEBRATE THREE STUDENT-FREE MONTHS."
THINK THE LIBRARIANS WILL COME?
SHOULD I WARN THEM ABOUT BILLY'S COLLAPSIBLE SLINGSHOT?
WHY NOT? THEY'RE THE GUESTS OF HONOR!
LET THEM FIND OUT THE HARD WAY.
BB

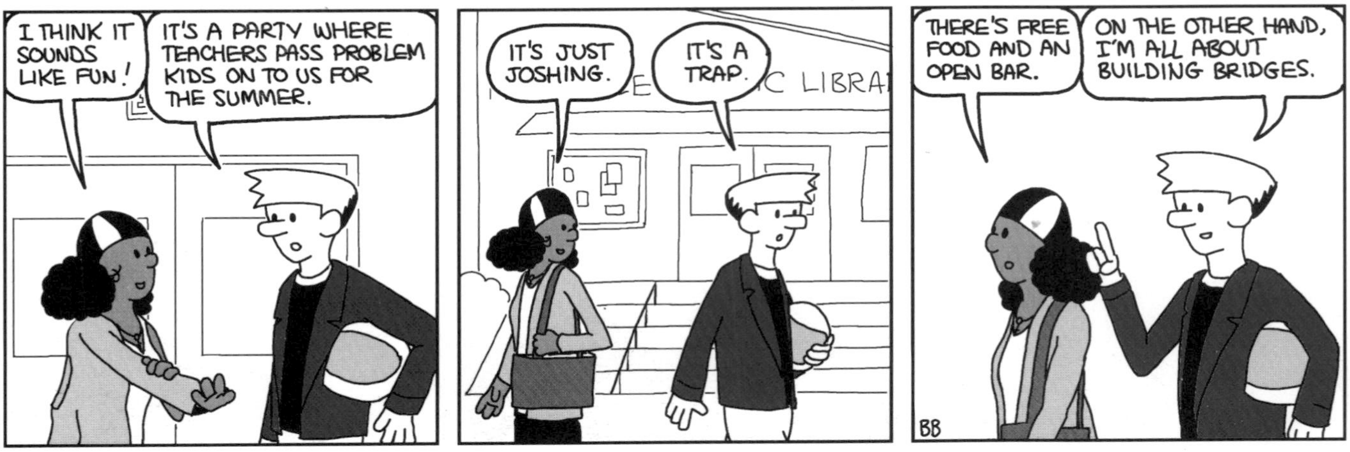
I THINK IT SOUNDS LIKE FUN!
IT'S A PARTY WHERE TEACHERS PASS PROBLEM KIDS ON TO US FOR THE SUMMER.
IT'S JUST JOSHING.
IT'S A TRAP.
THERE'S FREE FOOD AND AN OPEN BAR.
ON THE OTHER HAND, I'M ALL ABOUT BUILDING BRIDGES.
BB

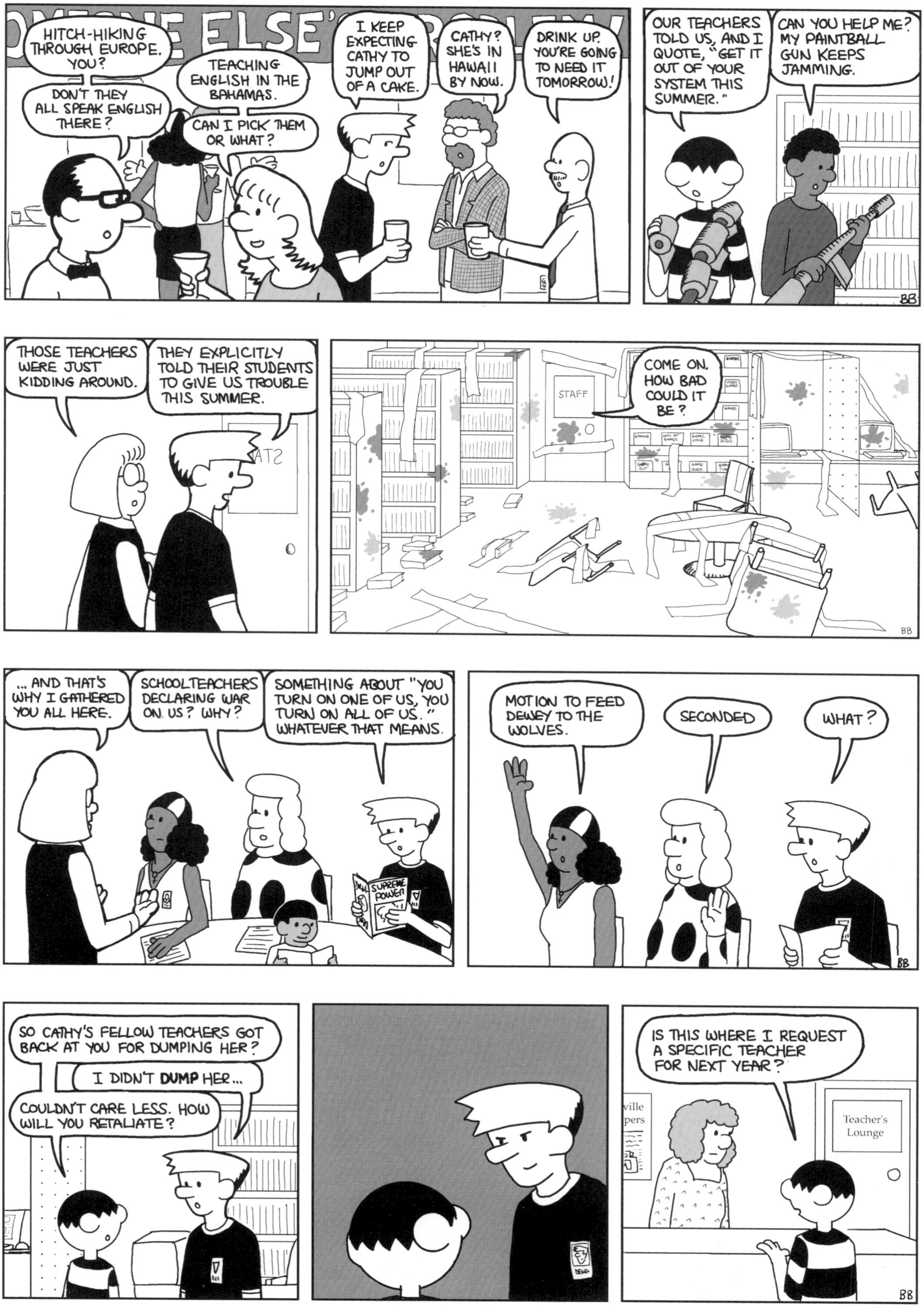
HITCH-HIKING THROUGH EUROPE. YOU?
DON'T THEY ALL SPEAK ENGLISH THERE?
TEACHING ENGLISH IN THE BAHAMAS.
CAN I PICK THEM OR WHAT?
I KEEP EXPECTING CATHY TO JUMP OUT OF A CAKE.
CATHY? SHE'S IN HAWAII BY NOW.
DRINK UP. YOU'RE GOING TO NEED IT TOMORROW!
OUR TEACHERS TOLD US, AND I QUOTE, "GET IT OUT OF YOUR SYSTEM THIS SUMMER."
CAN YOU HELP ME? MY PAINTBALL GUN KEEPS JAMMING.
BB
THOSE TEACHERS WERE JUST KIDDING AROUND.
THEY EXPLICITLY TOLD THEIR STUDENTS TO GIVE US TROUBLE THIS SUMMER.
STAFF
COME ON. HOW BAD COULD IT BE?
BB
... AND THAT'S WHY I GATHERED YOU ALL HERE.
SCHOOLTEACHERS DECLARING WAR ON US? WHY?
SOMETHING ABOUT "YOU TURN ON ONE OF US, YOU TURN ON ALL OF US." WHATEVER THAT MEANS.
SUPREME POWER
MOTION TO FEED DEWEY TO THE WOLVES.
SECONDED
WHAT?
BB
SO CATHY'S FELLOW TEACHERS GOT BACK AT YOU FOR DUMPING HER?
I DIDN'T **DUMP** HER...
COULDN'T CARE LESS. HOW WILL YOU RETALIATE?
IS THIS WHERE I REQUEST A SPECIFIC TEACHER FOR NEXT YEAR?
Teacher's Lounge
BB

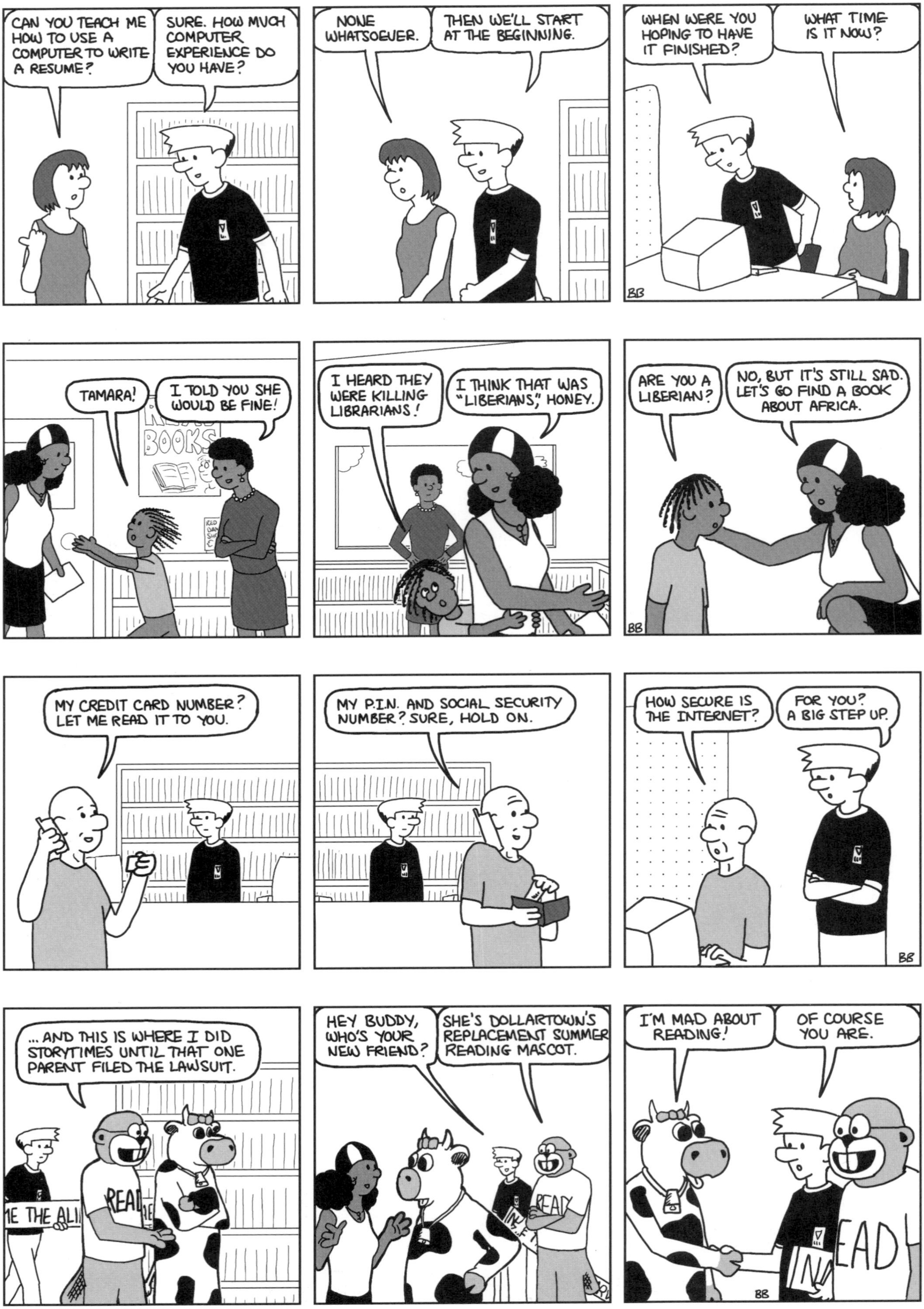
CAN YOU TEACH ME HOW TO USE A COMPUTER TO WRITE A RESUME?
SURE. HOW MUCH COMPUTER EXPERIENCE DO YOU HAVE?
NONE WHATSOEVER.
THEN WE'LL START AT THE BEGINNING.
WHEN WERE YOU HOPING TO HAVE IT FINISHED?
WHAT TIME IS IT NOW?
TAMARA!
I TOLD YOU SHE WOULD BE FINE!
BOOKS
I HEARD THEY WERE KILLING LIBRARIANS!
I THINK THAT WAS "LIBERIANS," HONEY.
ARE YOU A LIBERIAN?
NO, BUT IT'S STILL SAD. LET'S GO FIND A BOOK ABOUT AFRICA.
MY CREDIT CARD NUMBER? LET ME READ IT TO YOU.
MY P.I.N. AND SOCIAL SECURITY NUMBER? SURE, HOLD ON.
HOW SECURE IS THE INTERNET?
FOR YOU? A BIG STEP UP.
... AND THIS IS WHERE I DID STORYTIMES UNTIL THAT ONE PARENT FILED THE LAWSUIT.
READ
HEY BUDDY, WHO'S YOUR NEW FRIEND?
SHE'S DOLLARTOWN'S REPLACEMENT SUMMER READING MASCOT.
I'M MAD ABOUT READING!
OF COURSE YOU ARE.

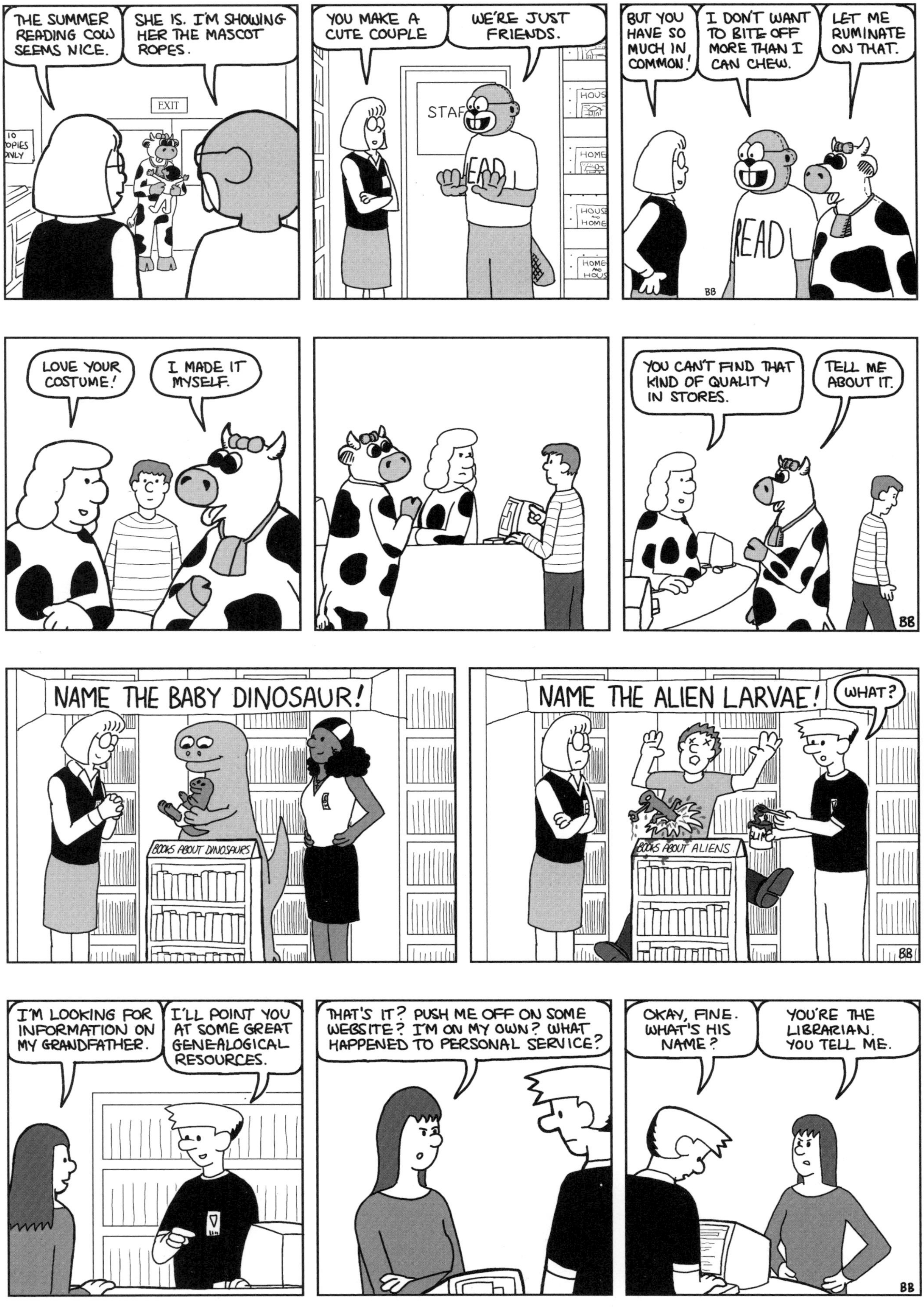
THE SUMMER READING COW SEEMS NICE.
SHE IS. I'M SHOWING HER THE MASCOT ROPES.
EXIT
10 COPIES ONLY
YOU MAKE A CUTE COUPLE
WE'RE JUST FRIENDS.
STAFF
READ
BUT YOU HAVE SO MUCH IN COMMON!
I DON'T WANT TO BITE OFF MORE THAN I CAN CHEW.
LET ME RUMINATE ON THAT.
READ
BB
LOVE YOUR COSTUME!
I MADE IT MYSELF.
YOU CAN'T FIND THAT KIND OF QUALITY IN STORES.
TELL ME ABOUT IT.
BB
NAME THE BABY DINOSAUR!
BOOKS ABOUT DINOSAURS
NAME THE ALIEN LARVAE!
WHAT?
BOOKS ABOUT ALIENS
BB
I'M LOOKING FOR INFORMATION ON MY GRANDFATHER.
I'LL POINT YOU AT SOME GREAT GENEALOGICAL RESOURCES.
THAT'S IT? PUSH ME OFF ON SOME WEBSITE? I'M ON MY OWN? WHAT HAPPENED TO PERSONAL SERVICE?
OKAY, FINE. WHAT'S HIS NAME?
YOU'RE THE LIBRARIAN. YOU TELL ME.
BB

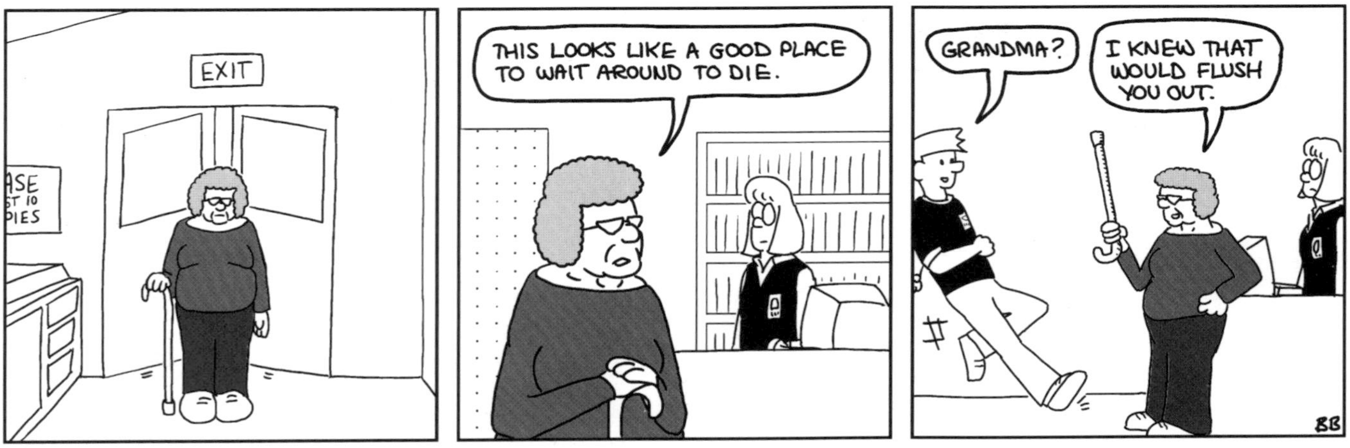

EXIT
THIS LOOKS LIKE A GOOD PLACE TO WAIT AROUND TO DIE.
GRANDMA?
I KNEW THAT WOULD FLUSH YOU OUT.
BB

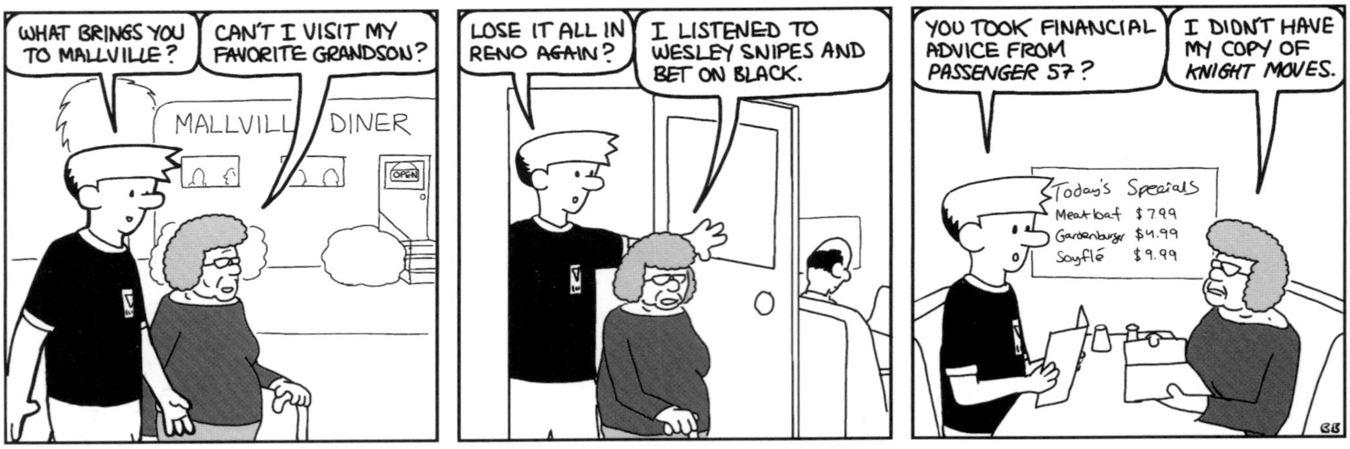

WHAT BRINGS YOU TO MALLVILLE?
CAN'T I VISIT MY FAVORITE GRANDSON?
OPEN
LOSE IT ALL IN RENO AGAIN?
I LISTENED TO WESLEY SNIPES AND BET ON BLACK.
YOU TOOK FINANCIAL ADVICE FROM *PASSENGER 57*?
I DIDN'T HAVE MY COPY OF *KNIGHT MOVES*.
Today's Specials
Meatloaf $7.99
Gardenburger $4.99
Souflé $9.99
BB

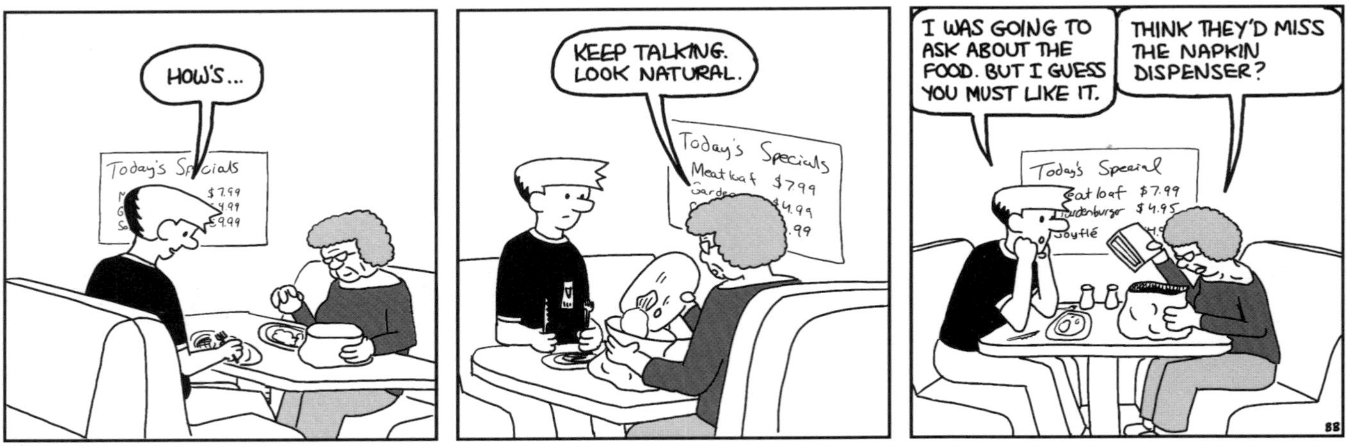

HOW'S...
KEEP TALKING. LOOK NATURAL.
I WAS GOING TO ASK ABOUT THE FOOD. BUT I GUESS YOU MUST LIKE IT.
THINK THEY'D MISS THE NAPKIN DISPENSER?
BB

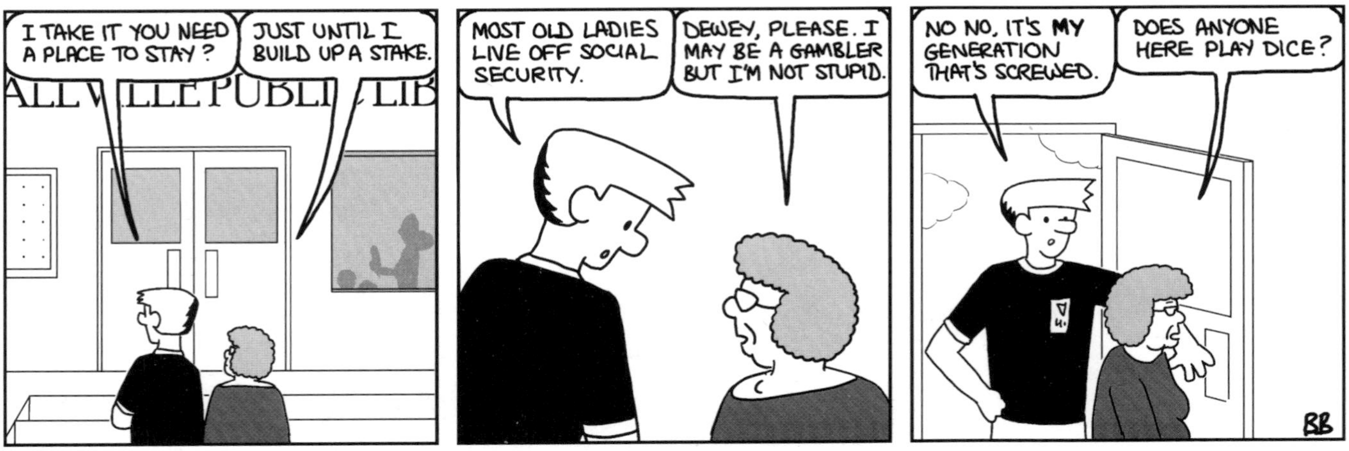

I TAKE IT YOU NEED A PLACE TO STAY?
JUST UNTIL I BUILD UP A STAKE.
MOST OLD LADIES LIVE OFF SOCIAL SECURITY.
DEWEY, PLEASE. I MAY BE A GAMBLER BUT I'M NOT STUPID.
NO NO, IT'S MY GENERATION THAT'S SCREWED.
DOES ANYONE HERE PLAY DICE?
BB

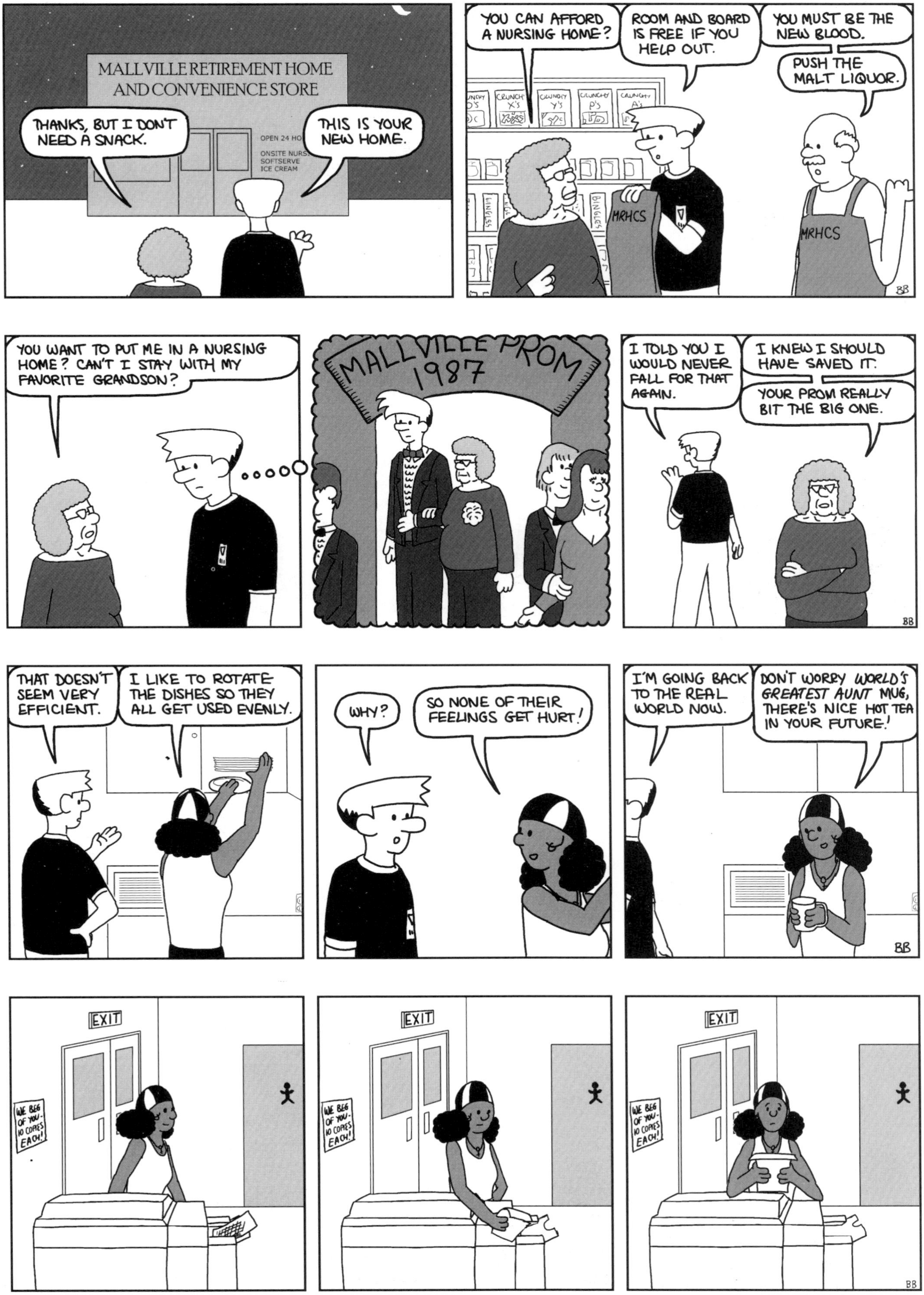
MALLVILLE RETIREMENT HOME AND CONVENIENCE STORE
THANKS, BUT I DON'T NEED A SNACK.
THIS IS YOUR NEW HOME.
SOFTSERVE ICE CREAM
YOU CAN AFFORD A NURSING HOME?
ROOM AND BOARD IS FREE IF YOU HELP OUT.
YOU MUST BE THE NEW BLOOD.
PUSH THE MALT LIQUOR.
MRHCS
MRHCS
YOU WANT TO PUT ME IN A NURSING HOME? CAN'T I STAY WITH MY FAVORITE GRANDSON?
MALLVILLE PROM 1987
I TOLD YOU I WOULD NEVER FALL FOR THAT AGAIN.
I KNEW I SHOULD HAVE SAVED IT.
YOUR PROM REALLY BIT THE BIG ONE.
THAT DOESN'T SEEM VERY EFFICIENT.
I LIKE TO ROTATE THE DISHES SO THEY ALL GET USED EVENLY.
WHY?
SO NONE OF THEIR FEELINGS GET HURT!
I'M GOING BACK TO THE REAL WORLD NOW.
DON'T WORRY *WORLD'S GREATEST AUNT* MUG, THERE'S NICE HOT TEA IN YOUR FUTURE!
EXIT
WE BEG OF YOU - 10 COPIES EACH!
EXIT
WE BEG OF YOU - 10 COPIES EACH!
EXIT
WE BEG OF YOU - 10 COPIES EACH!

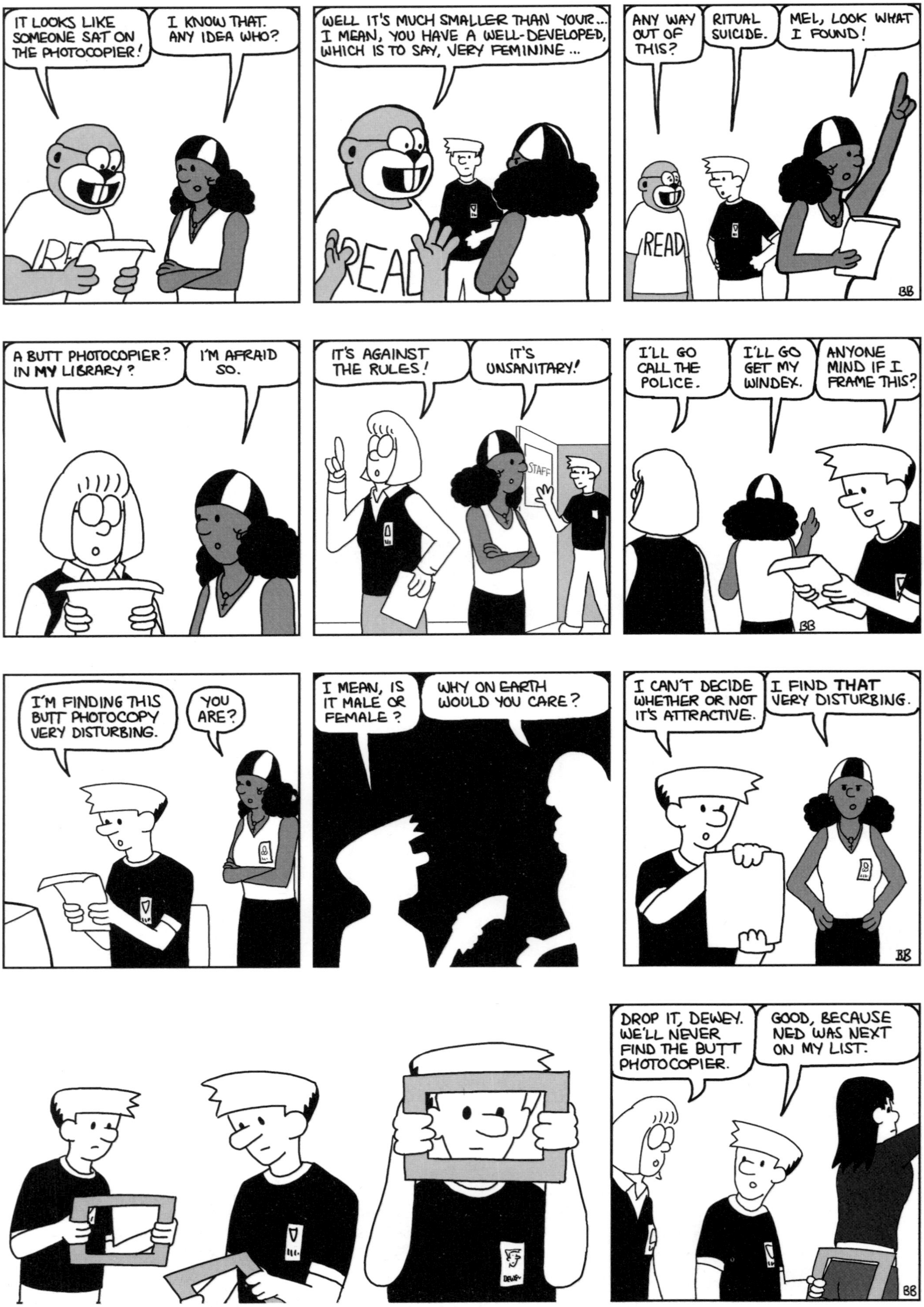
IT LOOKS LIKE SOMEONE SAT ON THE PHOTOCOPIER!
I KNOW THAT. ANY IDEA WHO?
READ
WELL IT'S MUCH SMALLER THAN YOUR... I MEAN, YOU HAVE A WELL-DEVELOPED, WHICH IS TO SAY, VERY FEMININE...
READ
ANY WAY OUT OF THIS?
RITUAL SUICIDE.
MEL, LOOK WHAT I FOUND!
READ
BB
A BUTT PHOTOCOPIER? IN MY LIBRARY?
I'M AFRAID SO.
IT'S AGAINST THE RULES!
IT'S UNSANITARY!
STAFF
I'LL GO CALL THE POLICE.
I'LL GO GET MY WINDEX.
ANYONE MIND IF I FRAME THIS?
BB
I'M FINDING THIS BUTT PHOTOCOPY VERY DISTURBING.
YOU ARE?
I MEAN, IS IT MALE OR FEMALE?
WHY ON EARTH WOULD YOU CARE?
I CAN'T DECIDE WHETHER OR NOT IT'S ATTRACTIVE.
I FIND THAT VERY DISTURBING.
BB
DROP IT, DEWEY. WE'LL NEVER FIND THE BUTT PHOTOCOPIER.
GOOD, BECAUSE NED WAS NEXT ON MY LIST.
BB

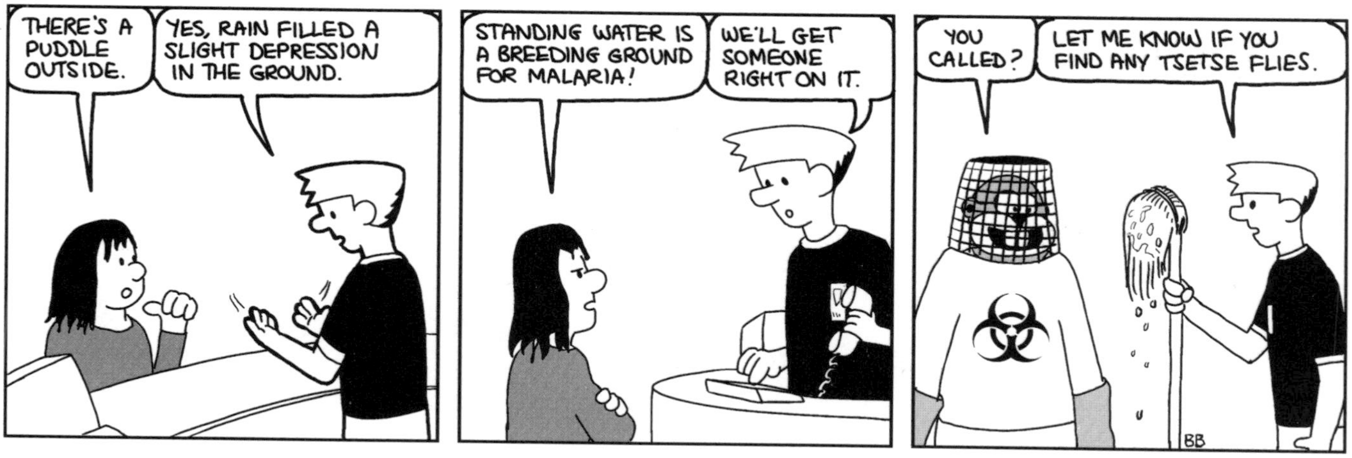
THERE'S A PUDDLE OUTSIDE.
YES, RAIN FILLED A SLIGHT DEPRESSION IN THE GROUND.
STANDING WATER IS A BREEDING GROUND FOR MALARIA!
WE'LL GET SOMEONE RIGHT ON IT.
YOU CALLED?
LET ME KNOW IF YOU FIND ANY TSETSE FLIES.
BB

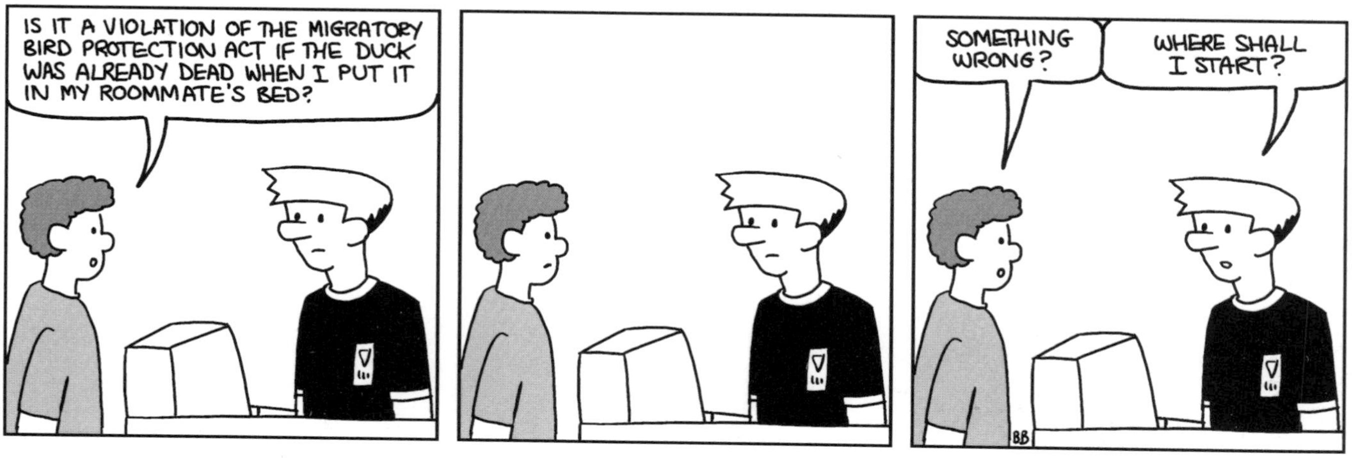
IS IT A VIOLATION OF THE MIGRATORY BIRD PROTECTION ACT IF THE DUCK WAS ALREADY DEAD WHEN I PUT IT IN MY ROOMMATE'S BED?
SOMETHING WRONG?
WHERE SHALL I START?
BB

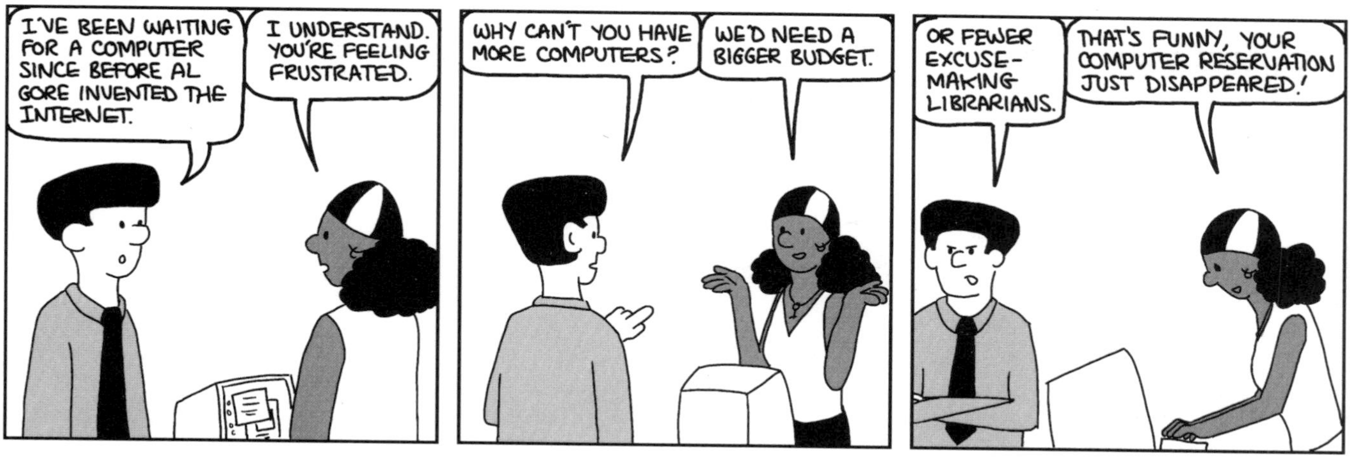
I'VE BEEN WAITING FOR A COMPUTER SINCE BEFORE AL GORE INVENTED THE INTERNET.
I UNDERSTAND. YOU'RE FEELING FRUSTRATED.
WHY CAN'T YOU HAVE MORE COMPUTERS?
WE'D NEED A BIGGER BUDGET.
OR FEWER EXCUSE-MAKING LIBRARIANS.
THAT'S FUNNY, YOUR COMPUTER RESERVATION JUST DISAPPEARED!

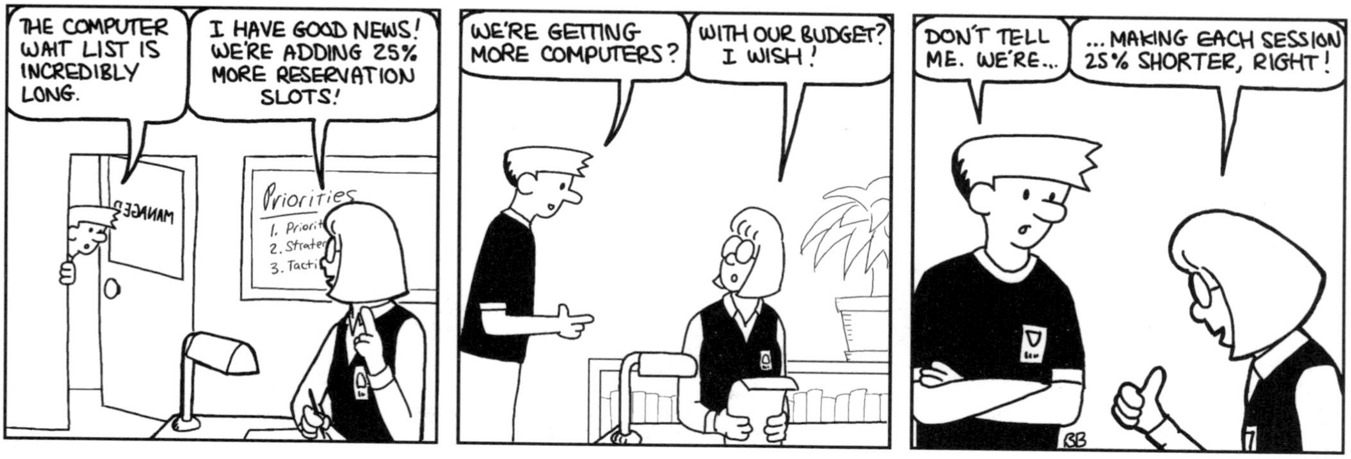
THE COMPUTER WAIT LIST IS INCREDIBLY LONG.
I HAVE GOOD NEWS! WE'RE ADDING 25% MORE RESERVATION SLOTS!
Priorities
WE'RE GETTING MORE COMPUTERS?
WITH OUR BUDGET? I WISH!
DON'T TELL ME. WE'RE...
...MAKING EACH SESSION 25% SHORTER, RIGHT!
BB

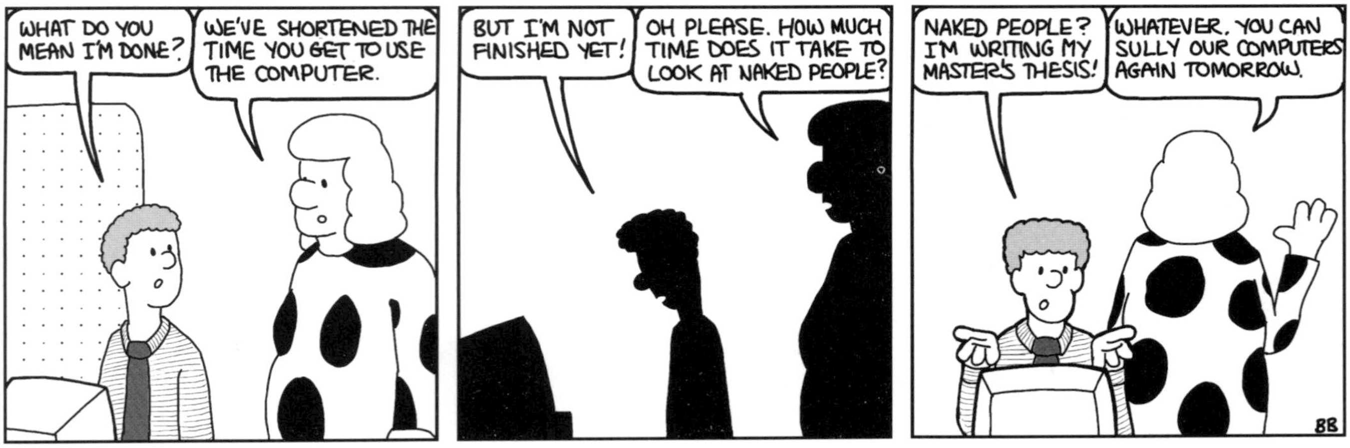
WHAT DO YOU MEAN I'M DONE?
WE'VE SHORTENED THE TIME YOU GET TO USE THE COMPUTER.
BUT I'M NOT FINISHED YET!
OH PLEASE. HOW MUCH TIME DOES IT TAKE TO LOOK AT NAKED PEOPLE?
NAKED PEOPLE? I'M WRITING MY MASTER'S THESIS!
WHATEVER. YOU CAN SULLY OUR COMPUTERS AGAIN TOMORROW.
BB

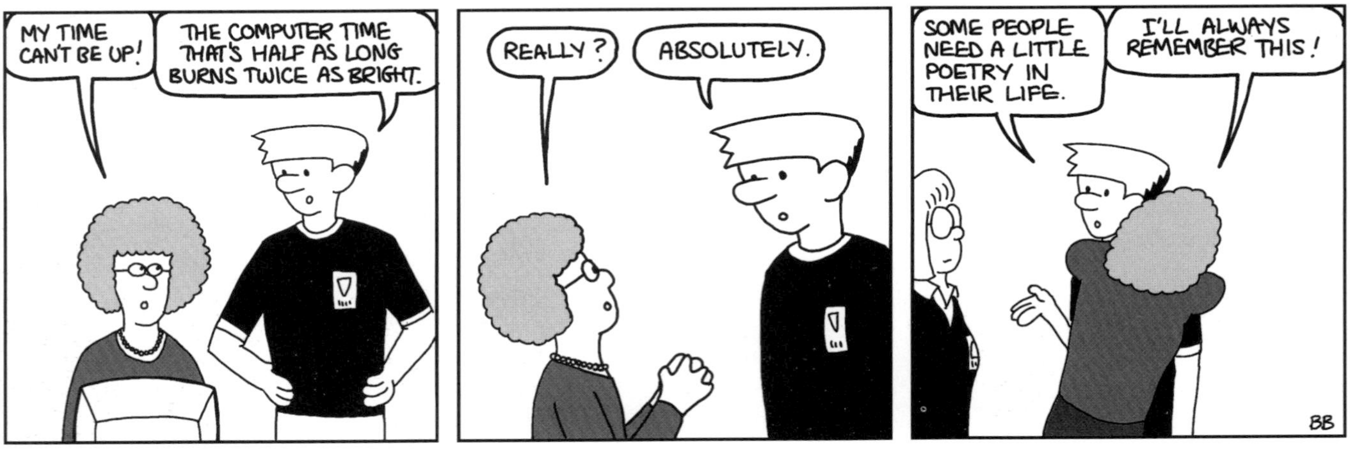
MY TIME CAN'T BE UP!
THE COMPUTER TIME THAT'S HALF AS LONG BURNS TWICE AS BRIGHT.
REALLY?
ABSOLUTELY.
SOME PEOPLE NEED A LITTLE POETRY IN THEIR LIFE.
I'LL ALWAYS REMEMBER THIS!
BB

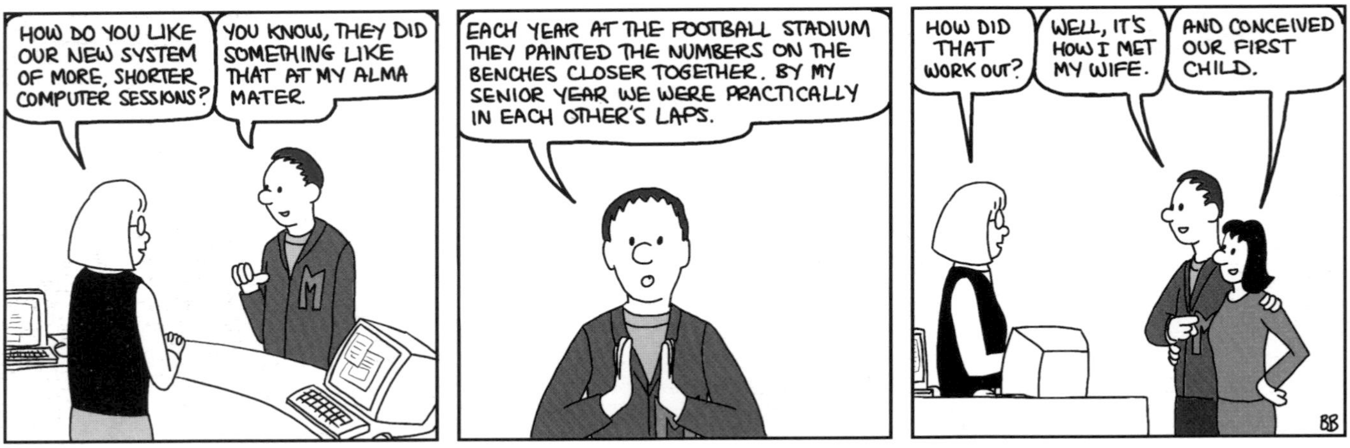
HOW DO YOU LIKE OUR NEW SYSTEM OF MORE, SHORTER COMPUTER SESSIONS?
YOU KNOW, THEY DID SOMETHING LIKE THAT AT MY ALMA MATER.
EACH YEAR AT THE FOOTBALL STADIUM THEY PAINTED THE NUMBERS ON THE BENCHES CLOSER TOGETHER. BY MY SENIOR YEAR WE WERE PRACTICALLY IN EACH OTHER'S LAPS.
HOW DID THAT WORK OUT?
WELL, IT'S HOW I MET MY WIFE.
AND CONCEIVED OUR FIRST CHILD.
BB

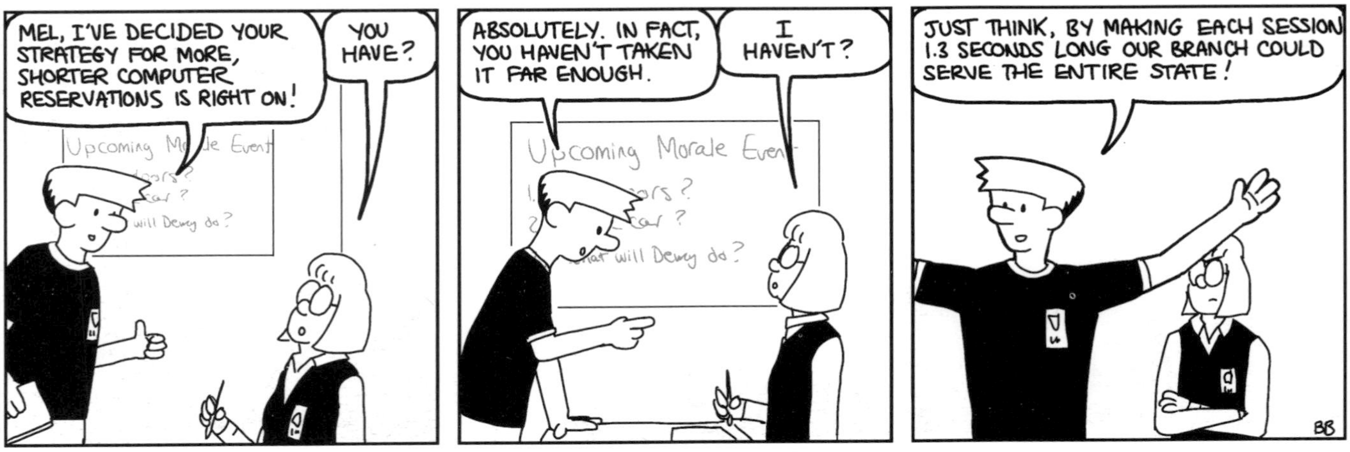
MEL, I'VE DECIDED YOUR STRATEGY FOR MORE, SHORTER COMPUTER RESERVATIONS IS RIGHT ON!
YOU HAVE?
ABSOLUTELY. IN FACT, YOU HAVEN'T TAKEN IT FAR ENOUGH.
I HAVEN'T?
JUST THINK, BY MAKING EACH SESSION 1.3 SECONDS LONG OUR BRANCH COULD SERVE THE ENTIRE STATE!
BB

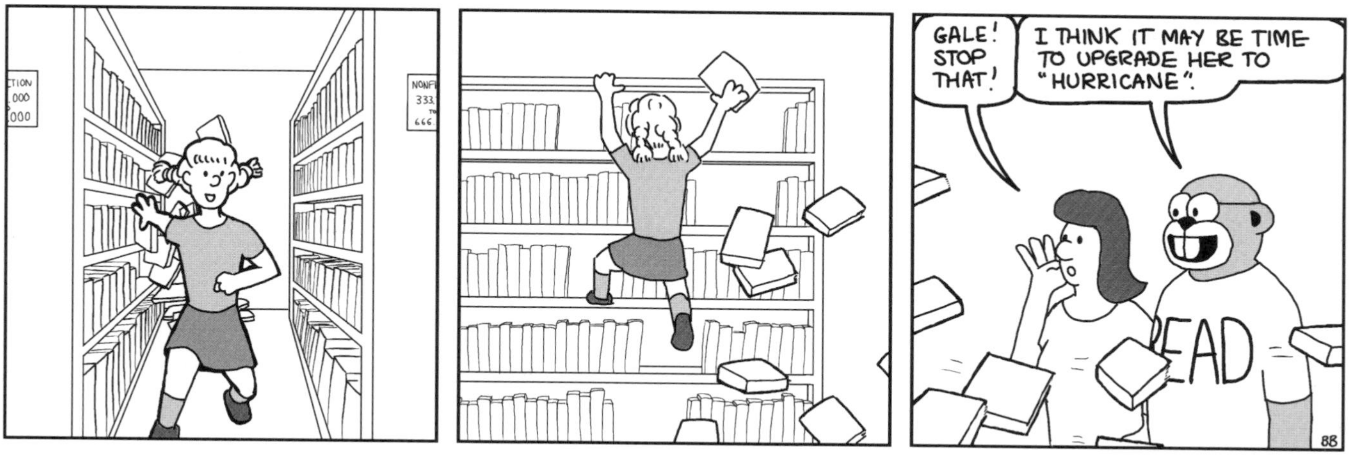
GALE! STOP THAT!
I THINK IT MAY BE TIME TO UPGRADE HER TO "HURRICANE".

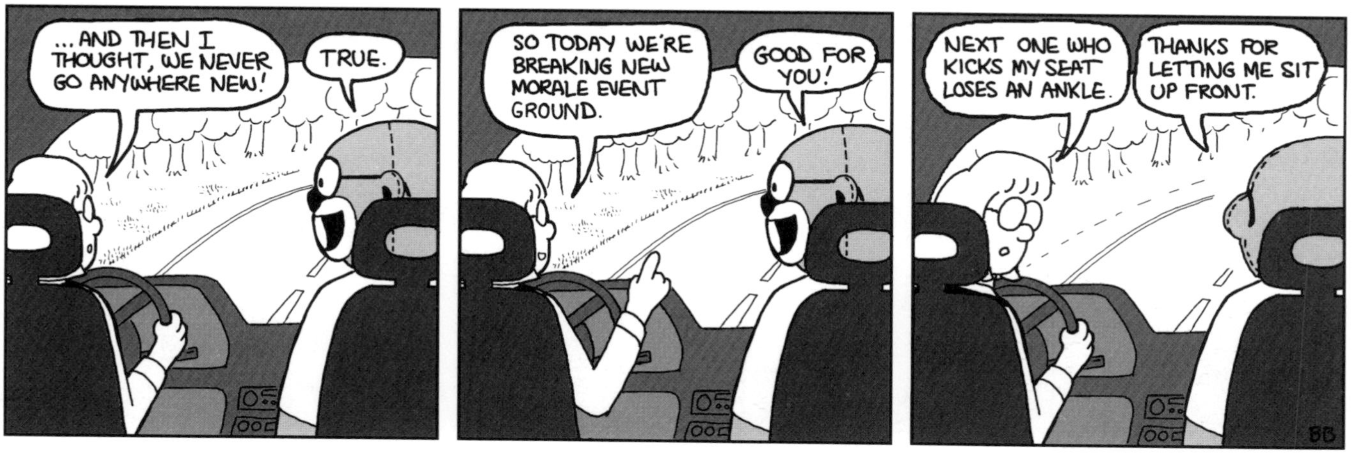
...AND THEN I THOUGHT, WE NEVER GO ANYWHERE NEW!
TRUE.
SO TODAY WE'RE BREAKING NEW MORALE EVENT GROUND.
GOOD FOR YOU!
NEXT ONE WHO KICKS MY SEAT LOSES AN ANKLE.
THANKS FOR LETTING ME SIT UP FRONT.

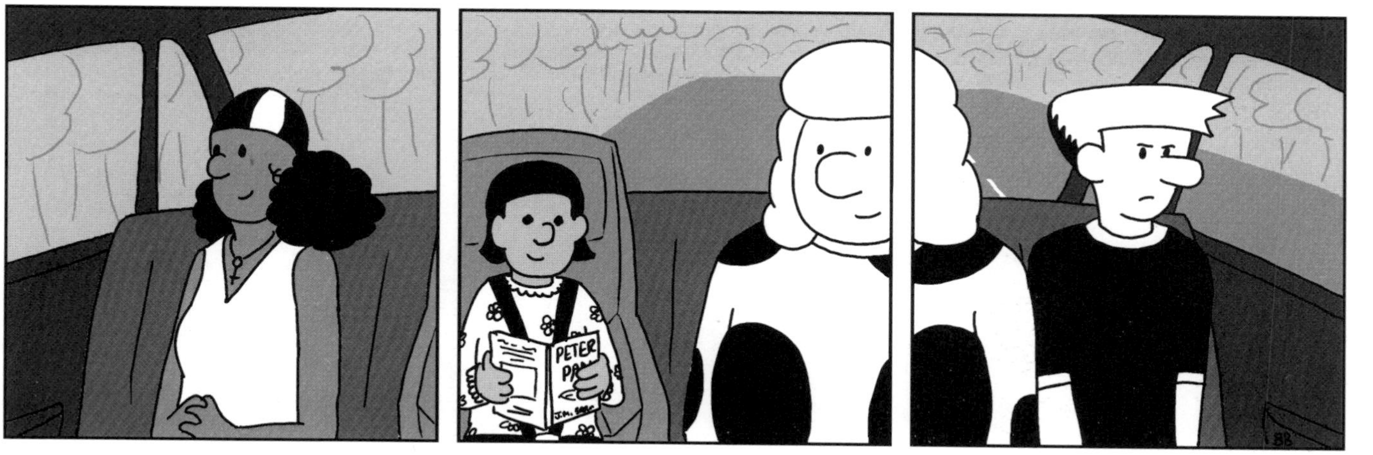
PETER PAN

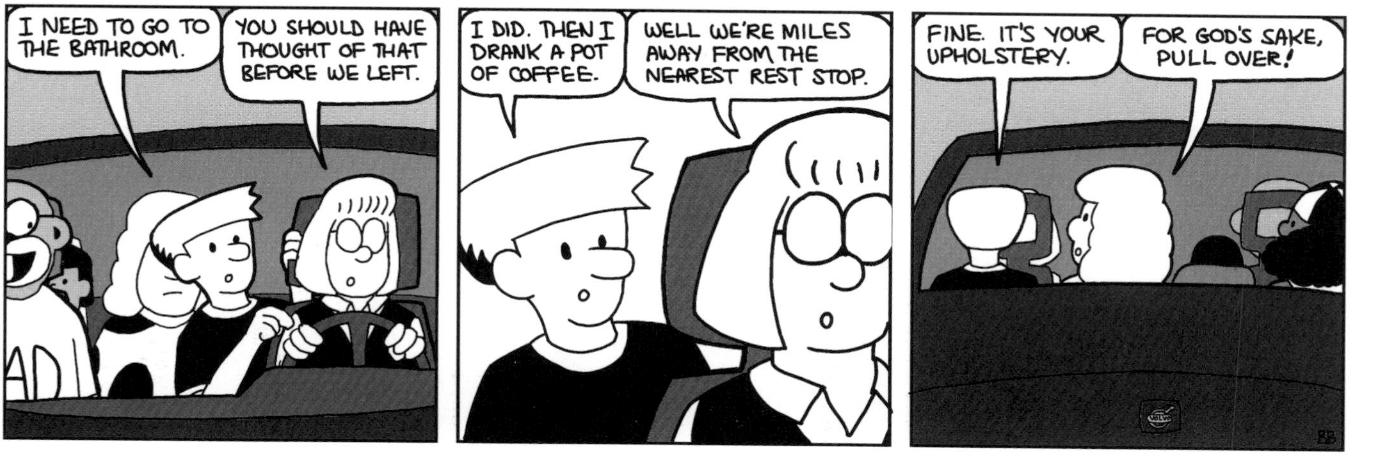
I NEED TO GO TO THE BATHROOM.
YOU SHOULD HAVE THOUGHT OF THAT BEFORE WE LEFT.
I DID. THEN I DRANK A POT OF COFFEE.
WELL WE'RE MILES AWAY FROM THE NEAREST REST STOP.
FINE. IT'S YOUR UPHOLSTERY.
FOR GOD'S SAKE, PULL OVER!

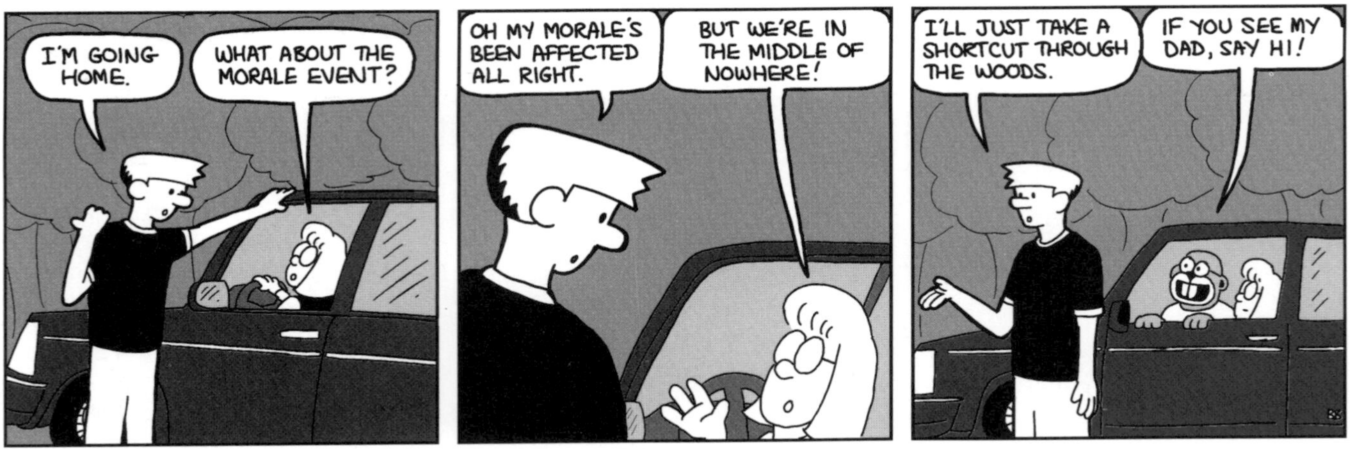
I'M GOING HOME.
WHAT ABOUT THE MORALE EVENT?
OH MY MORALE'S BEEN AFFECTED ALL RIGHT.
BUT WE'RE IN THE MIDDLE OF NOWHERE!
I'LL JUST TAKE A SHORTCUT THROUGH THE WOODS.
IF YOU SEE MY DAD, SAY HI!

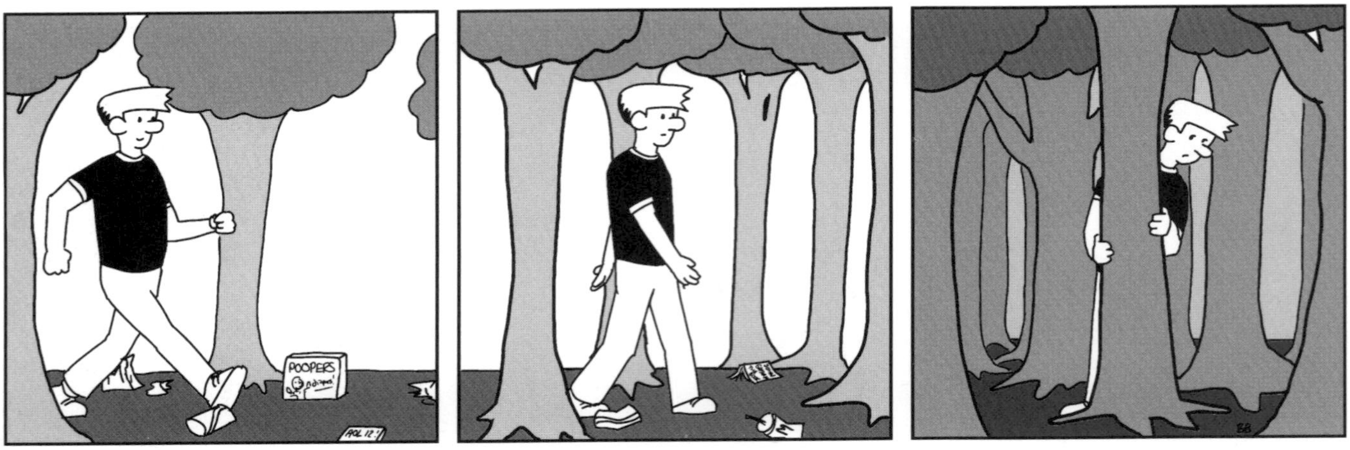
POOPERS

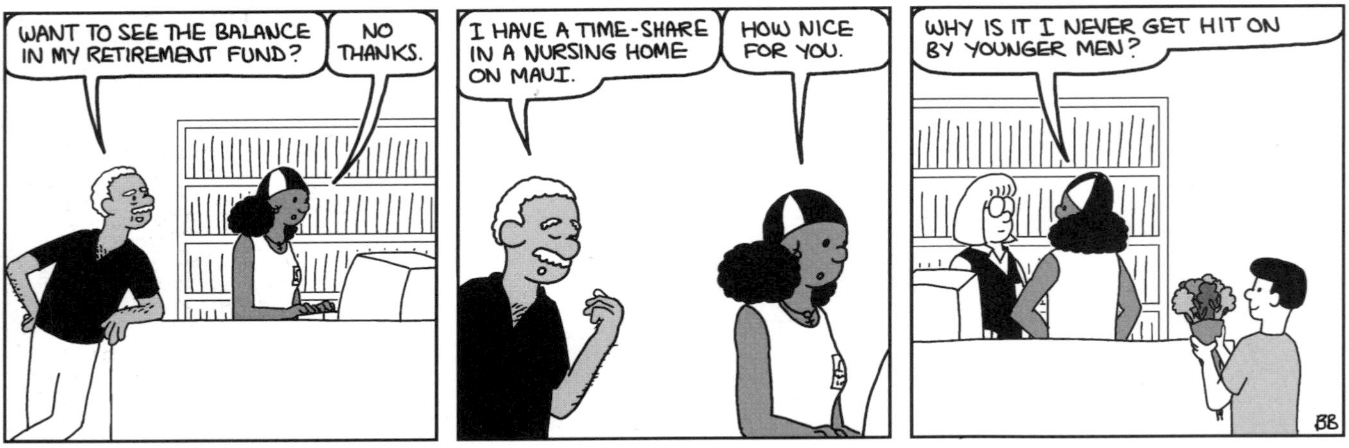
WANT TO SEE THE BALANCE IN MY RETIREMENT FUND?
NO THANKS.
I HAVE A TIME-SHARE IN A NURSING HOME ON MAUI.
HOW NICE FOR YOU.
WHY IS IT I NEVER GET HIT ON BY YOUNGER MEN?

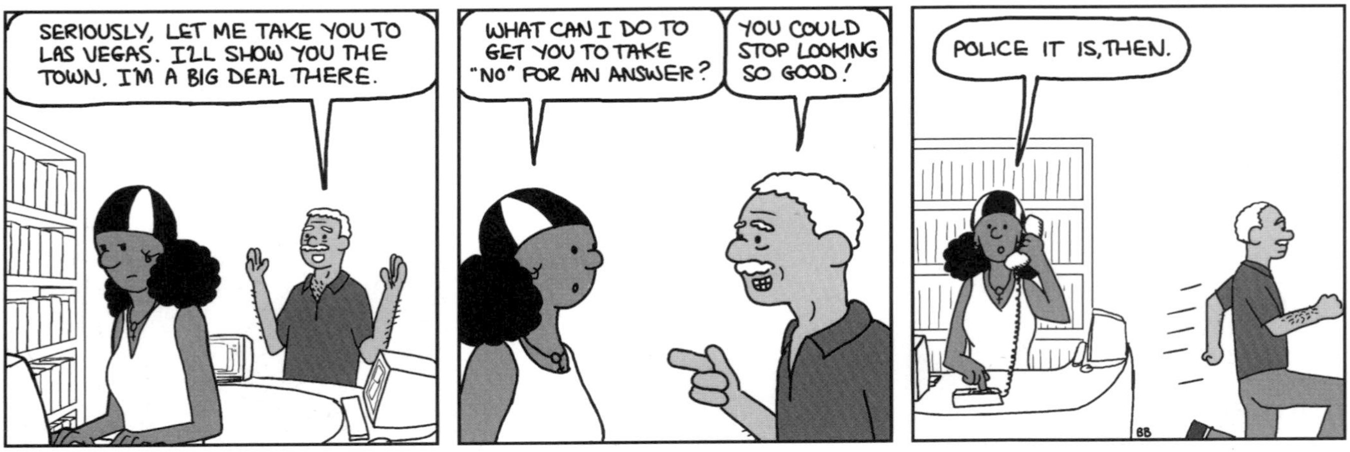
SERIOUSLY, LET ME TAKE YOU TO LAS VEGAS. I'LL SHOW YOU THE TOWN. I'M A BIG DEAL THERE.
WHAT CAN I DO TO GET YOU TO TAKE "NO" FOR AN ANSWER?
YOU COULD STOP LOOKING SO GOOD!
POLICE IT IS, THEN.

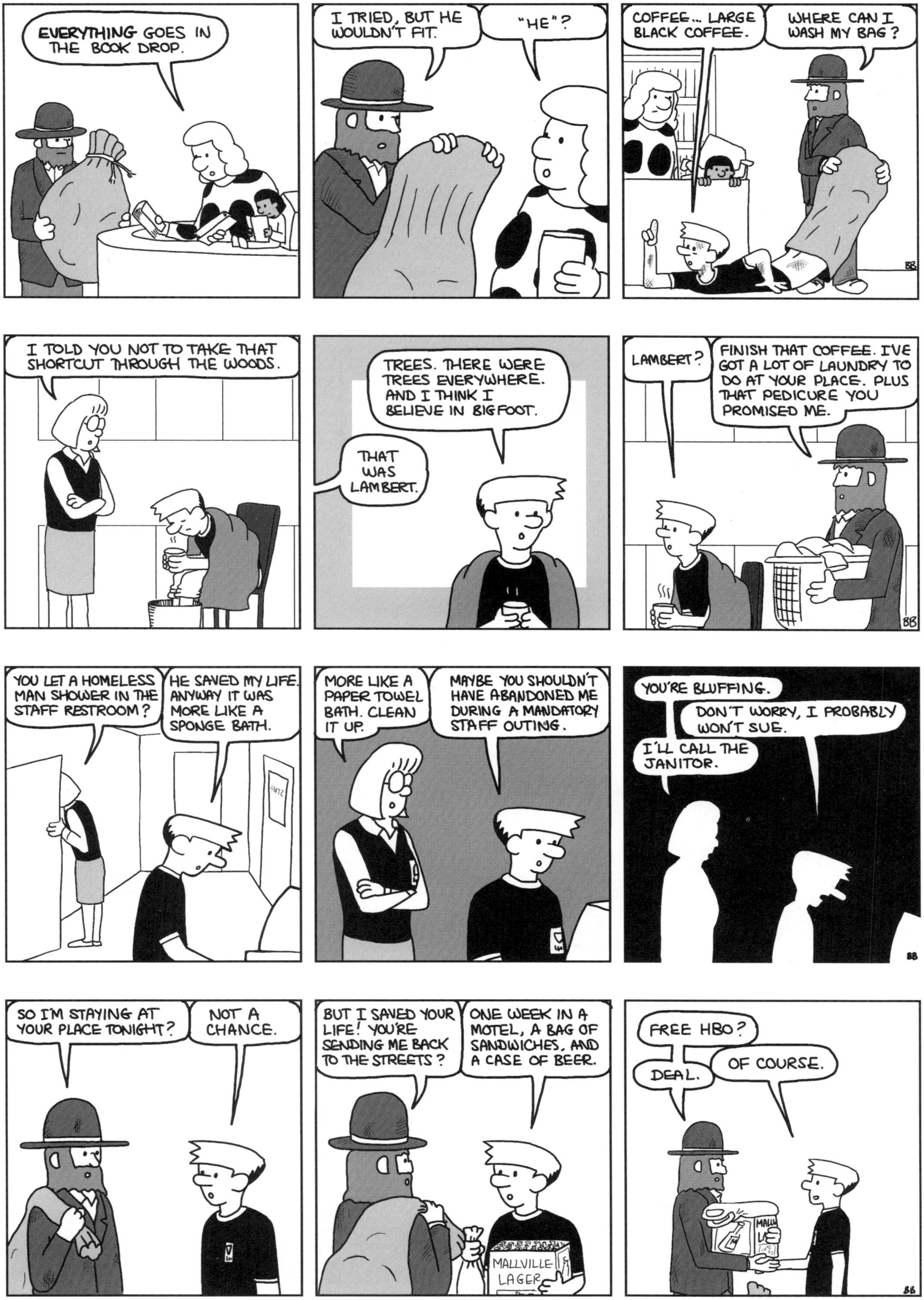
EVERYTHING GOES IN THE BOOK DROP.
I TRIED, BUT HE WOULDN'T FIT.
"HE"?
COFFEE... LARGE BLACK COFFEE.
WHERE CAN I WASH MY BAG?
I TOLD YOU NOT TO TAKE THAT SHORTCUT THROUGH THE WOODS.
TREES. THERE WERE TREES EVERYWHERE. AND I THINK I BELIEVE IN BIGFOOT.
THAT WAS LAMBERT.
LAMBERT?
FINISH THAT COFFEE. I'VE GOT A LOT OF LAUNDRY TO DO AT YOUR PLACE. PLUS THAT PEDICURE YOU PROMISED ME.
YOU LET A HOMELESS MAN SHOWER IN THE STAFF RESTROOM?
HE SAVED MY LIFE. ANYWAY IT WAS MORE LIKE A SPONGE BATH.
MORE LIKE A PAPER TOWEL BATH. CLEAN IT UP.
MAYBE YOU SHOULDN'T HAVE ABANDONED ME DURING A MANDATORY STAFF OUTING.
YOU'RE BLUFFING.
DON'T WORRY, I PROBABLY WON'T SUE.
I'LL CALL THE JANITOR.
SO I'M STAYING AT YOUR PLACE TONIGHT?
NOT A CHANCE.
BUT I SAVED YOUR LIFE! YOU'RE SENDING ME BACK TO THE STREETS?
ONE WEEK IN A MOTEL, A BAG OF SANDWICHES, AND A CASE OF BEER.
MALLVILLE LAGER
FREE HBO?
DEAL.
OF COURSE.

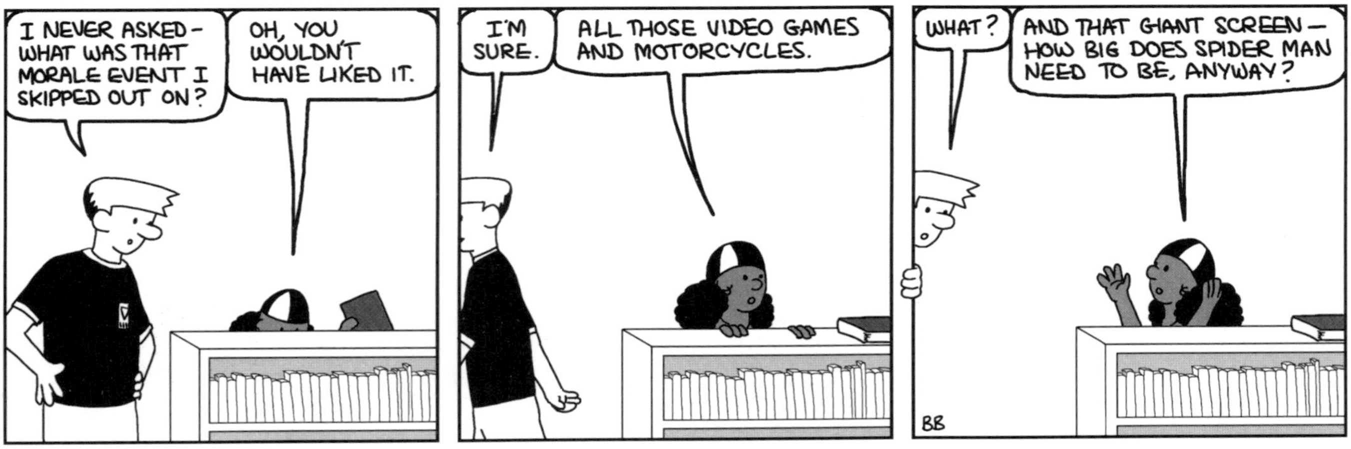
I NEVER ASKED - WHAT WAS THAT MORALE EVENT I SKIPPED OUT ON?
OH, YOU WOULDN'T HAVE LIKED IT.
I'M SURE.
ALL THOSE VIDEO GAMES AND MOTORCYCLES.
WHAT?
AND THAT GIANT SCREEN - HOW BIG DOES SPIDER MAN NEED TO BE, ANYWAY?
BB

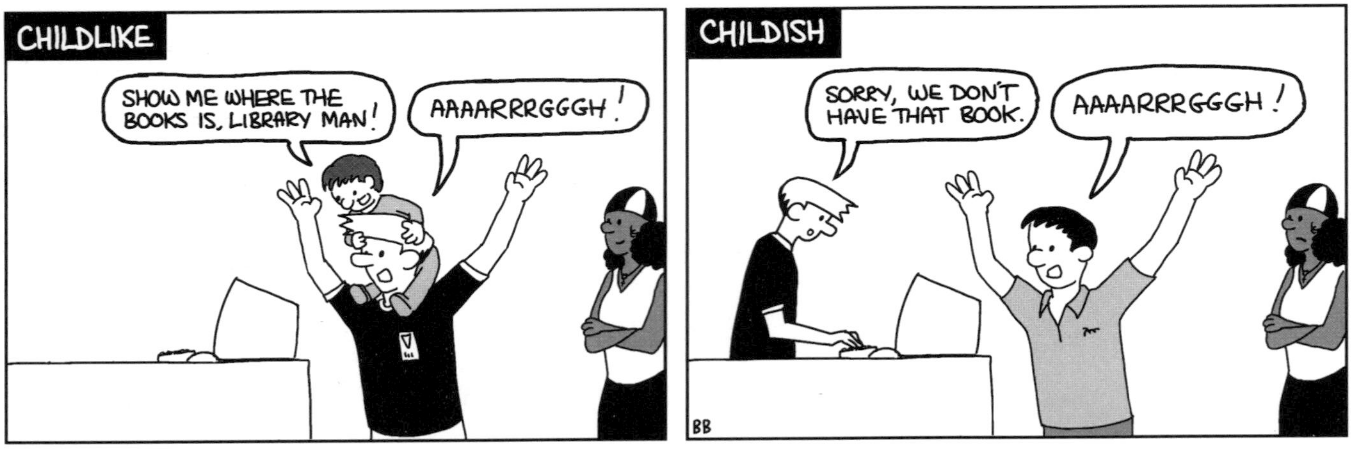
CHILDLIKE
SHOW ME WHERE THE BOOKS IS, LIBRARY MAN!
AAAARRRGGGH!
CHILDISH
SORRY, WE DON'T HAVE THAT BOOK.
AAAARRRGGGH!
BB

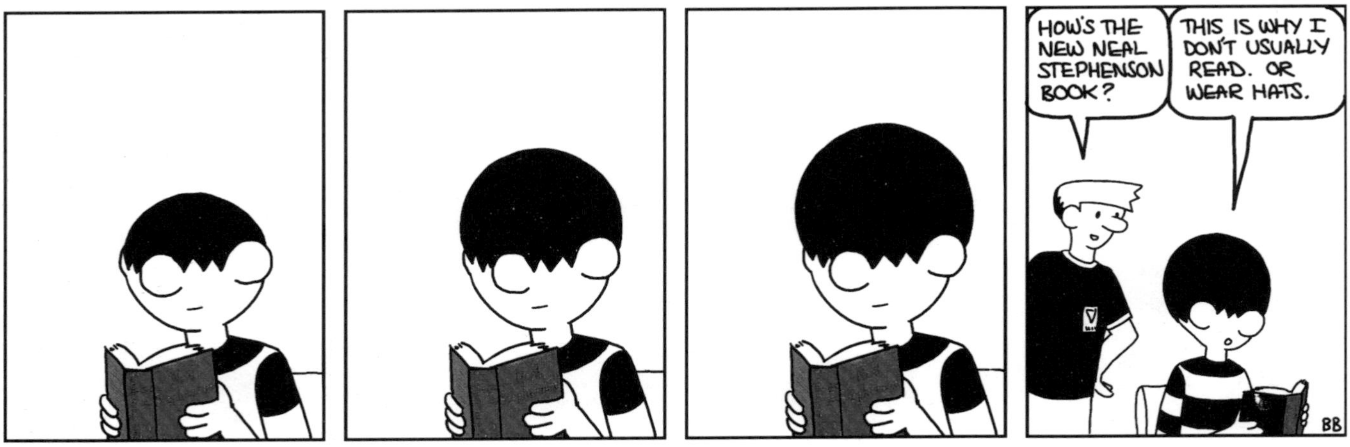
HOW'S THE NEW NEAL STEPHENSON BOOK?
THIS IS WHY I DON'T USUALLY READ. OR WEAR HATS.
BB

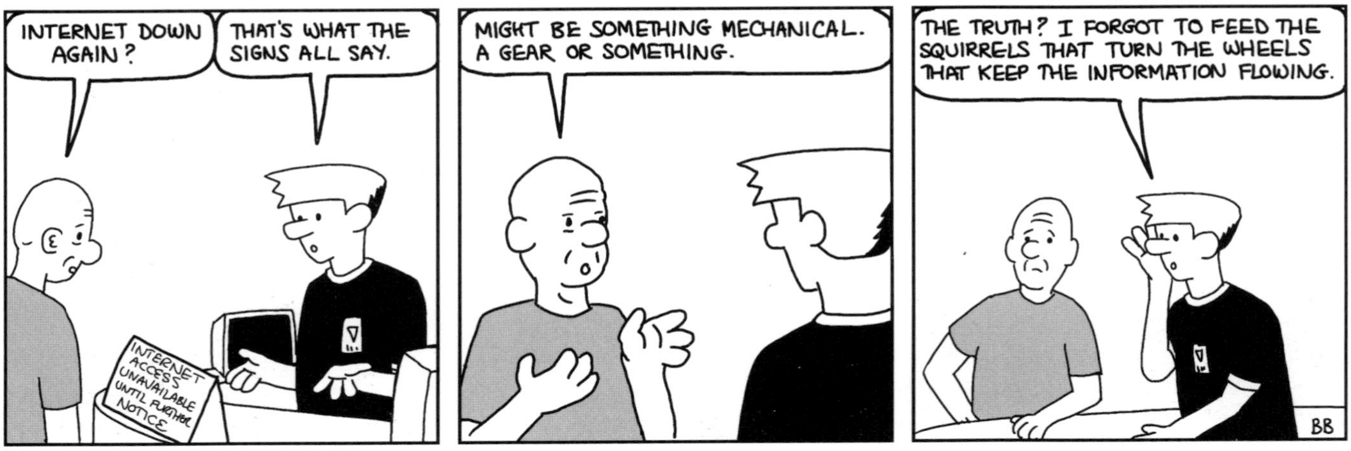
INTERNET DOWN AGAIN?
THAT'S WHAT THE SIGNS ALL SAY.
INTERNET ACCESS UNAVAILABLE UNTIL FURTHER NOTICE
MIGHT BE SOMETHING MECHANICAL. A GEAR OR SOMETHING.
THE TRUTH? I FORGOT TO FEED THE SQUIRRELS THAT TURN THE WHEELS THAT KEEP THE INFORMATION FLOWING.
BB

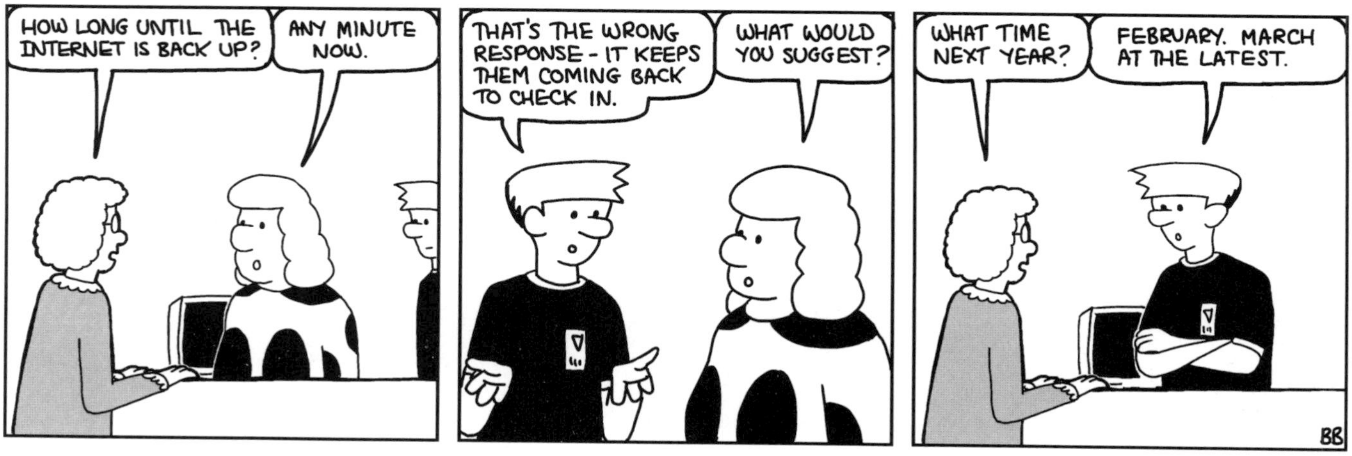
HOW LONG UNTIL THE INTERNET IS BACK UP?
ANY MINUTE NOW.
THAT'S THE WRONG RESPONSE - IT KEEPS THEM COMING BACK TO CHECK IN.
WHAT WOULD YOU SUGGEST?
WHAT TIME NEXT YEAR?
FEBRUARY. MARCH AT THE LATEST.
BB

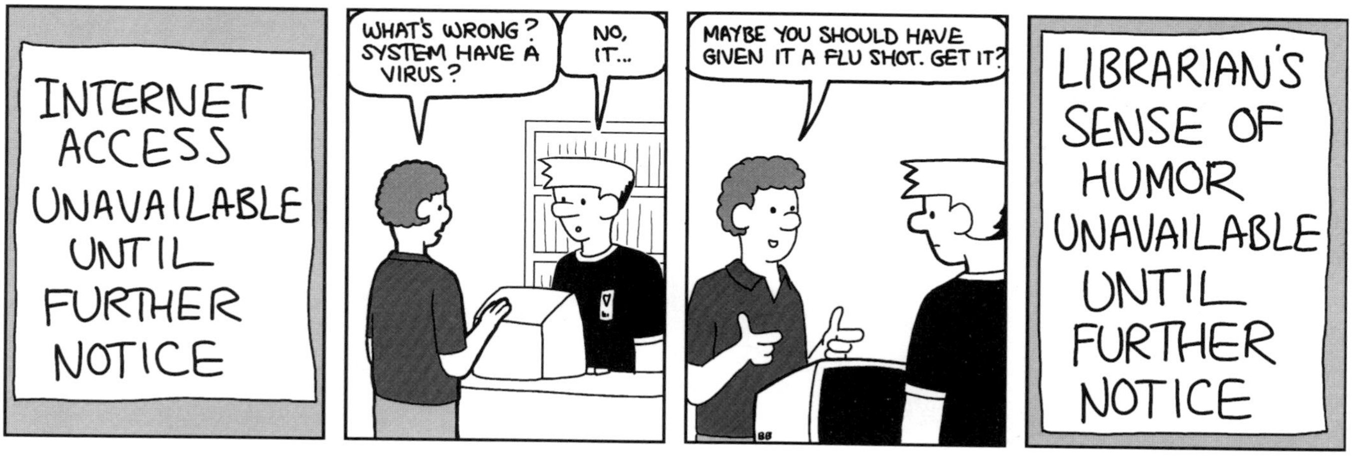
INTERNET ACCESS UNAVAILABLE UNTIL FURTHER NOTICE
WHAT'S WRONG? SYSTEM HAVE A VIRUS?
NO, IT...
MAYBE YOU SHOULD HAVE GIVEN IT A FLU SHOT. GET IT?
LIBRARIAN'S SENSE OF HUMOR UNAVAILABLE UNTIL FURTHER NOTICE

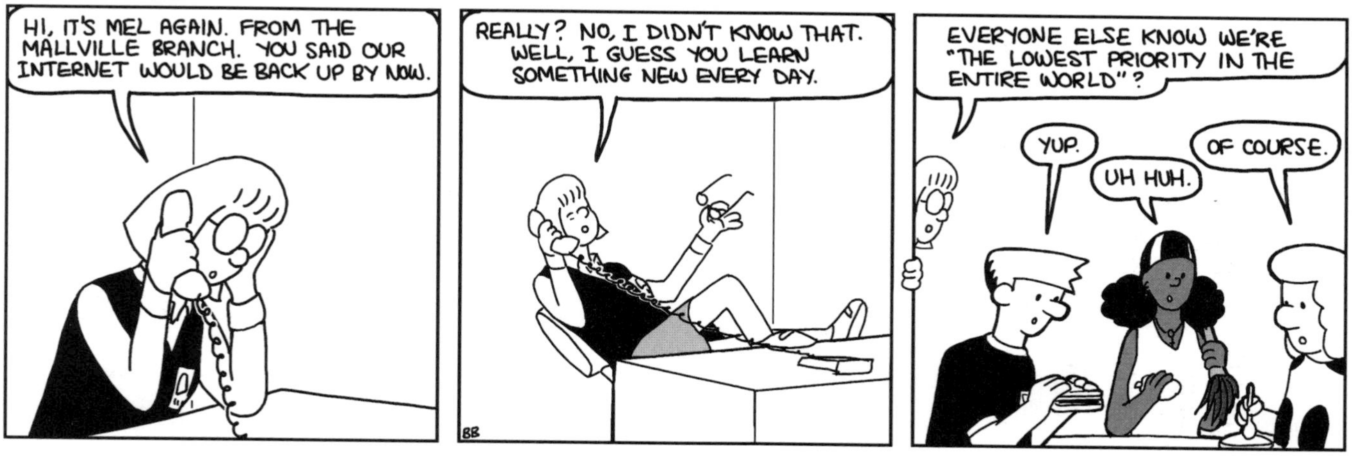
HI, IT'S MEL AGAIN. FROM THE MALLVILLE BRANCH. YOU SAID OUR INTERNET WOULD BE BACK UP BY NOW.
REALLY? NO, I DIDN'T KNOW THAT. WELL, I GUESS YOU LEARN SOMETHING NEW EVERY DAY.
EVERYONE ELSE KNOW WE'RE "THE LOWEST PRIORITY IN THE ENTIRE WORLD"?
YUP.
UH HUH.
OF COURSE.
BB

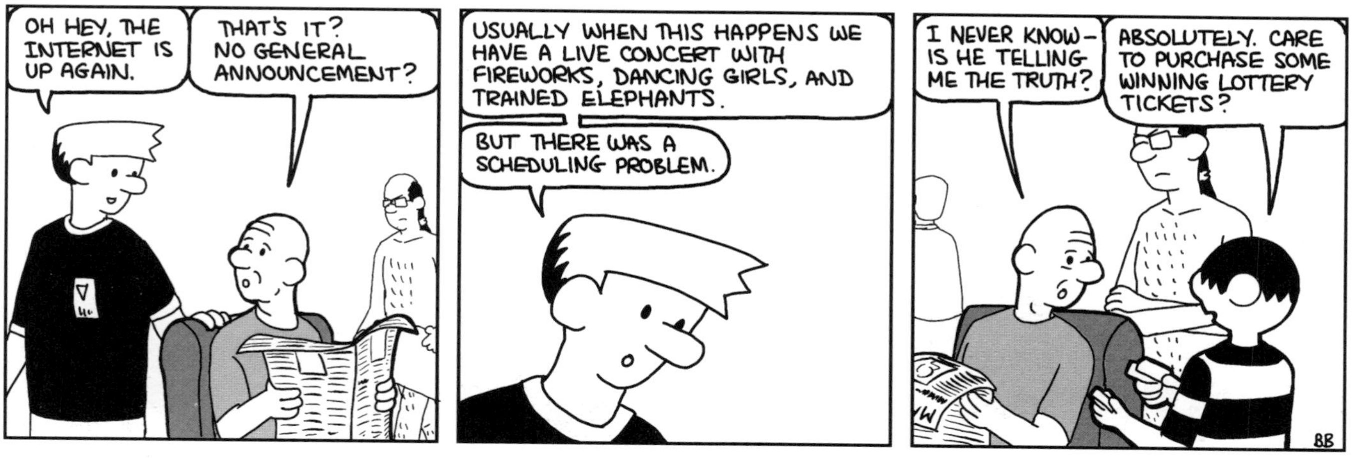
OH HEY, THE INTERNET IS UP AGAIN.
THAT'S IT? NO GENERAL ANNOUNCEMENT?
USUALLY WHEN THIS HAPPENS WE HAVE A LIVE CONCERT WITH FIREWORKS, DANCING GIRLS, AND TRAINED ELEPHANTS.
BUT THERE WAS A SCHEDULING PROBLEM.
I NEVER KNOW - IS HE TELLING ME THE TRUTH?
ABSOLUTELY. CARE TO PURCHASE SOME WINNING LOTTERY TICKETS?
BB

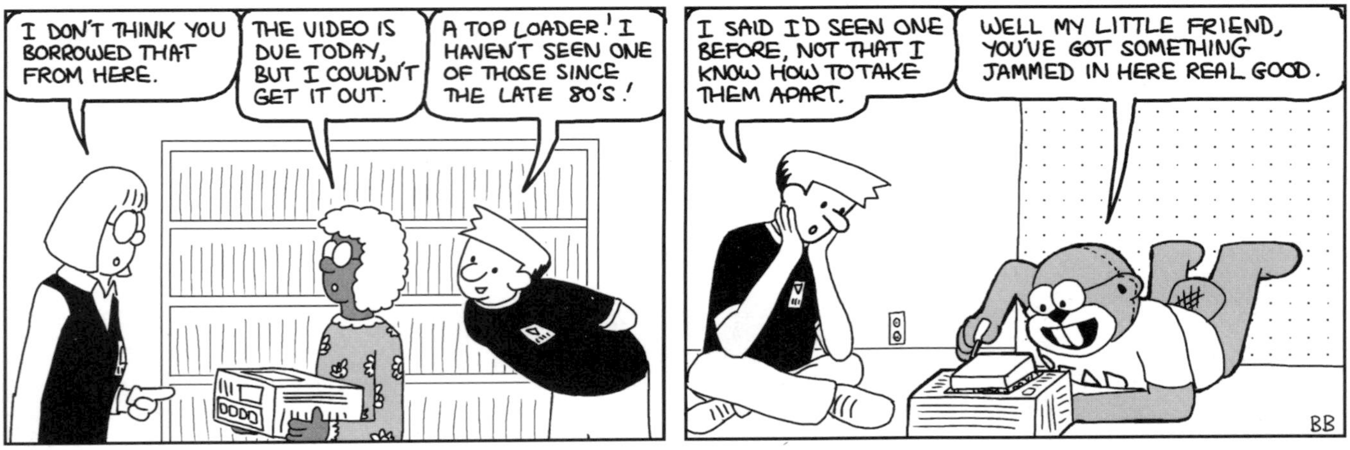
I DON'T THINK YOU BORROWED THAT FROM HERE.
THE VIDEO IS DUE TODAY, BUT I COULDN'T GET IT OUT.
A TOP LOADER! I HAVEN'T SEEN ONE OF THOSE SINCE THE LATE 80'S!
I SAID I'D SEEN ONE BEFORE, NOT THAT I KNOW HOW TO TAKE THEM APART.
WELL MY LITTLE FRIEND, YOU'VE GOT SOMETHING JAMMED IN HERE REAL GOOD.

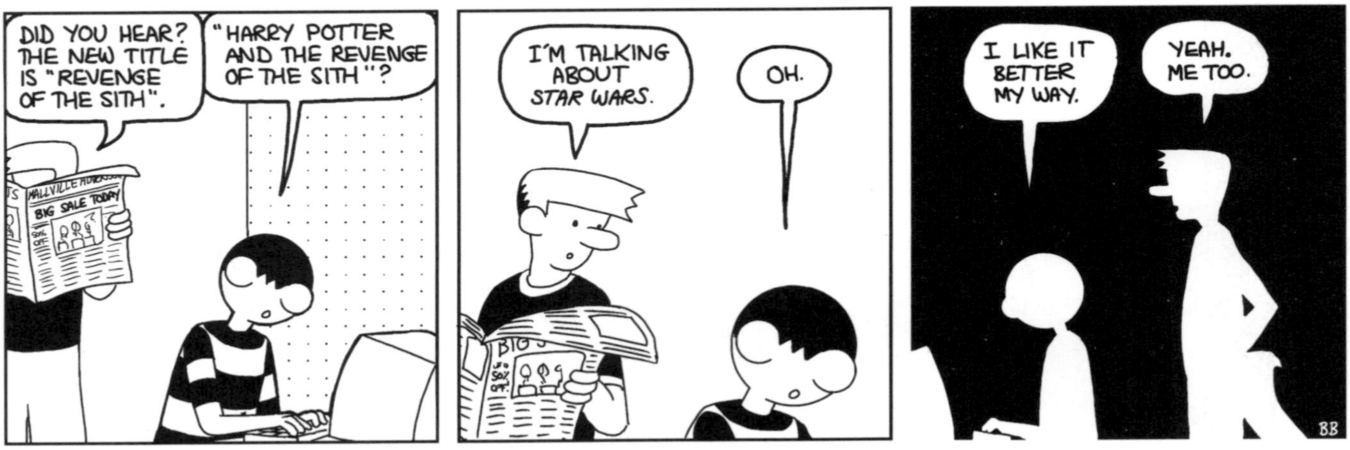
DID YOU HEAR? THE NEW TITLE IS "REVENGE OF THE SITH".
"HARRY POTTER AND THE REVENGE OF THE SITH"?
BIG SALE TODAY
I'M TALKING ABOUT *STAR WARS*.
OH.
I LIKE IT BETTER MY WAY.
YEAH. ME TOO.

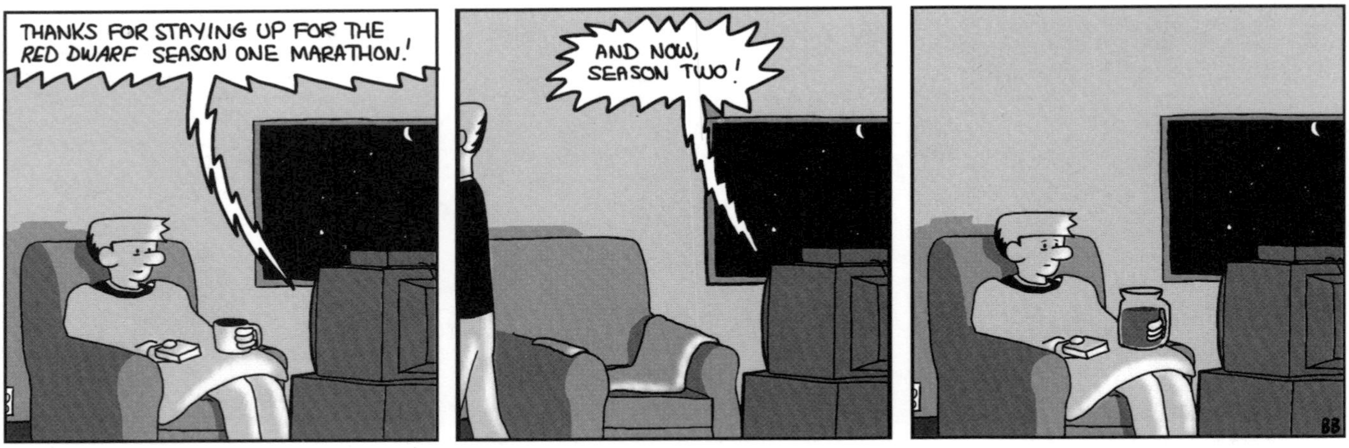
THANKS FOR STAYING UP FOR THE *RED DWARF* SEASON ONE MARATHON!
AND NOW, SEASON TWO!

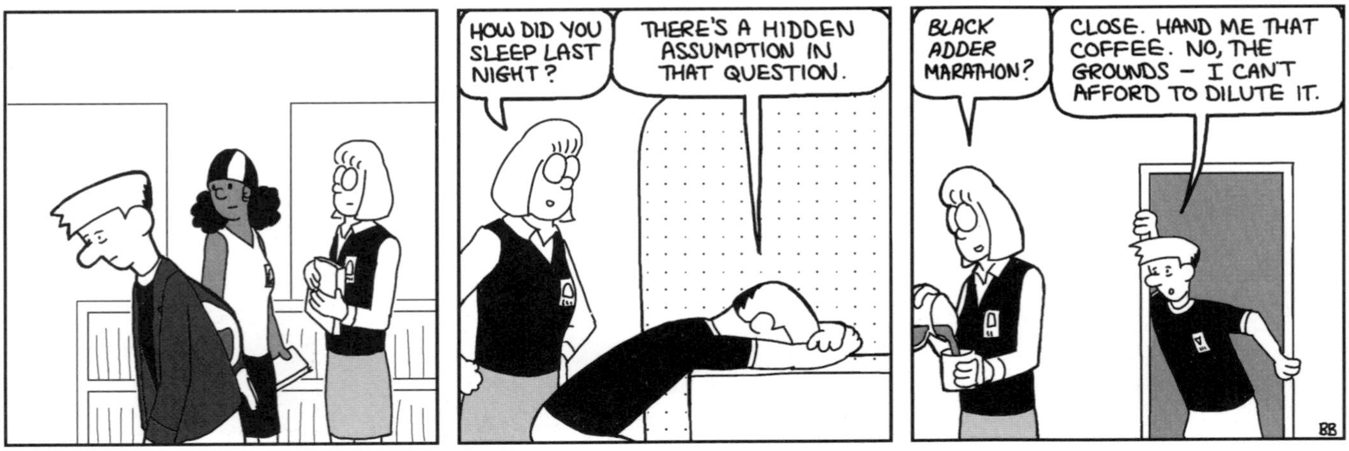
HOW DID YOU SLEEP LAST NIGHT?
THERE'S A HIDDEN ASSUMPTION IN THAT QUESTION.
BLACK ADDER MARATHON?
CLOSE. HAND ME THAT COFFEE. NO, THE GROUNDS – I CAN'T AFFORD TO DILUTE IT.

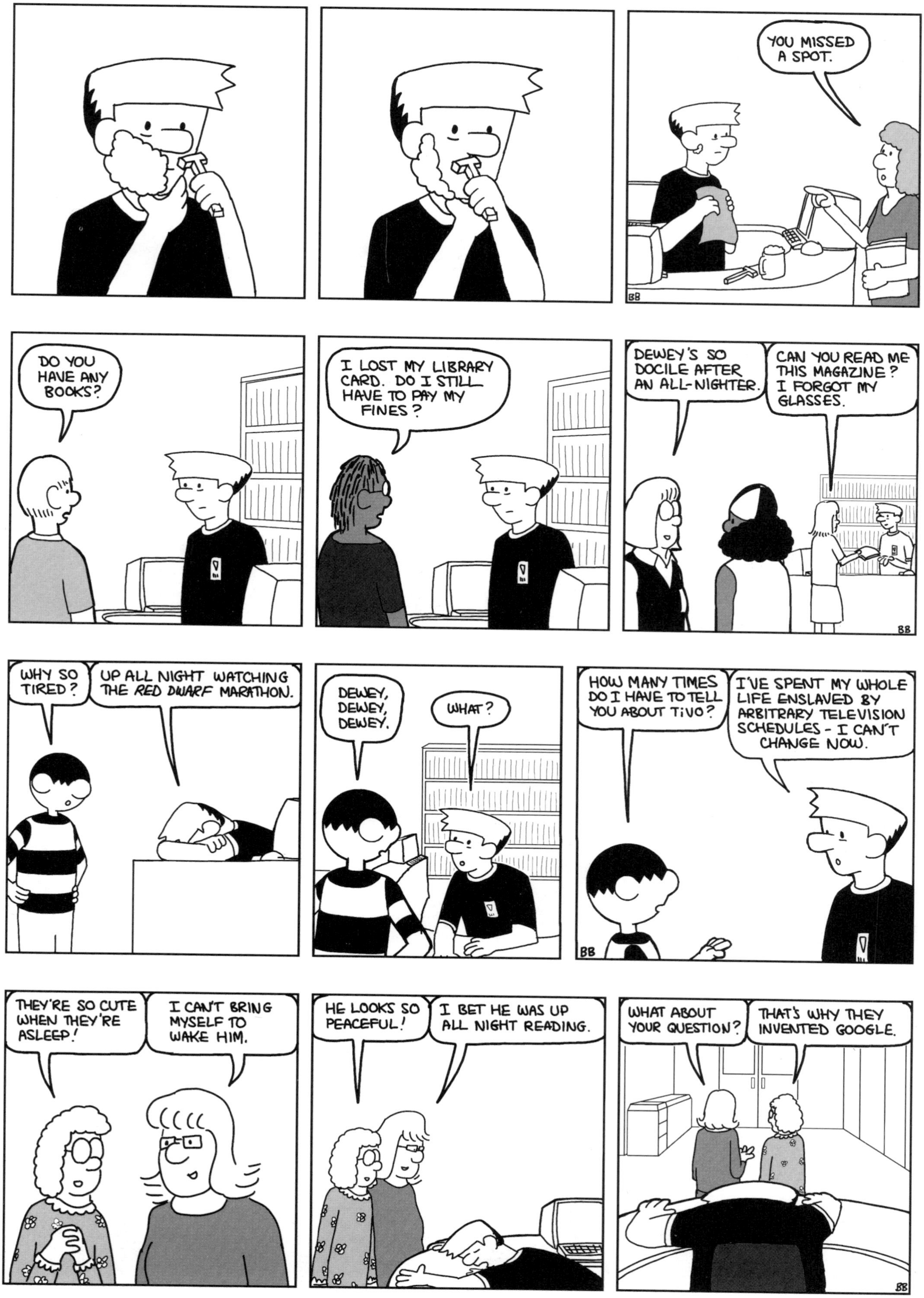
YOU MISSED A SPOT.
DO YOU HAVE ANY BOOKS?
I LOST MY LIBRARY CARD. DO I STILL HAVE TO PAY MY FINES?
DEWEY'S SO DOCILE AFTER AN ALL-NIGHTER.
CAN YOU READ ME THIS MAGAZINE? I FORGOT MY GLASSES.
WHY SO TIRED?
UP ALL NIGHT WATCHING THE RED DWARF MARATHON.
DEWEY, DEWEY, DEWEY.
WHAT?
HOW MANY TIMES DO I HAVE TO TELL YOU ABOUT TiVO?
I'VE SPENT MY WHOLE LIFE ENSLAVED BY ARBITRARY TELEVISION SCHEDULES - I CAN'T CHANGE NOW.
THEY'RE SO CUTE WHEN THEY'RE ASLEEP!
I CAN'T BRING MYSELF TO WAKE HIM.
HE LOOKS SO PEACEFUL!
I BET HE WAS UP ALL NIGHT READING.
WHAT ABOUT YOUR QUESTION?
THAT'S WHY THEY INVENTED GOOGLE.

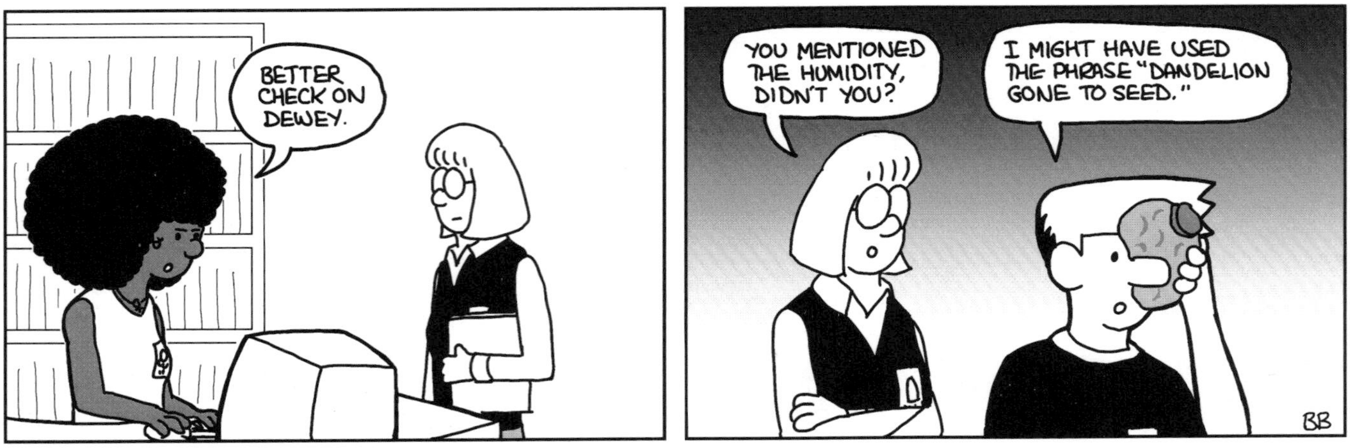
BETTER CHECK ON DEWEY.
YOU MENTIONED THE HUMIDITY, DIDN'T YOU?
I MIGHT HAVE USED THE PHRASE "DANDELION GONE TO SEED."
BB

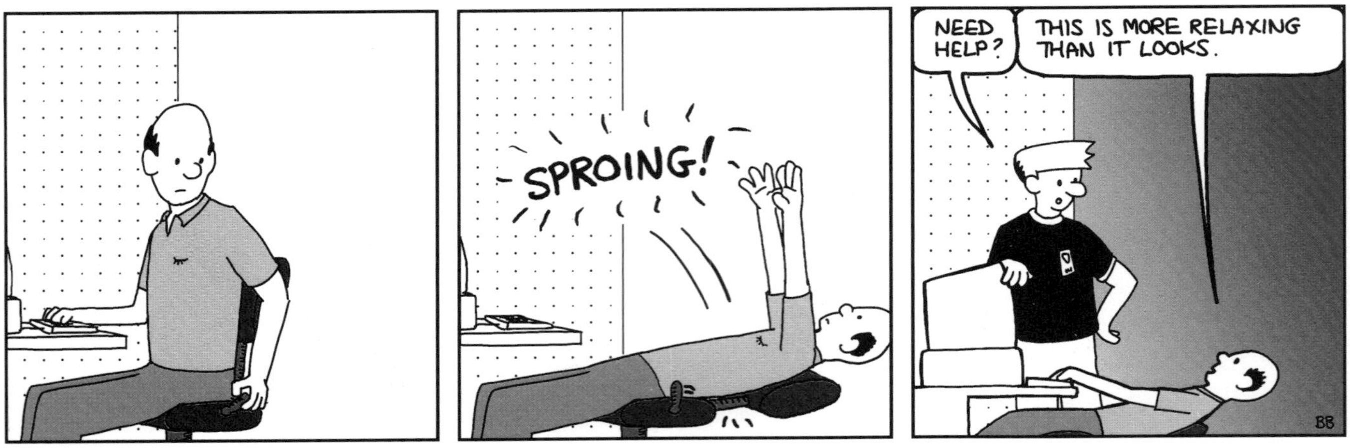
SPROING!
NEED HELP?
THIS IS MORE RELAXING THAN IT LOOKS.
BB

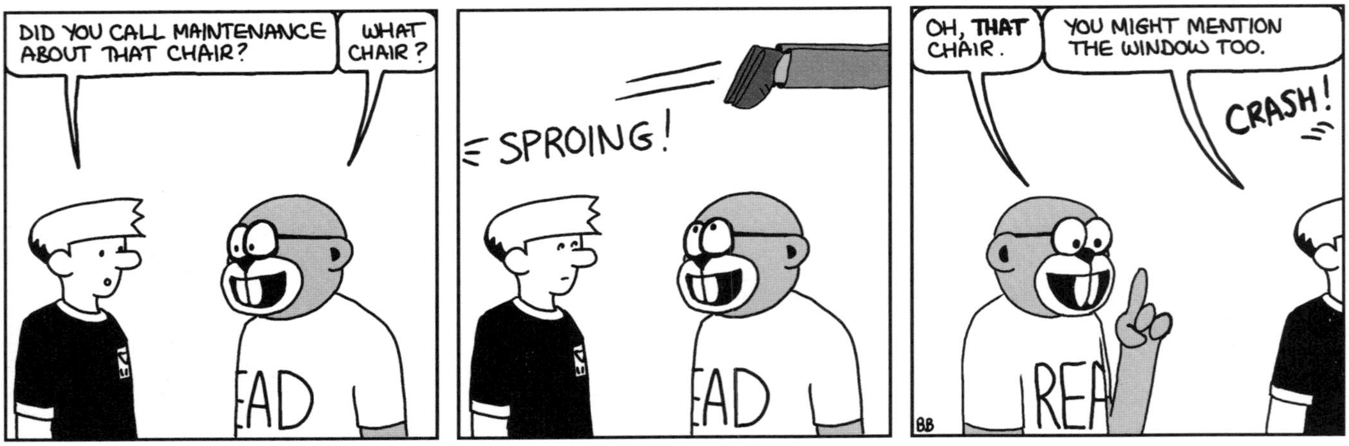
DID YOU CALL MAINTENANCE ABOUT THAT CHAIR?
WHAT CHAIR?
EAD
SPROING!
OH, THAT CHAIR.
YOU MIGHT MENTION THE WINDOW TOO.
CRASH!
REA
BB

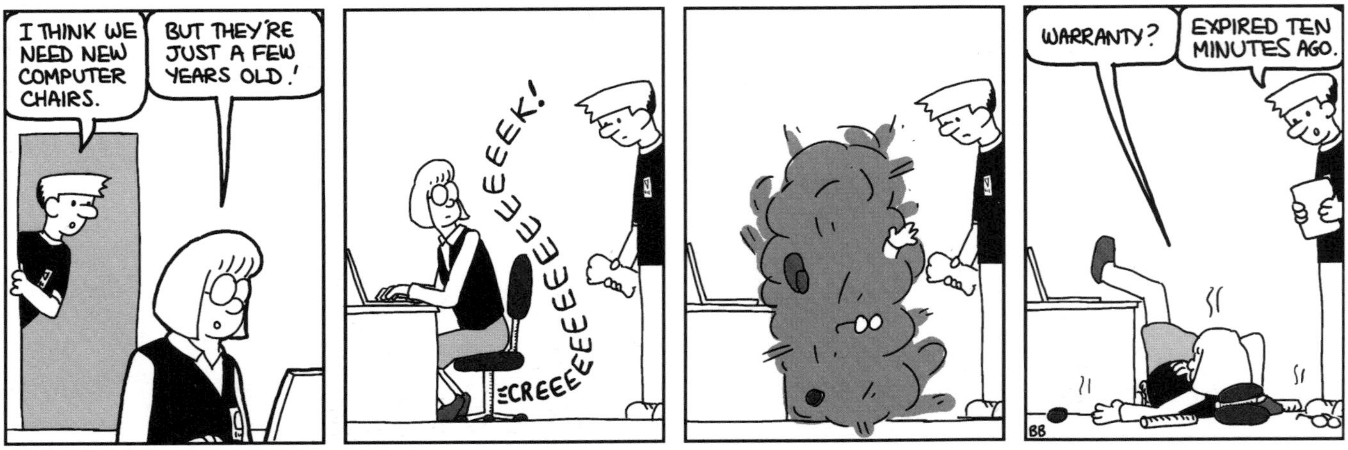
I THINK WE NEED NEW COMPUTER CHAIRS.
BUT THEY'RE JUST A FEW YEARS OLD!
CREEEEEEEEEEEK!
WARRANTY?
EXPIRED TEN MINUTES AGO.
BB

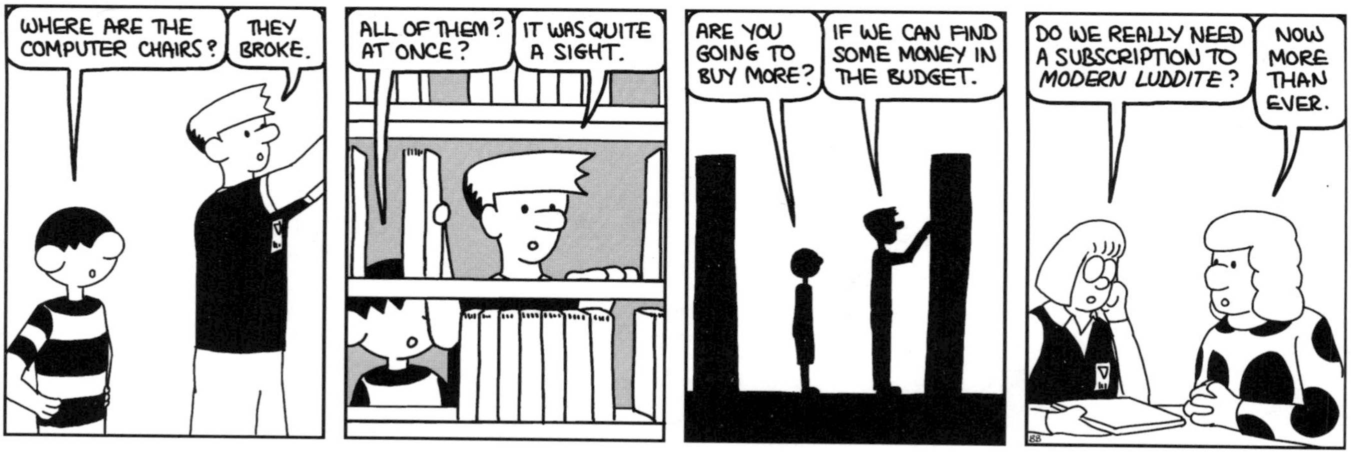
WHERE ARE THE COMPUTER CHAIRS?
THEY BROKE.
ALL OF THEM? AT ONCE?
IT WAS QUITE A SIGHT.
ARE YOU GOING TO BUY MORE?
IF WE CAN FIND SOME MONEY IN THE BUDGET.
DO WE REALLY NEED A SUBSCRIPTION TO *MODERN LUDDITE*?
NOW MORE THAN EVER.
BB

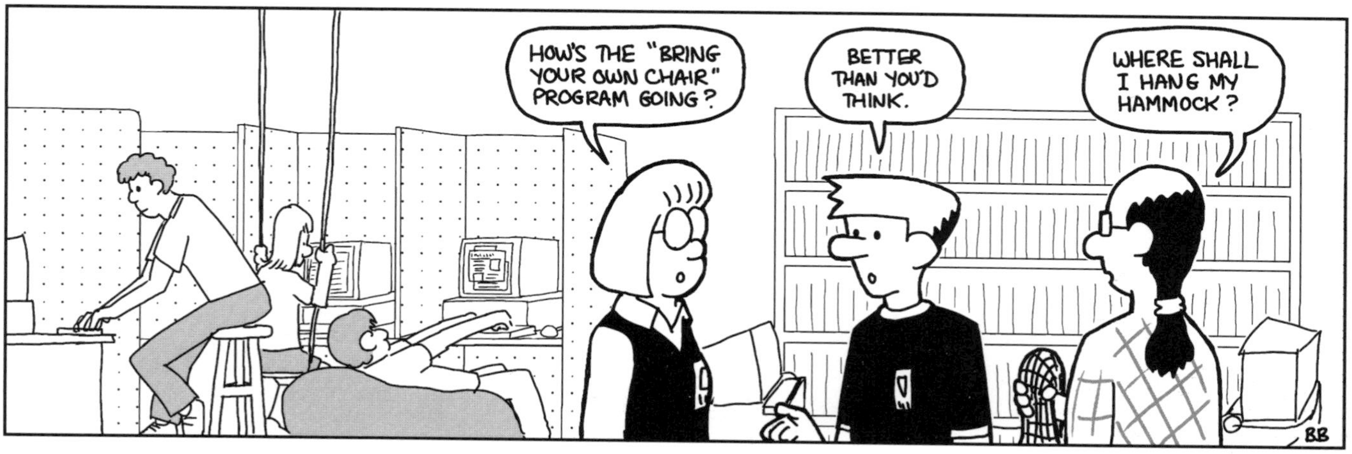
HOW'S THE "BRING YOUR OWN CHAIR" PROGRAM GOING?
BETTER THAN YOU'D THINK.
WHERE SHALL I HANG MY HAMMOCK?
BB

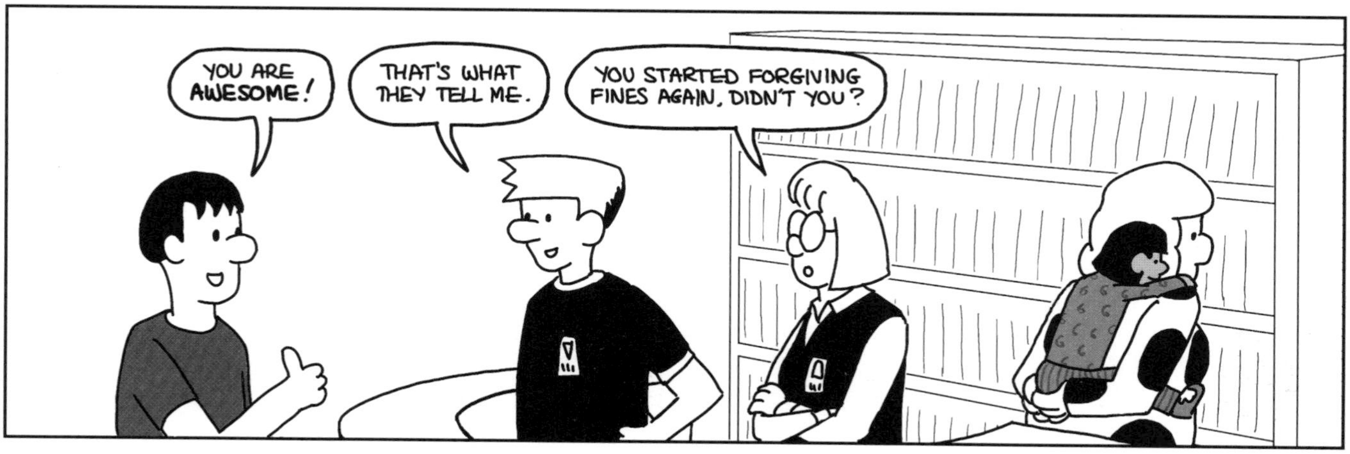
YOU ARE **AWESOME**!
THAT'S WHAT THEY TELL ME.
YOU STARTED FORGIVING FINES AGAIN, DIDN'T YOU?

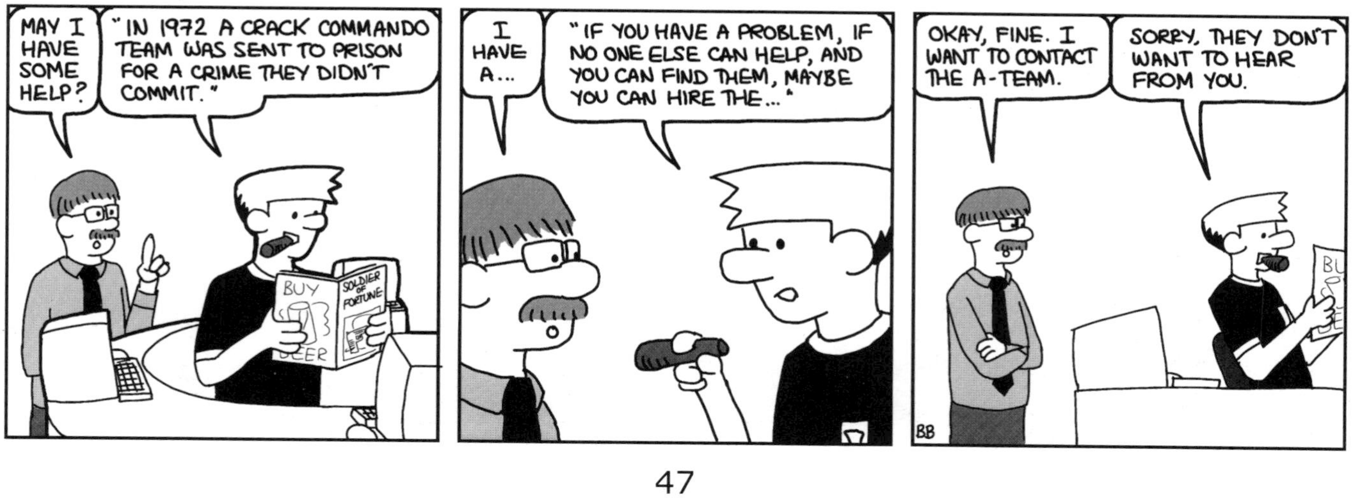
MAY I HAVE SOME HELP?
"IN 1972 A CRACK COMMANDO TEAM WAS SENT TO PRISON FOR A CRIME THEY DIDN'T COMMIT."
BUY BEER
SOLDIER OF FORTUNE
I HAVE A...
"IF YOU HAVE A PROBLEM, IF NO ONE ELSE CAN HELP, AND YOU CAN FIND THEM, MAYBE YOU CAN HIRE THE..."
OKAY, FINE. I WANT TO CONTACT THE A-TEAM.
SORRY, THEY DON'T WANT TO HEAR FROM YOU.
BB

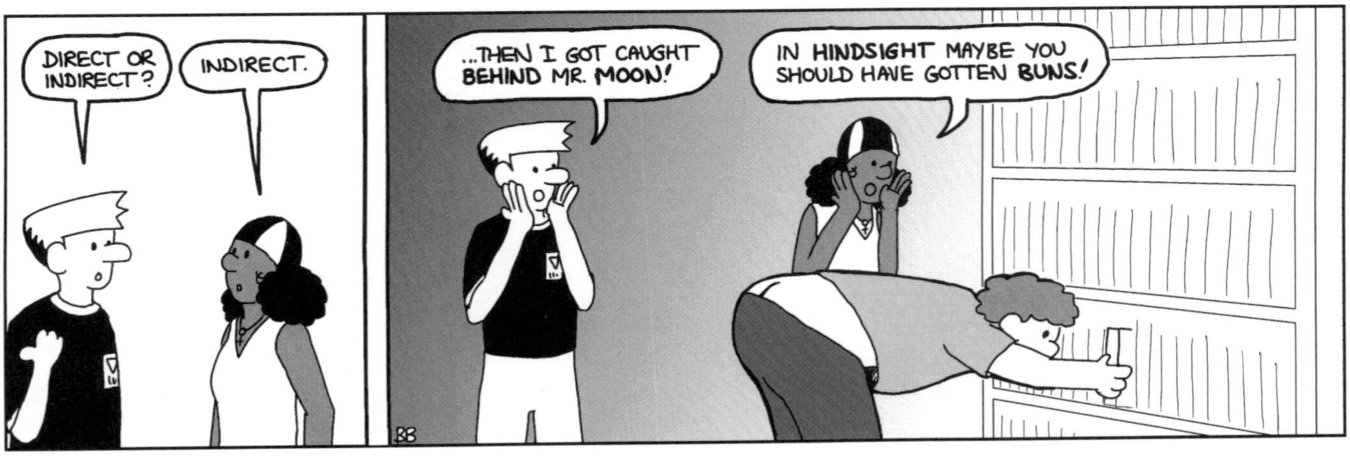
DIRECT OR INDIRECT?
INDIRECT.
...THEN I GOT CAUGHT BEHIND MR. MOON!
IN HINDSIGHT MAYBE YOU SHOULD HAVE GOTTEN BUNS!
BB

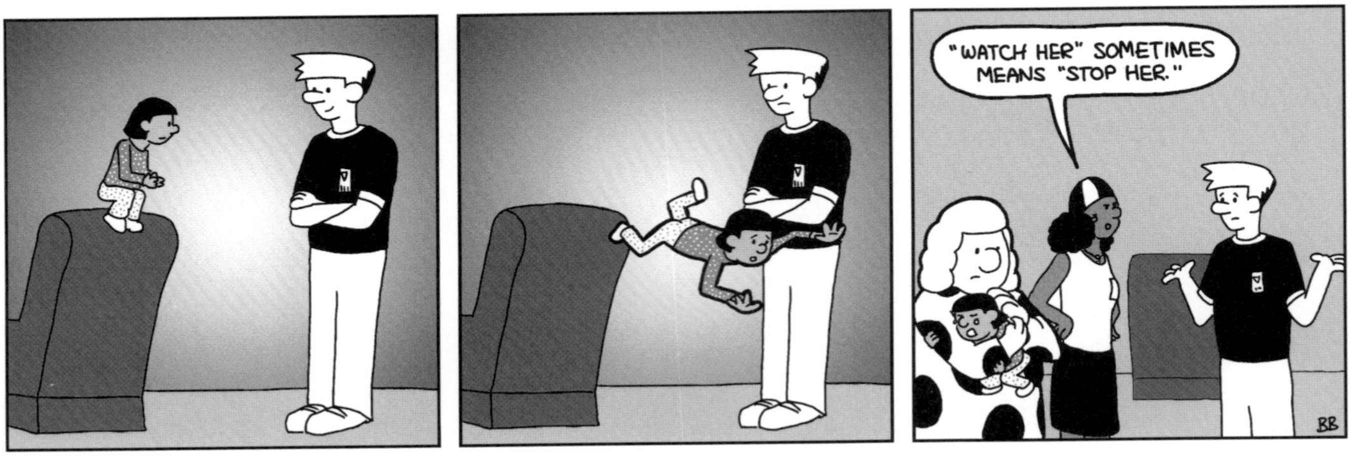
"WATCH HER" SOMETIMES MEANS "STOP HER."
BB

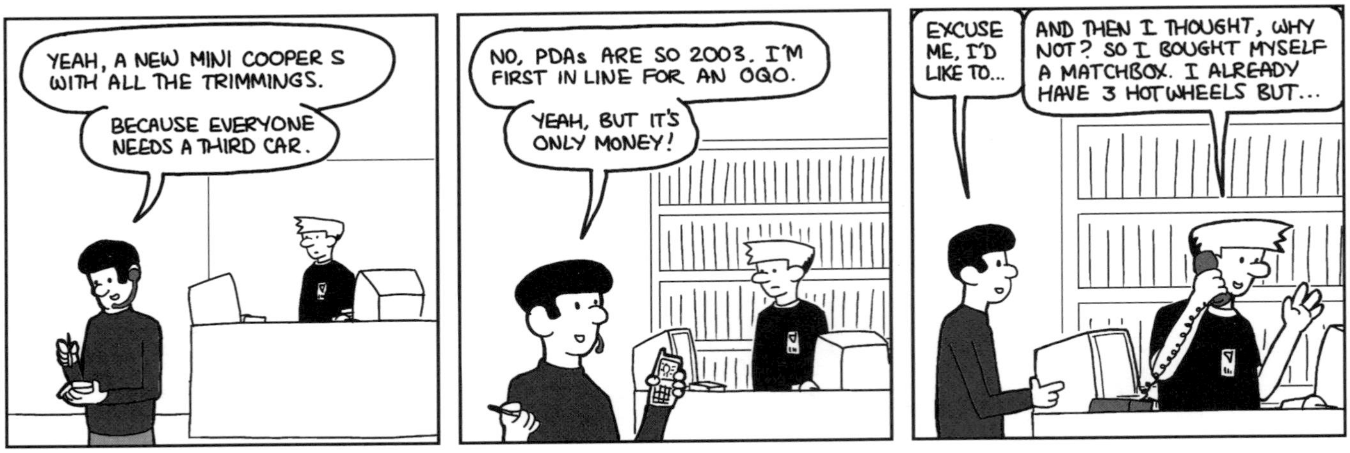
YEAH, A NEW MINI COOPER S WITH ALL THE TRIMMINGS.
BECAUSE EVERYONE NEEDS A THIRD CAR.
NO, PDAs ARE SO 2003. I'M FIRST IN LINE FOR AN OQO.
YEAH, BUT IT'S ONLY MONEY!
EXCUSE ME, I'D LIKE TO...
AND THEN I THOUGHT, WHY NOT? SO I BOUGHT MYSELF A MATCHBOX. I ALREADY HAVE 3 HOTWHEELS BUT...

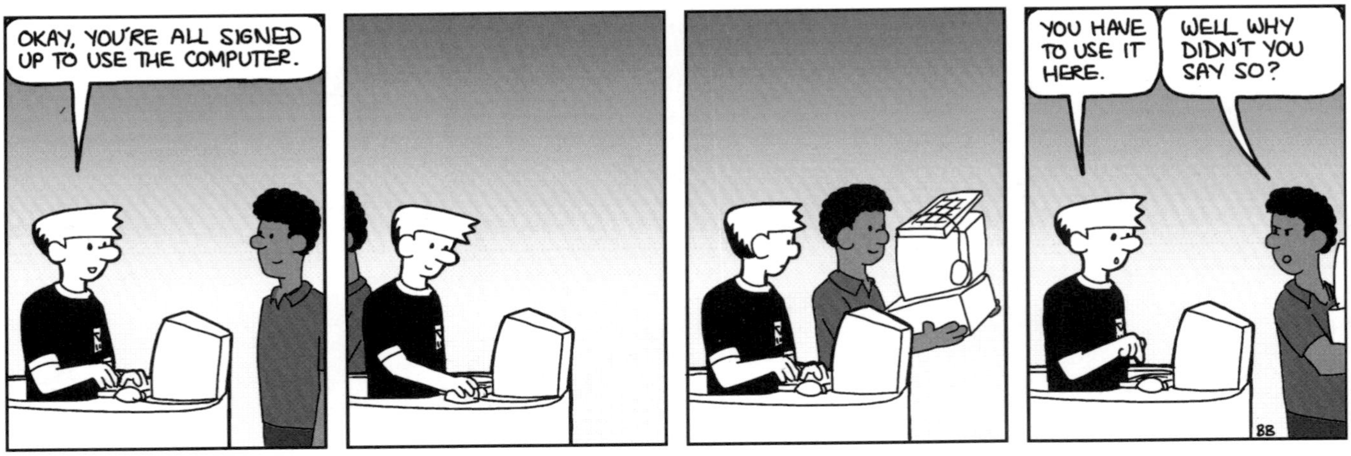
OKAY, YOU'RE ALL SIGNED UP TO USE THE COMPUTER.
YOU HAVE TO USE IT HERE.
WELL WHY DIDN'T YOU SAY SO?
BB

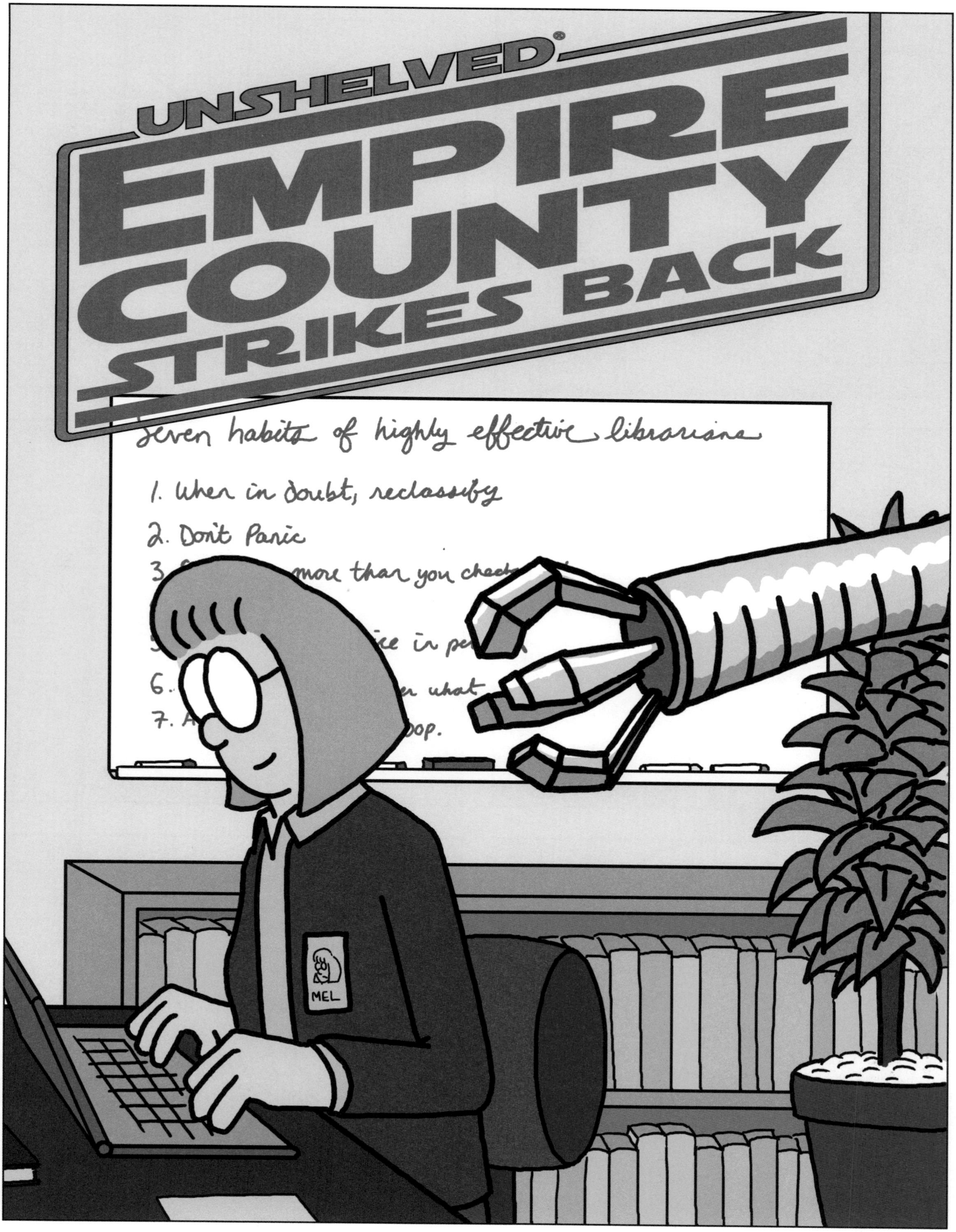
UNSHELVED®
EMPIRE COUNTY STRIKES BACK
Seven habits of highly effective librarians
1. When in doubt, reclassify
2. Don't Panic
MEL

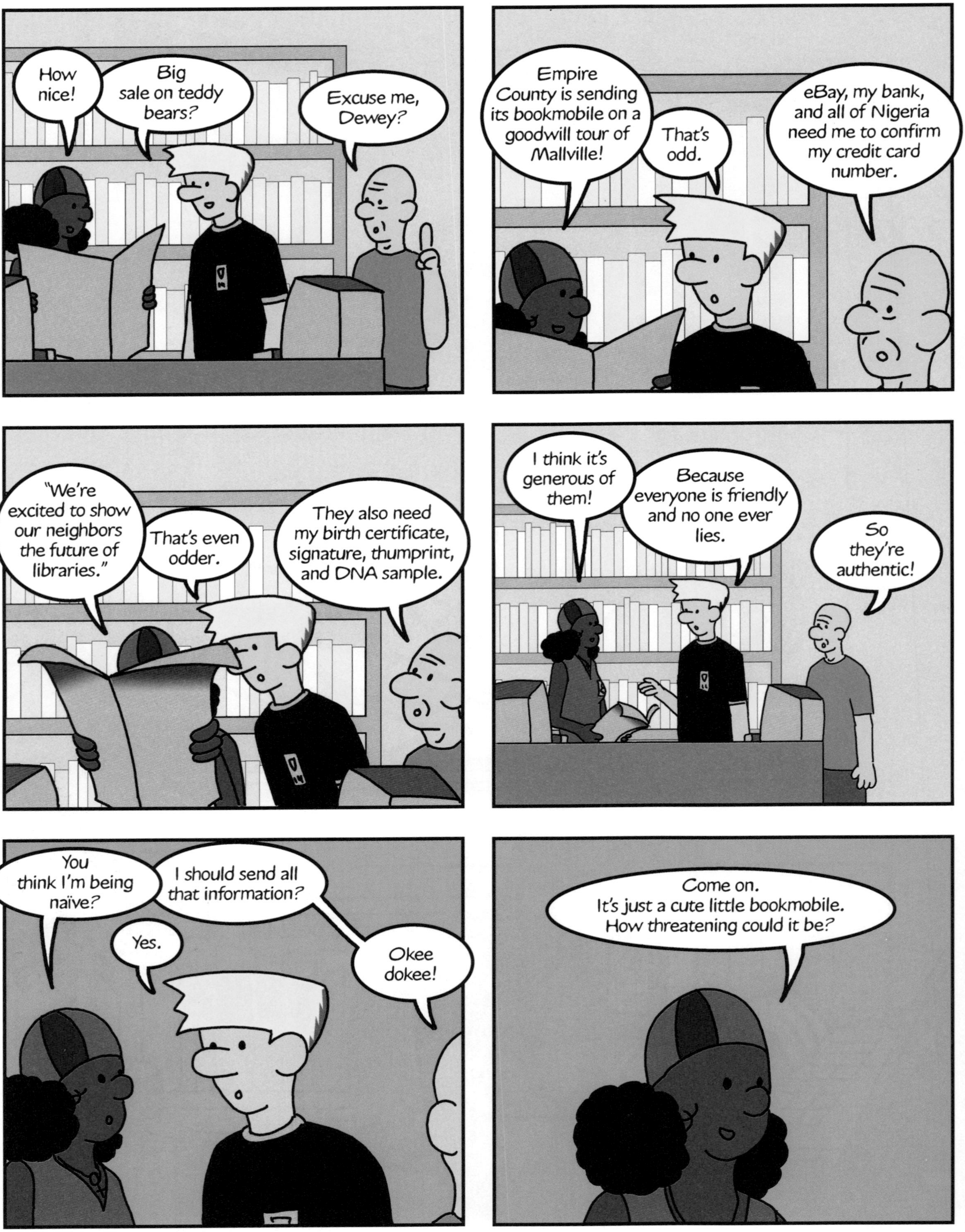
How nice!
Big sale on teddy bears?
Excuse me, Dewey?
Empire County is sending its bookmobile on a goodwill tour of Mallville!
That's odd.
eBay, my bank, and all of Nigeria need me to confirm my credit card number.
"We're excited to show our neighbors the future of libraries."
That's even odder.
They also need my birth certificate, signature, thumprint, and DNA sample.
I think it's generous of them!
Because everyone is friendly and no one ever lies.
So they're authentic!
You think I'm being naïve?
I should send all that information?
Yes.
Okee dokee!
Come on. It's just a cute little bookmobile. How threatening could it be?

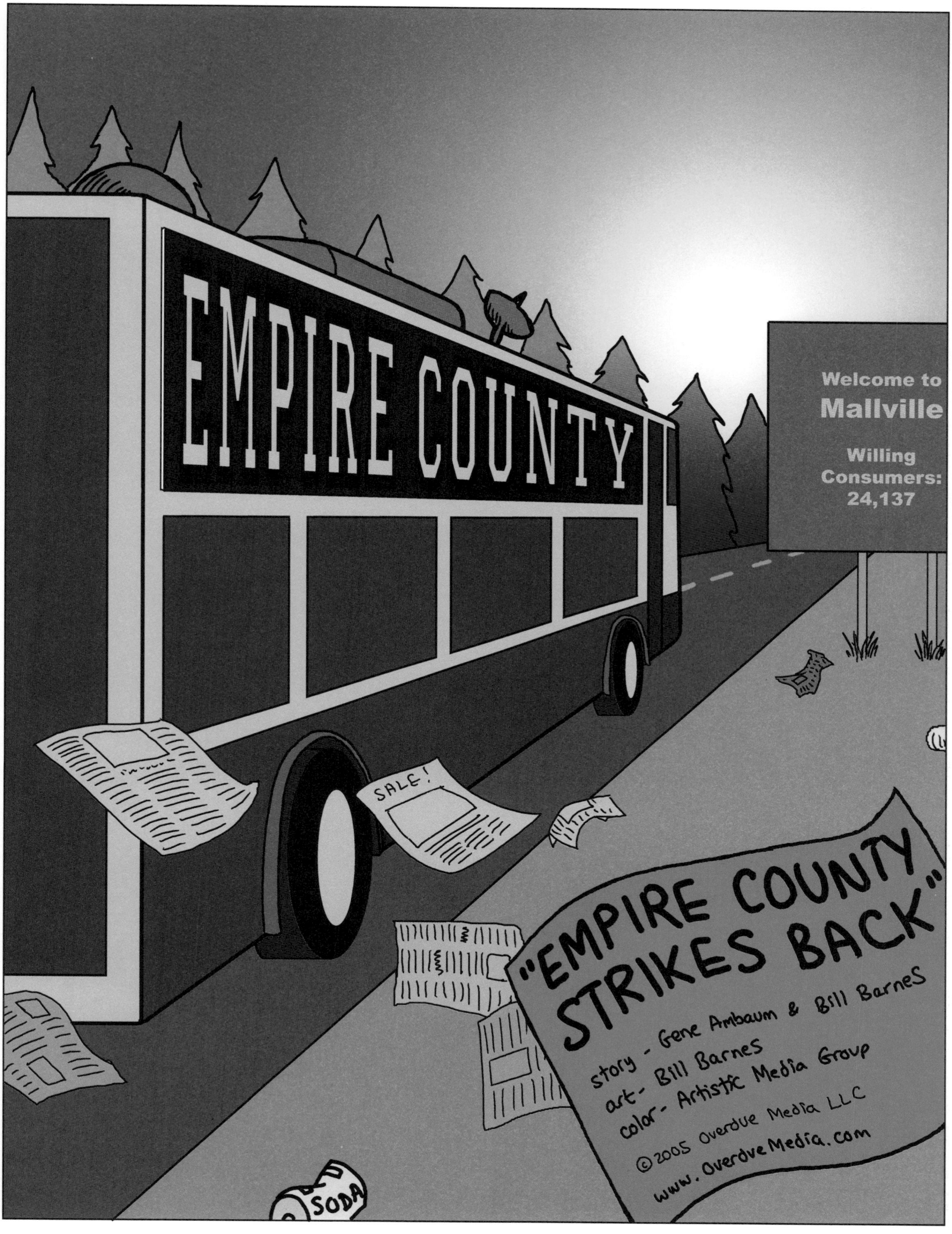
EMPIRE COUNTY
Welcome to
Mallville
Willing
Consumers:
24,137
SALE!
"EMPIRE COUNTY STRIKES BACK"
story - Gene Ambaum & Bill Barnes
art - Bill Barnes
color - Artistic Media Group
©2005 Overdue Media LLC
www.OverdueMedia.com
SODA

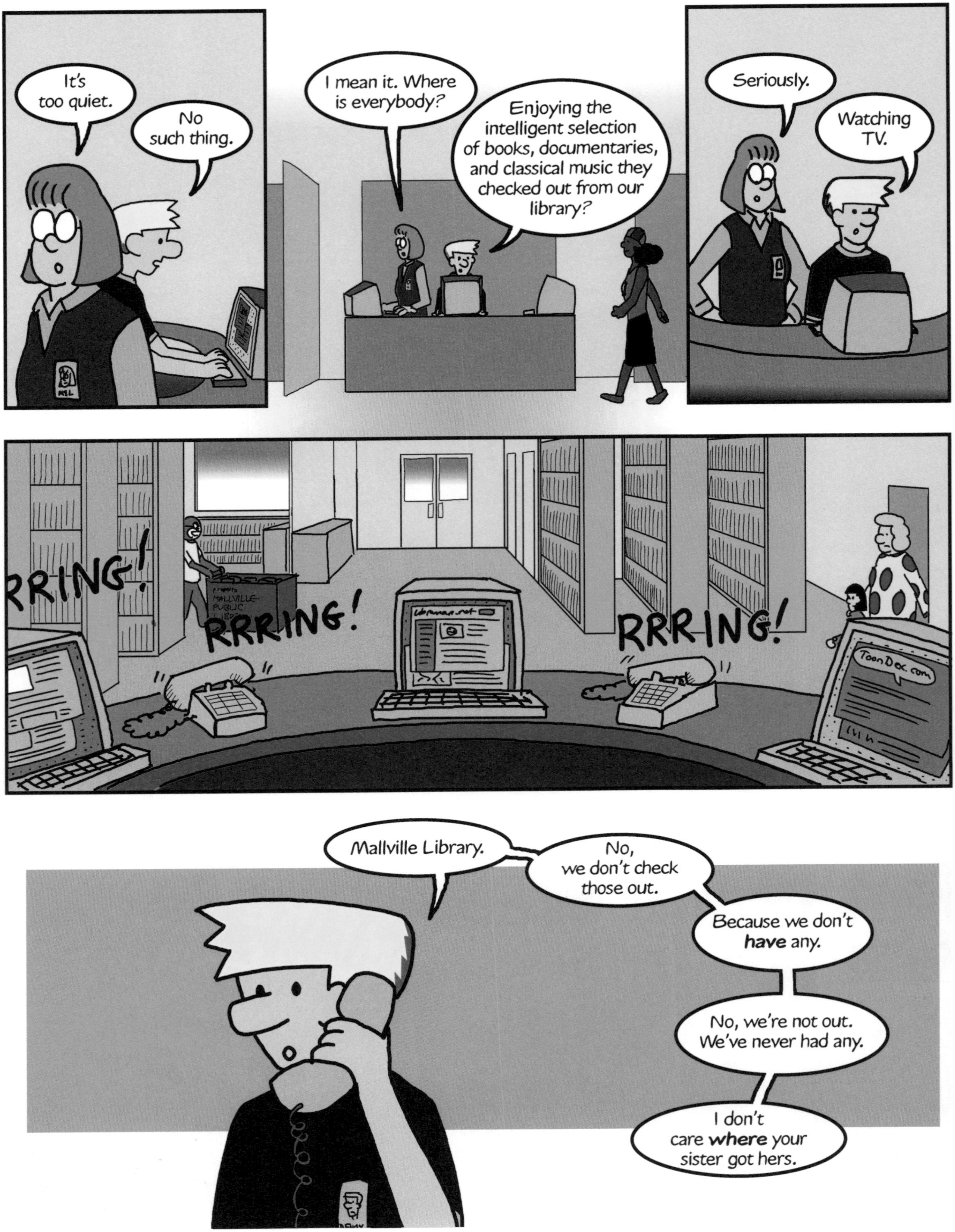

It's too quiet.
No such thing.
I mean it. Where is everybody?
Enjoying the intelligent selection of books, documentaries, and classical music they checked out from our library?
Seriously.
Watching TV.
RRING!
RRRING!
RRRING!
ToonDex.com
Mallville Library.
No, we don't check those out.
Because we don't **have** any.
No, we're not out. We've never had any.
I don't care **where** your sister got hers.

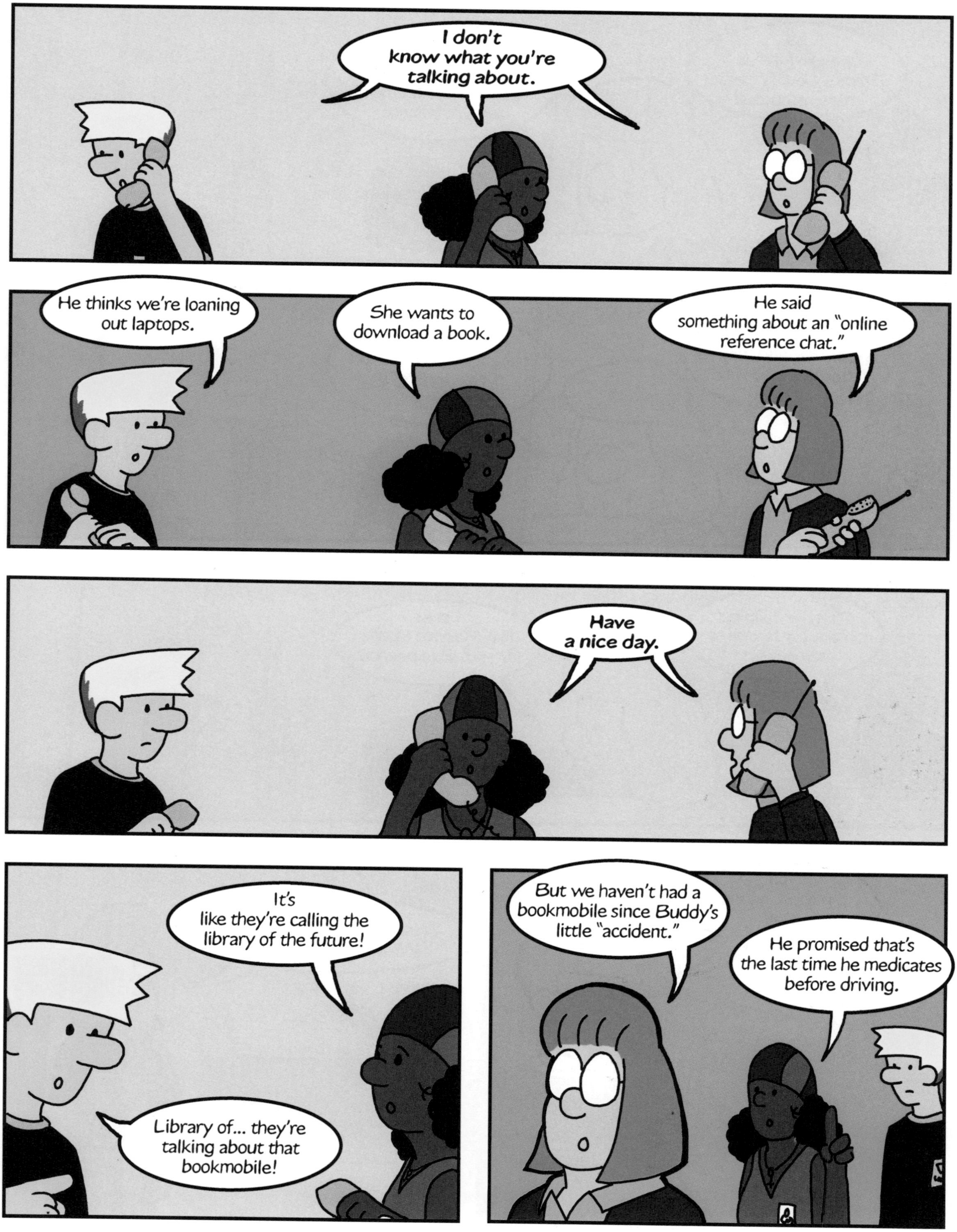
I don't know what you're talking about.
He thinks we're loaning out laptops.
She wants to download a book.
He said something about an "online reference chat."
Have a nice day.
It's like they're calling the library of the future!
Library of... they're talking about that bookmobile!
But we haven't had a bookmobile since Buddy's little "accident."
He promised that's the last time he medicates before driving.

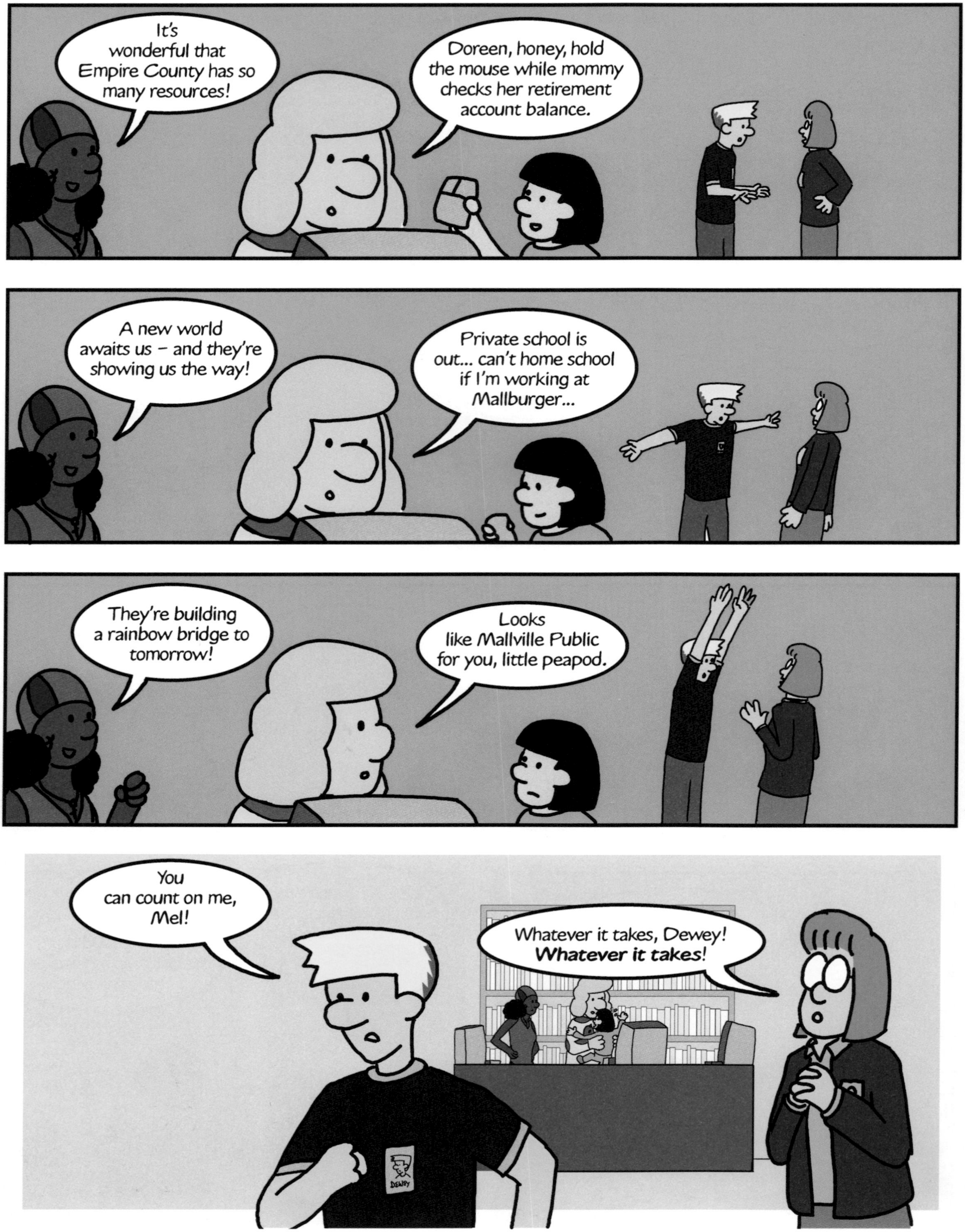
It's wonderful that Empire County has so many resources!
Doreen, honey, hold the mouse while mommy checks her retirement account balance.
A new world awaits us – and they're showing us the way!
Private school is out... can't home school if I'm working at Mallburger...
They're building a rainbow bridge to tomorrow!
Looks like Mallville Public for you, little peapod.
You can count on me, Mel!
Whatever it takes, Dewey! **Whatever it takes**!
DEWEY

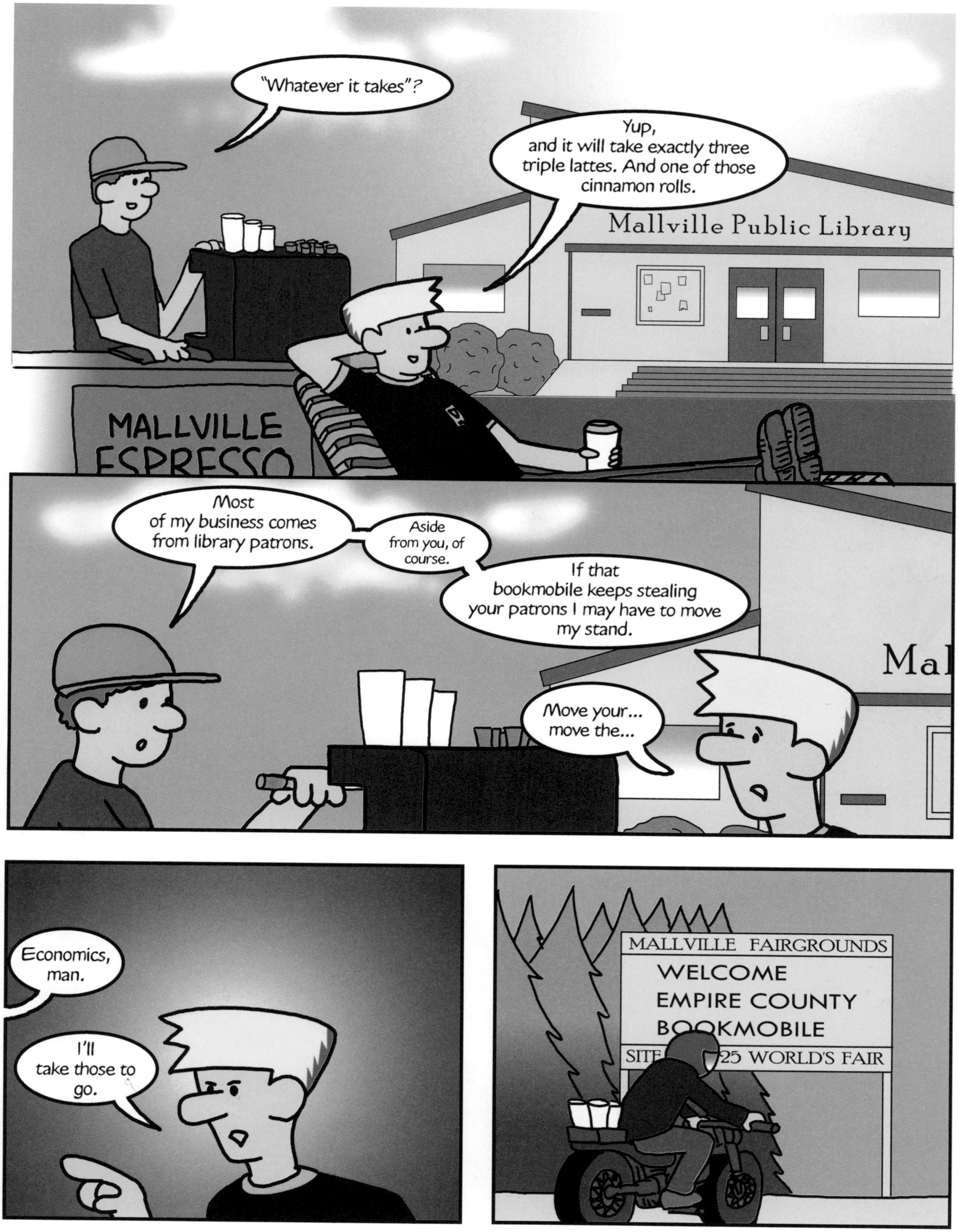
"Whatever it takes"?
Yup, and it will take exactly three triple lattes. And one of those cinnamon rolls.
Mallville Public Library
MALLVILLE ESPRESSO
Most of my business comes from library patrons.
Aside from you, of course.
If that bookmobile keeps stealing your patrons I may have to move my stand.
Move your... move the...
Economics, man.
I'll take those to go.
MALLVILLE FAIRGROUNDS
WELCOME
EMPIRE COUNTY
BOOKMOBILE
SITE
25 WORLD'S FAIR

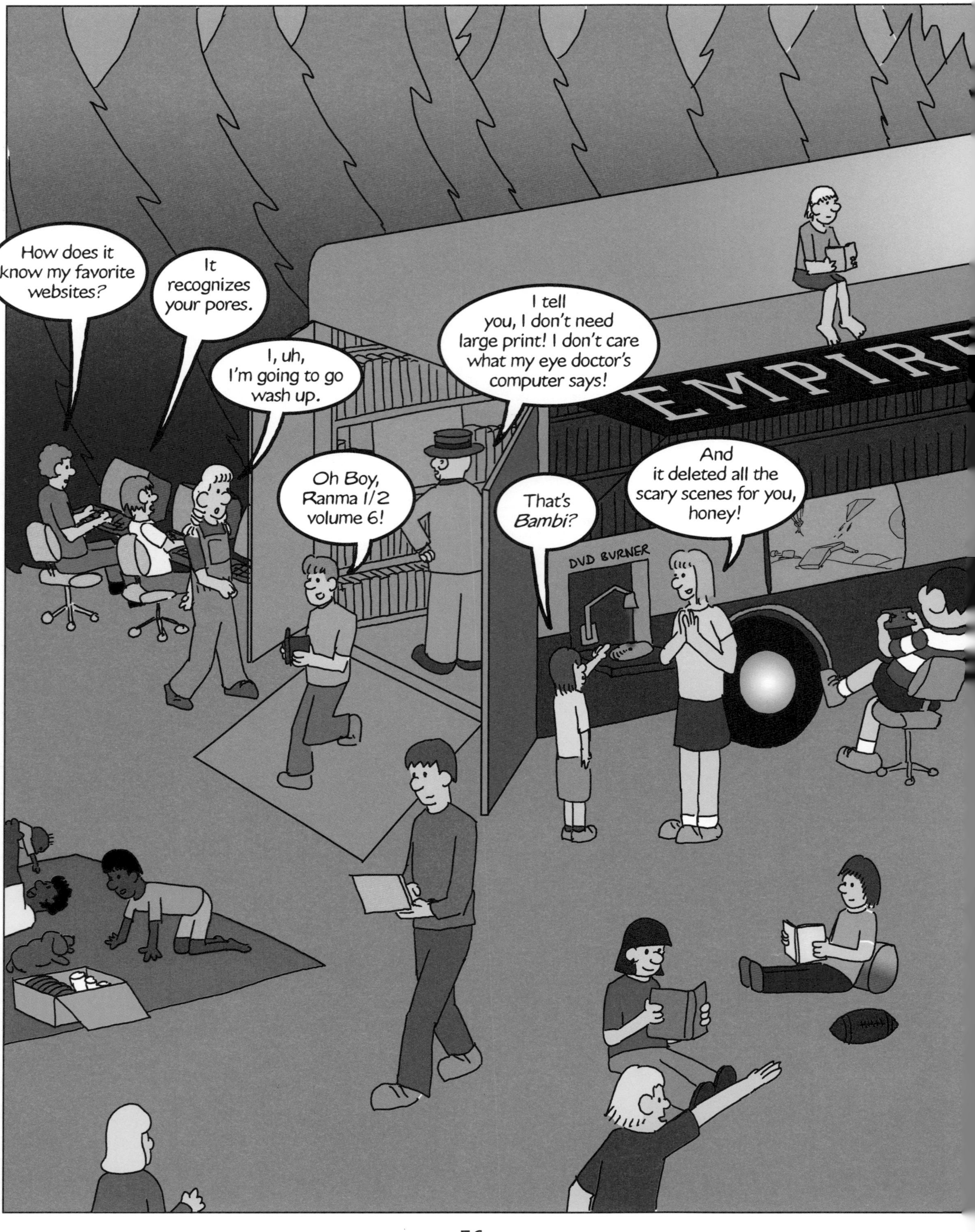
How does it know my favorite websites?
It recognizes your pores.
I, uh, I'm going to go wash up.
I tell you, I don't need large print! I don't care what my eye doctor's computer says!
EMPIRE
Oh Boy, Ranma 1/2 volume 6!
That's *Bambi*?
And it deleted all the scary scenes for you, honey!
DVD BURNER

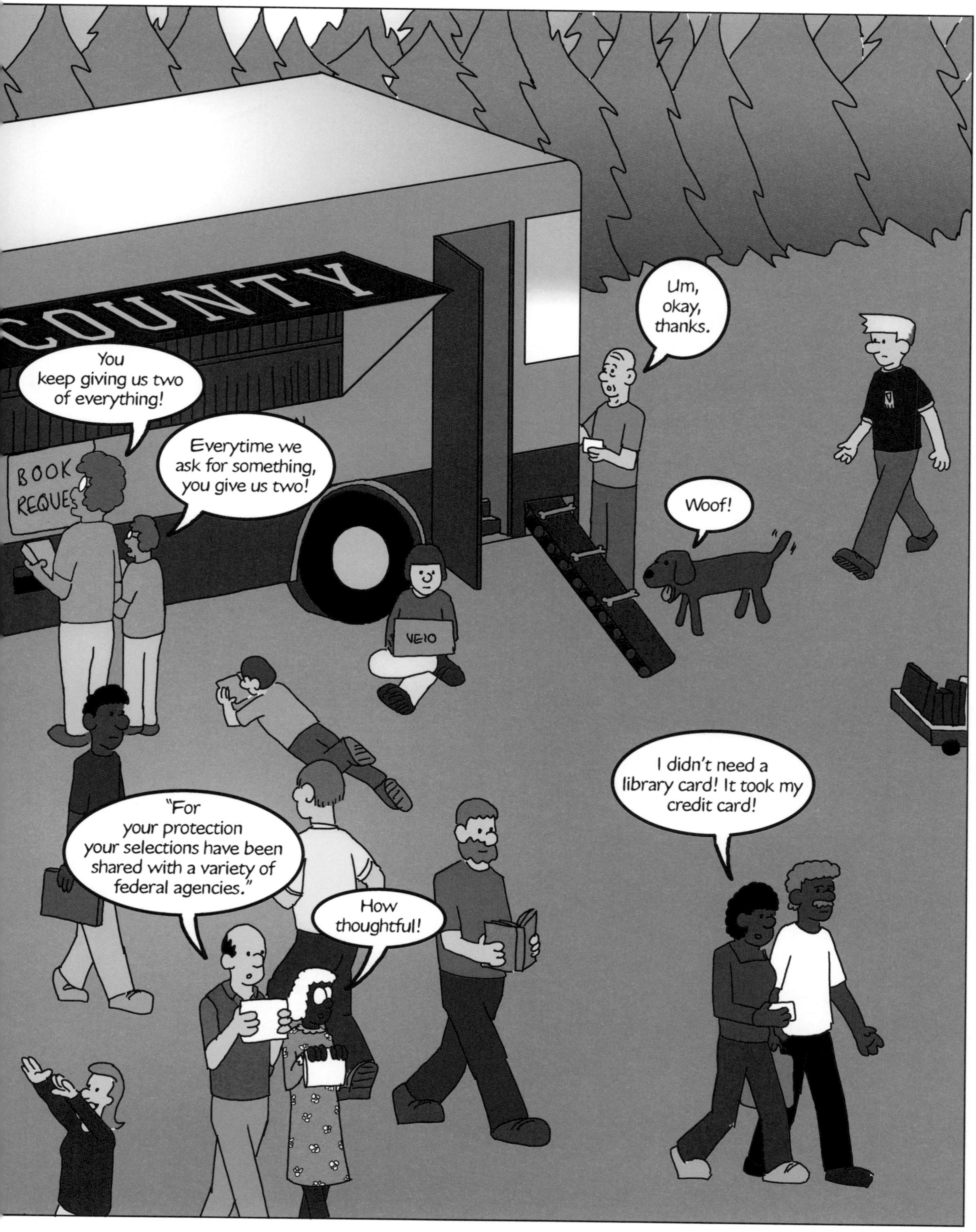
COUNTY
BOOK REQUES
You keep giving us two of everything!
Everytime we ask for something, you give us two!
Um, okay, thanks.
Woof!
I didn't need a library card! It took my credit card!
"For your protection your selections have been shared with a variety of federal agencies."
How thoughtful!

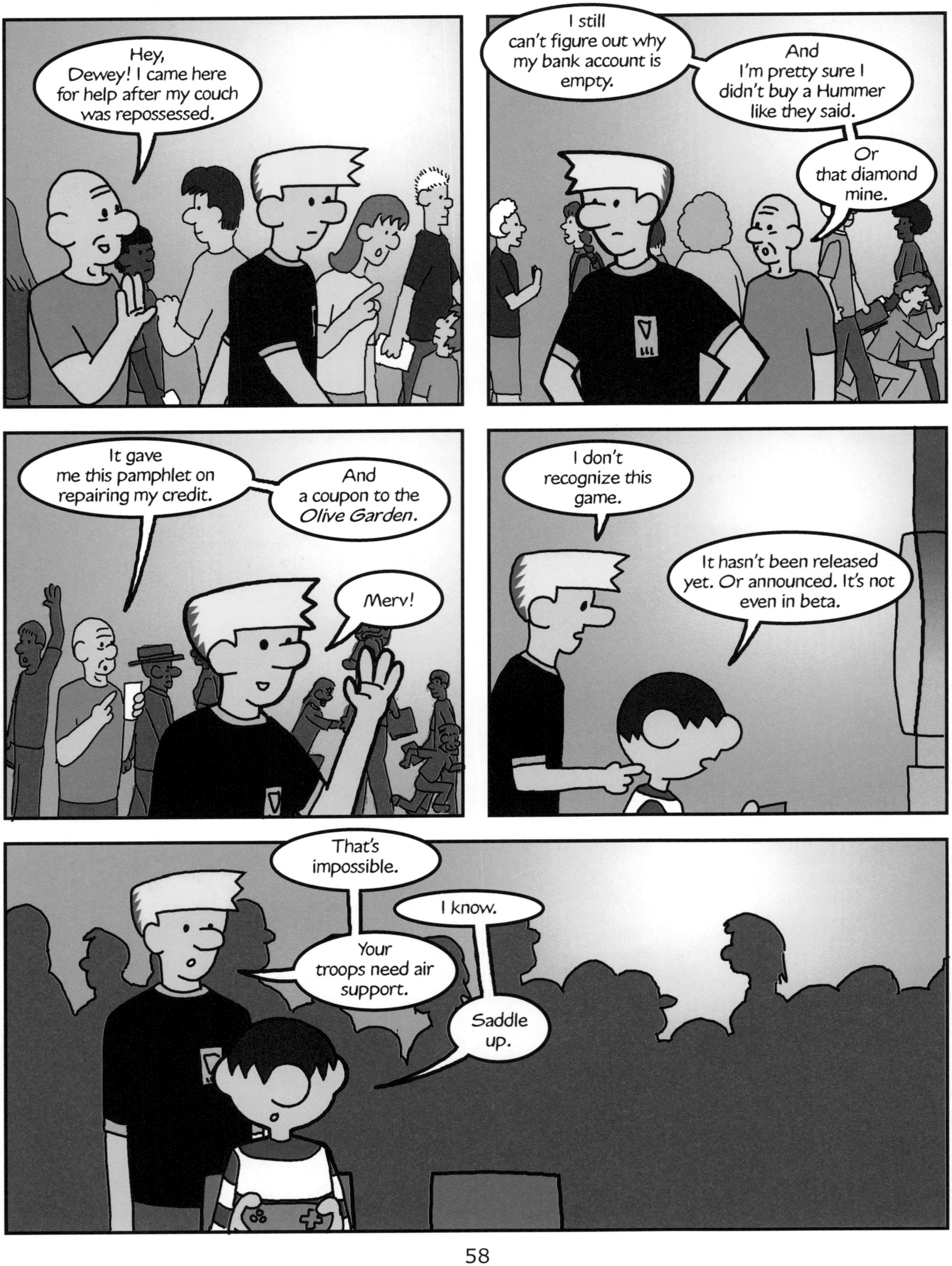
Hey, Dewey! I came here for help after my couch was repossessed.
I still can't figure out why my bank account is empty.
And I'm pretty sure I didn't buy a Hummer like they said.
Or that diamond mine.
It gave me this pamphlet on repairing my credit.
And a coupon to the *Olive Garden*.
Merv!
I don't recognize this game.
It hasn't been released yet. Or announced. It's not even in beta.
That's impossible.
I know.
Your troops need air support.
Saddle up.

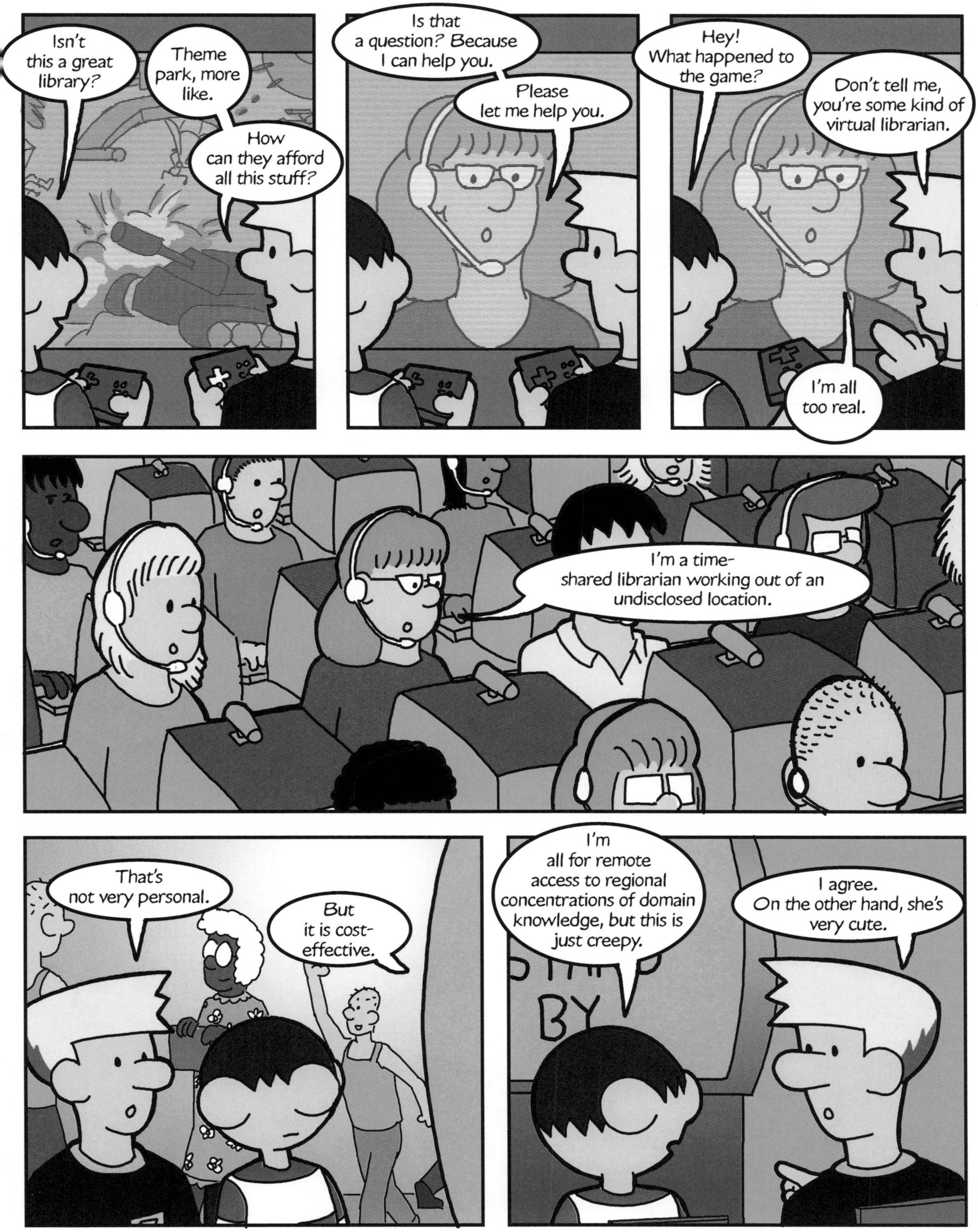
Isn't this a great library?
Theme park, more like.
How can they afford all this stuff?
Is that a question? Because I can help you.
Please let me help you.
Hey! What happened to the game?
Don't tell me, you're some kind of virtual librarian.
I'm all too real.
I'm a time-shared librarian working out of an undisclosed location.
That's not very personal.
But it is cost-effective.
I'm all for remote access to regional concentrations of domain knowledge, but this is just creepy.
I agree. On the other hand, she's very cute.

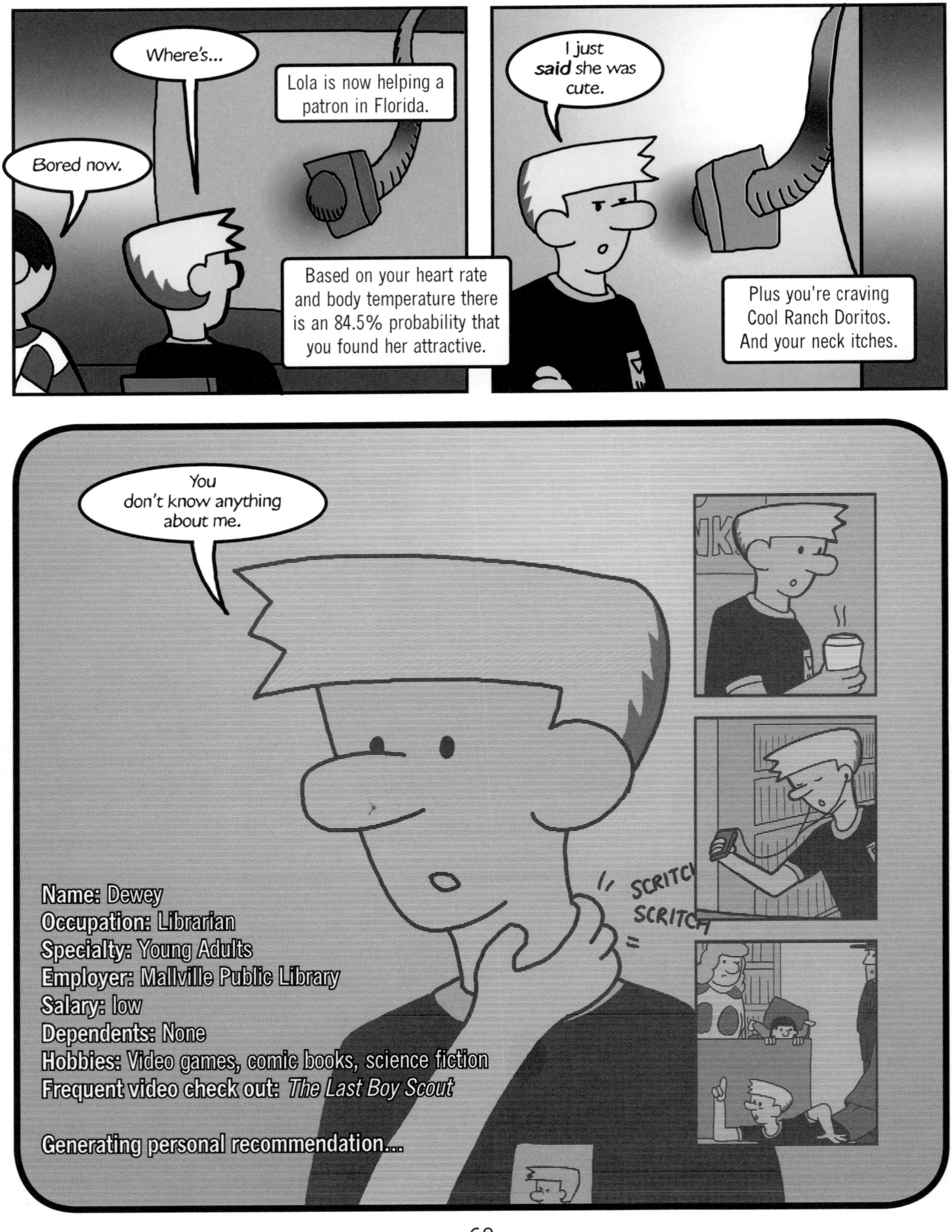
Where's...
Lola is now helping a patron in Florida.
Bored now.
Based on your heart rate and body temperature there is an 84.5% probability that you found her attractive.
I just *said* she was cute.
Plus you're craving Cool Ranch Doritos. And your neck itches.
You don't know anything about me.
SCRITCH
SCRITCH
Name: Dewey
Occupation: Librarian
Specialty: Young Adults
Employer: Mallville Public Library
Salary: low
Dependents: None
Hobbies: Video games, comic books, science fiction
Frequent video check out: *The Last Boy Scout*
Generating personal recommendation...

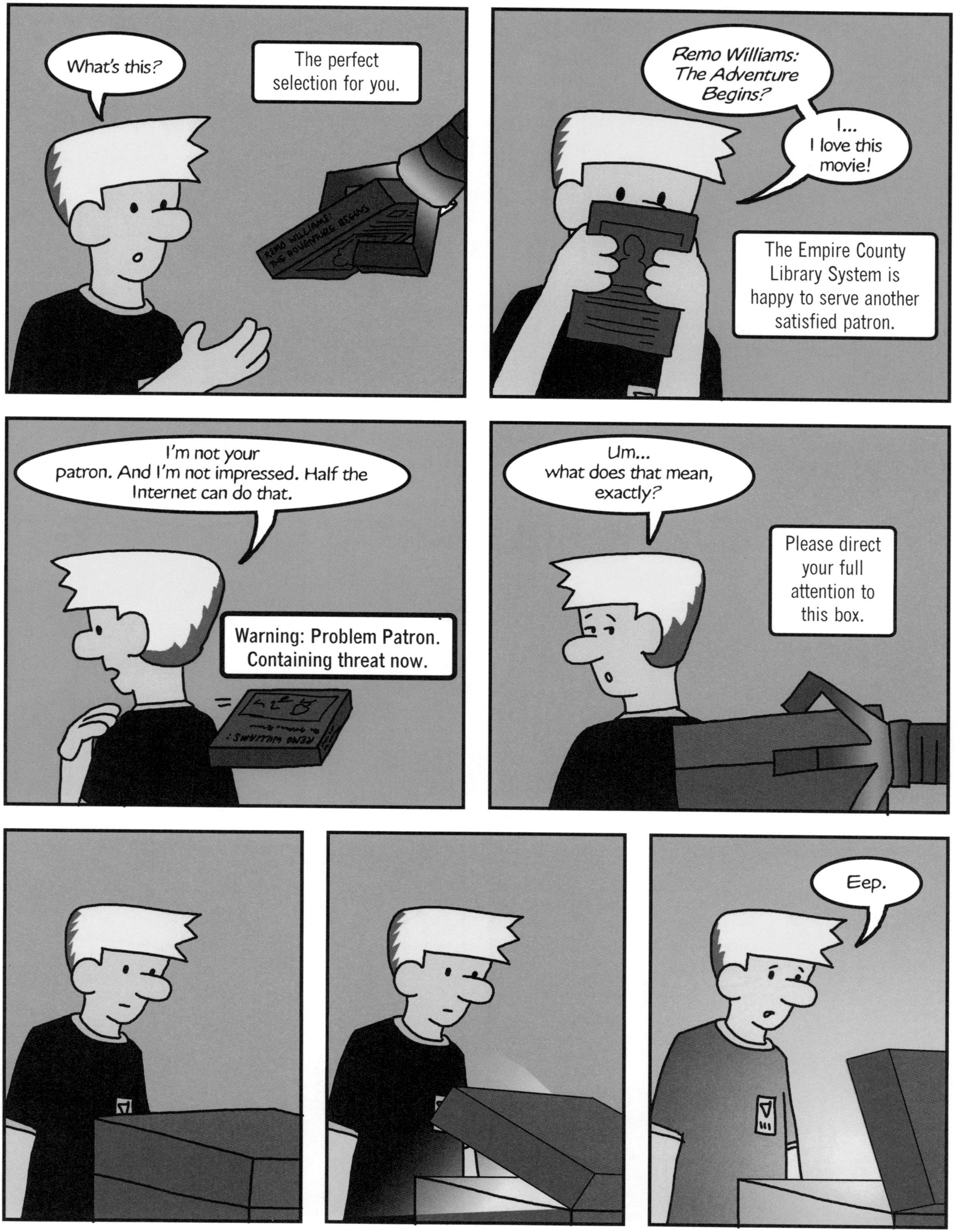
What's this?
The perfect selection for you.
Remo Williams: The Adventure Begins?
I... I love this movie!
The Empire County Library System is happy to serve another satisfied patron.
I'm not your patron. And I'm not impressed. Half the Internet can do that.
Warning: Problem Patron. Containing threat now.
Um... what does that mean, exactly?
Please direct your full attention to this box.
Eep.

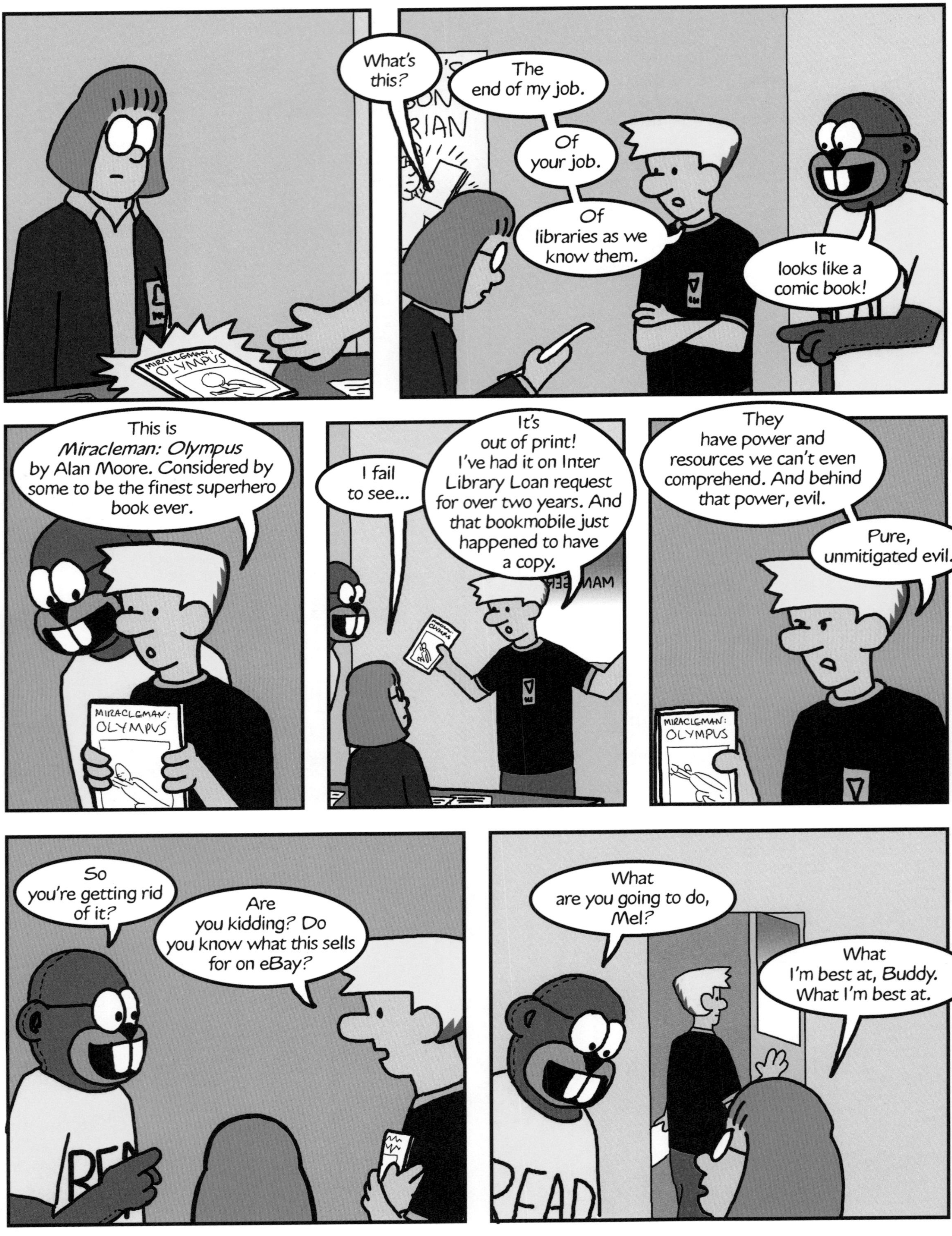
What's this?
The end of my job.
Of your job.
Of libraries as we know them.
It looks like a comic book!
MIRACLEMAN: OLYMPUS
This is *Miracleman: Olympus* by Alan Moore. Considered by some to be the finest superhero book ever.
I fail to see...
It's out of print! I've had it on Inter Library Loan request for over two years. And that bookmobile just happened to have a copy.
They have power and resources we can't even comprehend. And behind that power, evil.
Pure, unmitigated evil.
So you're getting rid of it?
Are you kidding? Do you know what this sells for on eBay?
What are you going to do, Mel?
What I'm best at, Buddy. What I'm best at.

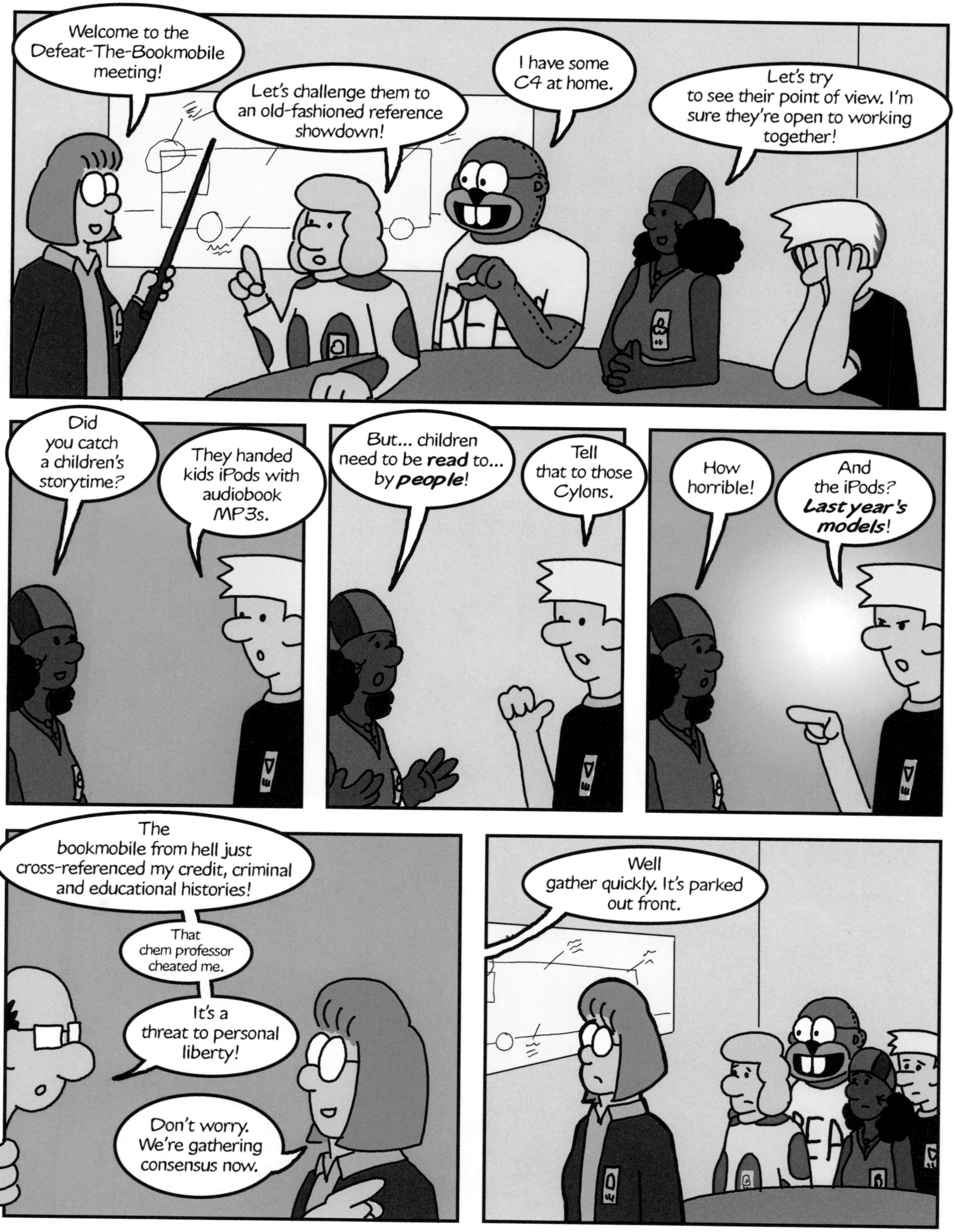
Welcome to the Defeat-The-Bookmobile meeting!
Let's challenge them to an old-fashioned reference showdown!
I have some C4 at home.
Let's try to see their point of view. I'm sure they're open to working together!
Did you catch a children's storytime?
They handed kids iPods with audiobook MP3s.
But... children need to be **read** to... by ***people***!
Tell that to those Cylons.
How horrible!
And the iPods? ***Last year's models***!
The bookmobile from hell just cross-referenced my credit, criminal and educational histories!
That chem professor cheated me.
It's a threat to personal liberty!
Don't worry. We're gathering consensus now.
Well gather quickly. It's parked out front.

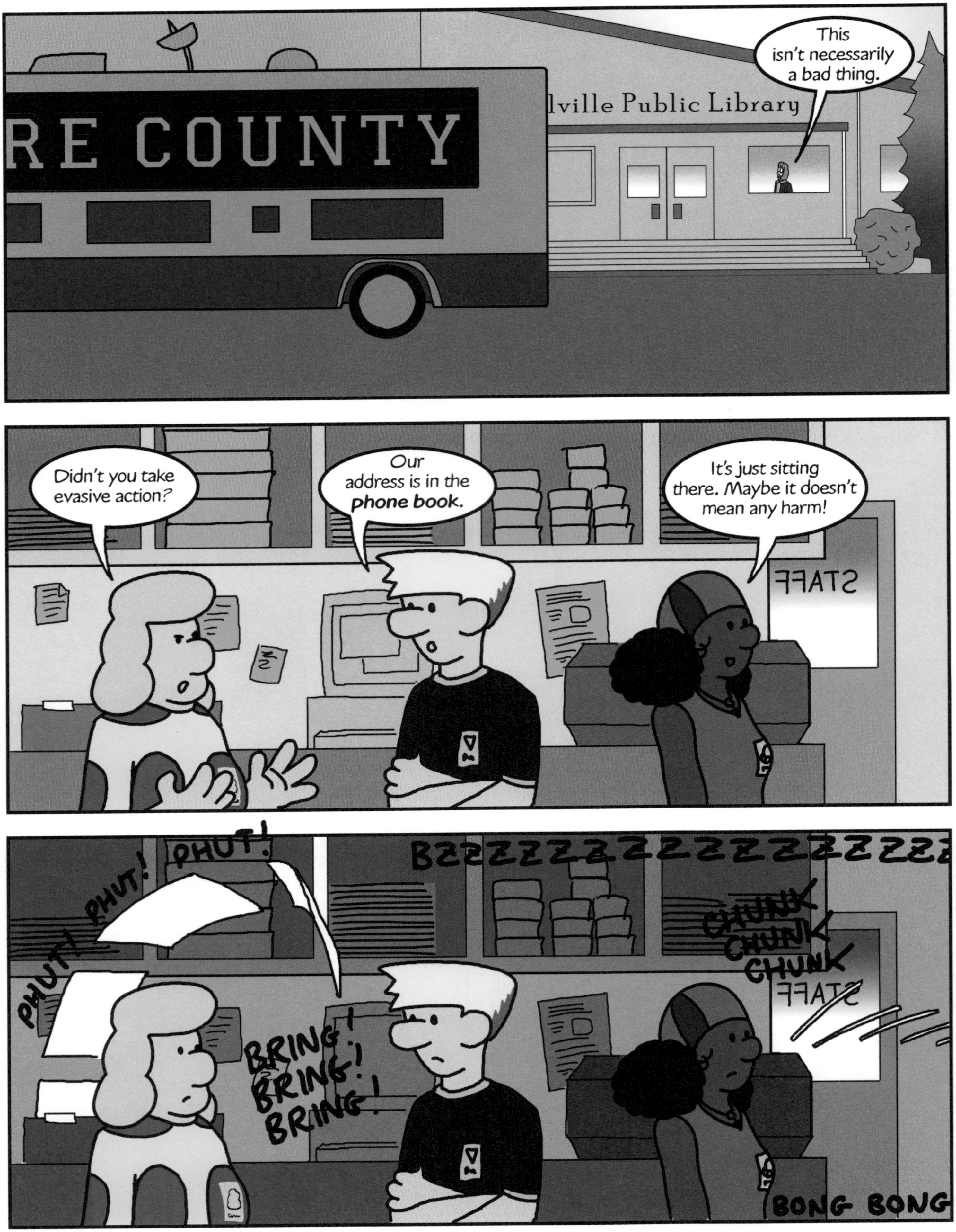
RE COUNTY
lville Public Library
This isn't necessarily a bad thing.
Didn't you take evasive action?
Our address is in the **phone book.**
It's just sitting there. Maybe it doesn't mean any harm!
STAFF
PHUT! PHUT! PHUT! PHUT!
BZZZZZZZZZZZZZZZZ
CHUNK CHUNK CHUNK
BRING! BRING! BRING!
BONG BONG

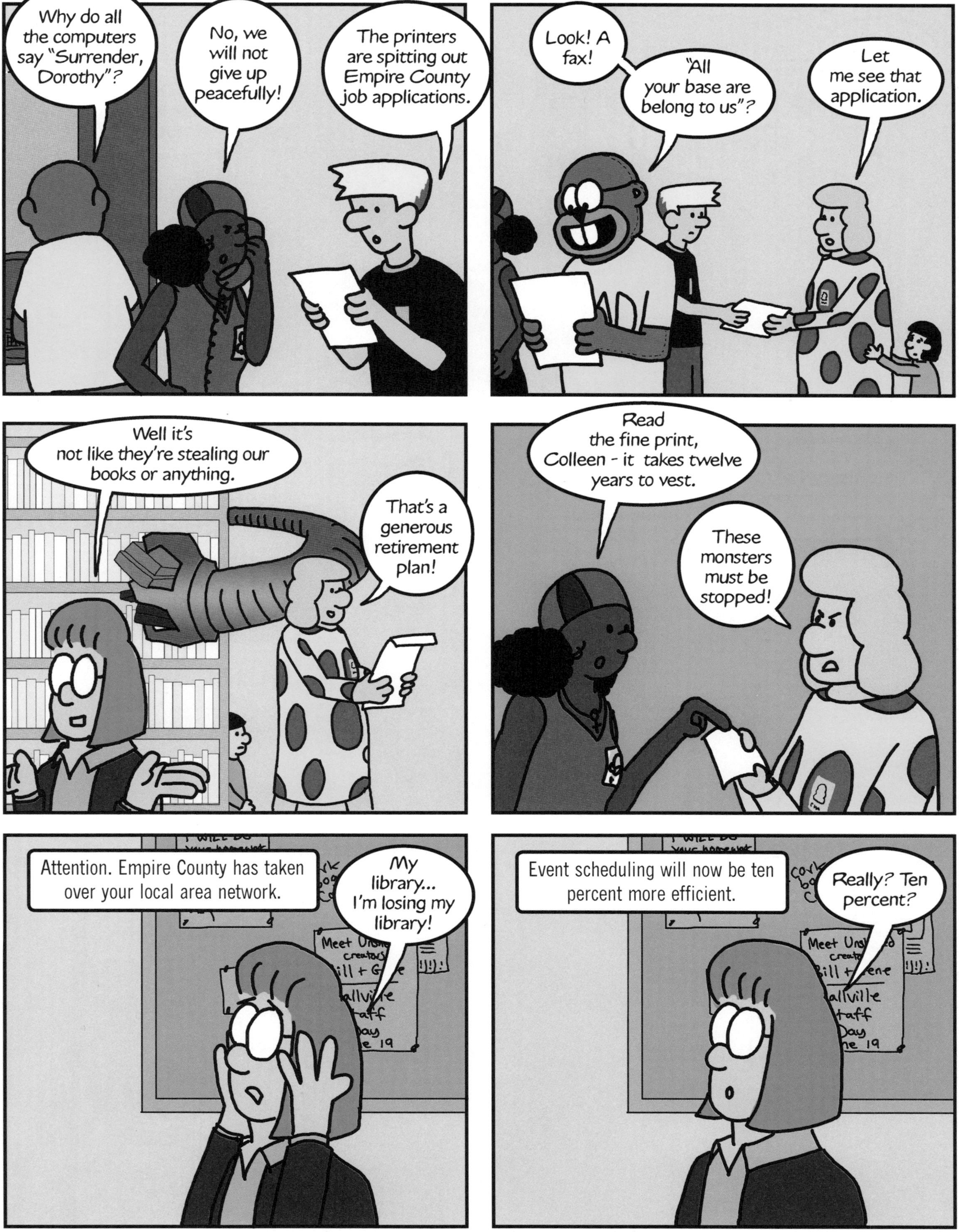
Why do all the computers say "Surrender, Dorothy"?
No, we will not give up peacefully!
The printers are spitting out Empire County job applications.
Look! A fax!
"All your base are belong to us"?
Let me see that application.
Well it's not like they're stealing our books or anything.
That's a generous retirement plan!
Read the fine print, Colleen - it takes twelve years to vest.
These monsters must be stopped!
Attention. Empire County has taken over your local area network.
My library... I'm losing my library!
Event scheduling will now be ten percent more efficient.
Really? Ten percent?

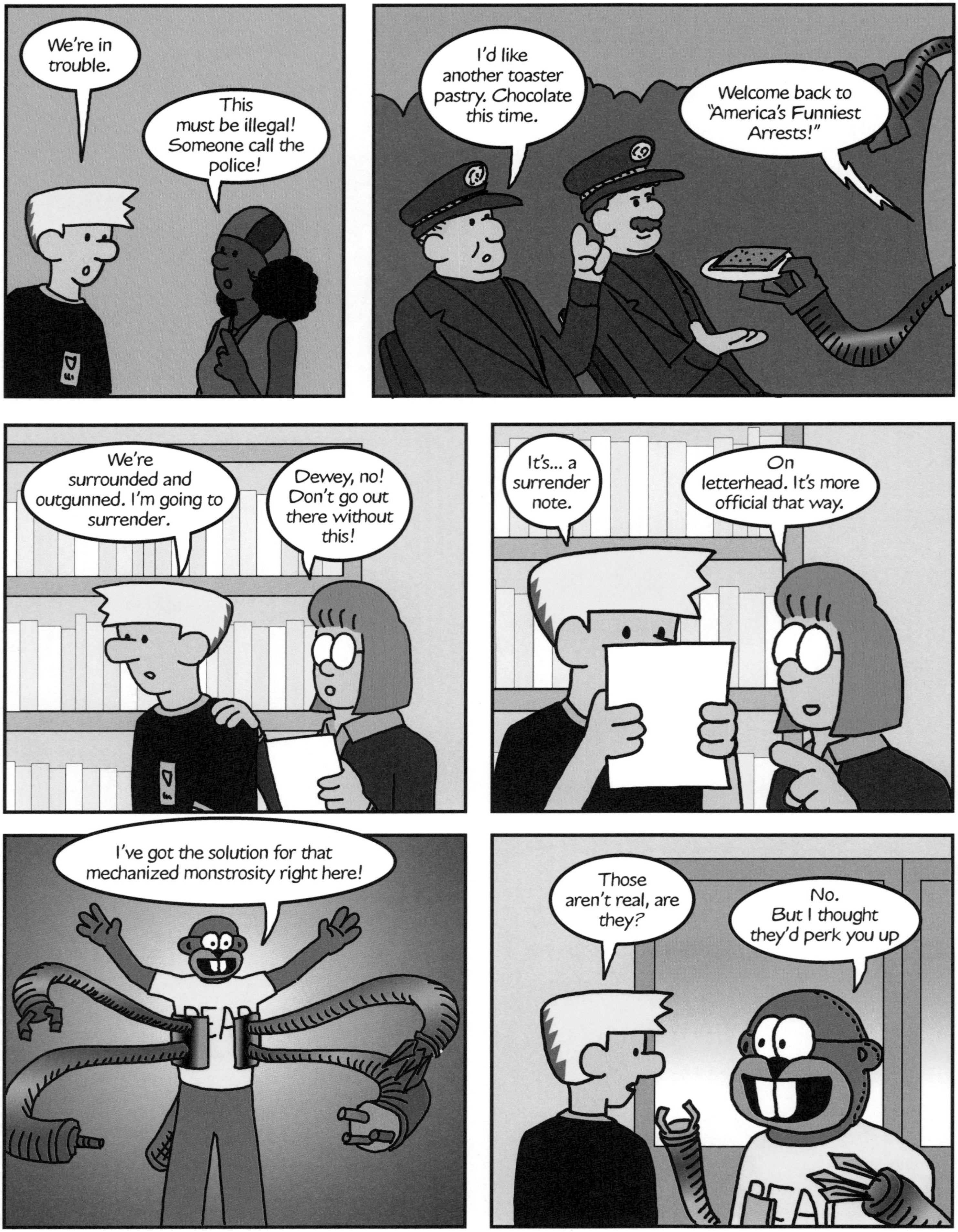

We're in trouble.
This must be illegal! Someone call the police!
I'd like another toaster pastry. Chocolate this time.
Welcome back to "America's Funniest Arrests!"
We're surrounded and outgunned. I'm going to surrender.
Dewey, no! Don't go out there without this!
It's... a surrender note.
On letterhead. It's more official that way.
I've got the solution for that mechanized monstrosity right here!
Those aren't real, are they?
No. But I thought they'd perk you up

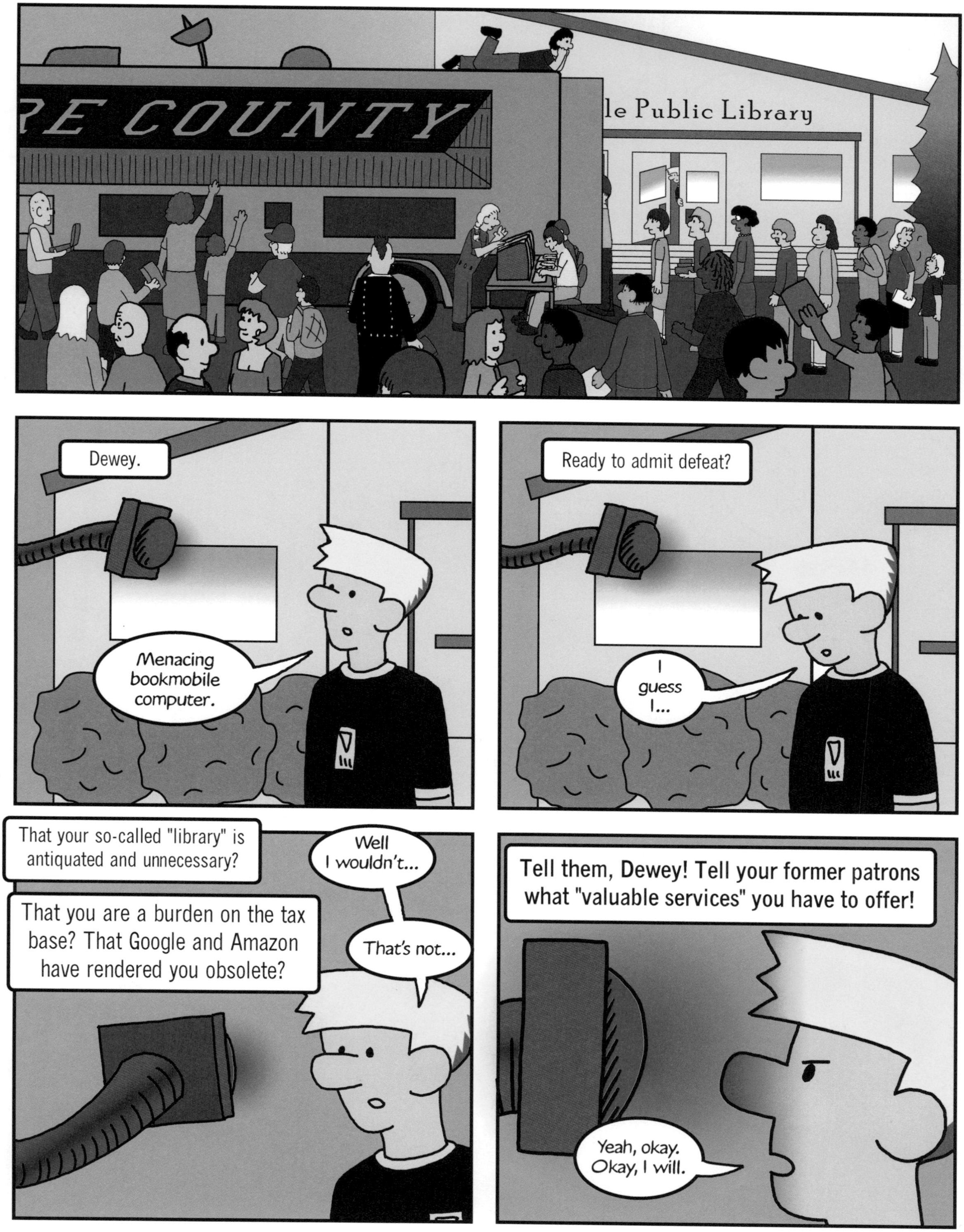
RE COUNTY
le Public Library
Dewey.
Menacing bookmobile computer.
Ready to admit defeat?
I guess I...
That your so-called "library" is antiquated and unnecessary?
Well I wouldn't...
That you are a burden on the tax base? That Google and Amazon have rendered you obsolete?
That's not...
Tell them, Dewey! Tell your former patrons what "valuable services" you have to offer!
Yeah, okay. Okay, I will.

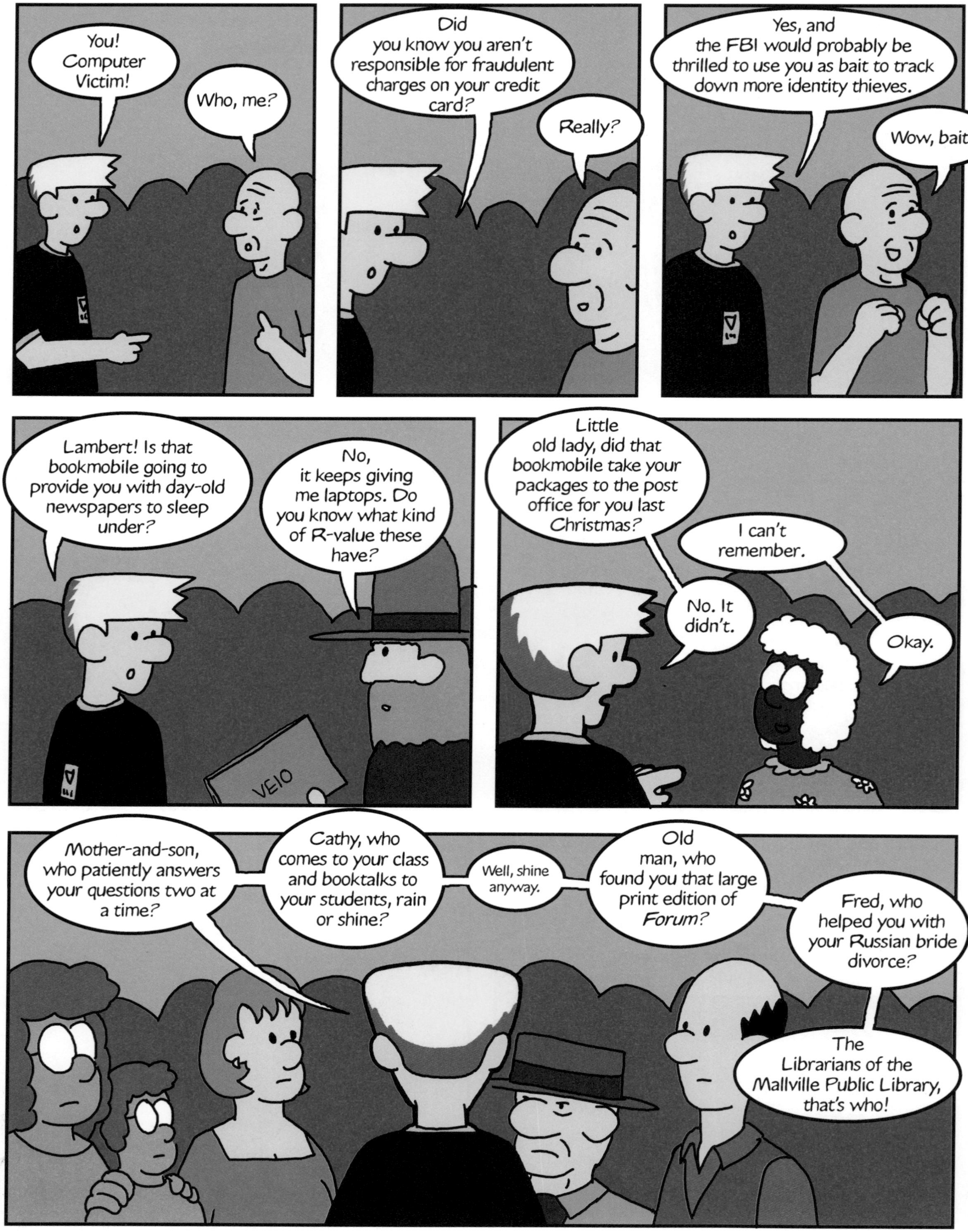
You! Computer Victim!
Who, me?
Did you know you aren't responsible for fraudulent charges on your credit card?
Really?
Yes, and the FBI would probably be thrilled to use you as bait to track down more identity thieves.
Wow, bait!
Lambert! Is that bookmobile going to provide you with day-old newspapers to sleep under?
No, it keeps giving me laptops. Do you know what kind of R-value these have?
VEIO
Little old lady, did that bookmobile take your packages to the post office for you last Christmas?
I can't remember.
No. It didn't.
Okay.
Mother-and-son, who patiently answers your questions two at a time?
Cathy, who comes to your class and booktalks to your students, rain or shine?
Well, shine anyway.
Old man, who found you that large print edition of *Forum*?
Fred, who helped you with your Russian bride divorce?
The Librarians of the Mallville Public Library, that's who!

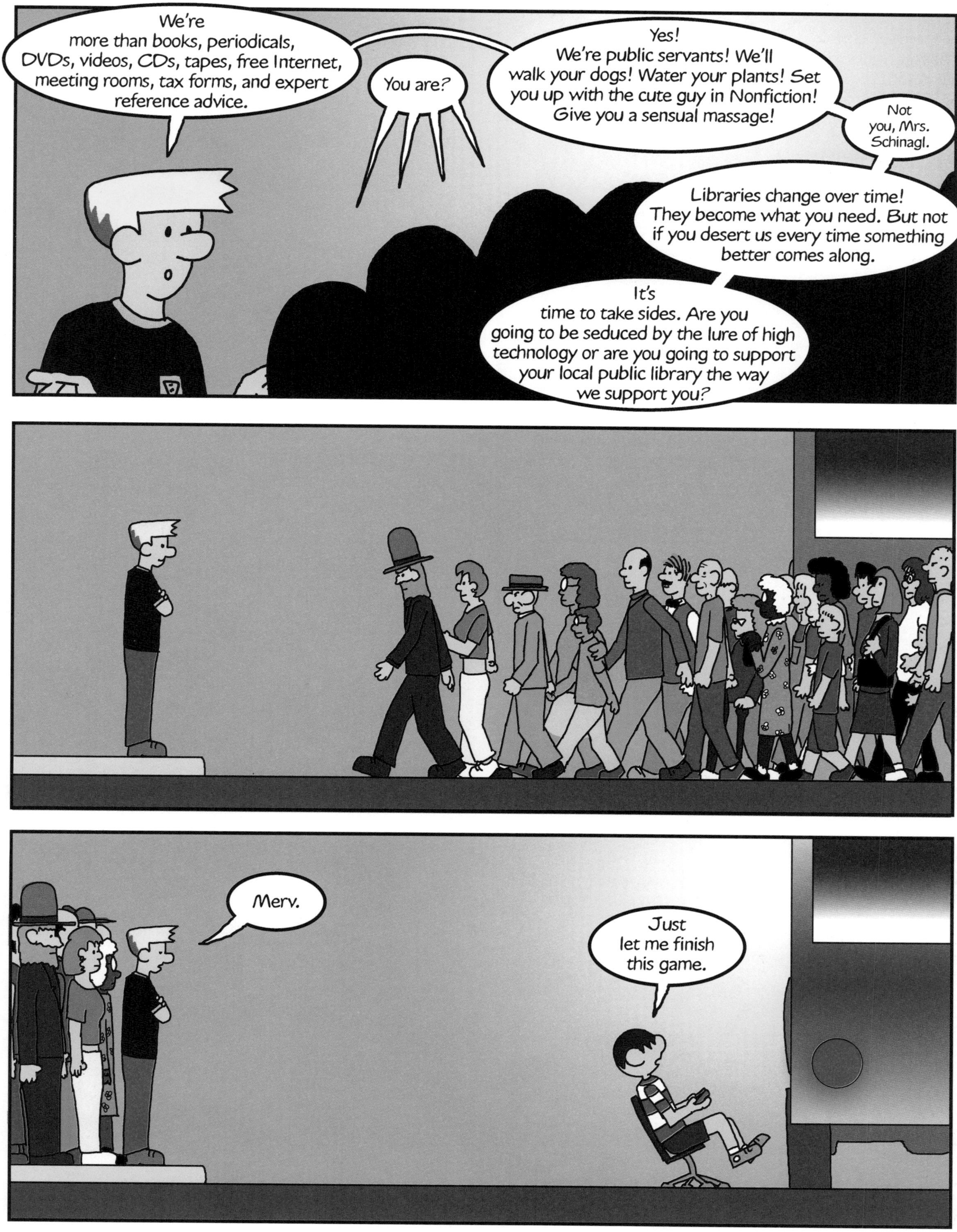
We're more than books, periodicals, DVDs, videos, CDs, tapes, free Internet, meeting rooms, tax forms, and expert reference advice.
You are?
Yes! We're public servants! We'll walk your dogs! Water your plants! Set you up with the cute guy in Nonfiction! Give you a sensual massage!
Not you, Mrs. Schinagl.
Libraries change over time! They become what you need. But not if you desert us every time something better comes along.
It's time to take sides. Are you going to be seduced by the lure of high technology or are you going to support your local public library the way we support you?
Merv.
Just let me finish this game.

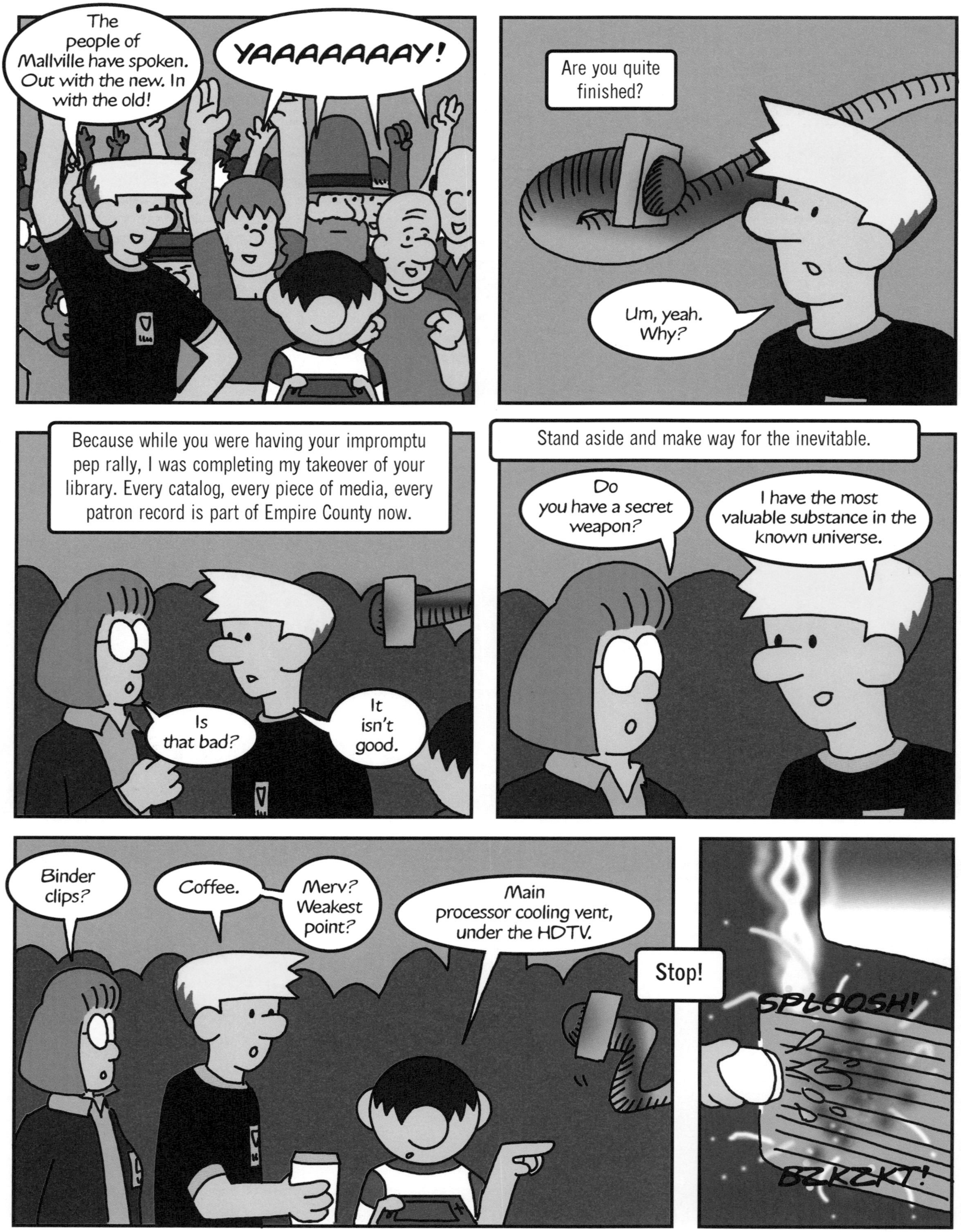
The people of Mallville have spoken. Out with the new. In with the old!
YAAAAAAAY!
Are you quite finished?
Um, yeah. Why?
Because while you were having your impromptu pep rally, I was completing my takeover of your library. Every catalog, every piece of media, every patron record is part of Empire County now.
Is that bad?
It isn't good.
Stand aside and make way for the inevitable.
Do you have a secret weapon?
I have the most valuable substance in the known universe.
Binder clips?
Coffee.
Merv? Weakest point?
Main processor cooling vent, under the HDTV.
Stop!
SPLOOSH!
BZKZKT!

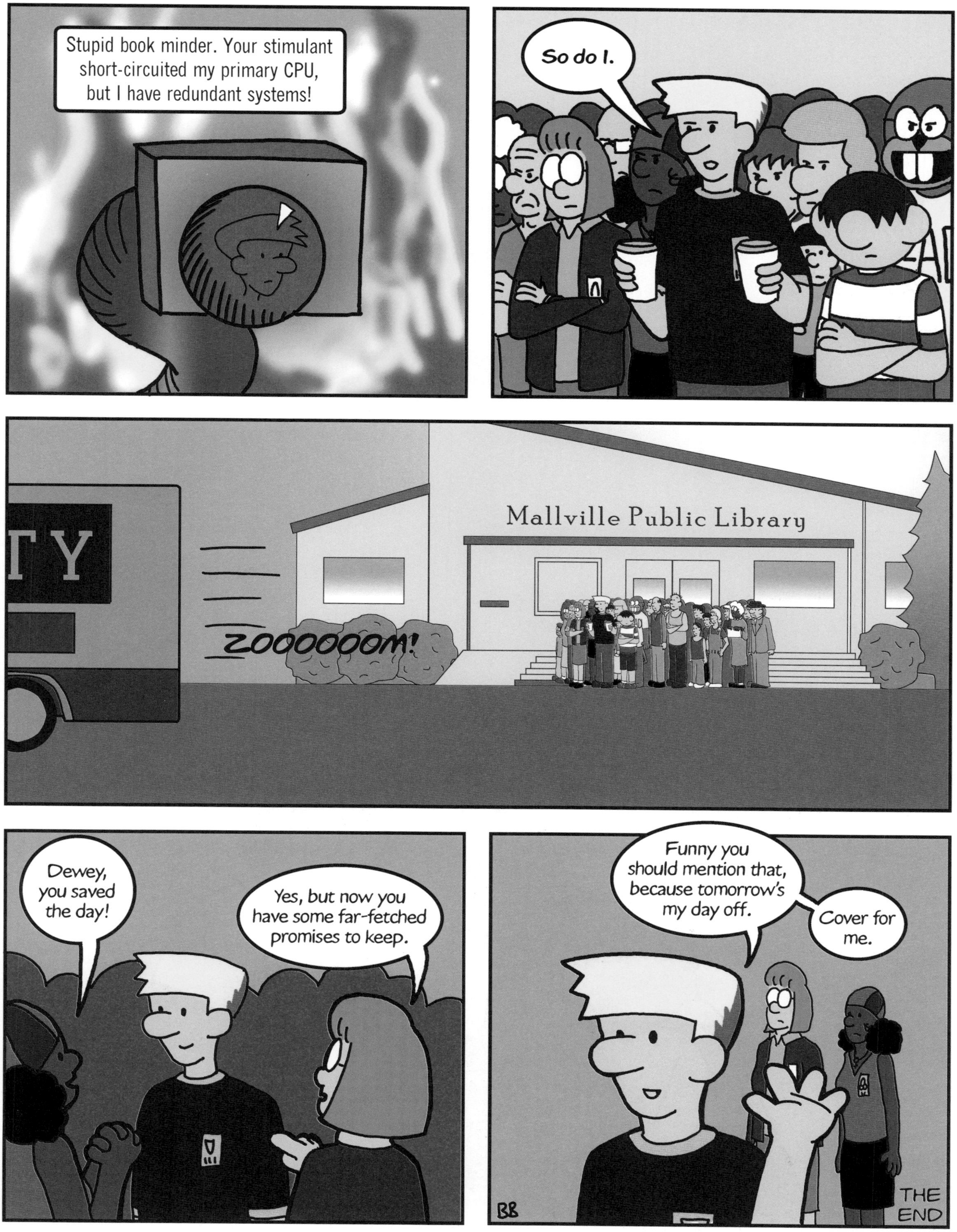

Stupid book minder. Your stimulant short-circuited my primary CPU, but I have redundant systems!
So do I.
TY
Mallville Public Library
ZOOOOOOM!
Dewey, you saved the day!
Yes, but now you have some far-fetched promises to keep.
Funny you should mention that, because tomorrow's my day off.
Cover for me.
BB
THE END

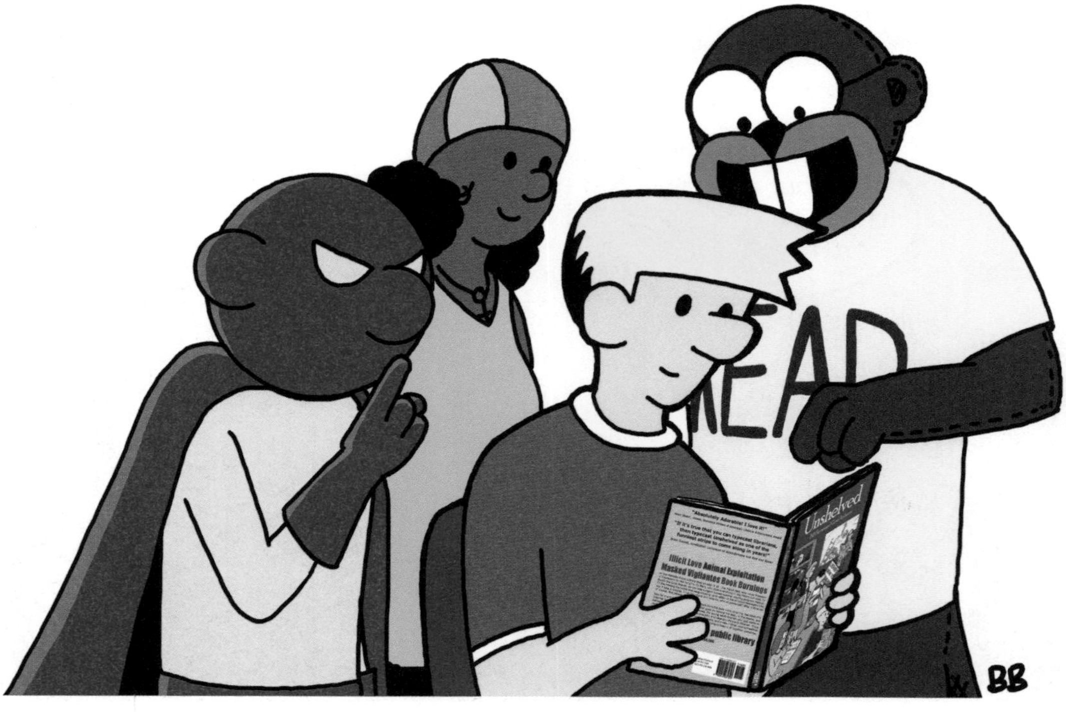
READ
"Absolutely Adorable! I love it!"
"If it's true that you can typecast librarians, then typecast Unshelved as one of the funniest strips to come along in years!"
Illicit Love Animal Exploitation
Masked Vigilantes Book Burnings
public library
Unshelved
BB

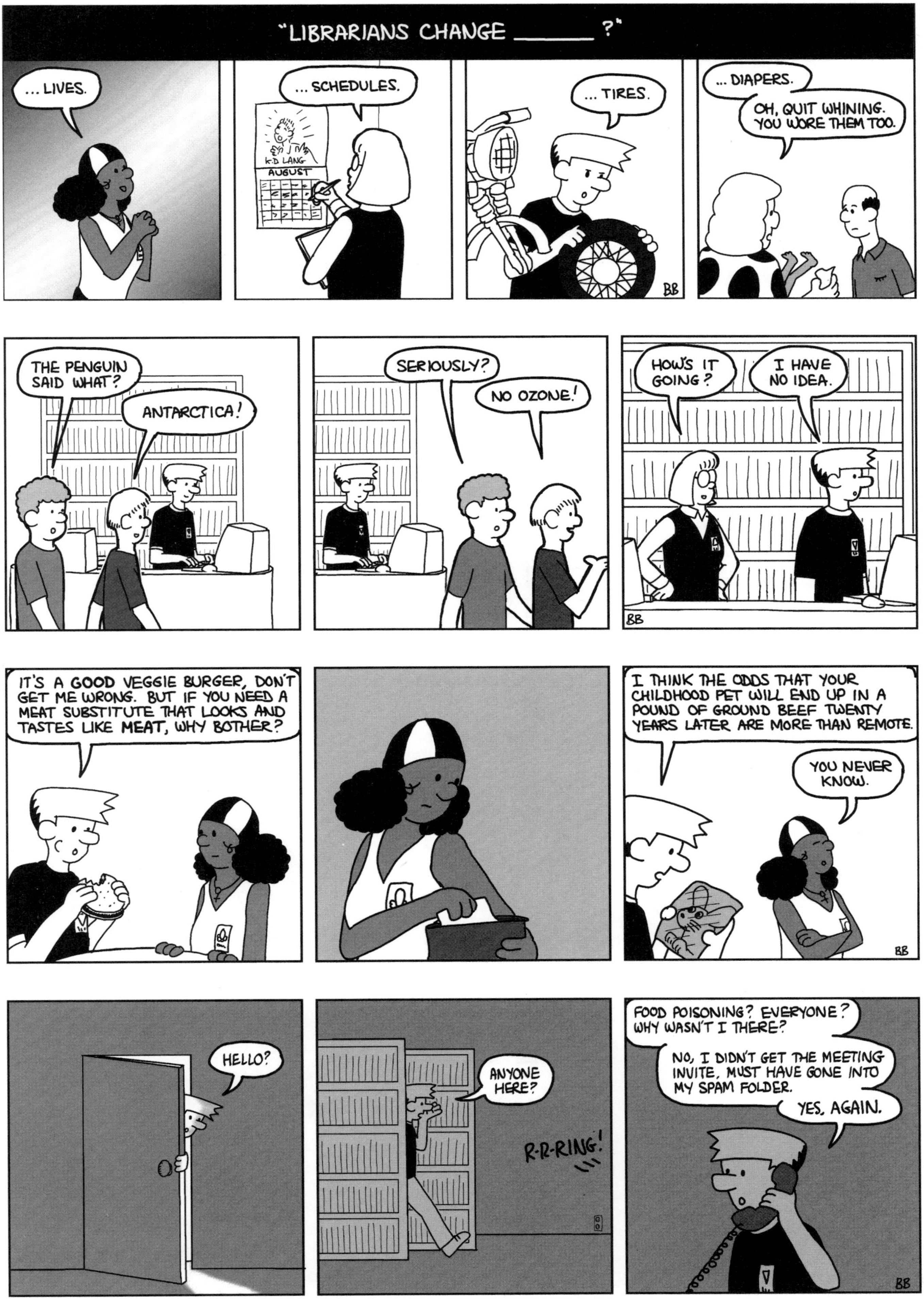
"LIBRARIANS CHANGE ______ ?"
... LIVES.
... SCHEDULES.
K.D LANG
AUGUST
... TIRES.
... DIAPERS.
OH, QUIT WHINING. YOU WORE THEM TOO.
BB
THE PENGUIN SAID WHAT?
ANTARCTICA!
SERIOUSLY?
NO OZONE!
HOW'S IT GOING?
I HAVE NO IDEA.
BB
IT'S A GOOD VEGGIE BURGER, DON'T GET ME WRONG. BUT IF YOU NEED A MEAT SUBSTITUTE THAT LOOKS AND TASTES LIKE MEAT, WHY BOTHER?
I THINK THE ODDS THAT YOUR CHILDHOOD PET WILL END UP IN A POUND OF GROUND BEEF TWENTY YEARS LATER ARE MORE THAN REMOTE.
YOU NEVER KNOW.
BB
HELLO?
ANYONE HERE?
R-R-RING!
FOOD POISONING? EVERYONE? WHY WASN'T I THERE?
NO, I DIDN'T GET THE MEETING INVITE, MUST HAVE GONE INTO MY SPAM FOLDER.
YES, AGAIN.
BB

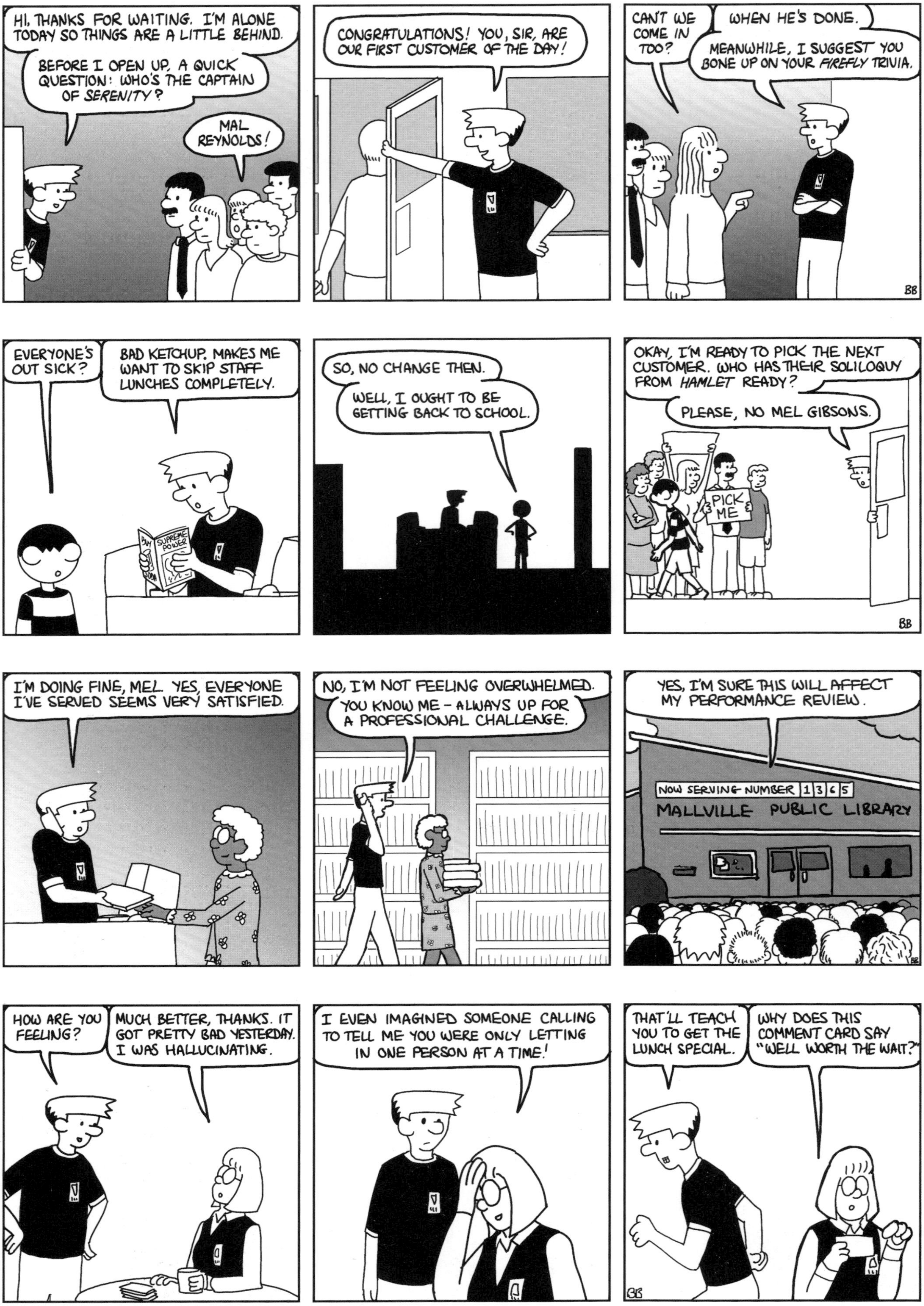
HI, THANKS FOR WAITING. I'M ALONE TODAY SO THINGS ARE A LITTLE BEHIND.
BEFORE I OPEN UP, A QUICK QUESTION: WHO'S THE CAPTAIN OF *SERENITY*?
MAL REYNOLDS!
CONGRATULATIONS! YOU, SIR, ARE OUR FIRST CUSTOMER OF THE DAY!
CAN'T WE COME IN TOO?
WHEN HE'S DONE.
MEANWHILE, I SUGGEST YOU BONE UP ON YOUR *FIREFLY* TRIVIA.
BB
EVERYONE'S OUT SICK?
BAD KETCHUP. MAKES ME WANT TO SKIP STAFF LUNCHES COMPLETELY.
SUPREME POWER
SO, NO CHANGE THEN.
WELL, I OUGHT TO BE GETTING BACK TO SCHOOL.
OKAY, I'M READY TO PICK THE NEXT CUSTOMER. WHO HAS THEIR SOLILOQUY FROM *HAMLET* READY?
PLEASE, NO MEL GIBSONS.
PICK ME
BB
I'M DOING FINE, MEL. YES, EVERYONE I'VE SERVED SEEMS VERY SATISFIED.
NO, I'M NOT FEELING OVERWHELMED.
YOU KNOW ME - ALWAYS UP FOR A PROFESSIONAL CHALLENGE.
YES, I'M SURE THIS WILL AFFECT MY PERFORMANCE REVIEW.
NOW SERVING NUMBER 1 3 6 5
MALLVILLE PUBLIC LIBRARY
BB
HOW ARE YOU FEELING?
MUCH BETTER, THANKS. IT GOT PRETTY BAD YESTERDAY. I WAS HALLUCINATING.
I EVEN IMAGINED SOMEONE CALLING TO TELL ME YOU WERE ONLY LETTING IN ONE PERSON AT A TIME!
THAT'LL TEACH YOU TO GET THE LUNCH SPECIAL.
WHY DOES THIS COMMENT CARD SAY "WELL WORTH THE WAIT?"
BB

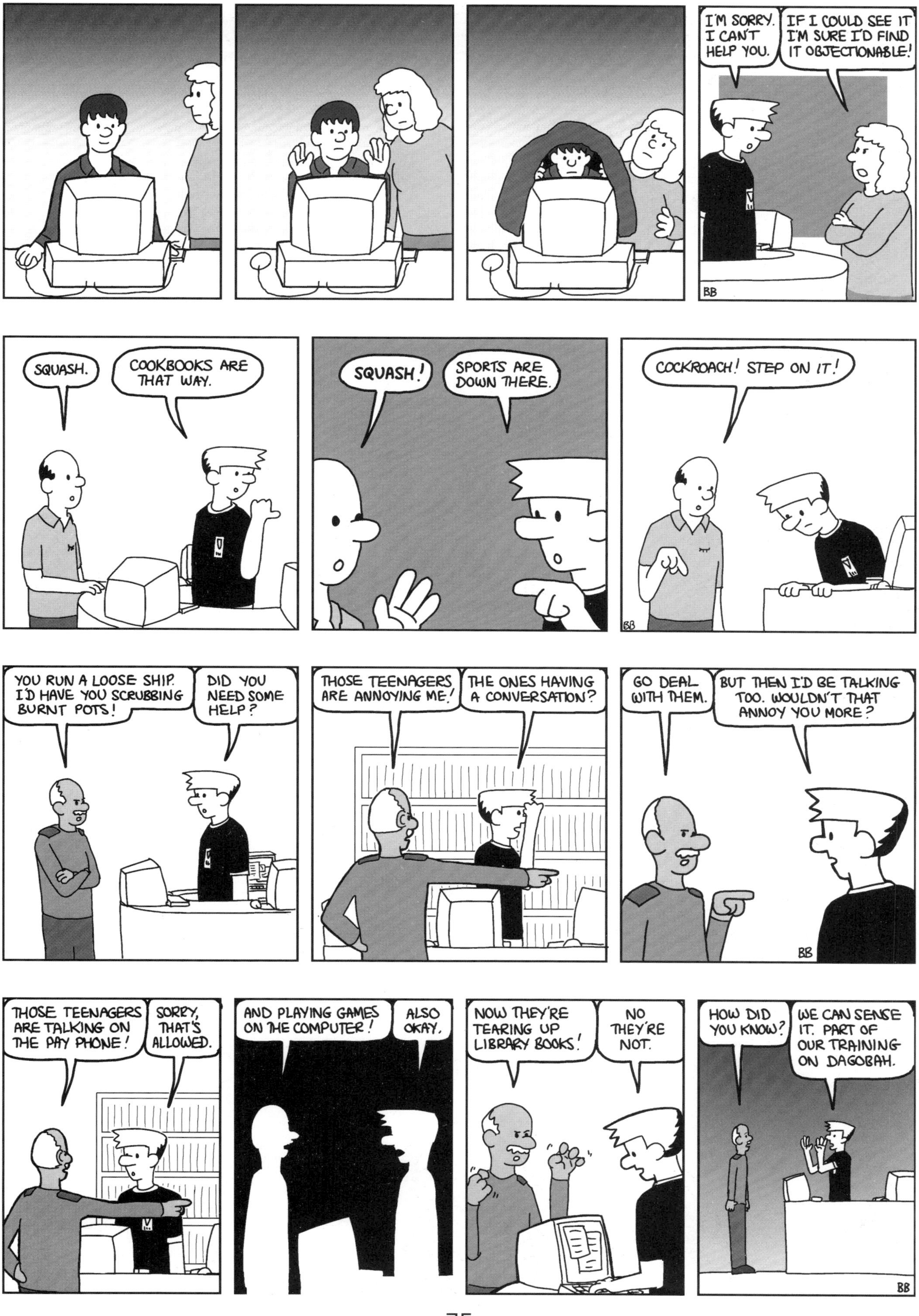
I'M SORRY. I CAN'T HELP YOU.
IF I COULD SEE IT I'M SURE I'D FIND IT OBJECTIONABLE!
BB
SQUASH.
COOKBOOKS ARE THAT WAY.
SQUASH!
SPORTS ARE DOWN THERE.
COCKROACH! STEP ON IT!
BB
YOU RUN A LOOSE SHIP. I'D HAVE YOU SCRUBBING BURNT POTS!
DID YOU NEED SOME HELP?
THOSE TEENAGERS ARE ANNOYING ME!
THE ONES HAVING A CONVERSATION?
GO DEAL WITH THEM.
BUT THEN I'D BE TALKING TOO. WOULDN'T THAT ANNOY YOU MORE?
BB
THOSE TEENAGERS ARE TALKING ON THE PAY PHONE!
SORRY, THAT'S ALLOWED.
AND PLAYING GAMES ON THE COMPUTER!
ALSO OKAY.
NOW THEY'RE TEARING UP LIBRARY BOOKS!
NO THEY'RE NOT.
HOW DID YOU KNOW?
WE CAN SENSE IT. PART OF OUR TRAINING ON DAGOBAH.
BB

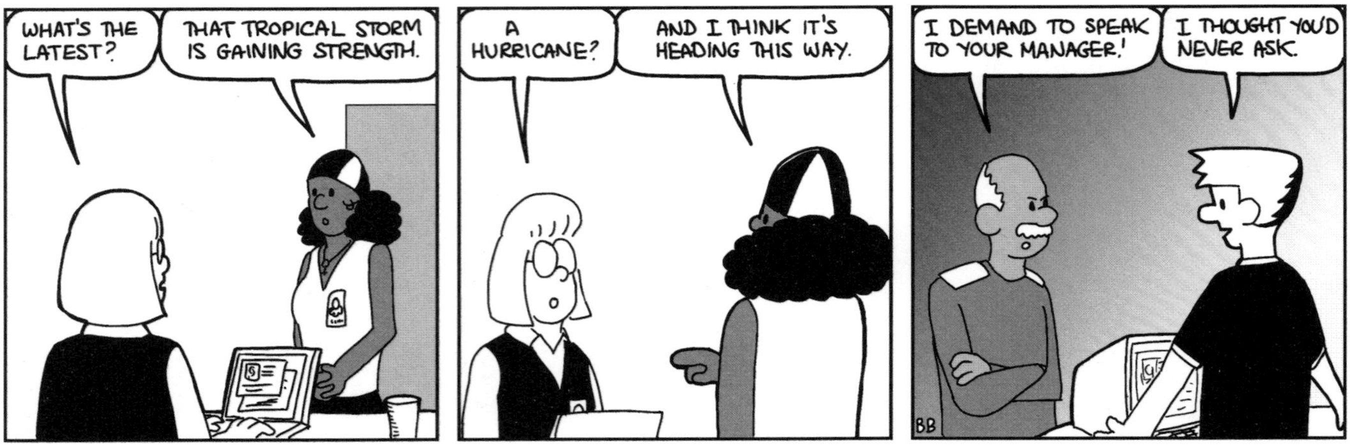
WHAT'S THE LATEST?
THAT TROPICAL STORM IS GAINING STRENGTH.
A HURRICANE?
AND I THINK IT'S HEADING THIS WAY.
I DEMAND TO SPEAK TO YOUR MANAGER!
I THOUGHT YOU'D NEVER ASK.
BB

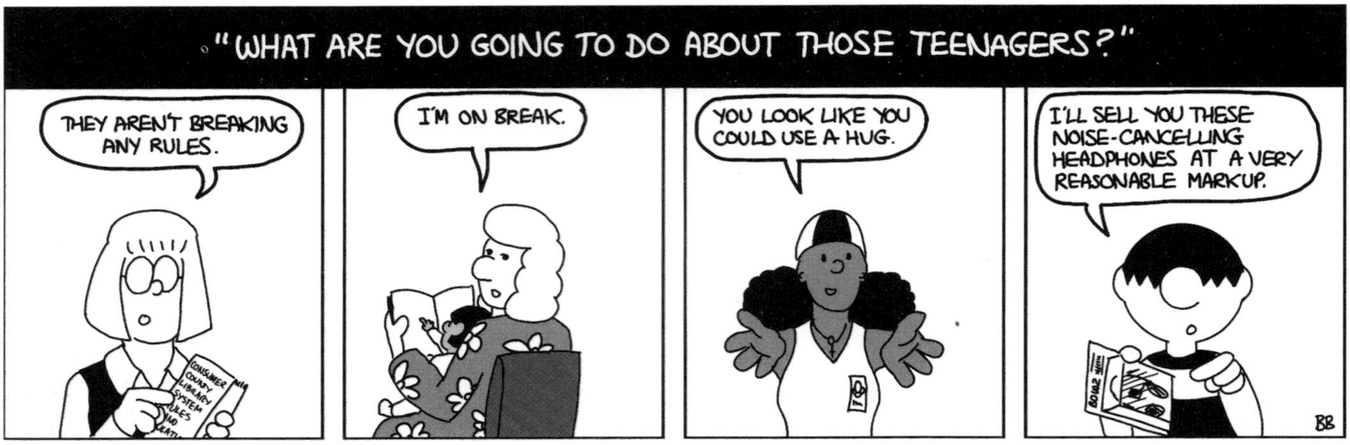
"WHAT ARE YOU GOING TO DO ABOUT THOSE TEENAGERS?"
THEY AREN'T BREAKING ANY RULES.
I'M ON BREAK.
YOU LOOK LIKE YOU COULD USE A HUG.
I'LL SELL YOU THESE NOISE-CANCELLING HEADPHONES AT A VERY REASONABLE MARKUP.
BB

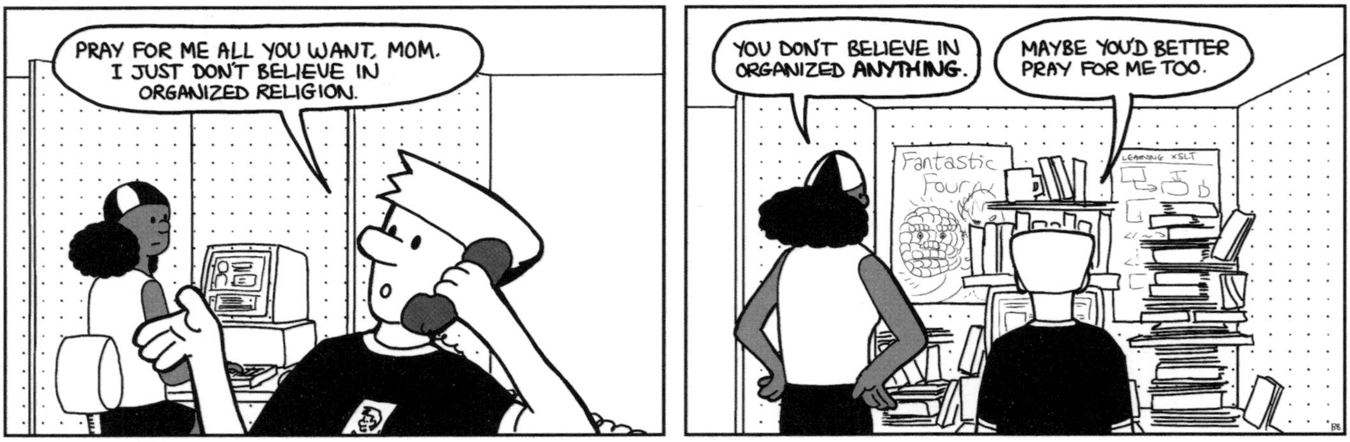
PRAY FOR ME ALL YOU WANT, MOM. I JUST DON'T BELIEVE IN ORGANIZED RELIGION.
YOU DON'T BELIEVE IN ORGANIZED **ANYTHING**.
MAYBE YOU'D BETTER PRAY FOR ME TOO.
BB

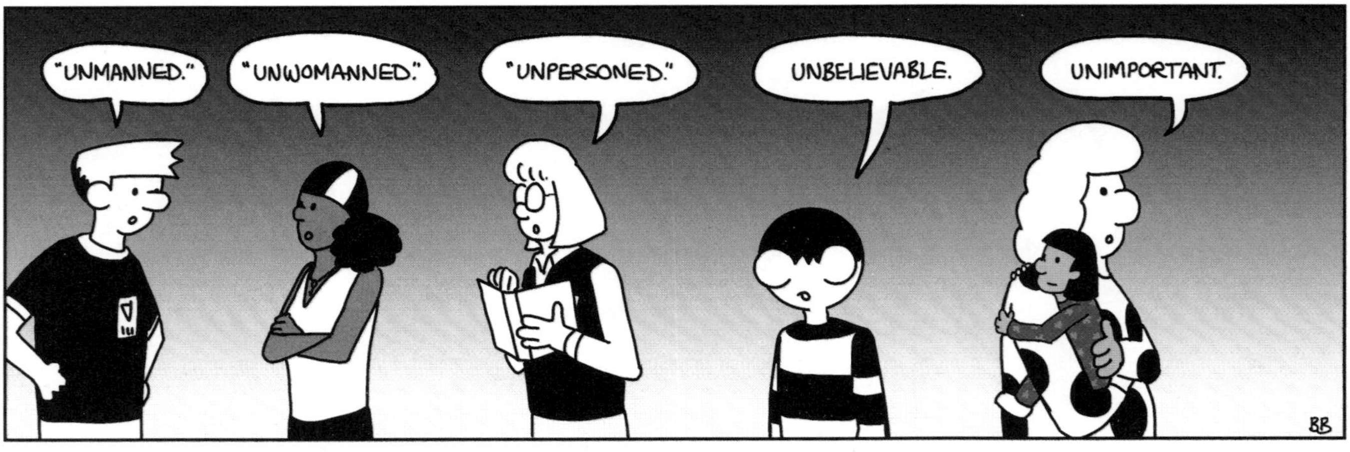
"UNMANNED."
"UNWOMANNED."
"UNPERSONED."
UNBELIEVABLE.
UNIMPORTANT.
BB

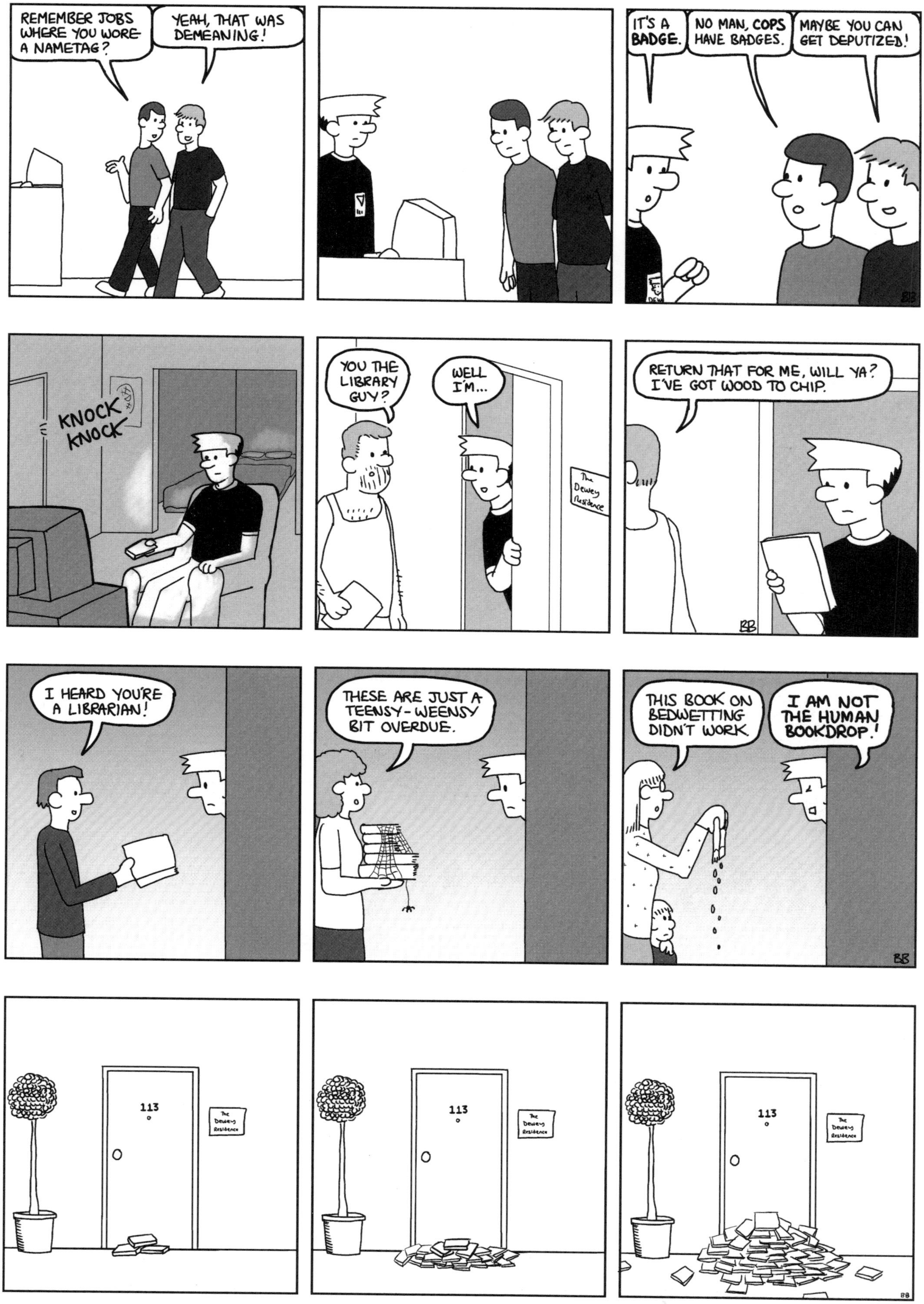
REMEMBER JOBS WHERE YOU WORE A NAMETAG?
YEAH, THAT WAS DEMEANING!
IT'S A BADGE.
NO MAN, COPS HAVE BADGES.
MAYBE YOU CAN GET DEPUTIZED!
KNOCK KNOCK
YOU THE LIBRARY GUY?
WELL I'M...
The Dewey Residence
RETURN THAT FOR ME, WILL YA? I'VE GOT WOOD TO CHIP.
I HEARD YOU'RE A LIBRARIAN!
THESE ARE JUST A TEENSY-WEENSY BIT OVERDUE.
THIS BOOK ON BEDWETTING DIDN'T WORK.
I AM NOT THE HUMAN BOOKDROP!
113
The Dewey Residence
113
The Dewey Residence
113
The Dewey Residence

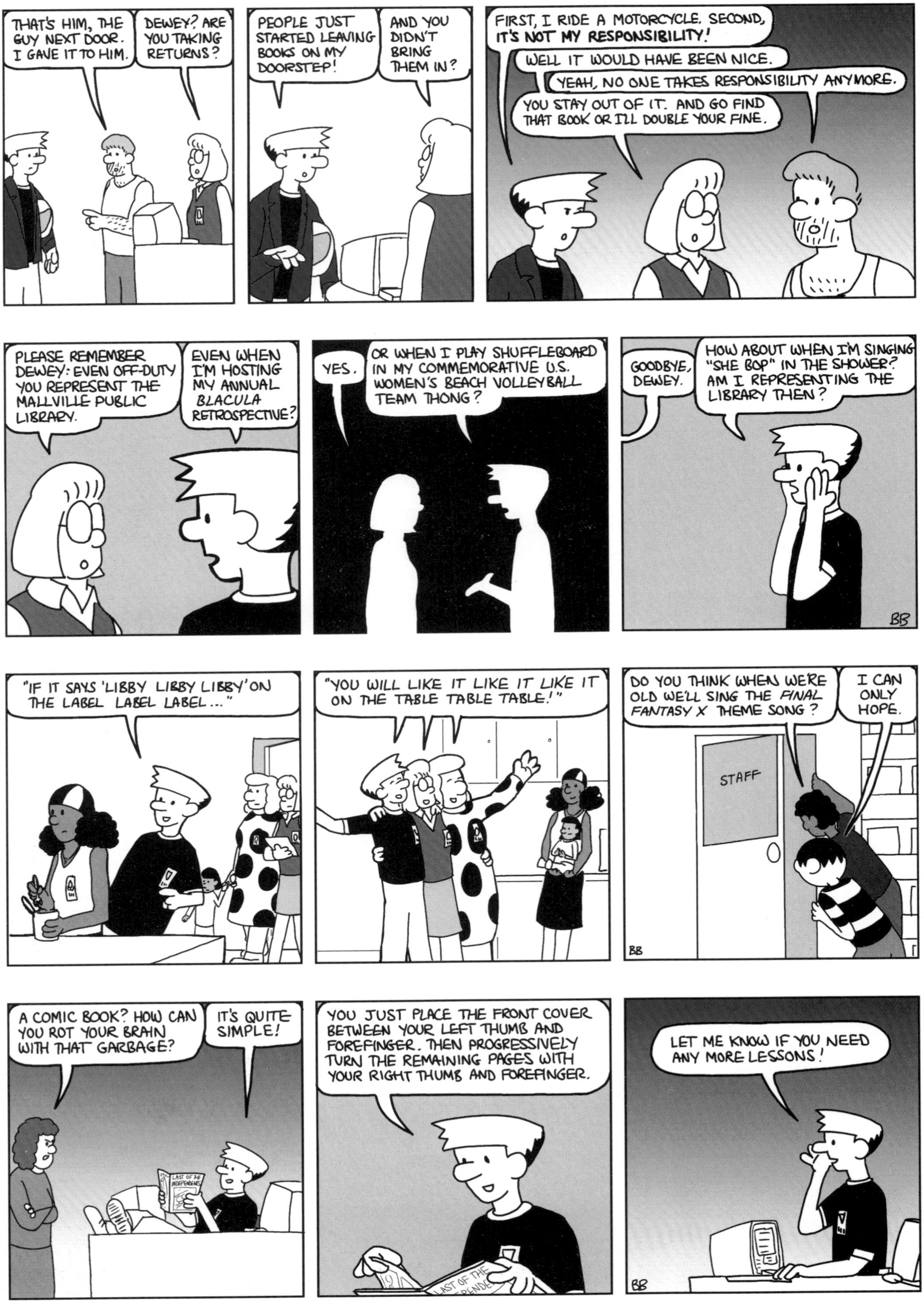
THAT'S HIM, THE GUY NEXT DOOR. I GAVE IT TO HIM.
DEWEY? ARE YOU TAKING RETURNS?
PEOPLE JUST STARTED LEAVING BOOKS ON MY DOORSTEP!
AND YOU DIDN'T BRING THEM IN?
FIRST, I RIDE A MOTORCYCLE. SECOND, **IT'S NOT MY RESPONSIBILITY!**
WELL IT WOULD HAVE BEEN NICE.
YEAH, NO ONE TAKES RESPONSIBILITY ANYMORE.
YOU STAY OUT OF IT. AND GO FIND THAT BOOK OR I'LL DOUBLE YOUR FINE.
PLEASE REMEMBER DEWEY: EVEN OFF-DUTY YOU REPRESENT THE MALLVILLE PUBLIC LIBRARY.
EVEN WHEN I'M HOSTING MY ANNUAL *BLACULA* RETROSPECTIVE?
YES.
OR WHEN I PLAY SHUFFLEBOARD IN MY COMMEMORATIVE U.S. WOMEN'S BEACH VOLLEYBALL TEAM THONG?
GOODBYE, DEWEY.
HOW ABOUT WHEN I'M SINGING "SHE BOP" IN THE SHOWER? AM I REPRESENTING THE LIBRARY THEN?
BB
"IF IT SAYS 'LIBBY LIBBY LIBBY' ON THE LABEL LABEL LABEL..."
"YOU WILL LIKE IT LIKE IT LIKE IT ON THE TABLE TABLE TABLE!"
DO YOU THINK WHEN WE'RE OLD WE'LL SING THE *FINAL FANTASY X* THEME SONG?
I CAN ONLY HOPE.
STAFF
BB
A COMIC BOOK? HOW CAN YOU ROT YOUR BRAIN WITH THAT GARBAGE?
IT'S QUITE SIMPLE!
LAST OF THE INDEPENDENTS
YOU JUST PLACE THE FRONT COVER BETWEEN YOUR LEFT THUMB AND FOREFINGER. THEN PROGRESSIVELY TURN THE REMAINING PAGES WITH YOUR RIGHT THUMB AND FOREFINGER.
LET ME KNOW IF YOU NEED ANY MORE LESSONS!
BB

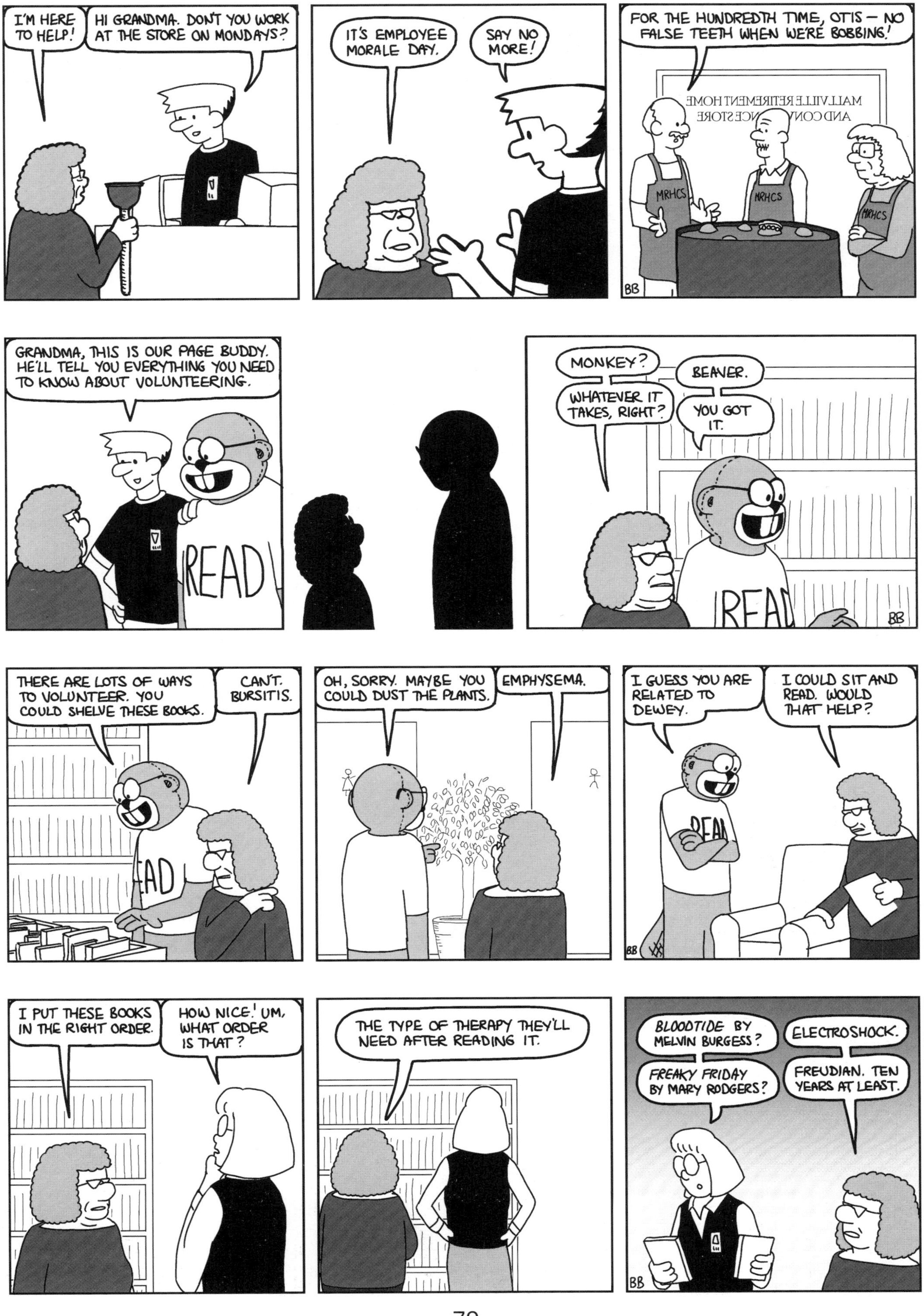
I'M HERE TO HELP!
HI GRANDMA. DON'T YOU WORK AT THE STORE ON MONDAYS?
IT'S EMPLOYEE MORALE DAY.
SAY NO MORE!
FOR THE HUNDREDTH TIME, OTIS — NO FALSE TEETH WHEN WE'RE BOBBING!
MALLVILLE RETIREMENT HOME AND CONV NCE STORE
MRHCS
MRHCS
MRHCS
BB
GRANDMA, THIS IS OUR PAGE BUDDY. HE'LL TELL YOU EVERYTHING YOU NEED TO KNOW ABOUT VOLUNTEERING.
READ
MONKEY?
WHATEVER IT TAKES, RIGHT?
BEAVER.
YOU GOT IT.
READ
BB
THERE ARE LOTS OF WAYS TO VOLUNTEER. YOU COULD SHELVE THESE BOOKS.
CAN'T. BURSITIS.
OH, SORRY. MAYBE YOU COULD DUST THE PLANTS.
EMPHYSEMA.
I GUESS YOU ARE RELATED TO DEWEY.
I COULD SIT AND READ. WOULD THAT HELP?
BB
I PUT THESE BOOKS IN THE RIGHT ORDER.
HOW NICE! UM, WHAT ORDER IS THAT?
THE TYPE OF THERAPY THEY'LL NEED AFTER READING IT.
BLOODTIDE BY MELVIN BURGESS?
ELECTROSHOCK.
FREAKY FRIDAY BY MARY RODGERS?
FREUDIAN. TEN YEARS AT LEAST.
BB

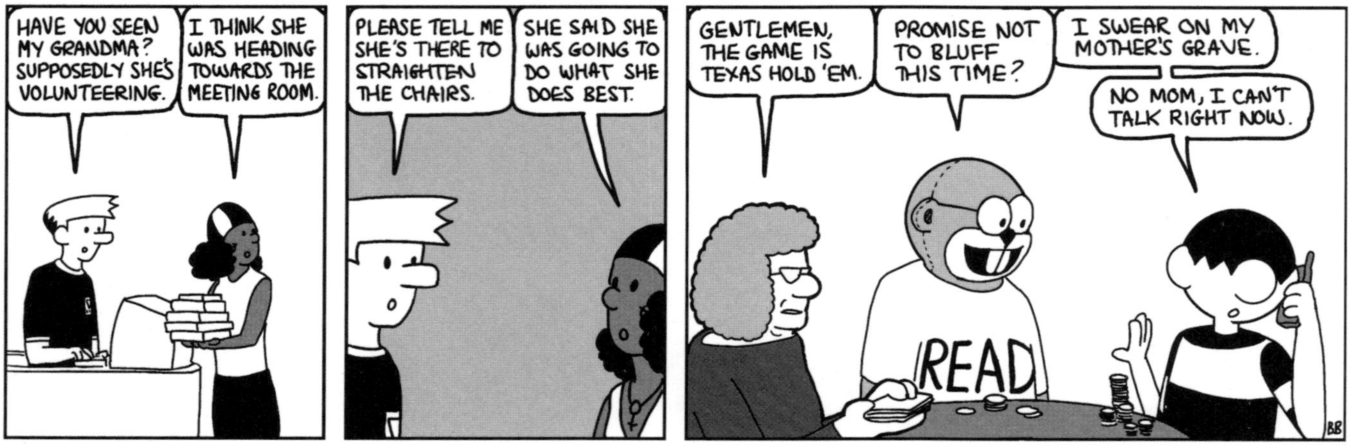
HAVE YOU SEEN MY GRANDMA? SUPPOSEDLY SHE'S VOLUNTEERING.
I THINK SHE WAS HEADING TOWARDS THE MEETING ROOM.
PLEASE TELL ME SHE'S THERE TO STRAIGHTEN THE CHAIRS.
SHE SAID SHE WAS GOING TO DO WHAT SHE DOES BEST.
GENTLEMEN, THE GAME IS TEXAS HOLD 'EM.
PROMISE NOT TO BLUFF THIS TIME?
I SWEAR ON MY MOTHER'S GRAVE.
NO MOM, I CAN'T TALK RIGHT NOW.
READ
BB

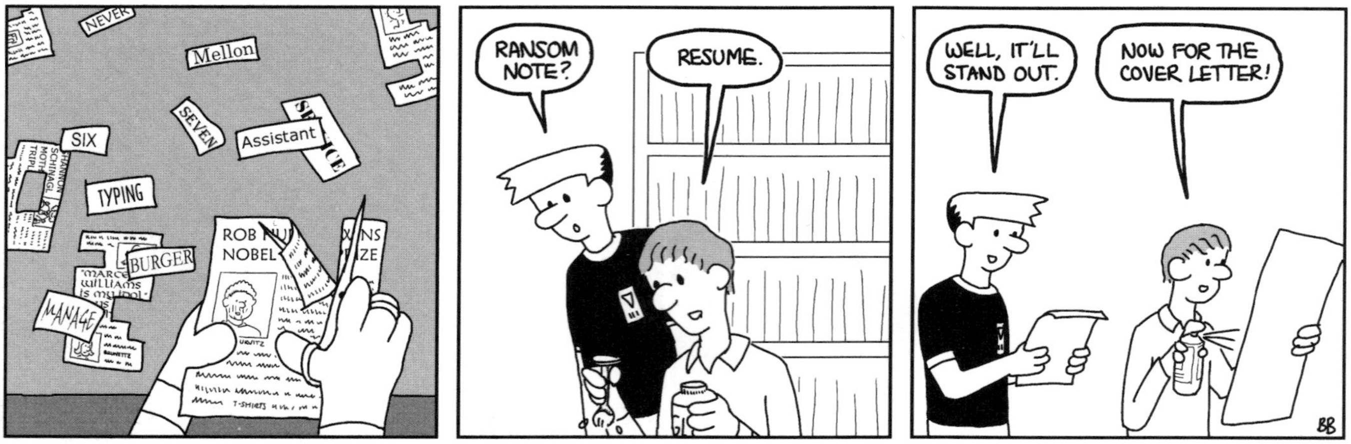
NEVER
Mellon
SIX
SEVEN
Assistant
TYPING
BURGER
MANAGE
RANSOM NOTE?
RESUME.
WELL, IT'LL STAND OUT.
NOW FOR THE COVER LETTER!
BB

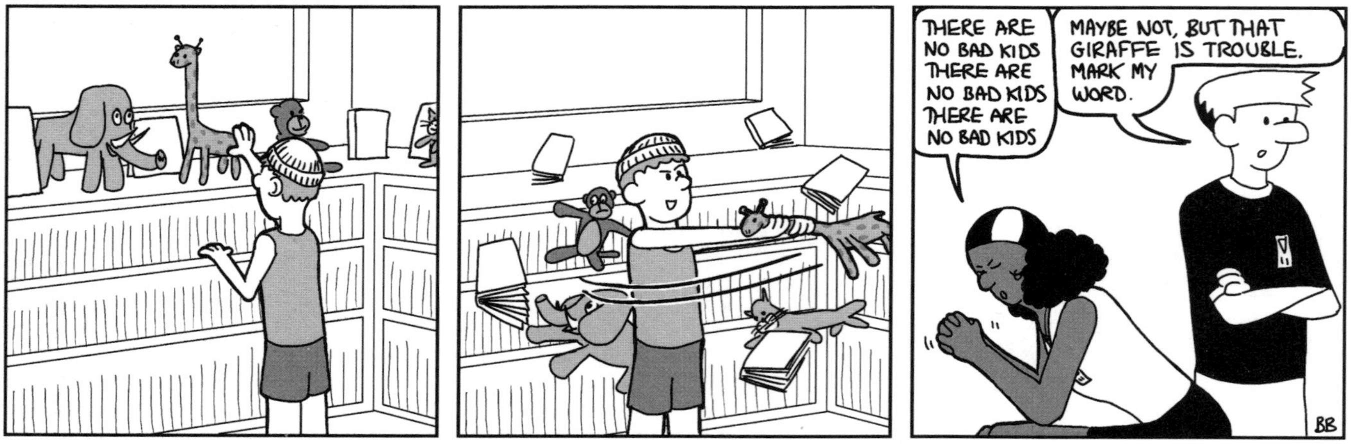
THERE ARE NO BAD KIDS THERE ARE NO BAD KIDS THERE ARE NO BAD KIDS
MAYBE NOT, BUT THAT GIRAFFE IS TROUBLE. MARK MY WORD.
BB

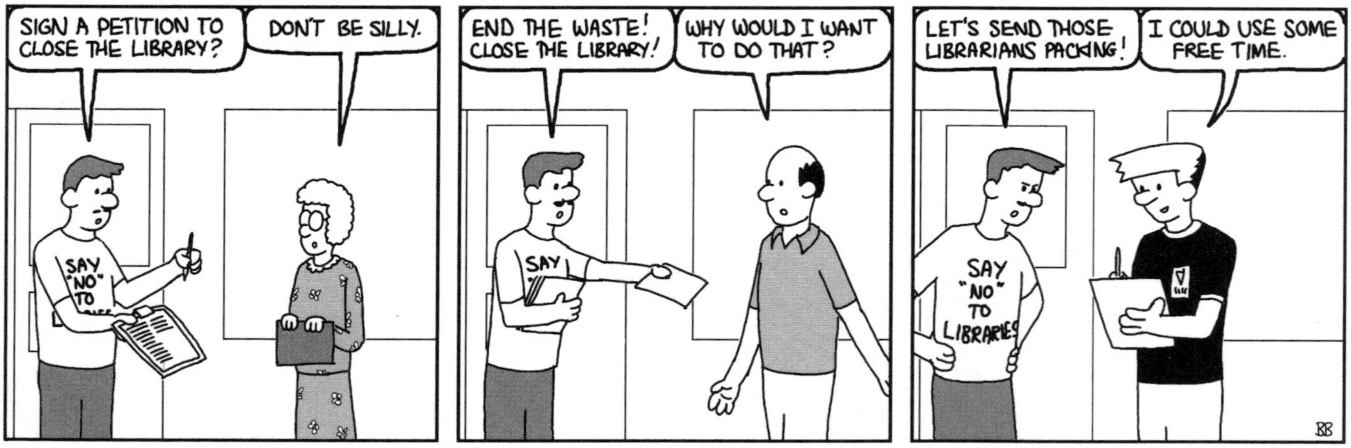
SIGN A PETITION TO CLOSE THE LIBRARY?
DON'T BE SILLY.
END THE WASTE! CLOSE THE LIBRARY!
WHY WOULD I WANT TO DO THAT?
LET'S SEND THOSE LIBRARIANS PACKING!
I COULD USE SOME FREE TIME.
SAY "NO" TO LIBRARIES
BB

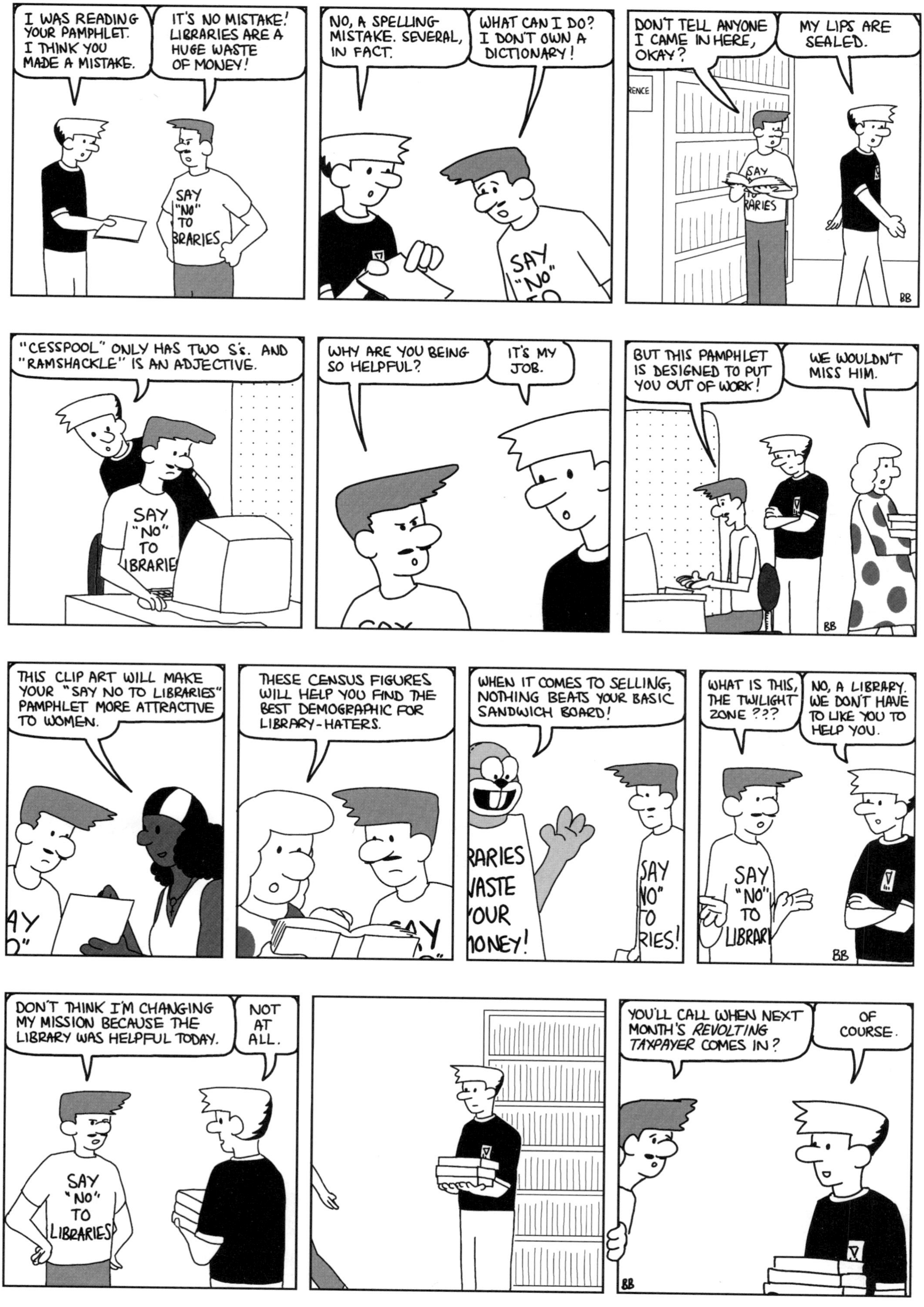
I WAS READING YOUR PAMPHLET. I THINK YOU MADE A MISTAKE.
IT'S NO MISTAKE! LIBRARIES ARE A HUGE WASTE OF MONEY!
NO, A SPELLING MISTAKE. SEVERAL, IN FACT.
WHAT CAN I DO? I DON'T OWN A DICTIONARY!
DON'T TELL ANYONE I CAME IN HERE, OKAY?
MY LIPS ARE SEALED.
BB
"CESSPOOL" ONLY HAS TWO S's. AND "RAMSHACKLE" IS AN ADJECTIVE.
WHY ARE YOU BEING SO HELPFUL?
IT'S MY JOB.
BUT THIS PAMPHLET IS DESIGNED TO PUT YOU OUT OF WORK!
WE WOULDN'T MISS HIM.
BB
THIS CLIP ART WILL MAKE YOUR "SAY NO TO LIBRARIES" PAMPHLET MORE ATTRACTIVE TO WOMEN.
THESE CENSUS FIGURES WILL HELP YOU FIND THE BEST DEMOGRAPHIC FOR LIBRARY-HATERS.
WHEN IT COMES TO SELLING, NOTHING BEATS YOUR BASIC SANDWICH BOARD!
RARIES WASTE YOUR MONEY!
WHAT IS THIS, THE TWILIGHT ZONE???
NO, A LIBRARY. WE DON'T HAVE TO LIKE YOU TO HELP YOU.
BB
DON'T THINK I'M CHANGING MY MISSION BECAUSE THE LIBRARY WAS HELPFUL TODAY.
NOT AT ALL.
SAY "NO" TO LIBRARIES
YOU'LL CALL WHEN NEXT MONTH'S *REVOLTING TAXPAYER* COMES IN?
OF COURSE.
BB

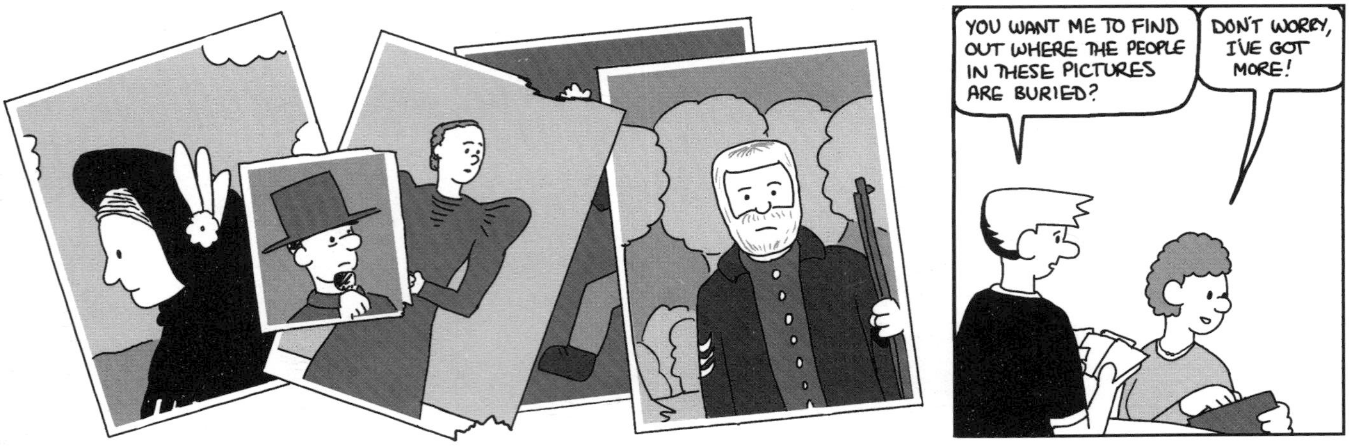
YOU WANT ME TO FIND OUT WHERE THE PEOPLE IN THESE PICTURES ARE BURIED?
DON'T WORRY, I'VE GOT MORE!

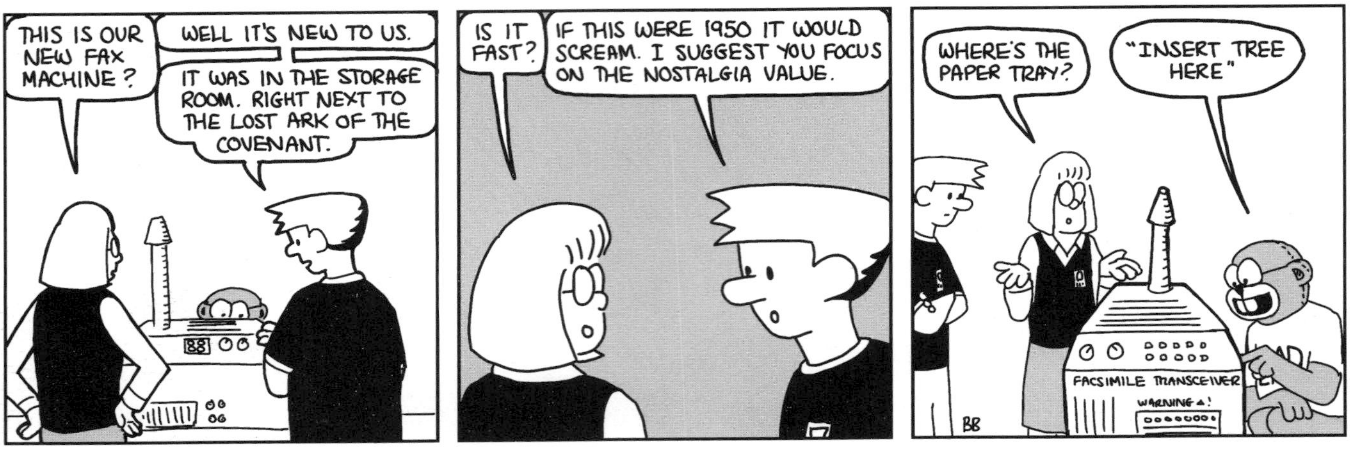
THIS IS OUR NEW FAX MACHINE?
WELL IT'S NEW TO US.
IT WAS IN THE STORAGE ROOM. RIGHT NEXT TO THE LOST ARK OF THE COVENANT.
IS IT FAST?
IF THIS WERE 1950 IT WOULD SCREAM. I SUGGEST YOU FOCUS ON THE NOSTALGIA VALUE.
WHERE'S THE PAPER TRAY?
"INSERT TREE HERE"
FACSIMILE TRANSCEIVER
WARNING!
BB

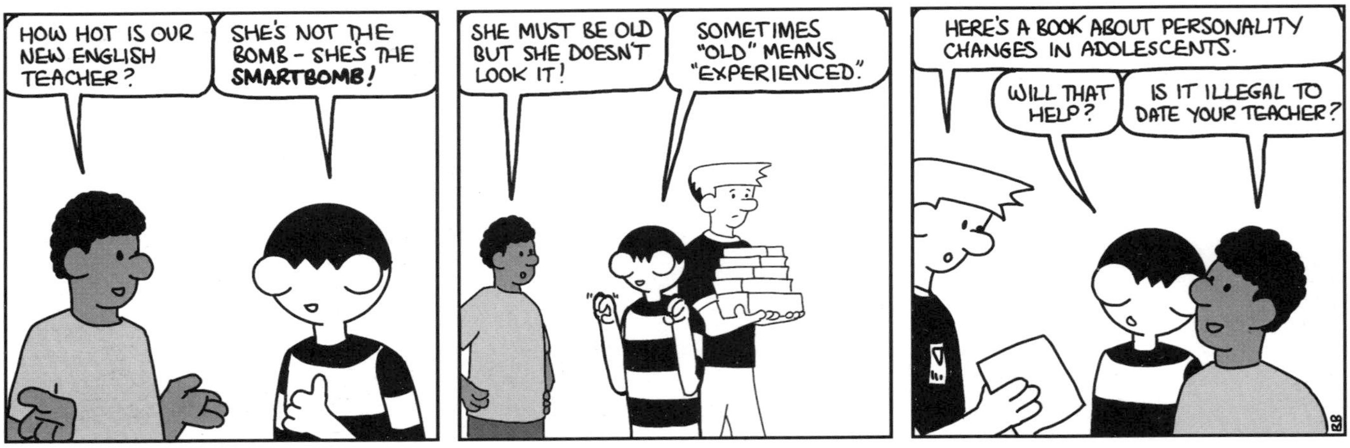
HOW HOT IS OUR NEW ENGLISH TEACHER?
SHE'S NOT THE BOMB - SHE'S THE **SMARTBOMB**!
SHE MUST BE OLD BUT SHE DOESN'T LOOK IT!
SOMETIMES "OLD" MEANS "EXPERIENCED."
HERE'S A BOOK ABOUT PERSONALITY CHANGES IN ADOLESCENTS.
WILL THAT HELP?
IS IT ILLEGAL TO DATE YOUR TEACHER?
BB

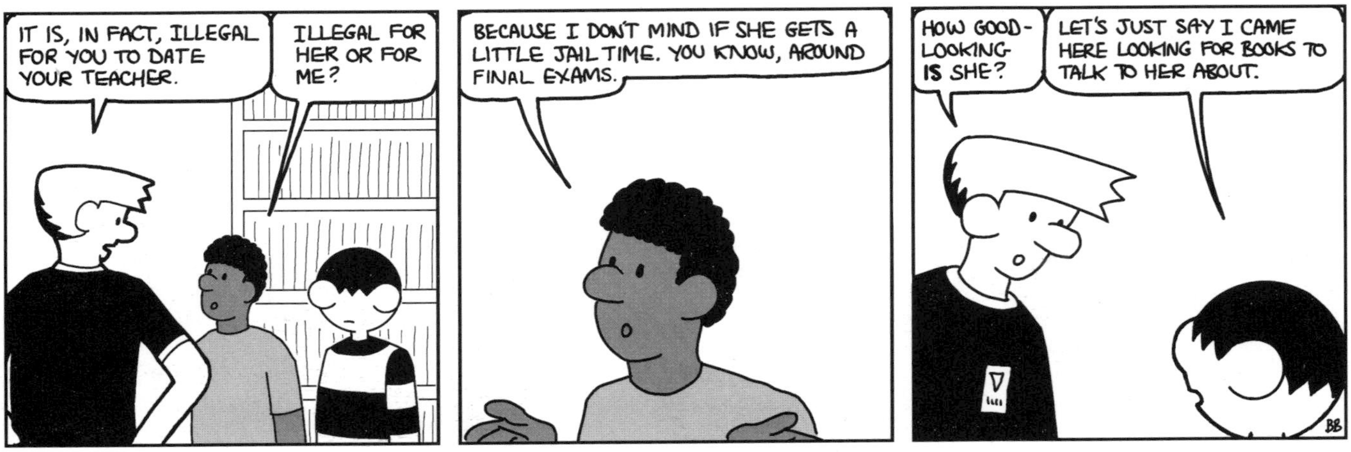
IT IS, IN FACT, ILLEGAL FOR YOU TO DATE YOUR TEACHER.
ILLEGAL FOR HER OR FOR ME?
BECAUSE I DON'T MIND IF SHE GETS A LITTLE JAIL TIME. YOU KNOW, AROUND FINAL EXAMS.
HOW GOOD-LOOKING **IS** SHE?
LET'S JUST SAY I CAME HERE LOOKING FOR BOOKS TO TALK TO HER ABOUT.
BB

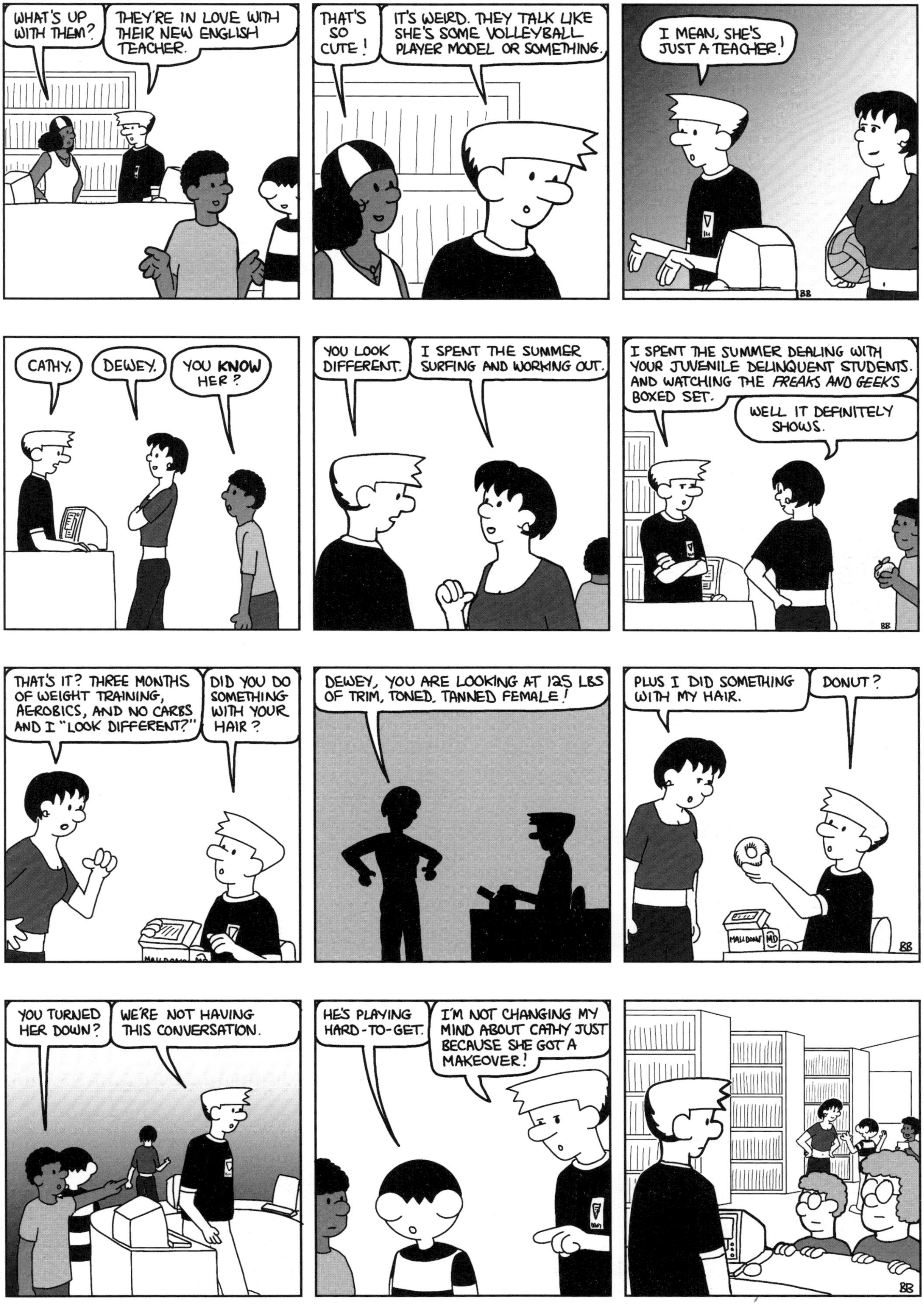
WHAT'S UP WITH THEM?
THEY'RE IN LOVE WITH THEIR NEW ENGLISH TEACHER.
THAT'S SO CUTE!
IT'S WEIRD. THEY TALK LIKE SHE'S SOME VOLLEYBALL PLAYER MODEL OR SOMETHING.
I MEAN, SHE'S JUST A TEACHER!
CATHY.
DEWEY.
YOU KNOW HER?
YOU LOOK DIFFERENT.
I SPENT THE SUMMER SURFING AND WORKING OUT.
I SPENT THE SUMMER DEALING WITH YOUR JUVENILE DELINQUENT STUDENTS. AND WATCHING THE FREAKS AND GEEKS BOXED SET.
WELL IT DEFINITELY SHOWS.
THAT'S IT? THREE MONTHS OF WEIGHT TRAINING, AEROBICS, AND NO CARBS AND I "LOOK DIFFERENT?"
DID YOU DO SOMETHING WITH YOUR HAIR?
DEWEY, YOU ARE LOOKING AT 125 LBS OF TRIM, TONED, TANNED FEMALE!
PLUS I DID SOMETHING WITH MY HAIR.
DONUT?
YOU TURNED HER DOWN?
WE'RE NOT HAVING THIS CONVERSATION.
HE'S PLAYING HARD-TO-GET.
I'M NOT CHANGING MY MIND ABOUT CATHY JUST BECAUSE SHE GOT A MAKEOVER!

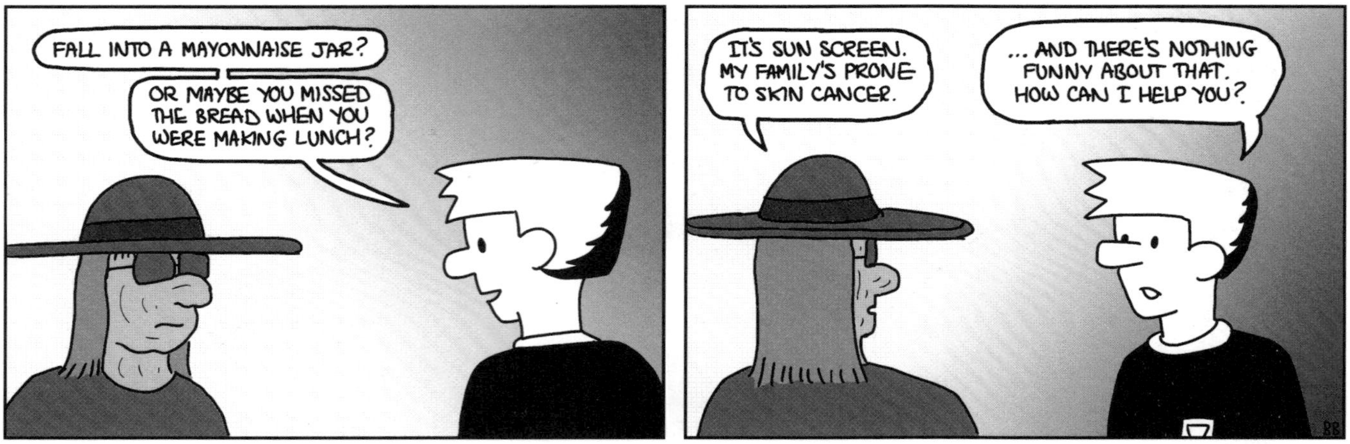
FALL INTO A MAYONNAISE JAR?
OR MAYBE YOU MISSED THE BREAD WHEN YOU WERE MAKING LUNCH?
IT'S SUN SCREEN. MY FAMILY'S PRONE TO SKIN CANCER.
... AND THERE'S NOTHING FUNNY ABOUT THAT. HOW CAN I HELP YOU?
BB

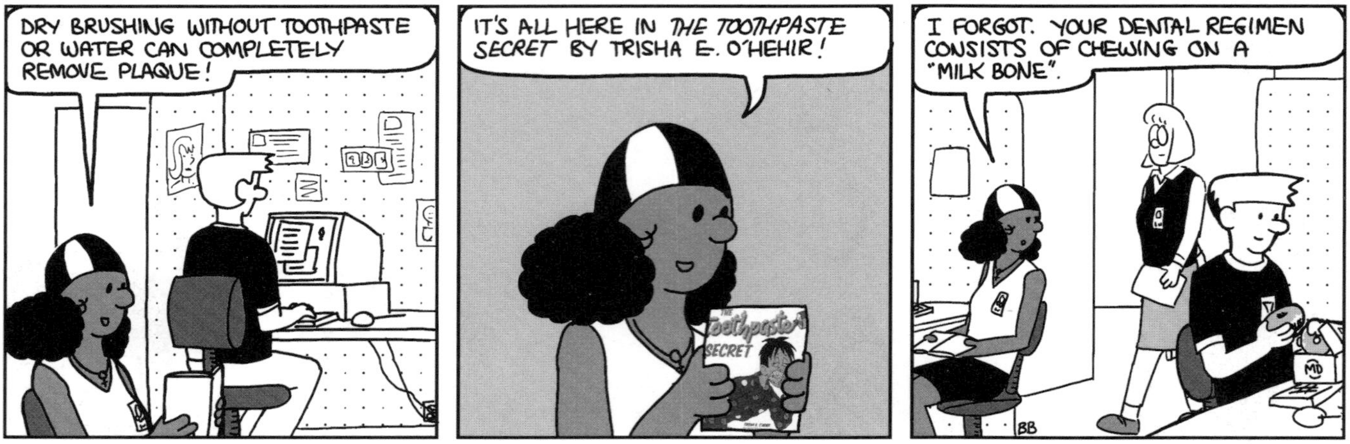
DRY BRUSHING WITHOUT TOOTHPASTE OR WATER CAN COMPLETELY REMOVE PLAQUE!
IT'S ALL HERE IN *THE TOOTHPASTE SECRET* BY TRISHA E. O'HEHIR!
Toothpaste SECRET
I FORGOT. YOUR DENTAL REGIMEN CONSISTS OF CHEWING ON A "MILK BONE".
MD
BB

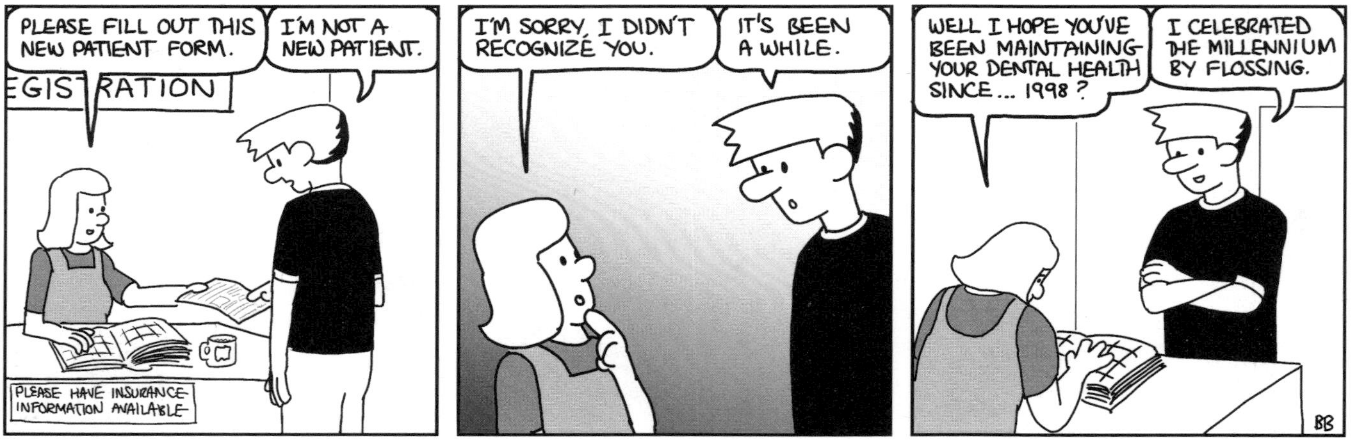
PLEASE FILL OUT THIS NEW PATIENT FORM.
I'M NOT A NEW PATIENT.
EGIS RATION
PLEASE HAVE INSURANCE INFORMATION AVAILABLE
I'M SORRY, I DIDN'T RECOGNIZE YOU.
IT'S BEEN A WHILE.
WELL I HOPE YOU'VE BEEN MAINTAINING YOUR DENTAL HEALTH SINCE ... 1998?
I CELEBRATED THE MILLENNIUM BY FLOSSING.
BB

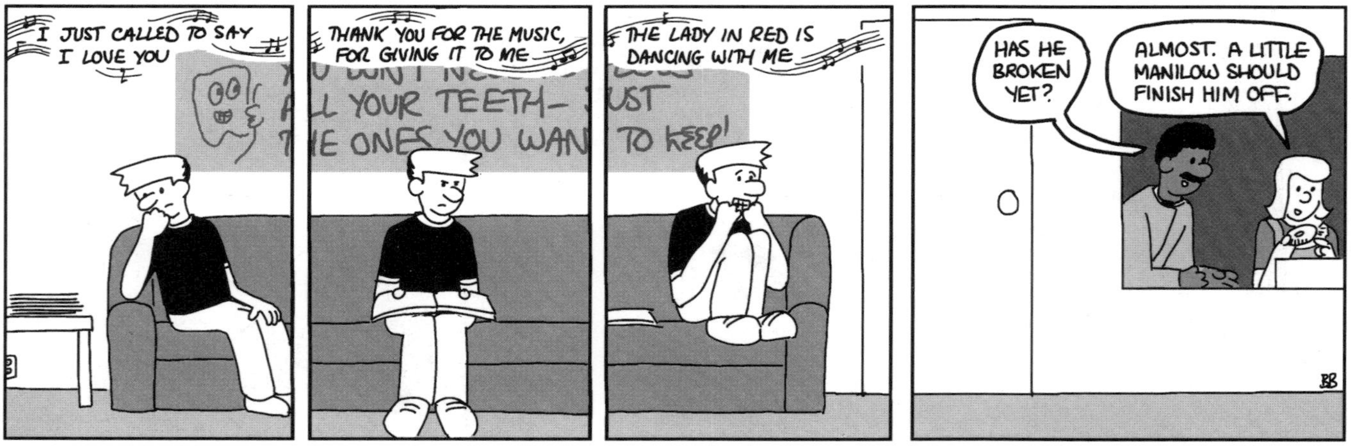
I JUST CALLED TO SAY I LOVE YOU
THANK YOU FOR THE MUSIC, FOR GIVING IT TO ME
THE LADY IN RED IS DANCING WITH ME
HAS HE BROKEN YET?
ALMOST. A LITTLE MANILOW SHOULD FINISH HIM OFF.
BB

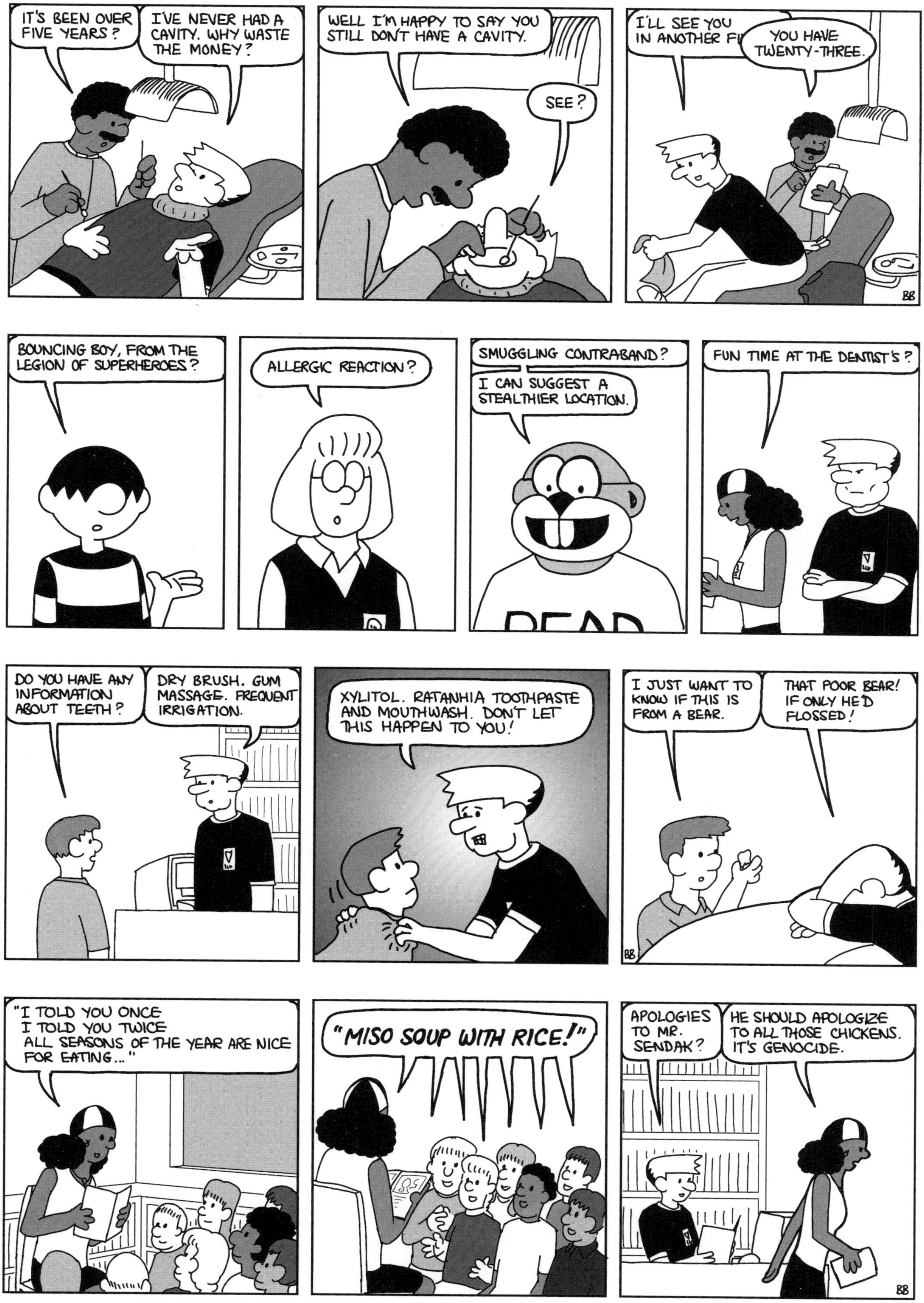
IT'S BEEN OVER FIVE YEARS?
I'VE NEVER HAD A CAVITY. WHY WASTE THE MONEY?
WELL I'M HAPPY TO SAY YOU STILL DON'T HAVE A CAVITY.
SEE?
I'LL SEE YOU IN ANOTHER FI
YOU HAVE TWENTY-THREE.
BOUNCING BOY, FROM THE LEGION OF SUPERHEROES?
ALLERGIC REACTION?
SMUGGLING CONTRABAND?
I CAN SUGGEST A STEALTHIER LOCATION.
FUN TIME AT THE DENTIST'S?
DO YOU HAVE ANY INFORMATION ABOUT TEETH?
DRY BRUSH. GUM MASSAGE. FREQUENT IRRIGATION.
XYLITOL. RATANHIA TOOTHPASTE AND MOUTHWASH. DON'T LET THIS HAPPEN TO YOU!
I JUST WANT TO KNOW IF THIS IS FROM A BEAR.
THAT POOR BEAR! IF ONLY HE'D FLOSSED!
"I TOLD YOU ONCE
I TOLD YOU TWICE
ALL SEASONS OF THE YEAR ARE NICE
FOR EATING..."
"MISO SOUP WITH RICE!"
APOLOGIES TO MR. SENDAK?
HE SHOULD APOLOGIZE TO ALL THOSE CHICKENS. IT'S GENOCIDE.

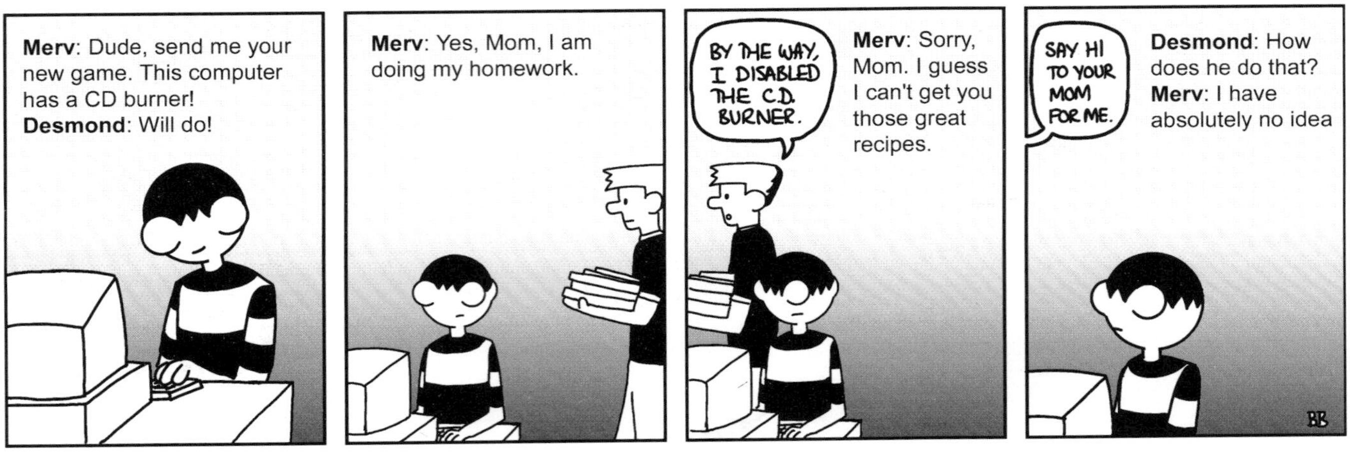
Merv: Dude, send me your new game. This computer has a CD burner!
Desmond: Will do!
Merv: Yes, Mom, I am doing my homework.
BY THE WAY, I DISABLED THE C.D. BURNER.
Merv: Sorry, Mom. I guess I can't get you those great recipes.
SAY HI TO YOUR MOM FOR ME.
Desmond: How does he do that?
Merv: I have absolutely no idea
BB

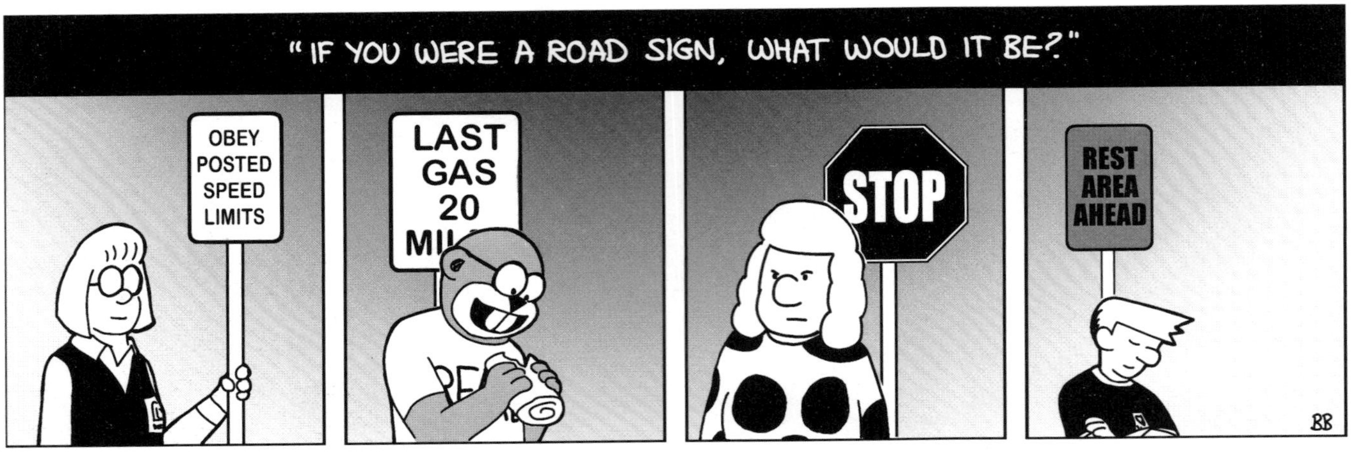
"IF YOU WERE A ROAD SIGN, WHAT WOULD IT BE?"
OBEY POSTED SPEED LIMITS
LAST GAS 20 MI
STOP
REST AREA AHEAD
BB

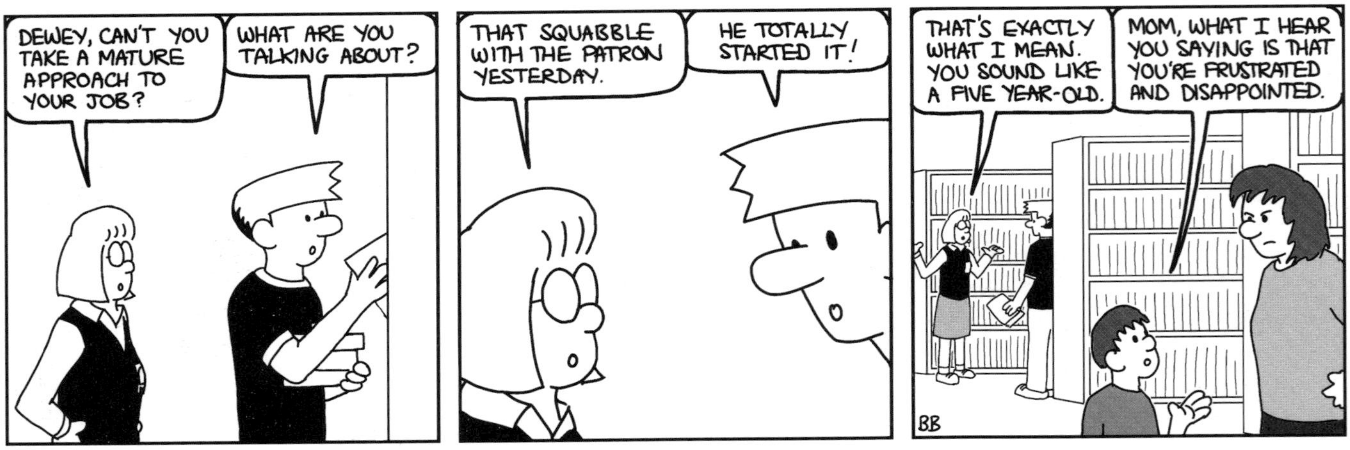
DEWEY, CAN'T YOU TAKE A MATURE APPROACH TO YOUR JOB?
WHAT ARE YOU TALKING ABOUT?
THAT SQUABBLE WITH THE PATRON YESTERDAY.
HE TOTALLY STARTED IT!
THAT'S EXACTLY WHAT I MEAN. YOU SOUND LIKE A FIVE YEAR-OLD.
MOM, WHAT I HEAR YOU SAYING IS THAT YOU'RE FRUSTRATED AND DISAPPOINTED.
BB

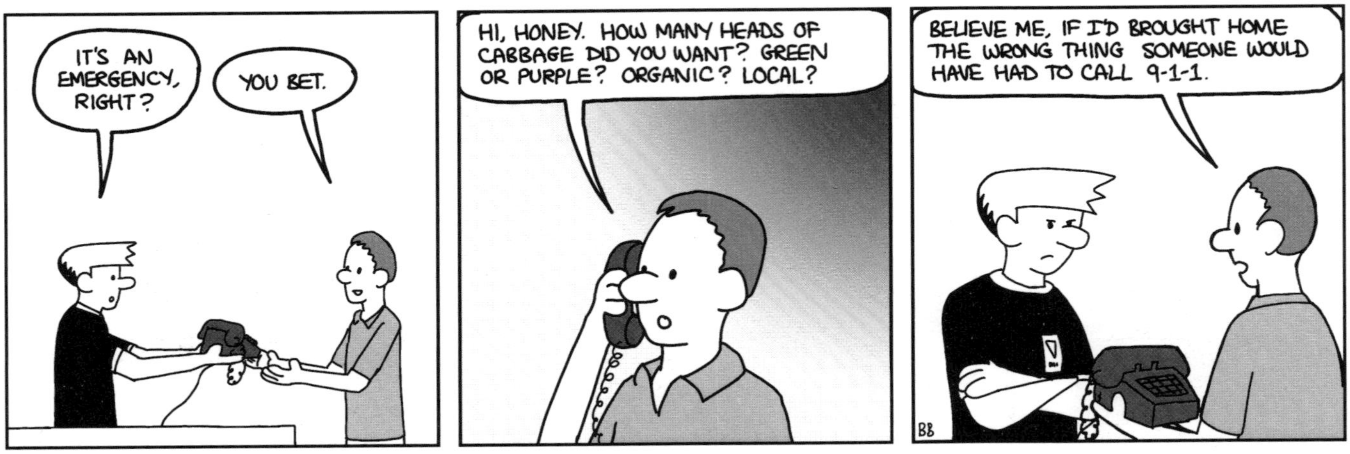
IT'S AN EMERGENCY, RIGHT?
YOU BET.
HI, HONEY. HOW MANY HEADS OF CABBAGE DID YOU WANT? GREEN OR PURPLE? ORGANIC? LOCAL?
BELIEVE ME, IF I'D BROUGHT HOME THE WRONG THING SOMEONE WOULD HAVE HAD TO CALL 9-1-1.
BB

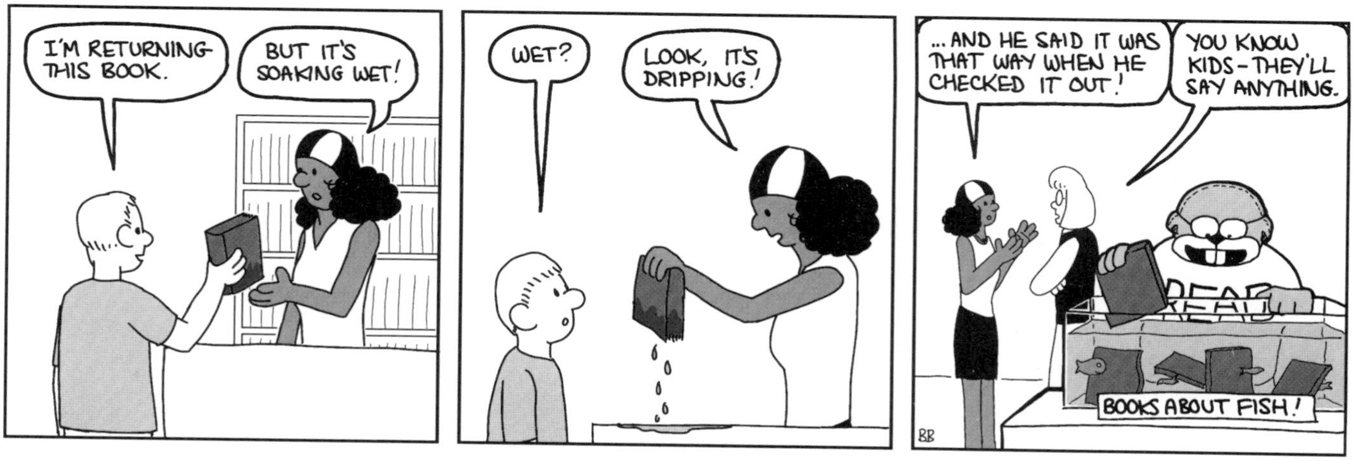
I'M RETURNING THIS BOOK.
BUT IT'S SOAKING WET!
WET?
LOOK, IT'S DRIPPING!
...AND HE SAID IT WAS THAT WAY WHEN HE CHECKED IT OUT!
YOU KNOW KIDS - THEY'LL SAY ANYTHING.
BOOKS ABOUT FISH!
BB

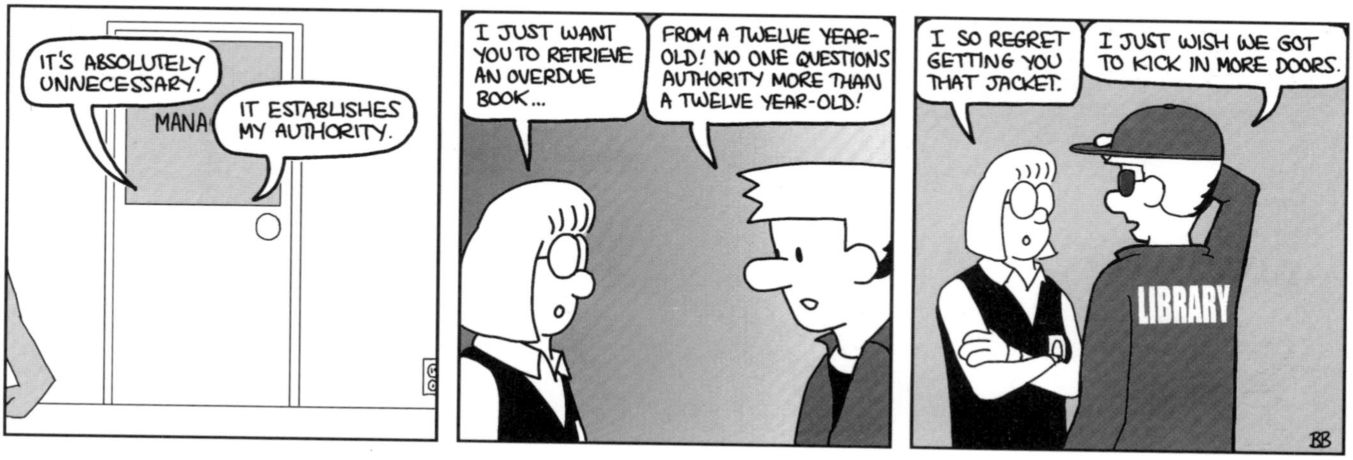
IT'S ABSOLUTELY UNNECESSARY.
MANA
IT ESTABLISHES MY AUTHORITY.
I JUST WANT YOU TO RETRIEVE AN OVERDUE BOOK...
FROM A TWELVE YEAR-OLD! NO ONE QUESTIONS AUTHORITY MORE THAN A TWELVE YEAR-OLD!
I SO REGRET GETTING YOU THAT JACKET.
I JUST WISH WE GOT TO KICK IN MORE DOORS.
LIBRARY
BB

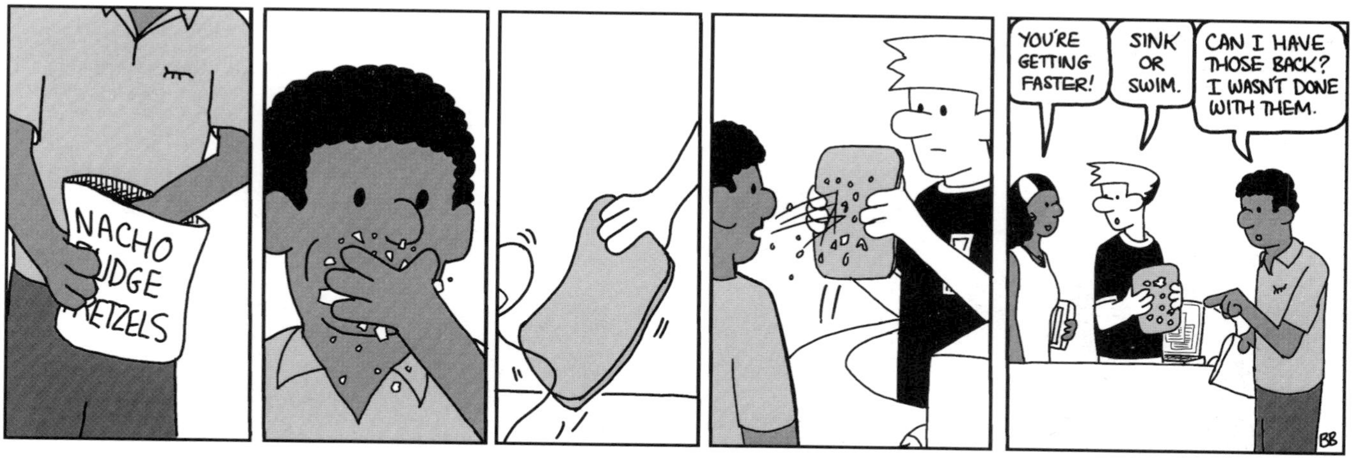
NACHO
UDGE
ETZELS
YOU'RE GETTING FASTER!
SINK OR SWIM.
CAN I HAVE THOSE BACK? I WASN'T DONE WITH THEM.
BB

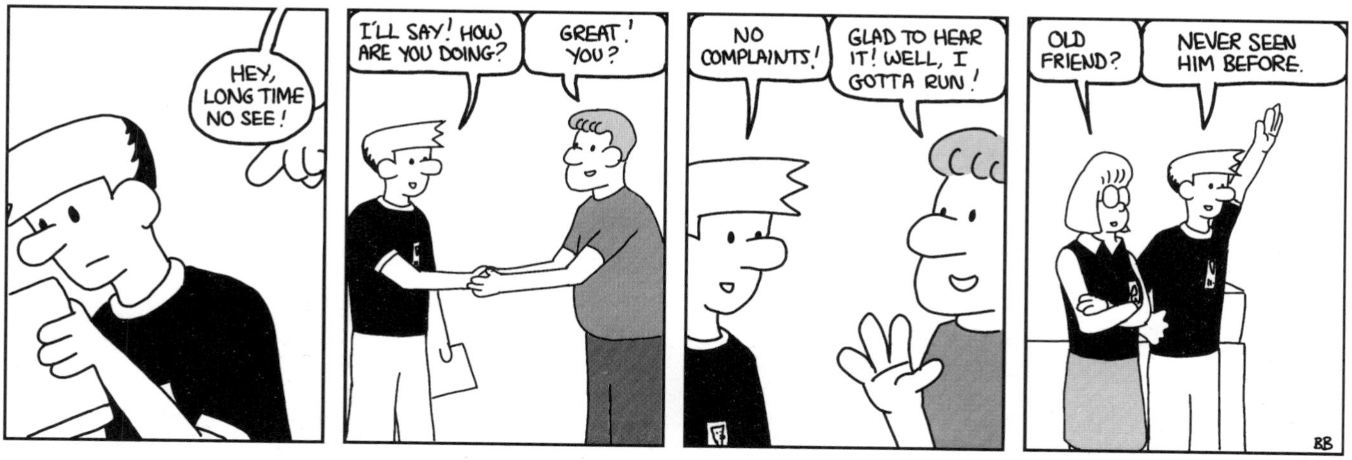
HEY, LONG TIME NO SEE!
I'LL SAY! HOW ARE YOU DOING?
GREAT! YOU?
NO COMPLAINTS!
GLAD TO HEAR IT! WELL, I GOTTA RUN!
OLD FRIEND?
NEVER SEEN HIM BEFORE.
BB

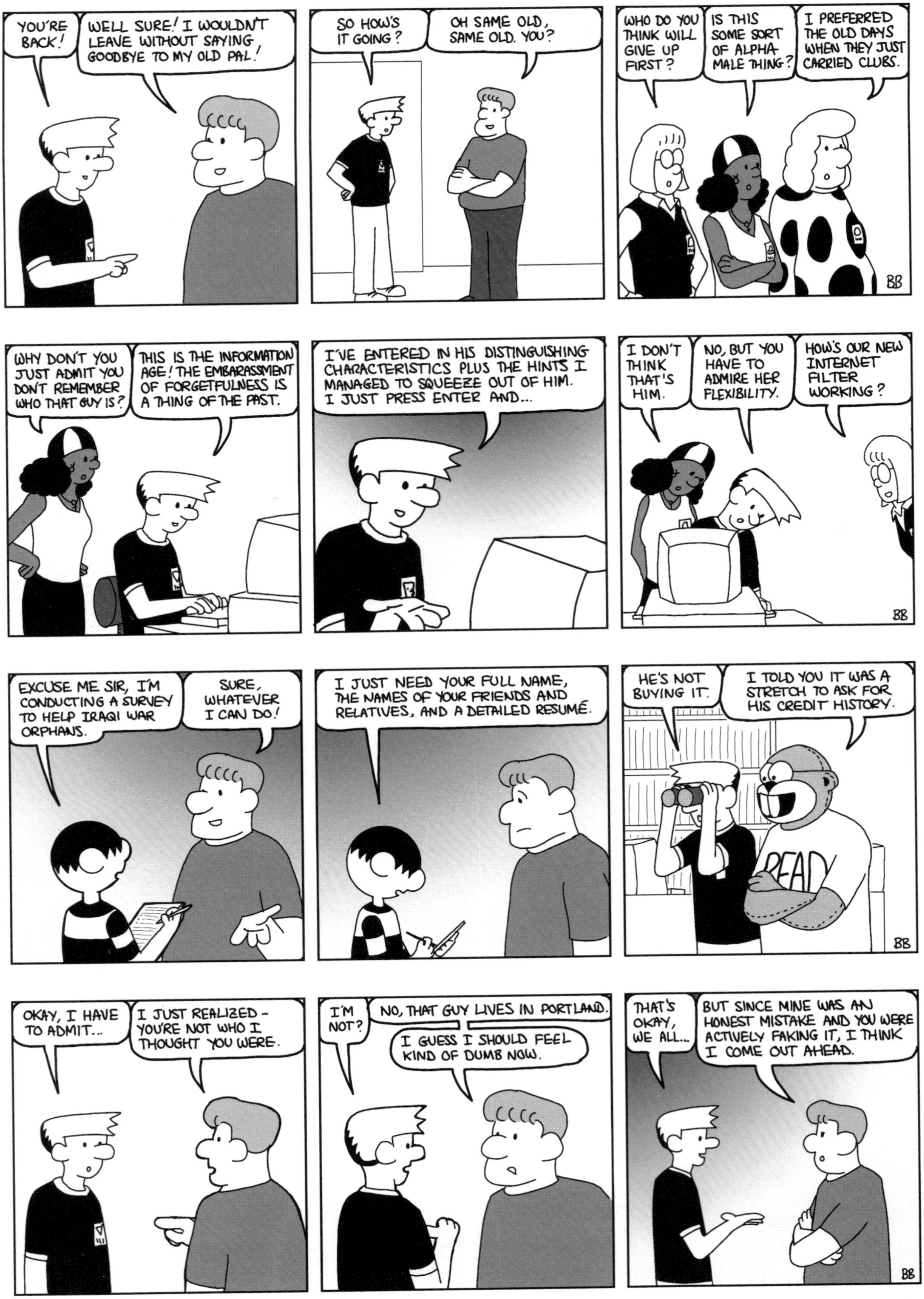
YOU'RE BACK!
WELL SURE! I WOULDN'T LEAVE WITHOUT SAYING GOODBYE TO MY OLD PAL!
SO HOW'S IT GOING?
OH SAME OLD, SAME OLD. YOU?
WHO DO YOU THINK WILL GIVE UP FIRST?
IS THIS SOME SORT OF ALPHA MALE THING?
I PREFERRED THE OLD DAYS WHEN THEY JUST CARRIED CLUBS.
BB
WHY DON'T YOU JUST ADMIT YOU DON'T REMEMBER WHO THAT GUY IS?
THIS IS THE INFORMATION AGE! THE EMBARASSMENT OF FORGETFULNESS IS A THING OF THE PAST.
I'VE ENTERED IN HIS DISTINGUISHING CHARACTERISTICS PLUS THE HINTS I MANAGED TO SQUEEZE OUT OF HIM. I JUST PRESS ENTER AND...
I DON'T THINK THAT'S HIM.
NO, BUT YOU HAVE TO ADMIRE HER FLEXIBILITY.
HOW'S OUR NEW INTERNET FILTER WORKING?
BB
EXCUSE ME SIR, I'M CONDUCTING A SURVEY TO HELP IRAQI WAR ORPHANS.
SURE, WHATEVER I CAN DO!
I JUST NEED YOUR FULL NAME, THE NAMES OF YOUR FRIENDS AND RELATIVES, AND A DETAILED RESUMÉ.
HE'S NOT BUYING IT.
I TOLD YOU IT WAS A STRETCH TO ASK FOR HIS CREDIT HISTORY.
READ
BB
OKAY, I HAVE TO ADMIT...
I JUST REALIZED - YOU'RE NOT WHO I THOUGHT YOU WERE.
I'M NOT?
NO, THAT GUY LIVES IN PORTLAND.
I GUESS I SHOULD FEEL KIND OF DUMB NOW.
THAT'S OKAY, WE ALL...
BUT SINCE MINE WAS AN HONEST MISTAKE AND YOU WERE ACTIVELY FAKING IT, I THINK I COME OUT AHEAD.
BB

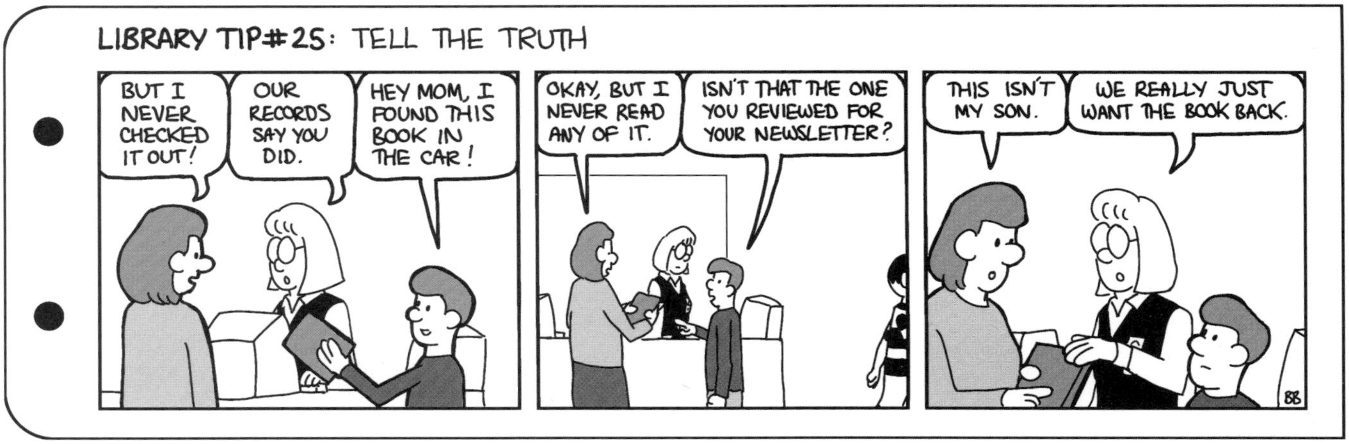
LIBRARY TIP #25: TELL THE TRUTH
BUT I NEVER CHECKED IT OUT!
OUR RECORDS SAY YOU DID.
HEY MOM, I FOUND THIS BOOK IN THE CAR!
OKAY, BUT I NEVER READ ANY OF IT.
ISN'T THAT THE ONE YOU REVIEWED FOR YOUR NEWSLETTER?
THIS ISN'T MY SON.
WE REALLY JUST WANT THE BOOK BACK.

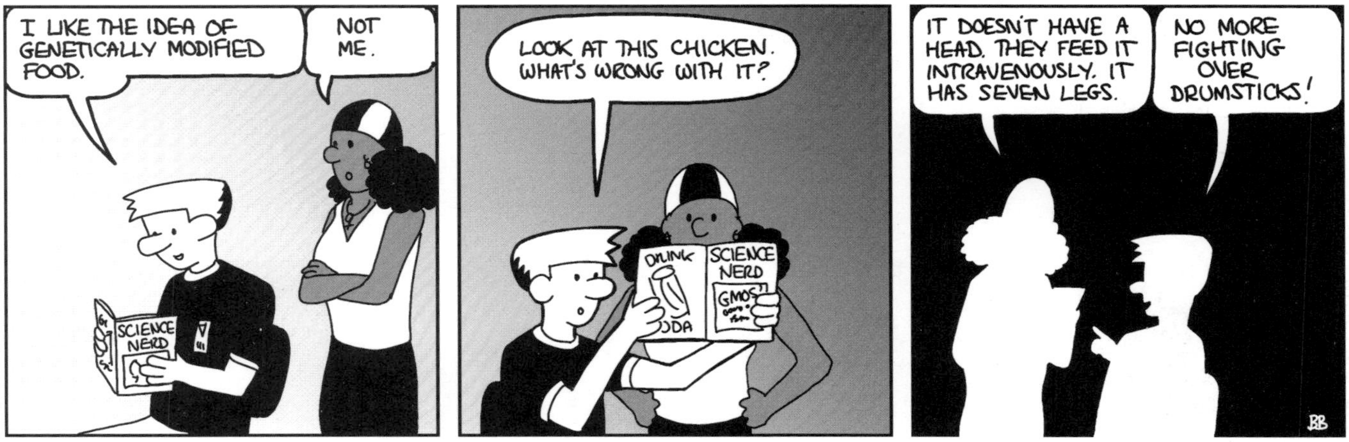
I LIKE THE IDEA OF GENETICALLY MODIFIED FOOD.
NOT ME.
LOOK AT THIS CHICKEN. WHAT'S WRONG WITH IT?
IT DOESN'T HAVE A HEAD. THEY FEED IT INTRAVENOUSLY. IT HAS SEVEN LEGS.
NO MORE FIGHTING OVER DRUMSTICKS!

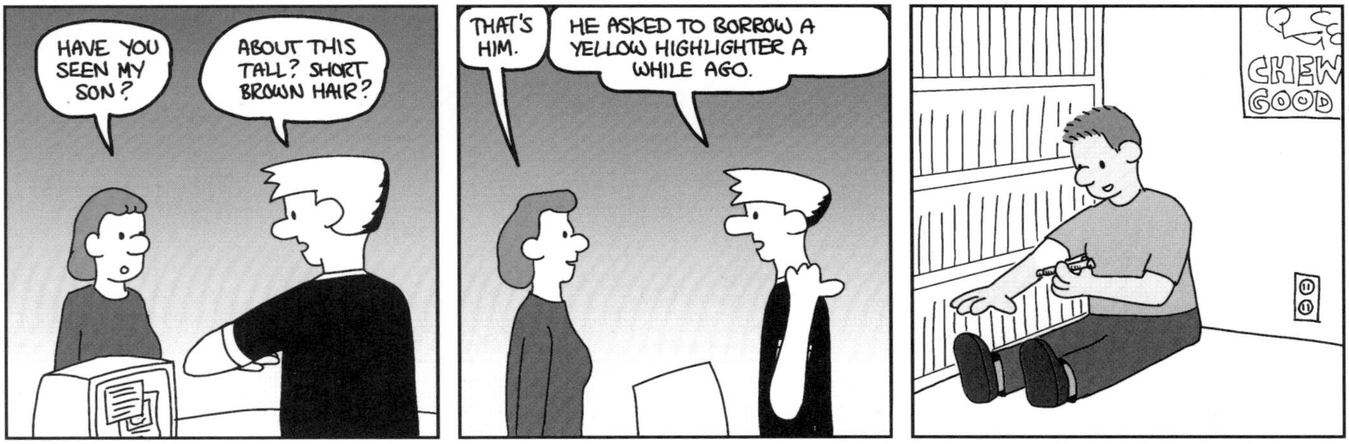
HAVE YOU SEEN MY SON?
ABOUT THIS TALL? SHORT BROWN HAIR?
THAT'S HIM.
HE ASKED TO BORROW A YELLOW HIGHLIGHTER A WHILE AGO.

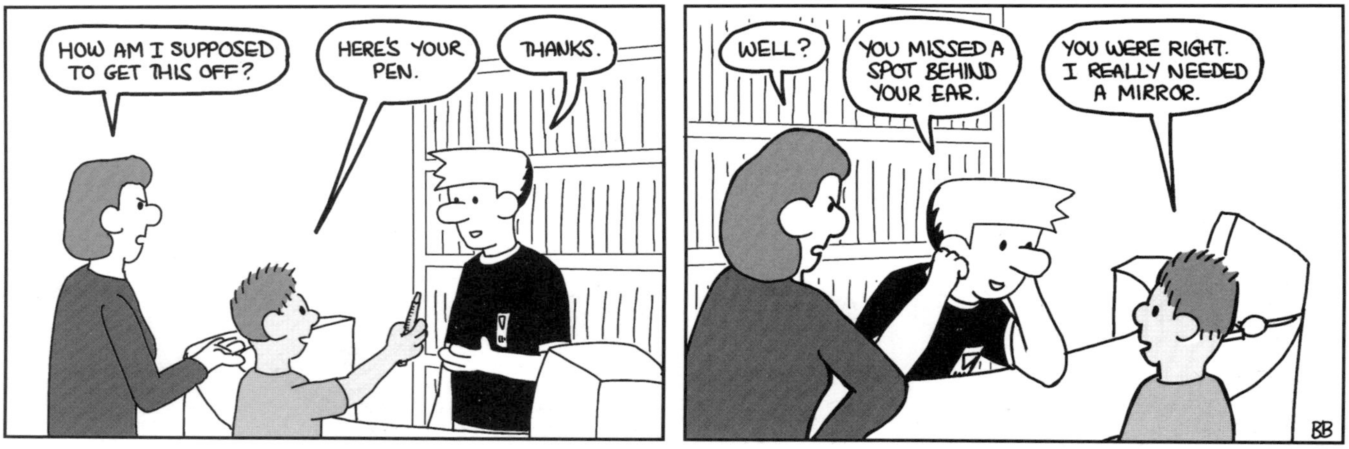
HOW AM I SUPPOSED TO GET THIS OFF?
HERE'S YOUR PEN.
THANKS.
WELL?
YOU MISSED A SPOT BEHIND YOUR EAR.
YOU WERE RIGHT. I REALLY NEEDED A MIRROR.

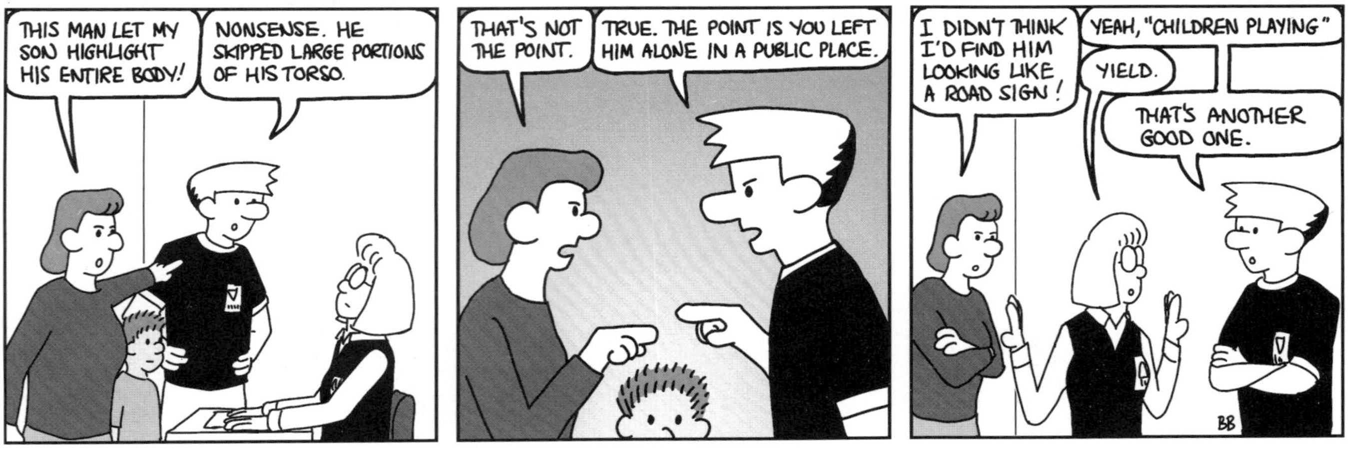
THIS MAN LET MY SON HIGHLIGHT HIS ENTIRE BODY!
NONSENSE. HE SKIPPED LARGE PORTIONS OF HIS TORSO.
THAT'S NOT THE POINT.
TRUE. THE POINT IS YOU LEFT HIM ALONE IN A PUBLIC PLACE.
I DIDN'T THINK I'D FIND HIM LOOKING LIKE A ROAD SIGN!
YEAH, "CHILDREN PLAYING"
YIELD.
THAT'S ANOTHER GOOD ONE.
BB

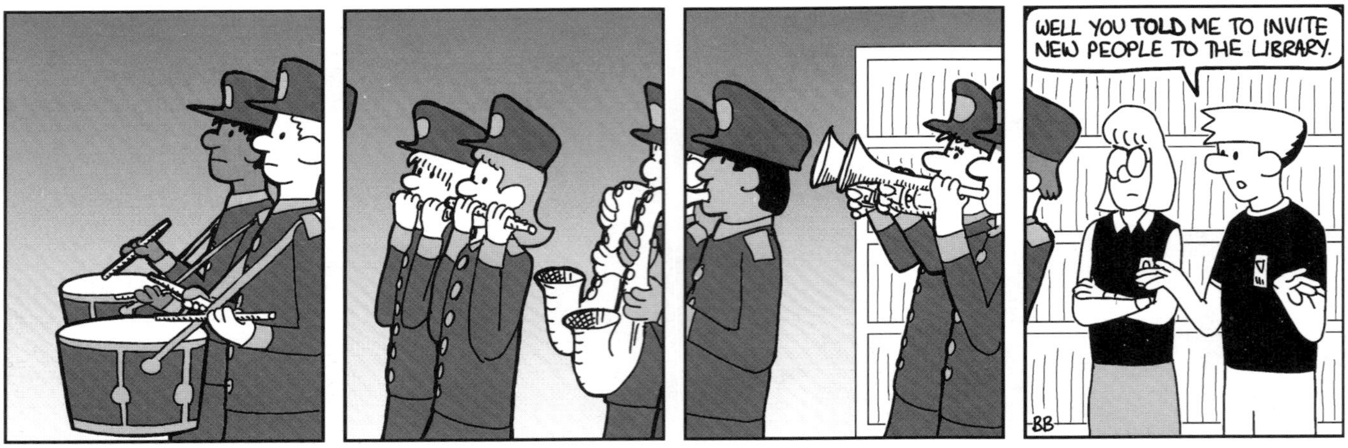
WELL YOU **TOLD** ME TO INVITE NEW PEOPLE TO THE LIBRARY.
BB

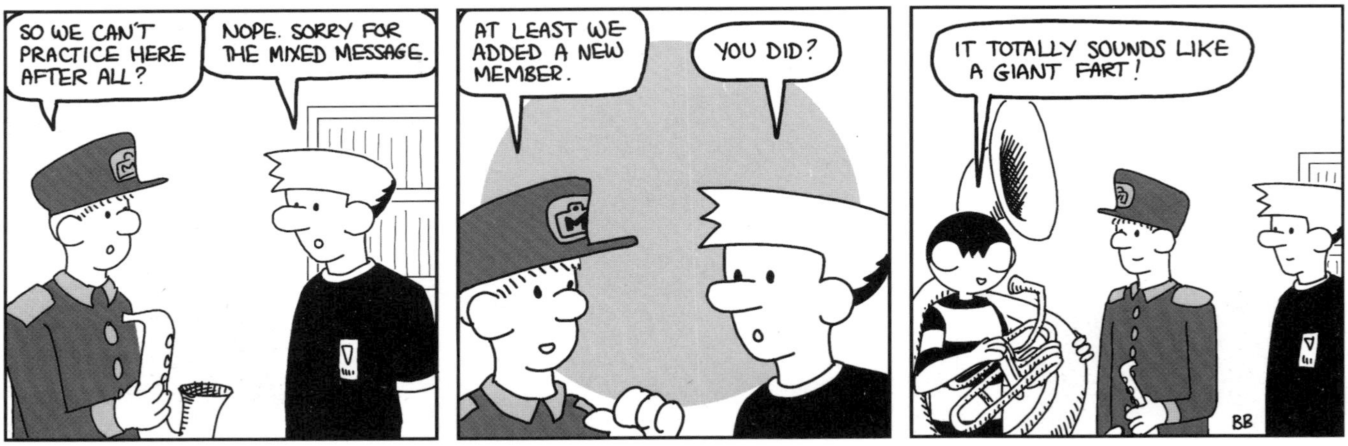
SO WE CAN'T PRACTICE HERE AFTER ALL?
NOPE. SORRY FOR THE MIXED MESSAGE.
AT LEAST WE ADDED A NEW MEMBER.
YOU DID?
IT TOTALLY SOUNDS LIKE A GIANT FART!
BB

LIBRARY TIP #26: JUST READ IT

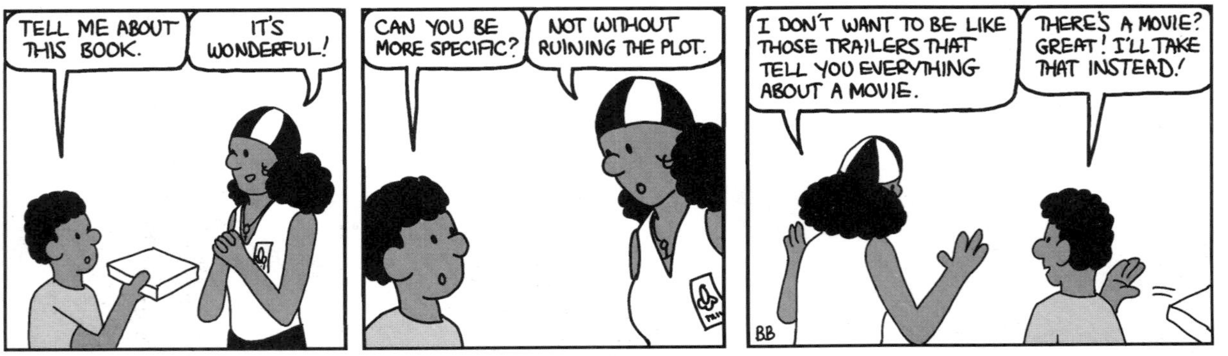
TELL ME ABOUT THIS BOOK.
IT'S WONDERFUL!
CAN YOU BE MORE SPECIFIC?
NOT WITHOUT RUINING THE PLOT.
I DON'T WANT TO BE LIKE THOSE TRAILERS THAT TELL YOU EVERYTHING ABOUT A MOVIE.
THERE'S A MOVIE? GREAT! I'LL TAKE THAT INSTEAD!
BB

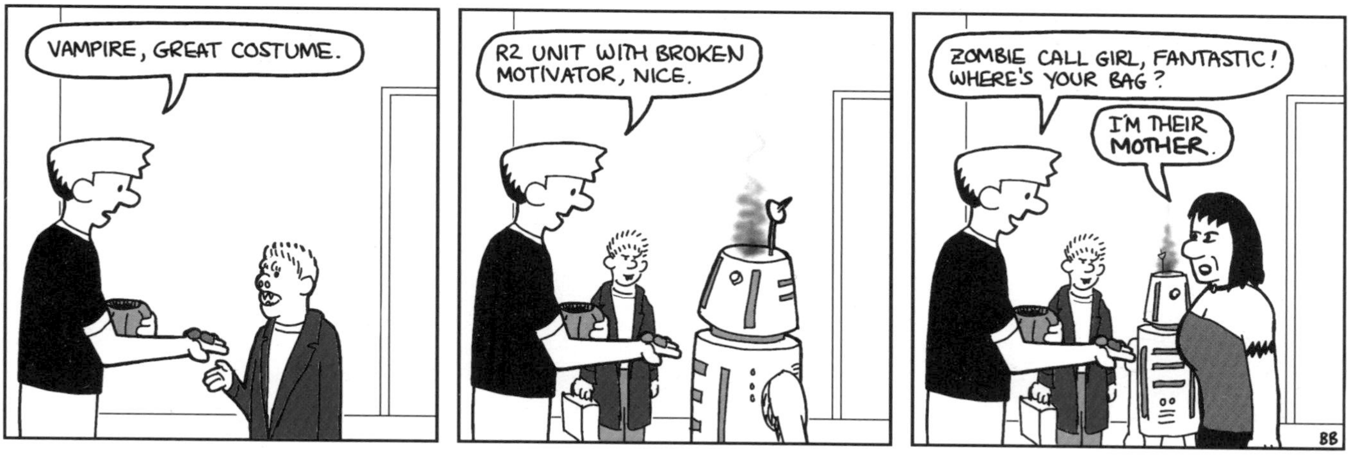
VAMPIRE, GREAT COSTUME.
R2 UNIT WITH BROKEN MOTIVATOR, NICE.
ZOMBIE CALL GIRL, FANTASTIC! WHERE'S YOUR BAG?
I'M THEIR MOTHER.
BB

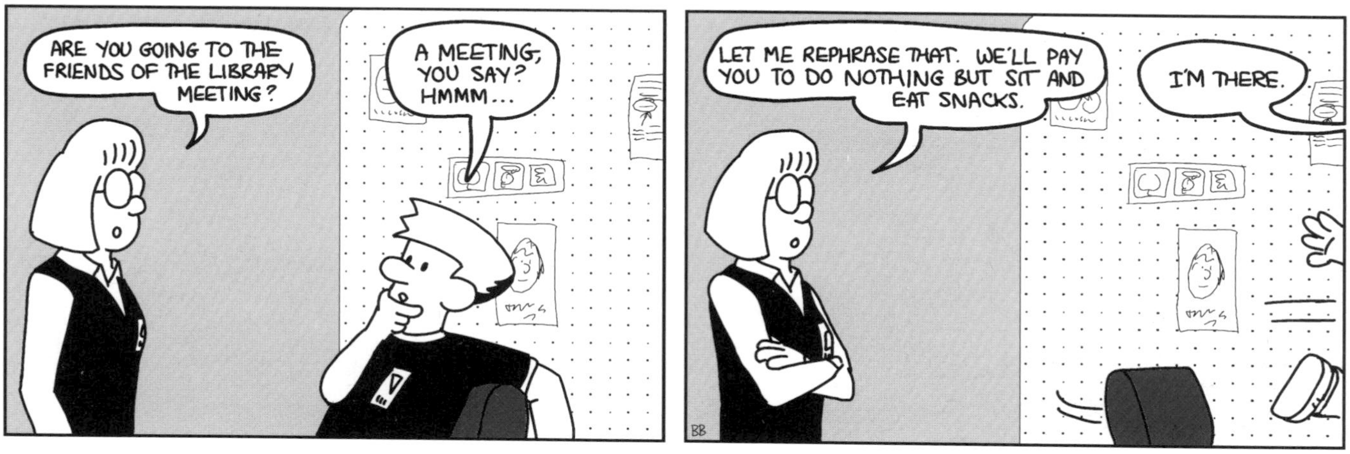
ARE YOU GOING TO THE FRIENDS OF THE LIBRARY MEETING?
A MEETING, YOU SAY? HMMM...
LET ME REPHRASE THAT. WE'LL PAY YOU TO DO NOTHING BUT SIT AND EAT SNACKS.
I'M THERE.
BB

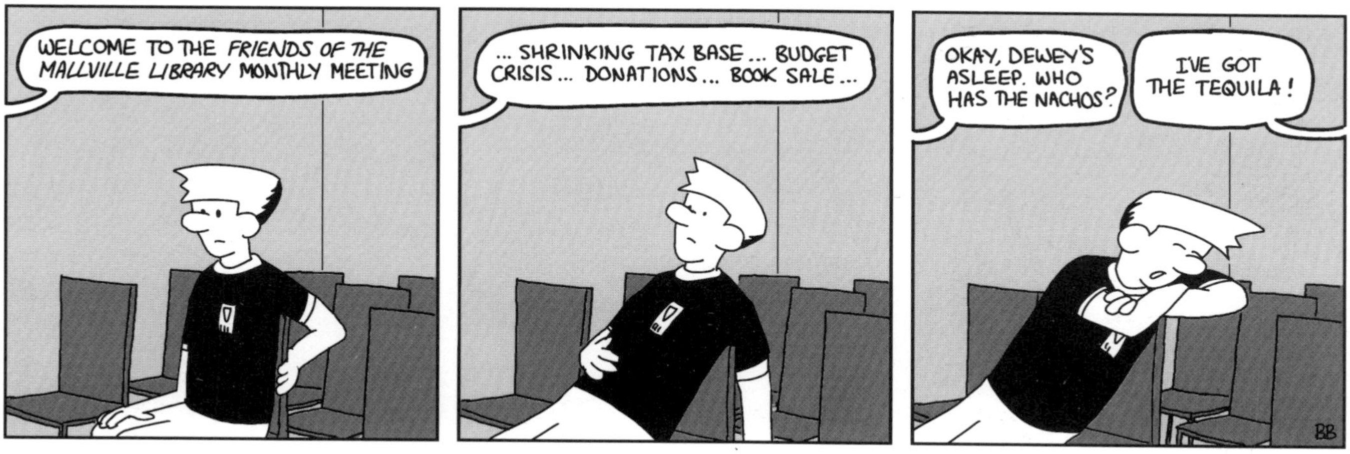
WELCOME TO THE *FRIENDS OF THE MALLVILLE LIBRARY* MONTHLY MEETING
... SHRINKING TAX BASE ... BUDGET CRISIS ... DONATIONS ... BOOK SALE ...
OKAY, DEWEY'S ASLEEP. WHO HAS THE NACHOS?
I'VE GOT THE TEQUILA!
BB

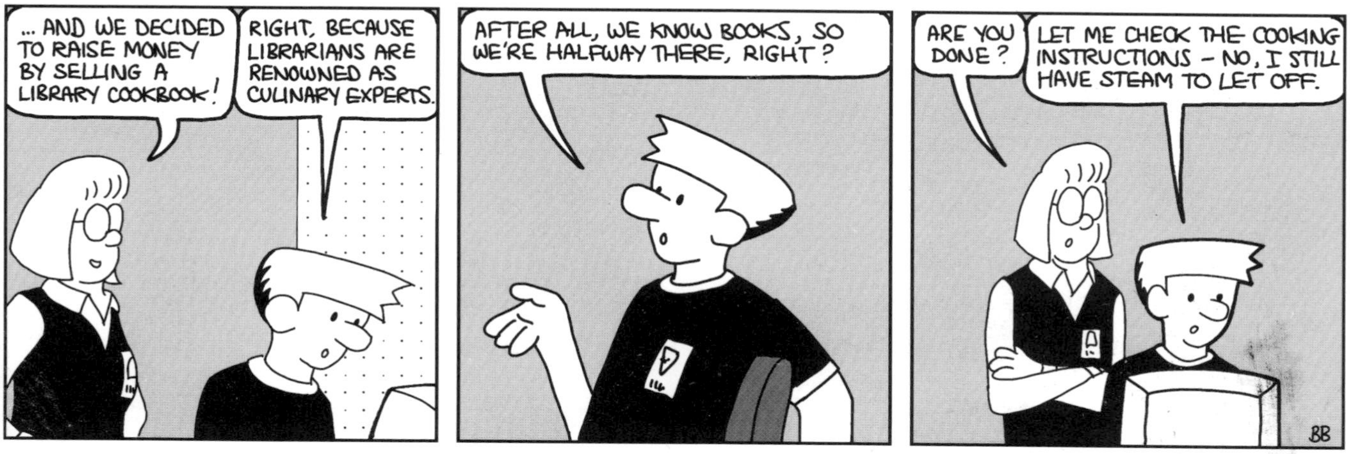
... AND WE DECIDED TO RAISE MONEY BY SELLING A LIBRARY COOKBOOK!
RIGHT, BECAUSE LIBRARIANS ARE RENOWNED AS CULINARY EXPERTS.
AFTER ALL, WE KNOW BOOKS, SO WE'RE HALFWAY THERE, RIGHT?
ARE YOU DONE?
LET ME CHECK THE COOKING INSTRUCTIONS - NO, I STILL HAVE STEAM TO LET OFF.
BB

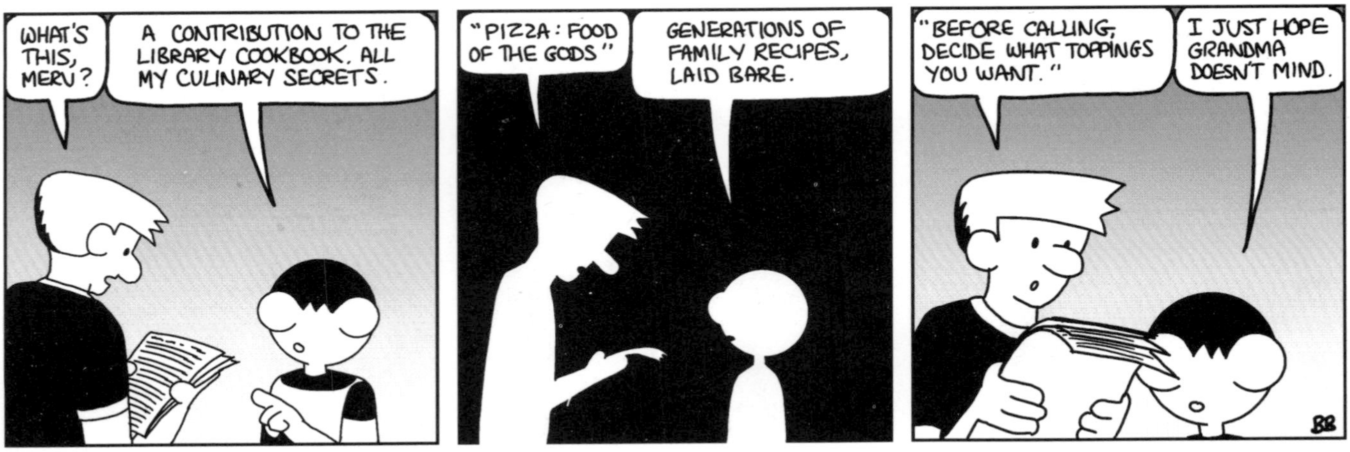
WHAT'S THIS, MERV?
A CONTRIBUTION TO THE LIBRARY COOKBOOK. ALL MY CULINARY SECRETS.
"PIZZA: FOOD OF THE GODS"
GENERATIONS OF FAMILY RECIPES, LAID BARE.
"BEFORE CALLING, DECIDE WHAT TOPPINGS YOU WANT."
I JUST HOPE GRANDMA DOESN'T MIND.

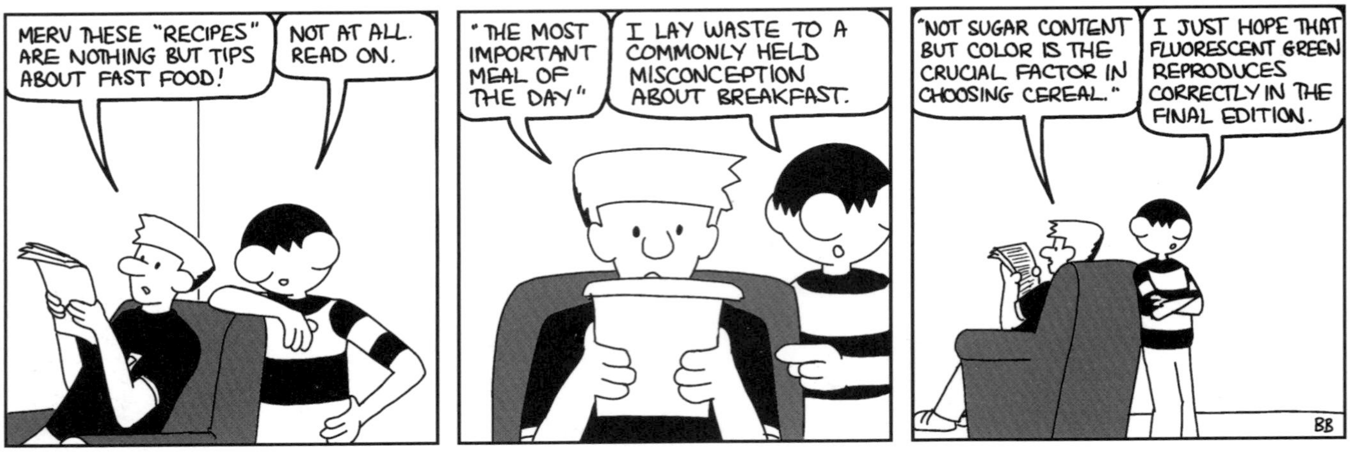
MERV THESE "RECIPES" ARE NOTHING BUT TIPS ABOUT FAST FOOD!
NOT AT ALL. READ ON.
"THE MOST IMPORTANT MEAL OF THE DAY"
I LAY WASTE TO A COMMONLY HELD MISCONCEPTION ABOUT BREAKFAST.
"NOT SUGAR CONTENT BUT COLOR IS THE CRUCIAL FACTOR IN CHOOSING CEREAL."
I JUST HOPE THAT FLUORESCENT GREEN REPRODUCES CORRECTLY IN THE FINAL EDITION.

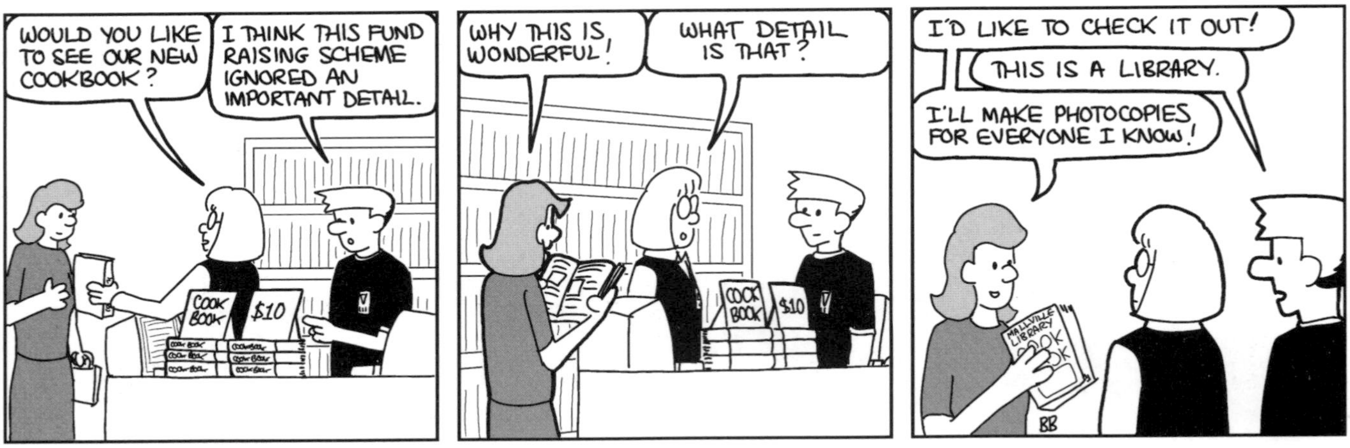
WOULD YOU LIKE TO SEE OUR NEW COOKBOOK?
I THINK THIS FUND RAISING SCHEME IGNORED AN IMPORTANT DETAIL.
COOK BOOK
$10
WHY THIS IS WONDERFUL!
WHAT DETAIL IS THAT?
I'D LIKE TO CHECK IT OUT!
THIS IS A LIBRARY.
I'LL MAKE PHOTOCOPIES FOR EVERYONE I KNOW!

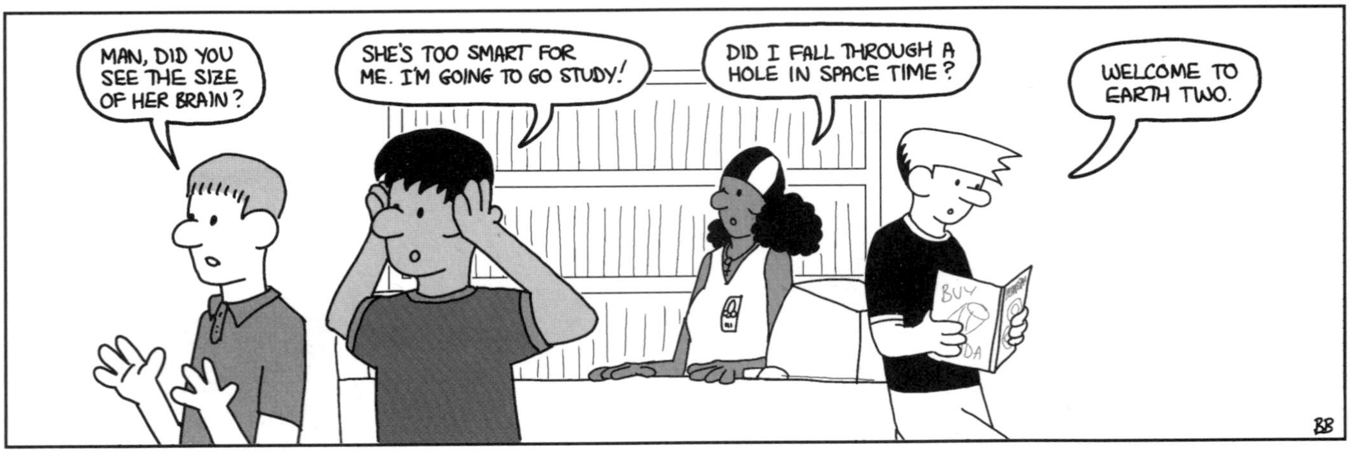
MAN, DID YOU SEE THE SIZE OF HER BRAIN?
SHE'S TOO SMART FOR ME. I'M GOING TO GO STUDY!
DID I FALL THROUGH A HOLE IN SPACE TIME?
WELCOME TO EARTH TWO.

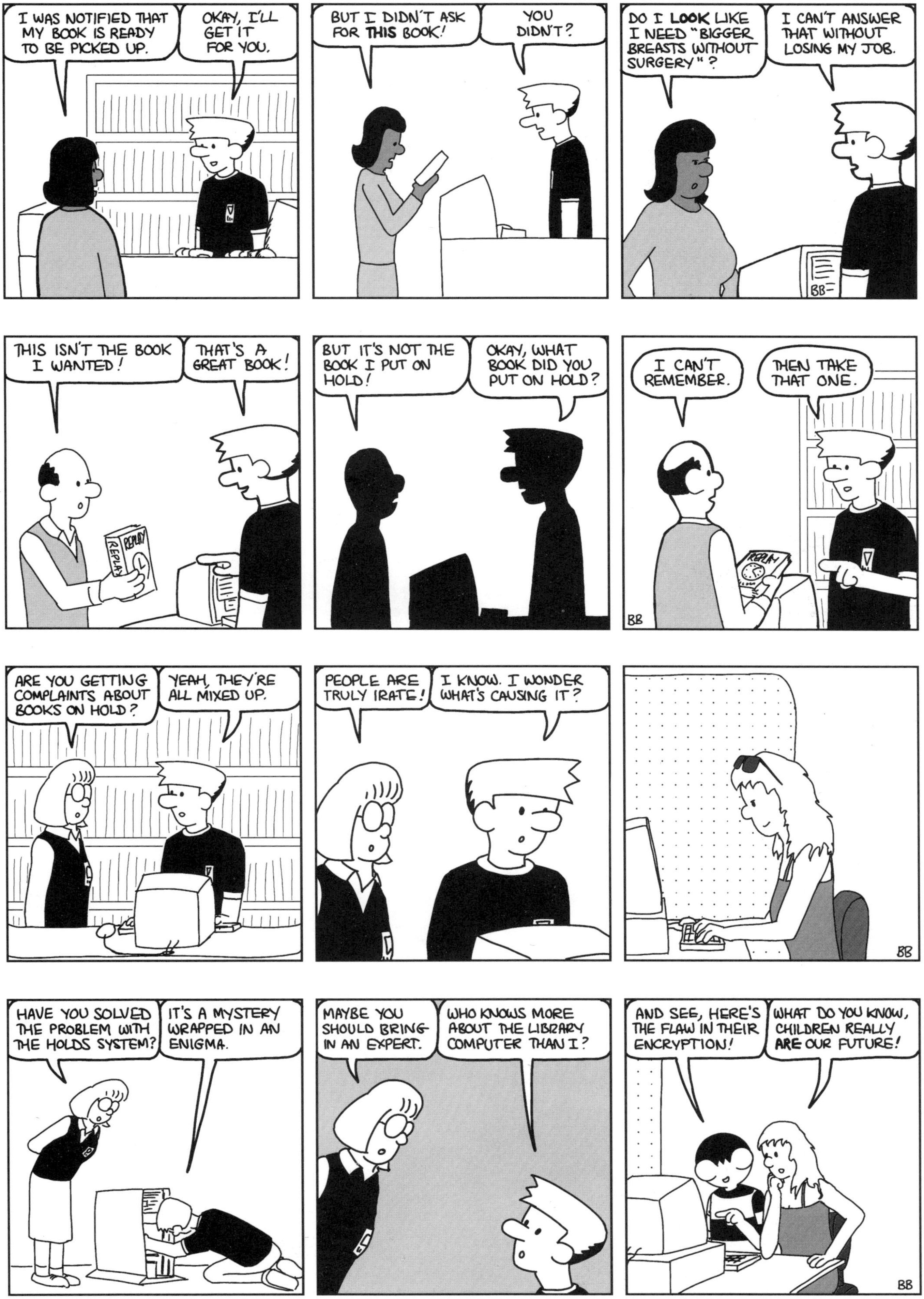

I WAS NOTIFIED THAT MY BOOK IS READY TO BE PICKED UP.
OKAY, I'LL GET IT FOR YOU.
BUT I DIDN'T ASK FOR **THIS** BOOK!
YOU DIDN'T?
DO I **LOOK** LIKE I NEED "BIGGER BREASTS WITHOUT SURGERY"?
I CAN'T ANSWER THAT WITHOUT LOSING MY JOB.
BB
THIS ISN'T THE BOOK I WANTED!
THAT'S A GREAT BOOK!
REPLAY
BUT IT'S NOT THE BOOK I PUT ON HOLD!
OKAY, WHAT BOOK DID YOU PUT ON HOLD?
I CAN'T REMEMBER.
THEN TAKE THAT ONE.
BB
ARE YOU GETTING COMPLAINTS ABOUT BOOKS ON HOLD?
YEAH, THEY'RE ALL MIXED UP.
PEOPLE ARE TRULY IRATE!
I KNOW. I WONDER WHAT'S CAUSING IT?
BB
HAVE YOU SOLVED THE PROBLEM WITH THE HOLDS SYSTEM?
IT'S A MYSTERY WRAPPED IN AN ENIGMA.
MAYBE YOU SHOULD BRING IN AN EXPERT.
WHO KNOWS MORE ABOUT THE LIBRARY COMPUTER THAN I?
AND SEE, HERE'S THE FLAW IN THEIR ENCRYPTION!
WHAT DO YOU KNOW, CHILDREN REALLY **ARE** OUR FUTURE!
BB

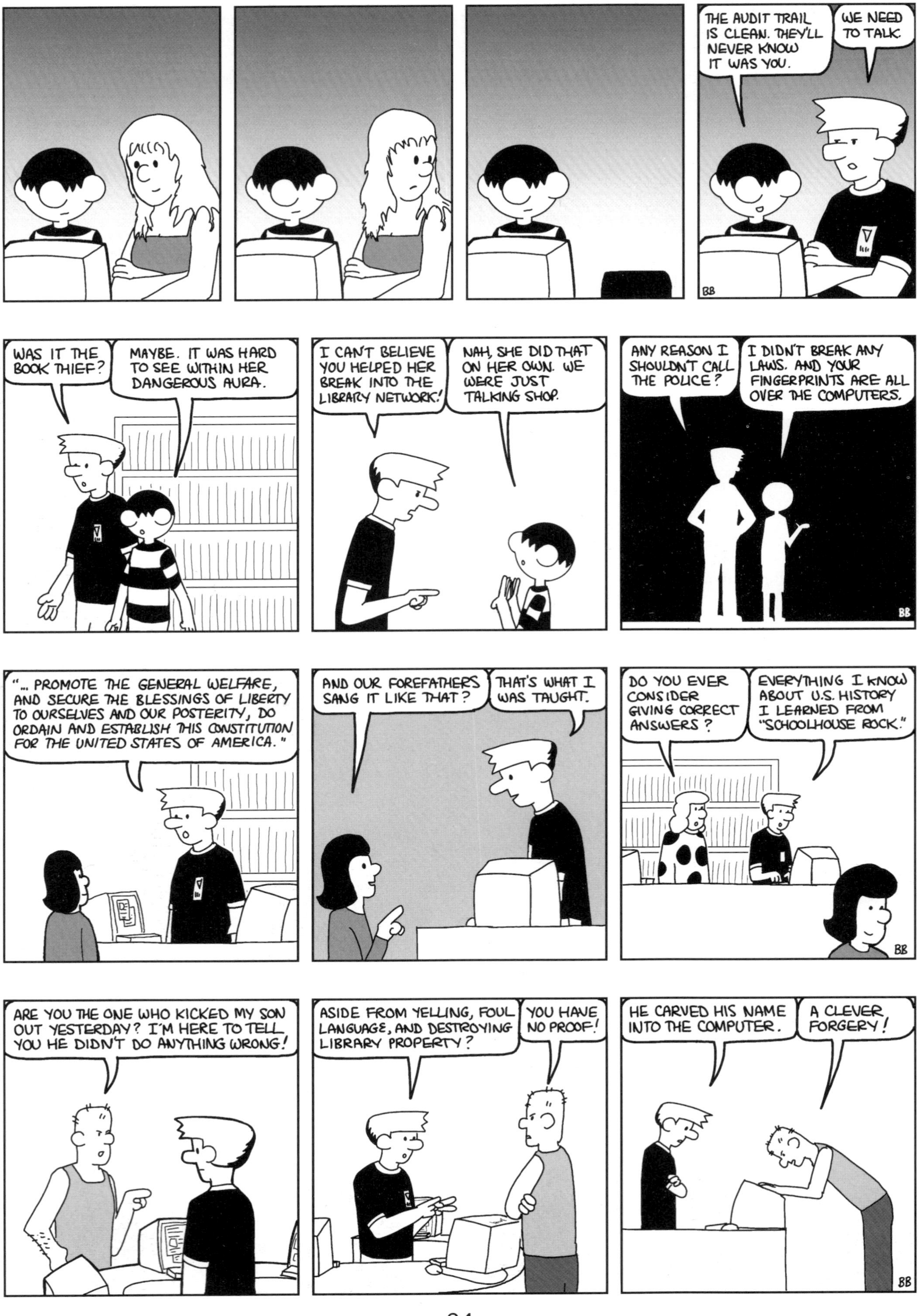
THE AUDIT TRAIL IS CLEAN. THEY'LL NEVER KNOW IT WAS YOU.
WE NEED TO TALK.
BB
WAS IT THE BOOK THIEF?
MAYBE. IT WAS HARD TO SEE WITHIN HER DANGEROUS AURA.
I CAN'T BELIEVE YOU HELPED HER BREAK INTO THE LIBRARY NETWORK!
NAH, SHE DID THAT ON HER OWN. WE WERE JUST TALKING SHOP.
ANY REASON I SHOULDN'T CALL THE POLICE?
I DIDN'T BREAK ANY LAWS. AND YOUR FINGERPRINTS ARE ALL OVER THE COMPUTERS.
BB
"... PROMOTE THE GENERAL WELFARE, AND SECURE THE BLESSINGS OF LIBERTY TO OURSELVES AND OUR POSTERITY, DO ORDAIN AND ESTABLISH THIS CONSTITUTION FOR THE UNITED STATES OF AMERICA."
AND OUR FOREFATHERS SANG IT LIKE THAT?
THAT'S WHAT I WAS TAUGHT.
DO YOU EVER CONSIDER GIVING CORRECT ANSWERS?
EVERYTHING I KNOW ABOUT U.S. HISTORY I LEARNED FROM "SCHOOLHOUSE ROCK."
BB
ARE YOU THE ONE WHO KICKED MY SON OUT YESTERDAY? I'M HERE TO TELL YOU HE DIDN'T DO ANYTHING WRONG!
ASIDE FROM YELLING, FOUL LANGUAGE, AND DESTROYING LIBRARY PROPERTY?
YOU HAVE NO PROOF!
HE CARVED HIS NAME INTO THE COMPUTER.
A CLEVER FORGERY!
BB

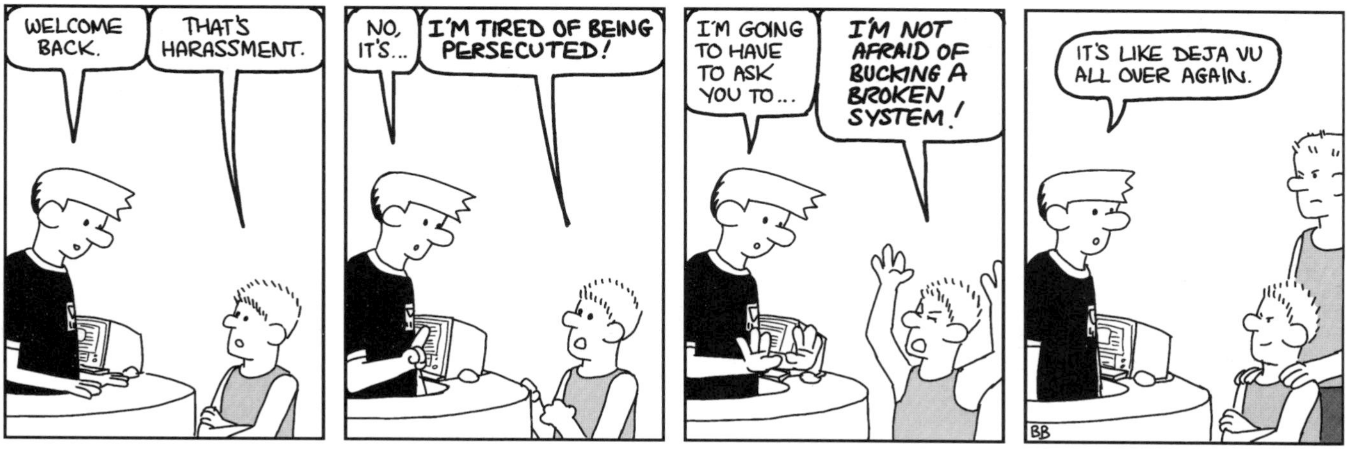
WELCOME BACK.
THAT'S HARASSMENT.
NO, IT'S...
I'M TIRED OF BEING PERSECUTED!
I'M GOING TO HAVE TO ASK YOU TO...
I'M NOT AFRAID OF BUCKING A BROKEN SYSTEM!
IT'S LIKE DEJA VU ALL OVER AGAIN.
BB

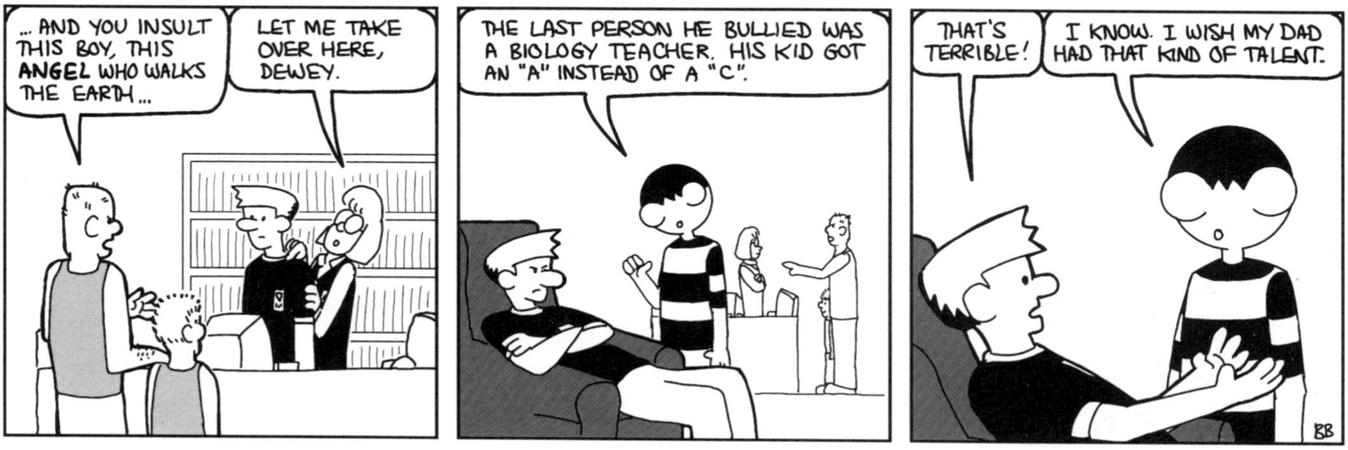
... AND YOU INSULT THIS BOY, THIS ANGEL WHO WALKS THE EARTH...
LET ME TAKE OVER HERE, DEWEY.
THE LAST PERSON HE BULLIED WAS A BIOLOGY TEACHER. HIS KID GOT AN "A" INSTEAD OF A "C".
THAT'S TERRIBLE!
I KNOW. I WISH MY DAD HAD THAT KIND OF TALENT.
BB

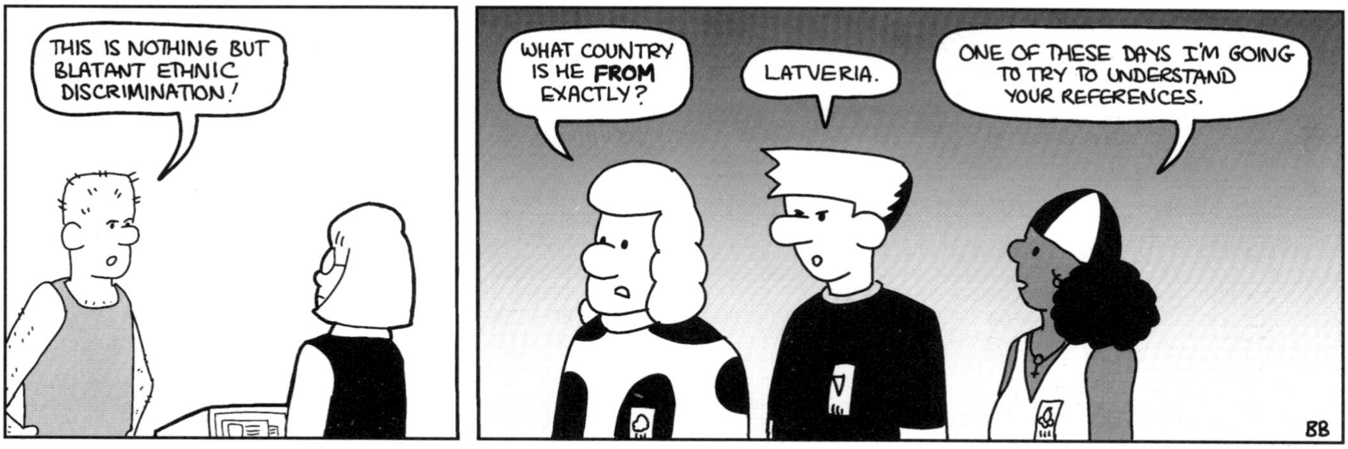
THIS IS NOTHING BUT BLATANT ETHNIC DISCRIMINATION!
WHAT COUNTRY IS HE FROM EXACTLY?
LATVERIA.
ONE OF THESE DAYS I'M GOING TO TRY TO UNDERSTAND YOUR REFERENCES.
BB

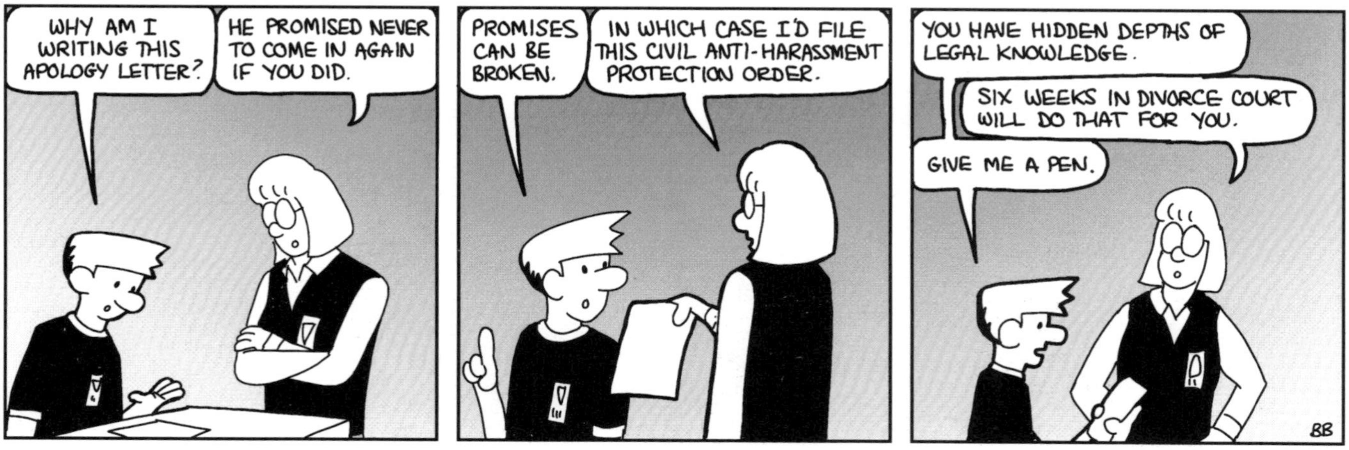
WHY AM I WRITING THIS APOLOGY LETTER?
HE PROMISED NEVER TO COME IN AGAIN IF YOU DID.
PROMISES CAN BE BROKEN.
IN WHICH CASE I'D FILE THIS CIVIL ANTI-HARASSMENT PROTECTION ORDER.
YOU HAVE HIDDEN DEPTHS OF LEGAL KNOWLEDGE.
SIX WEEKS IN DIVORCE COURT WILL DO THAT FOR YOU.
GIVE ME A PEN.
BB

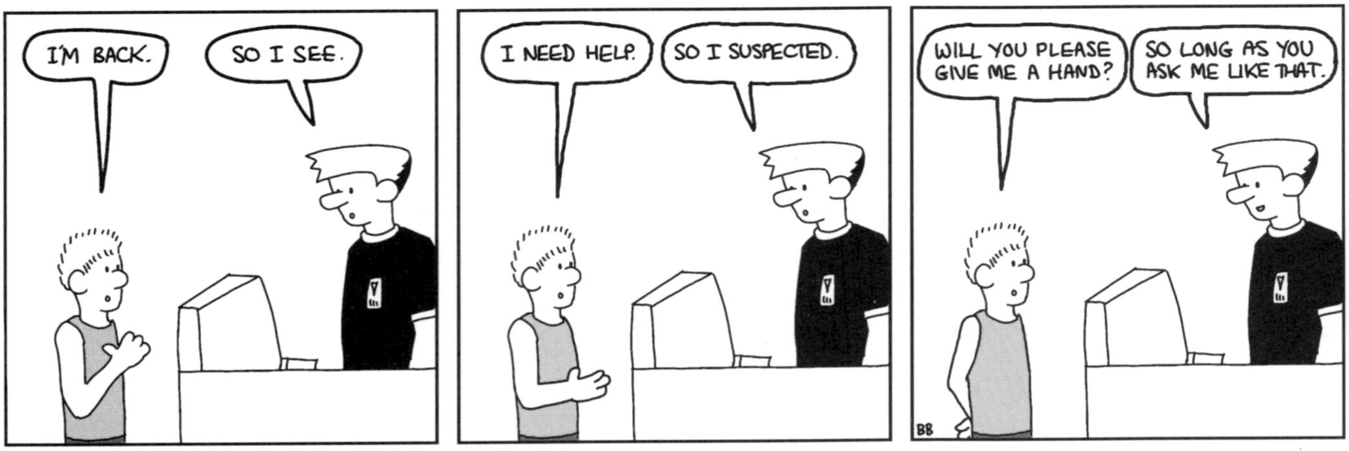
I'M BACK.
SO I SEE.
I NEED HELP.
SO I SUSPECTED.
WILL YOU PLEASE GIVE ME A HAND?
SO LONG AS YOU ASK ME LIKE THAT.
BB

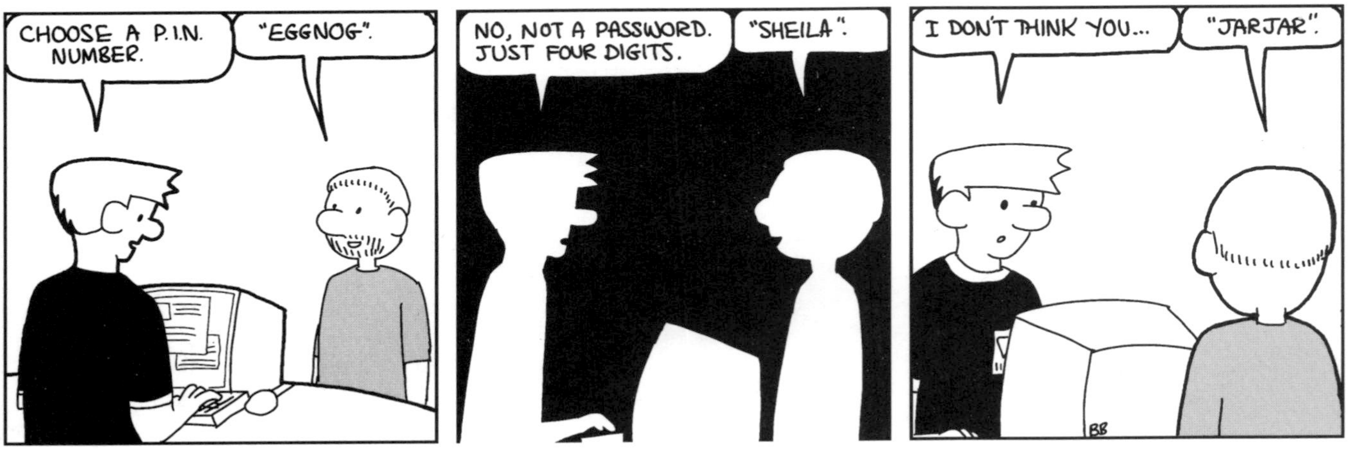
CHOOSE A P.I.N. NUMBER.
"EGGNOG".
NO, NOT A PASSWORD. JUST FOUR DIGITS.
"SHEILA".
I DON'T THINK YOU...
"JARJAR".
BB

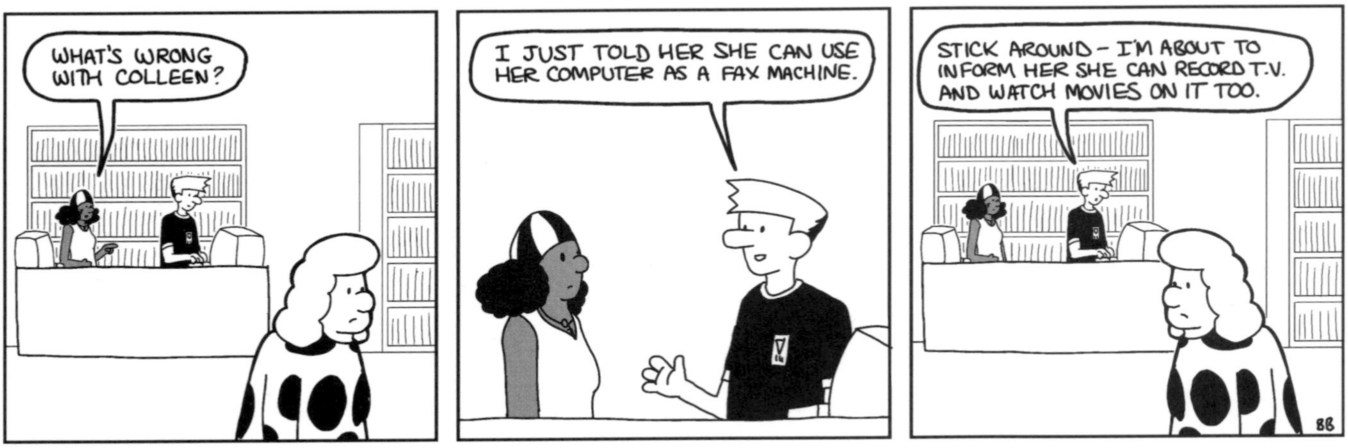
WHAT'S WRONG WITH COLLEEN?
I JUST TOLD HER SHE CAN USE HER COMPUTER AS A FAX MACHINE.
STICK AROUND – I'M ABOUT TO INFORM HER SHE CAN RECORD T.V. AND WATCH MOVIES ON IT TOO.
BB

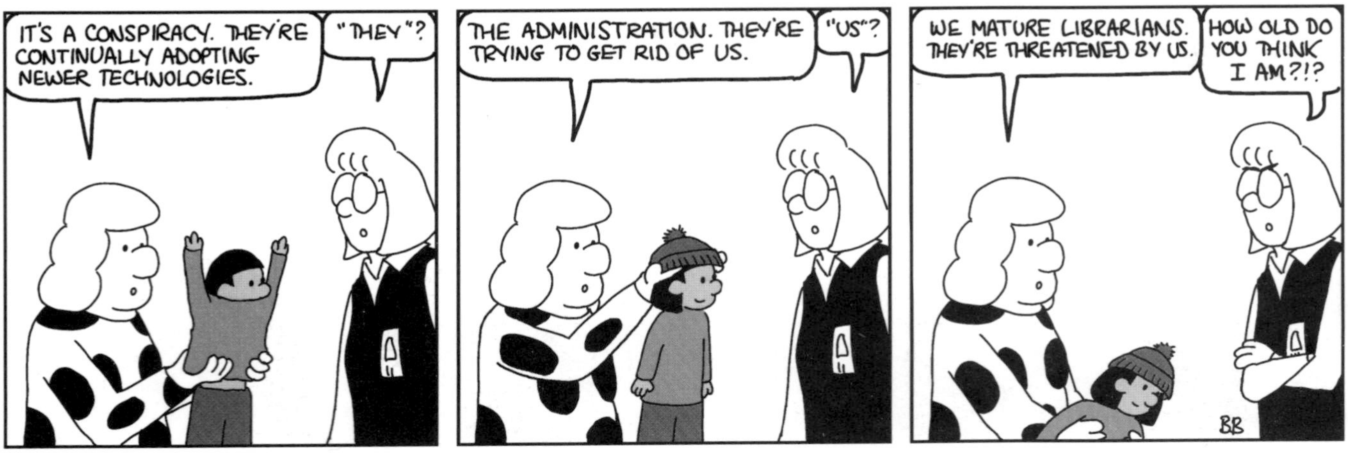
IT'S A CONSPIRACY. THEY'RE CONTINUALLY ADOPTING NEWER TECHNOLOGIES.
"THEY"?
THE ADMINISTRATION. THEY'RE TRYING TO GET RID OF US.
"US"?
WE MATURE LIBRARIANS. THEY'RE THREATENED BY US.
HOW OLD DO YOU THINK I AM?!?
BB

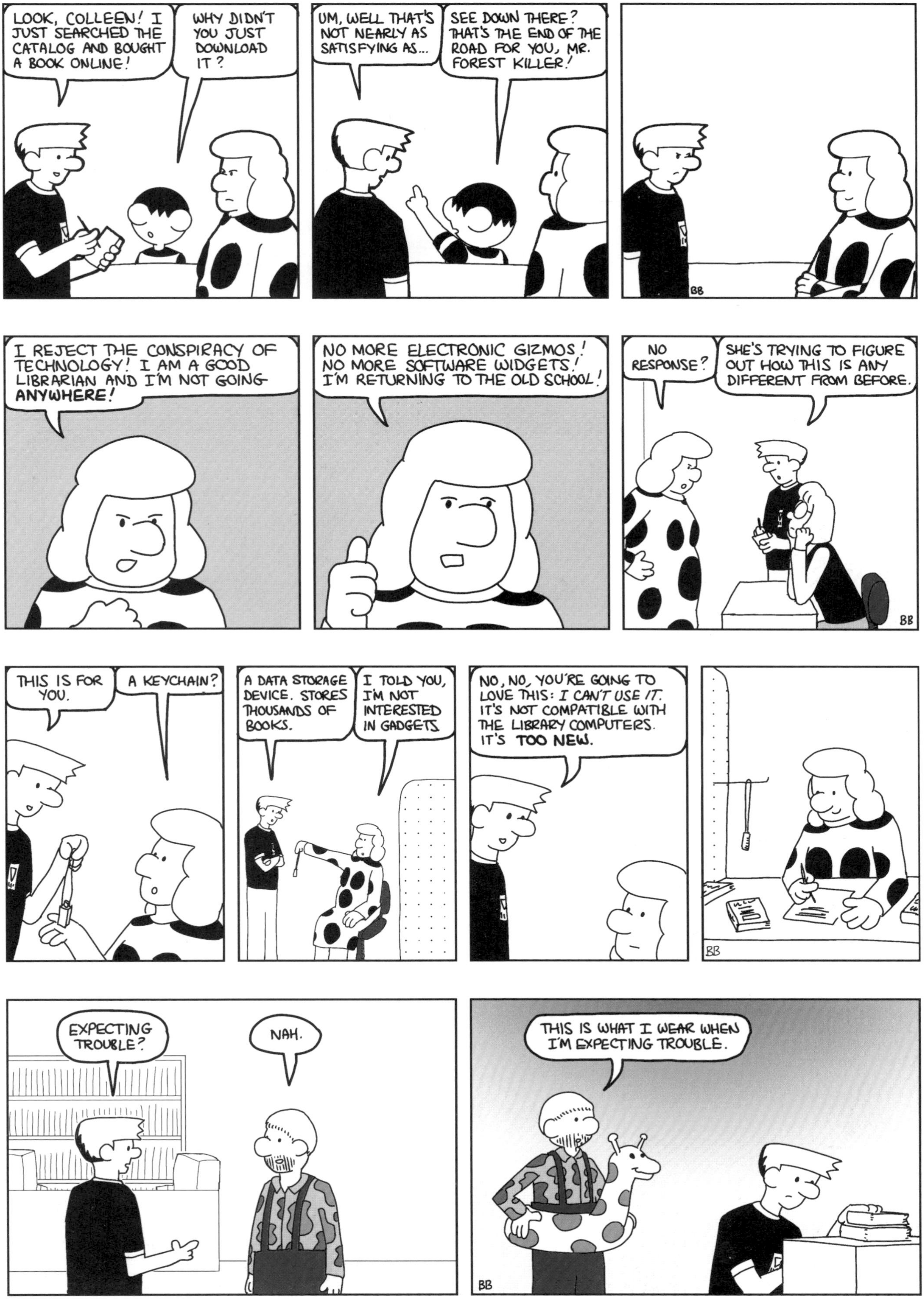
LOOK, COLLEEN! I JUST SEARCHED THE CATALOG AND BOUGHT A BOOK ONLINE!
WHY DIDN'T YOU JUST DOWNLOAD IT?
UM, WELL THAT'S NOT NEARLY AS SATISFYING AS...
SEE DOWN THERE? THAT'S THE END OF THE ROAD FOR YOU, MR. FOREST KILLER!
BB
I REJECT THE CONSPIRACY OF TECHNOLOGY! I AM A GOOD LIBRARIAN AND I'M NOT GOING ANYWHERE!
NO MORE ELECTRONIC GIZMOS! NO MORE SOFTWARE WIDGETS! I'M RETURNING TO THE OLD SCHOOL!
NO RESPONSE?
SHE'S TRYING TO FIGURE OUT HOW THIS IS ANY DIFFERENT FROM BEFORE.
BB
THIS IS FOR YOU.
A KEYCHAIN?
A DATA STORAGE DEVICE. STORES THOUSANDS OF BOOKS.
I TOLD YOU, I'M NOT INTERESTED IN GADGETS.
NO, NO, YOU'RE GOING TO LOVE THIS: I CAN'T USE IT. IT'S NOT COMPATIBLE WITH THE LIBRARY COMPUTERS. IT'S TOO NEW.
BB
EXPECTING TROUBLE?
NAH.
THIS IS WHAT I WEAR WHEN I'M EXPECTING TROUBLE.
BB

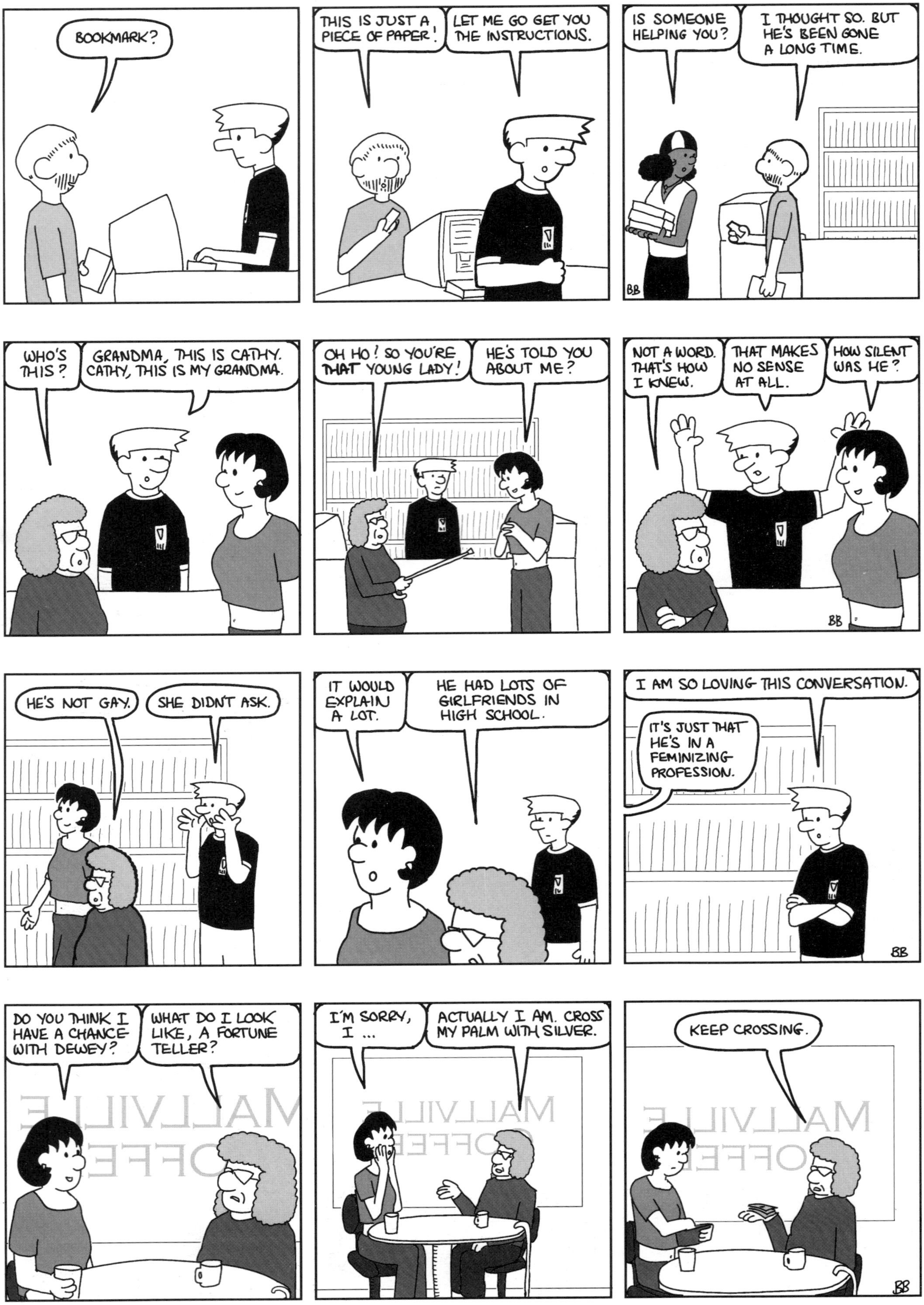
BOOKMARK?
THIS IS JUST A PIECE OF PAPER!
LET ME GO GET YOU THE INSTRUCTIONS.
IS SOMEONE HELPING YOU?
I THOUGHT SO. BUT HE'S BEEN GONE A LONG TIME.
BB
WHO'S THIS?
GRANDMA, THIS IS CATHY. CATHY, THIS IS MY GRANDMA.
OH HO! SO YOU'RE THAT YOUNG LADY!
HE'S TOLD YOU ABOUT ME?
NOT A WORD. THAT'S HOW I KNEW.
THAT MAKES NO SENSE AT ALL.
HOW SILENT WAS HE?
BB
HE'S NOT GAY.
SHE DIDN'T ASK.
IT WOULD EXPLAIN A LOT.
HE HAD LOTS OF GIRLFRIENDS IN HIGH SCHOOL.
I AM SO LOVING THIS CONVERSATION.
IT'S JUST THAT HE'S IN A FEMINIZING PROFESSION.
BB
DO YOU THINK I HAVE A CHANCE WITH DEWEY?
WHAT DO I LOOK LIKE, A FORTUNE TELLER?
I'M SORRY, I ...
ACTUALLY I AM. CROSS MY PALM WITH SILVER.
KEEP CROSSING.
BB

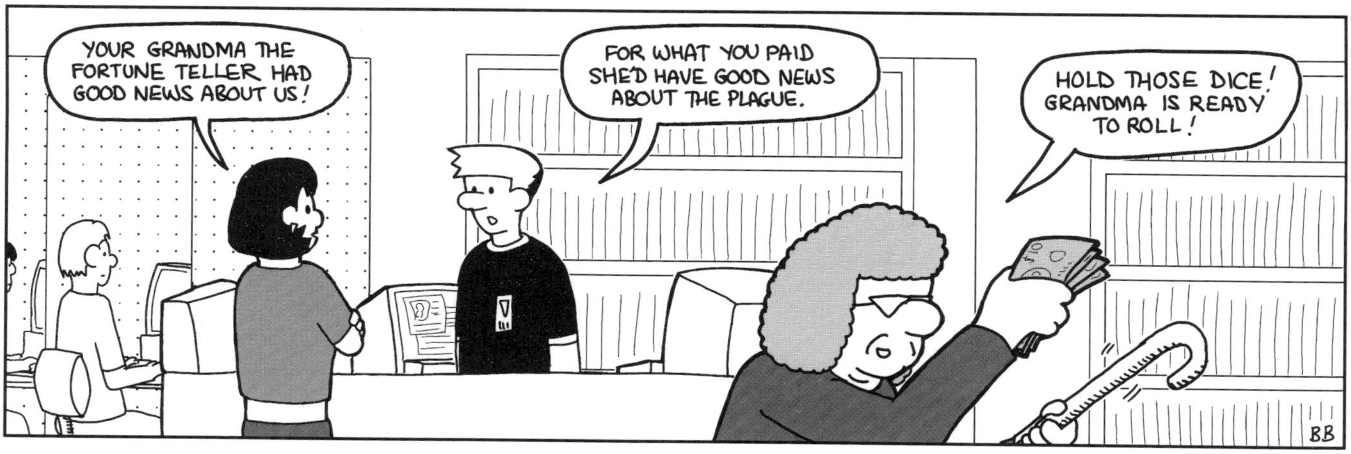
YOUR GRANDMA THE FORTUNE TELLER HAD GOOD NEWS ABOUT US!
FOR WHAT YOU PAID SHE'D HAVE GOOD NEWS ABOUT THE PLAGUE.
HOLD THOSE DICE! GRANDMA IS READY TO ROLL!
BB

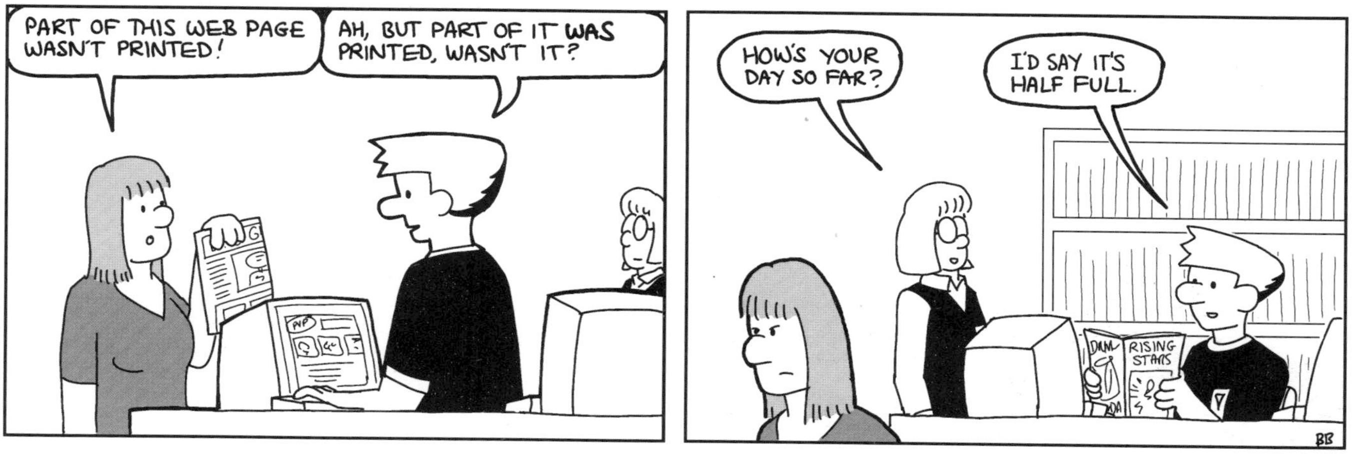
PART OF THIS WEB PAGE WASN'T PRINTED!
AH, BUT PART OF IT **WAS** PRINTED, WASN'T IT?
HOW'S YOUR DAY SO FAR?
I'D SAY IT'S HALF FULL.
RISING STARS
BB

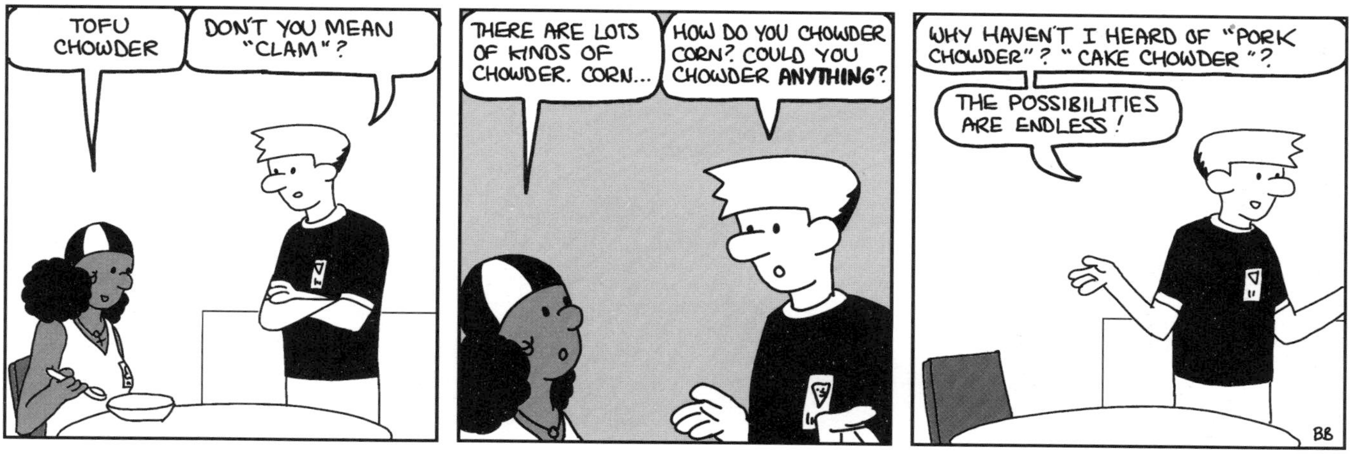
TOFU CHOWDER
DON'T YOU MEAN "CLAM"?
THERE ARE LOTS OF KINDS OF CHOWDER. CORN...
HOW DO YOU CHOWDER CORN? COULD YOU CHOWDER **ANYTHING**?
WHY HAVEN'T I HEARD OF "PORK CHOWDER"? "CAKE CHOWDER"?
THE POSSIBILITIES ARE ENDLESS!
BB

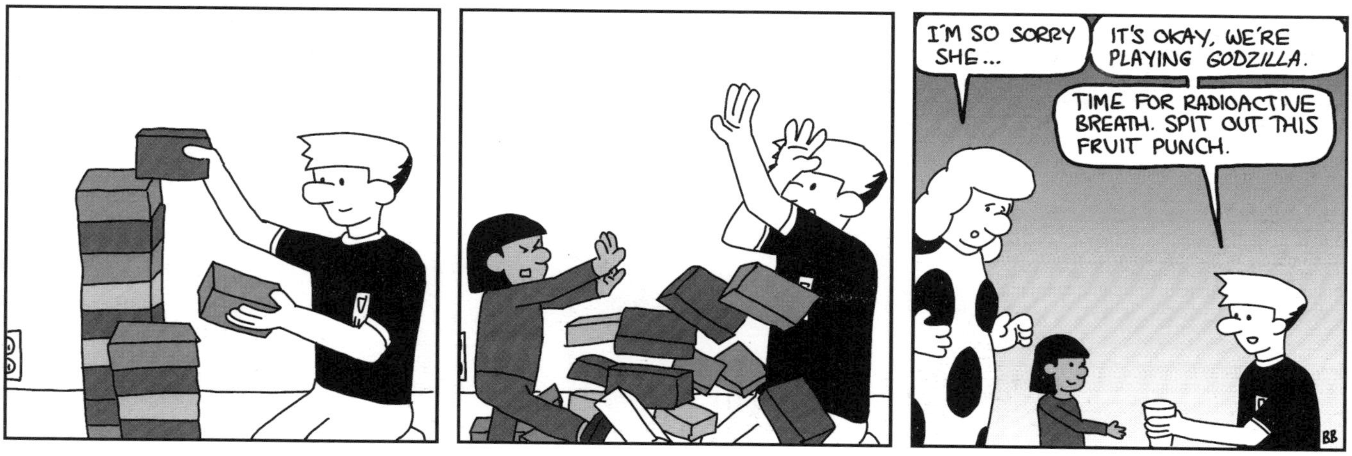
I'M SO SORRY SHE...
IT'S OKAY, WE'RE PLAYING *GODZILLA*.
TIME FOR RADIOACTIVE BREATH. SPIT OUT THIS FRUIT PUNCH.
BB

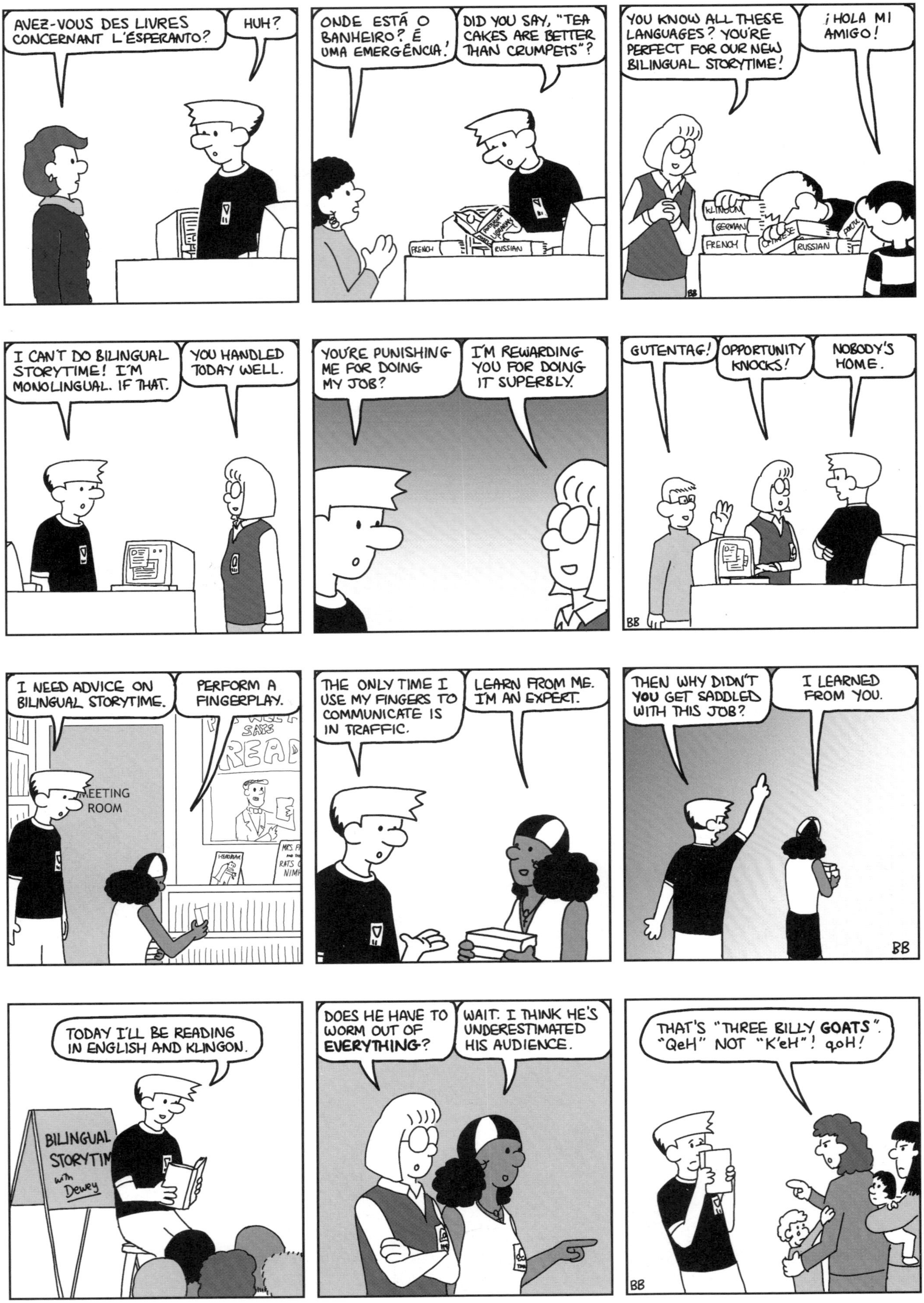
AVEZ-VOUS DES LIVRES CONCERNANT L'ESPERANTO?
HUH?
ONDE ESTÁ O BANHEIRO? É UMA EMERGÊNCIA!
DID YOU SAY, "TEA CAKES ARE BETTER THAN CRUMPETS"?
FRENCH
RUSSIAN
YOU KNOW ALL THESE LANGUAGES? YOU'RE PERFECT FOR OUR NEW BILINGUAL STORYTIME!
¡HOLA MI AMIGO!
KLINGON
GERMAN
FRENCH
RUSSIAN
I CAN'T DO BILINGUAL STORYTIME! I'M MONOLINGUAL. IF THAT.
YOU HANDLED TODAY WELL.
YOU'RE PUNISHING ME FOR DOING MY JOB?
I'M REWARDING YOU FOR DOING IT SUPERBLY.
GUTENTAG!
OPPORTUNITY KNOCKS!
NOBODY'S HOME.
I NEED ADVICE ON BILINGUAL STORYTIME.
PERFORM A FINGERPLAY.
MEETING ROOM
THE ONLY TIME I USE MY FINGERS TO COMMUNICATE IS IN TRAFFIC.
LEARN FROM ME. I'M AN EXPERT.
THEN WHY DIDN'T **YOU** GET SADDLED WITH THIS JOB?
I LEARNED FROM YOU.
TODAY I'LL BE READING IN ENGLISH AND KLINGON.
BILINGUAL STORYTIM
with Dewey
DOES HE HAVE TO WORM OUT OF **EVERYTHING**?
WAIT. I THINK HE'S UNDERESTIMATED HIS AUDIENCE.
THAT'S "THREE BILLY **GOATS**". "QeH" NOT "K'eH"! qoH!

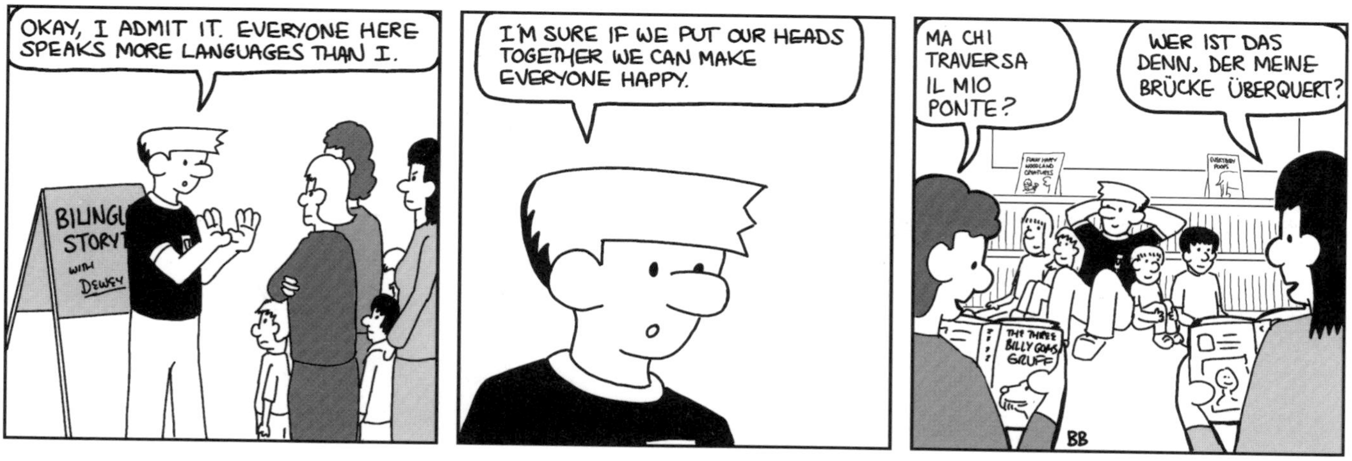
OKAY, I ADMIT IT. EVERYONE HERE SPEAKS MORE LANGUAGES THAN I.
I'M SURE IF WE PUT OUR HEADS TOGETHER WE CAN MAKE EVERYONE HAPPY.
MA CHI TRAVERSA IL MIO PONTE?
WER IST DAS DENN, DER MEINE BRÜCKE ÜBERQUERT?
THE THREE BILLY GOATS GRUFF

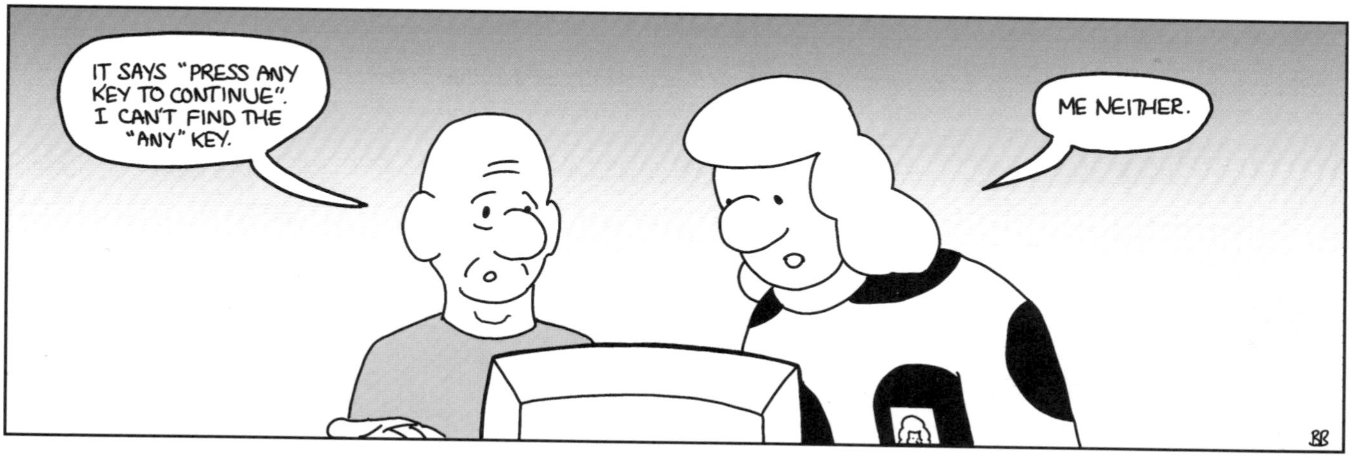
IT SAYS "PRESS ANY KEY TO CONTINUE". I CAN'T FIND THE "ANY" KEY.
ME NEITHER.

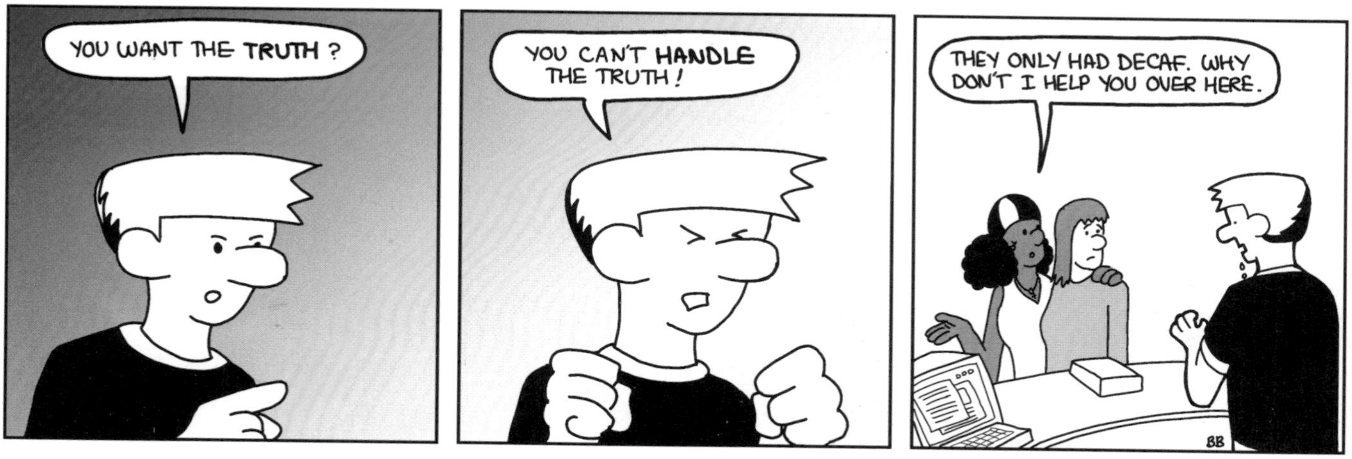
YOU WANT THE **TRUTH** ?
YOU CAN'T **HANDLE** THE TRUTH!
THEY ONLY HAD DECAF. WHY DON'T I HELP YOU OVER HERE.

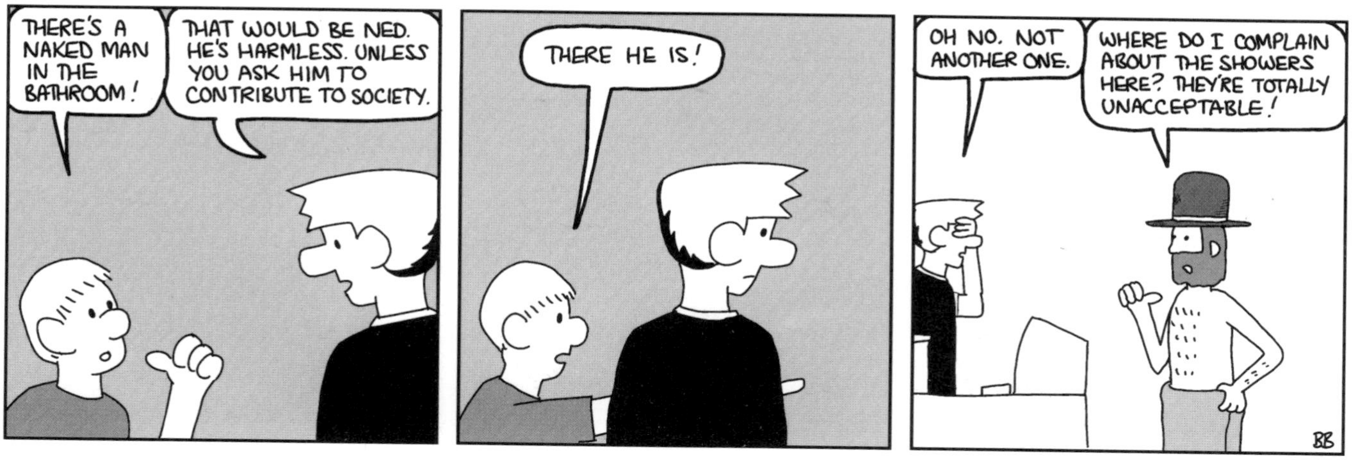
THERE'S A NAKED MAN IN THE BATHROOM!
THAT WOULD BE NED. HE'S HARMLESS. UNLESS YOU ASK HIM TO CONTRIBUTE TO SOCIETY.
THERE HE IS!
OH NO. NOT ANOTHER ONE.
WHERE DO I COMPLAIN ABOUT THE SHOWERS HERE? THEY'RE TOTALLY UNACCEPTABLE!

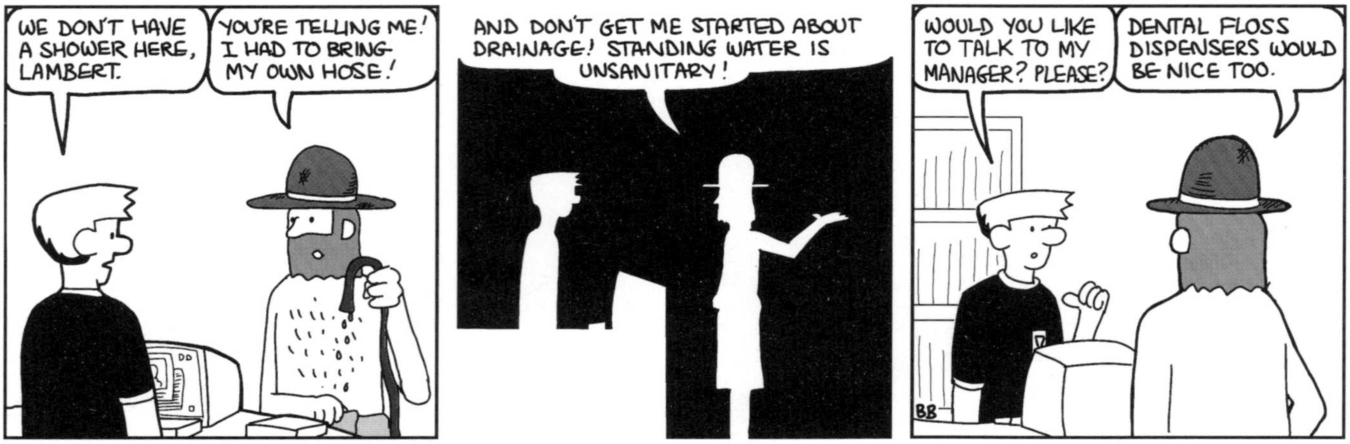
WE DON'T HAVE A SHOWER HERE, LAMBERT.
YOU'RE TELLING ME! I HAD TO BRING MY OWN HOSE!
AND DON'T GET ME STARTED ABOUT DRAINAGE! STANDING WATER IS UNSANITARY!
WOULD YOU LIKE TO TALK TO MY MANAGER? PLEASE?
DENTAL FLOSS DISPENSERS WOULD BE NICE TOO.
BB

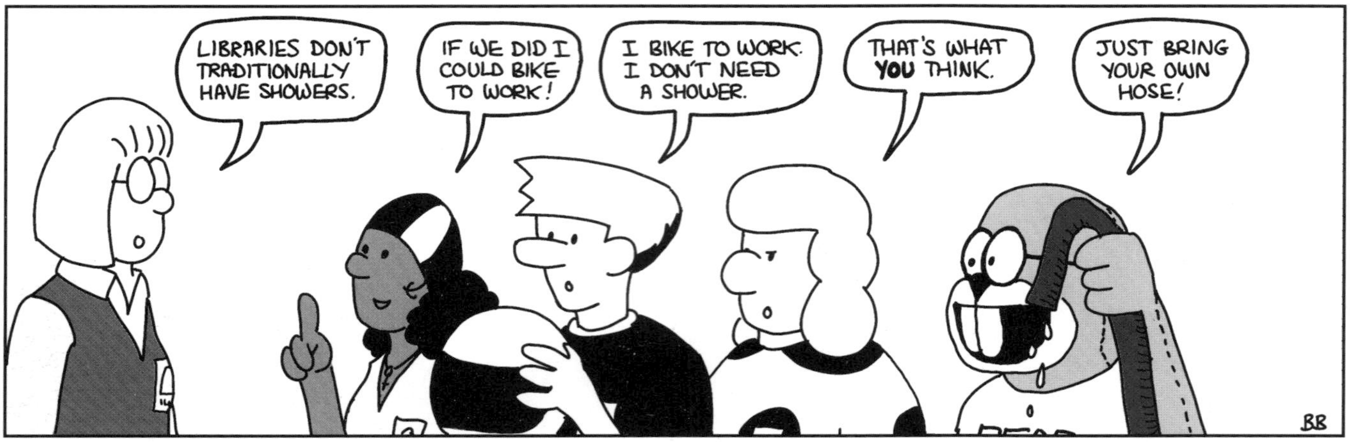
LIBRARIES DON'T TRADITIONALLY HAVE SHOWERS.
IF WE DID I COULD BIKE TO WORK!
I BIKE TO WORK. I DON'T NEED A SHOWER.
THAT'S WHAT **YOU** THINK.
JUST BRING YOUR OWN HOSE!
BB

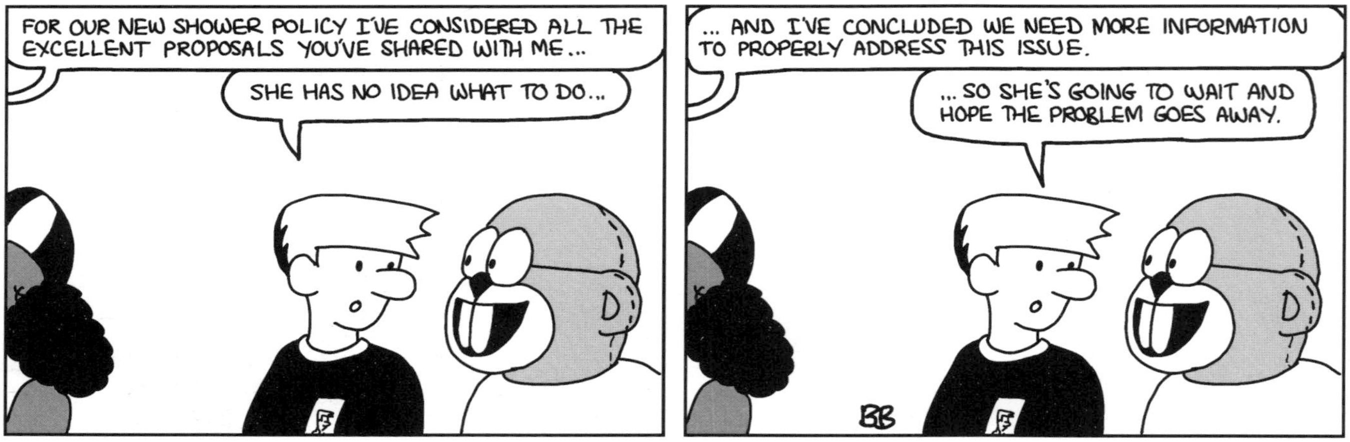
FOR OUR NEW SHOWER POLICY I'VE CONSIDERED ALL THE EXCELLENT PROPOSALS YOU'VE SHARED WITH ME...
SHE HAS NO IDEA WHAT TO DO...
... AND I'VE CONCLUDED WE NEED MORE INFORMATION TO PROPERLY ADDRESS THIS ISSUE.
... SO SHE'S GOING TO WAIT AND HOPE THE PROBLEM GOES AWAY.
BB

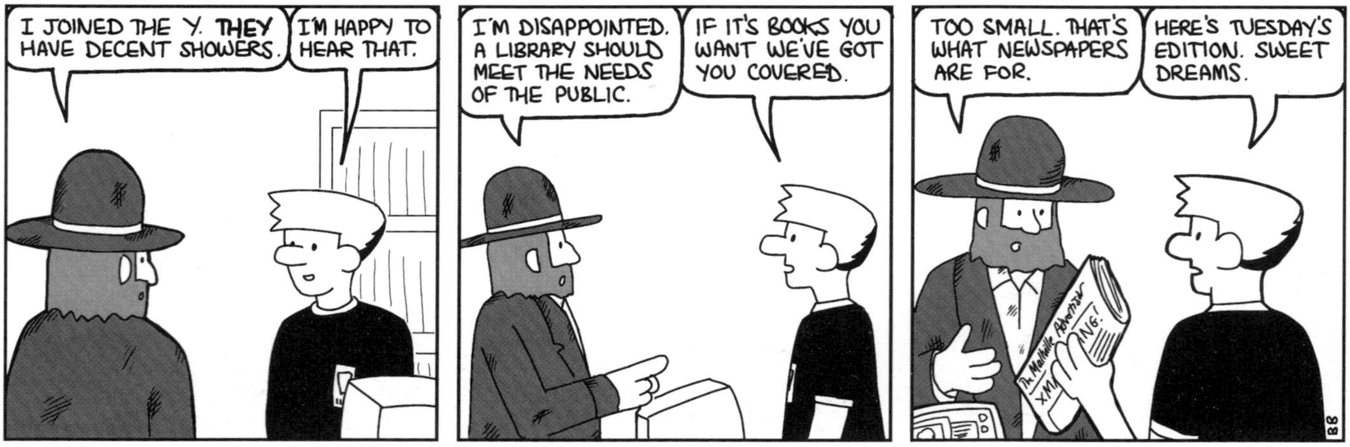
I JOINED THE Y. **THEY** HAVE DECENT SHOWERS.
I'M HAPPY TO HEAR THAT.
I'M DISAPPOINTED. A LIBRARY SHOULD MEET THE NEEDS OF THE PUBLIC.
IF IT'S BOOKS YOU WANT WE'VE GOT YOU COVERED.
TOO SMALL. THAT'S WHAT NEWSPAPERS ARE FOR.
HERE'S TUESDAY'S EDITION. SWEET DREAMS.
BB

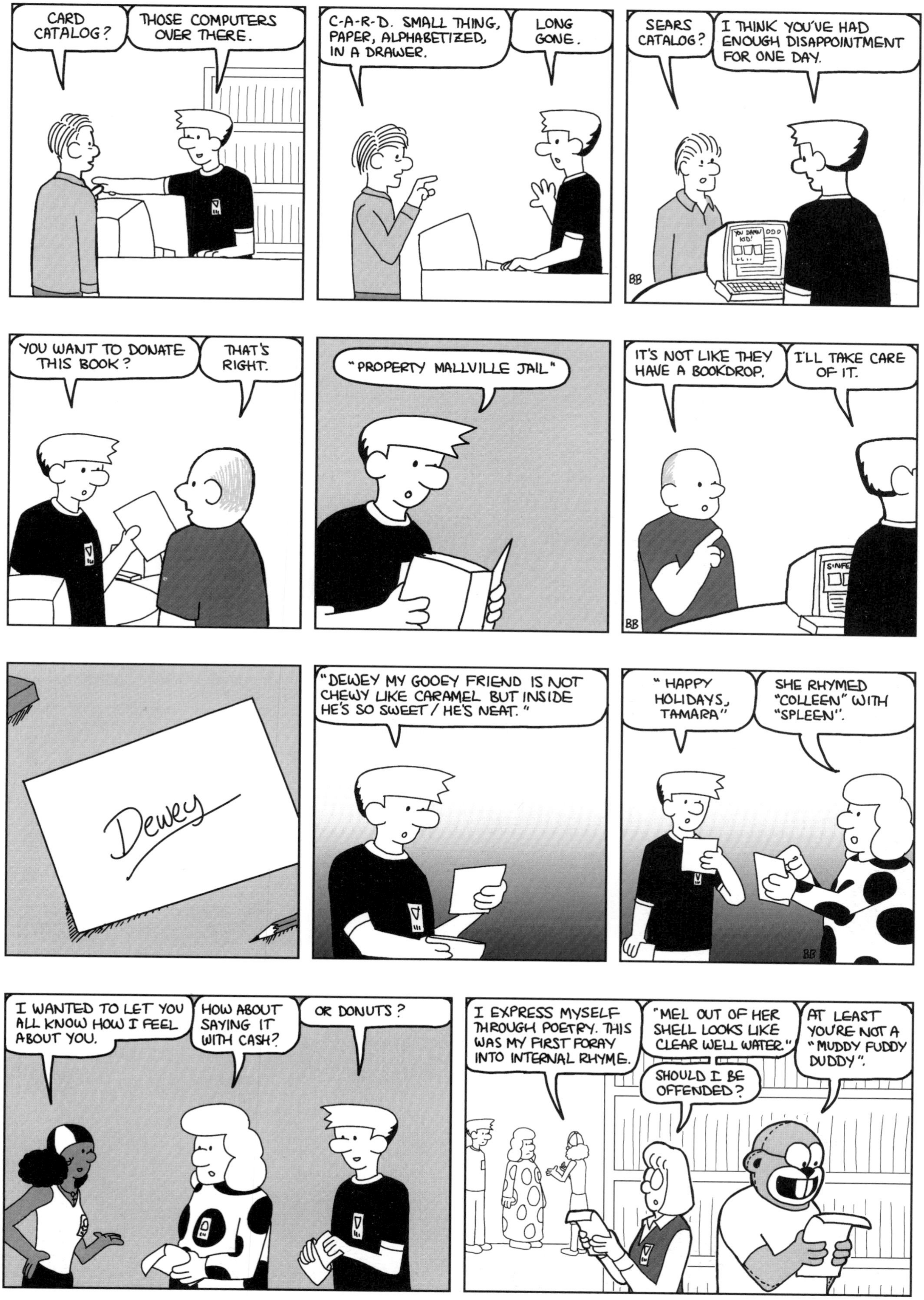
CARD CATALOG?
THOSE COMPUTERS OVER THERE.
C-A-R-D. SMALL THING, PAPER, ALPHABETIZED, IN A DRAWER.
LONG GONE.
SEARS CATALOG?
I THINK YOU'VE HAD ENOUGH DISAPPOINTMENT FOR ONE DAY.
BB
YOU WANT TO DONATE THIS BOOK?
THAT'S RIGHT.
"PROPERTY MALLVILLE JAIL"
IT'S NOT LIKE THEY HAVE A BOOKDROP.
I'LL TAKE CARE OF IT.
BB
Dewey
"DEWEY MY GOOEY FRIEND IS NOT CHEWY LIKE CARAMEL BUT INSIDE HE'S SO SWEET / HE'S NEAT."
"HAPPY HOLIDAYS, TAMARA"
SHE RHYMED "COLLEEN" WITH "SPLEEN".
BB
I WANTED TO LET YOU ALL KNOW HOW I FEEL ABOUT YOU.
HOW ABOUT SAYING IT WITH CASH?
OR DONUTS?
I EXPRESS MYSELF THROUGH POETRY. THIS WAS MY FIRST FORAY INTO INTERNAL RHYME.
"MEL OUT OF HER SHELL LOOKS LIKE CLEAR WELL WATER."
SHOULD I BE OFFENDED?
AT LEAST YOU'RE NOT A "MUDDY FUDDY DUDDY".

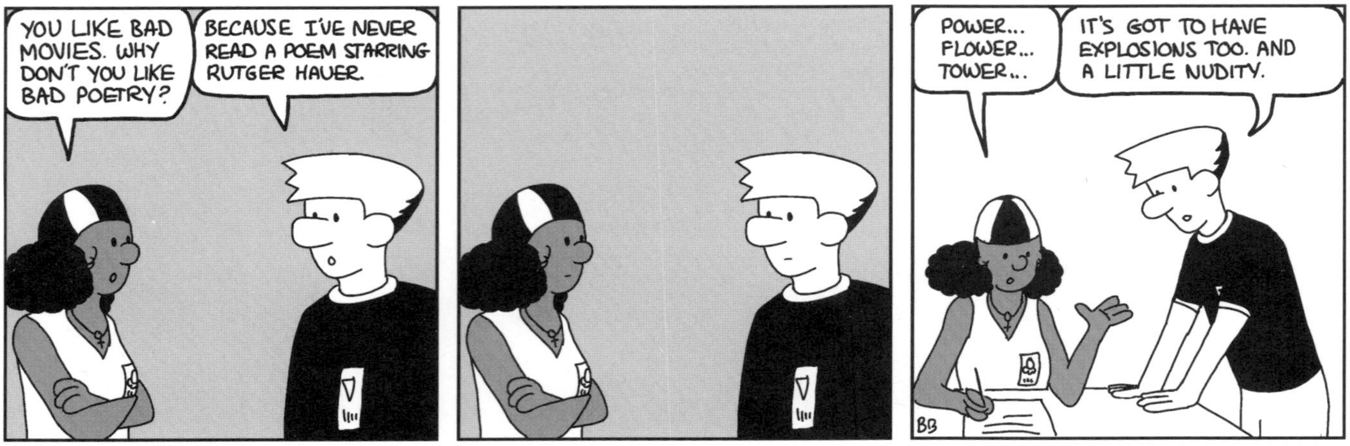
YOU LIKE BAD MOVIES. WHY DON'T YOU LIKE BAD POETRY?
BECAUSE I'VE NEVER READ A POEM STARRING RUTGER HAUER.
POWER... FLOWER... TOWER...
IT'S GOT TO HAVE EXPLOSIONS TOO. AND A LITTLE NUDITY.
BB

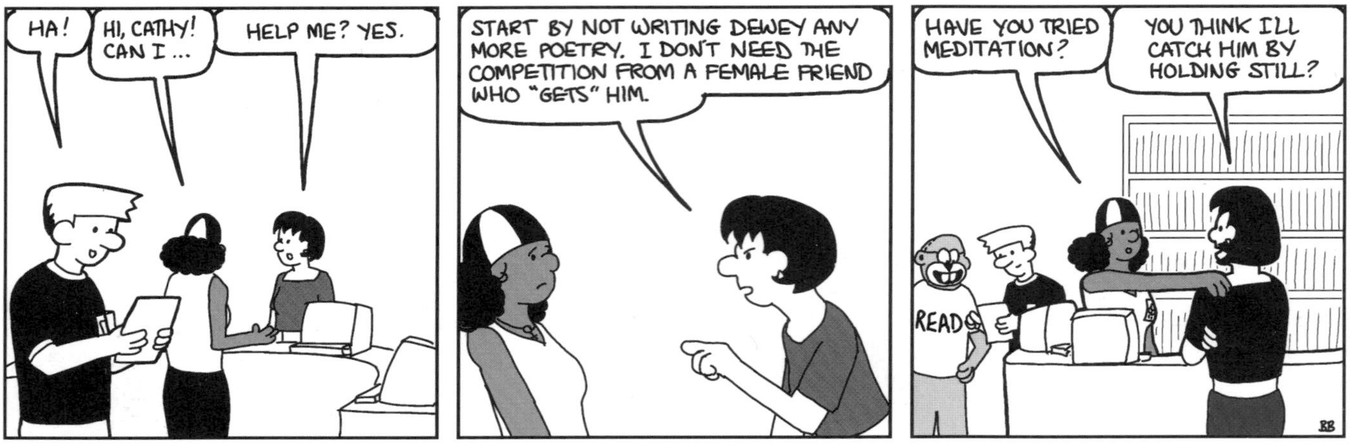
HA!
HI, CATHY! CAN I ...
HELP ME? YES.
START BY NOT WRITING DEWEY ANY MORE POETRY. I DON'T NEED THE COMPETITION FROM A FEMALE FRIEND WHO "GETS" HIM.
HAVE YOU TRIED MEDITATION?
YOU THINK I'LL CATCH HIM BY HOLDING STILL?
READ
BB

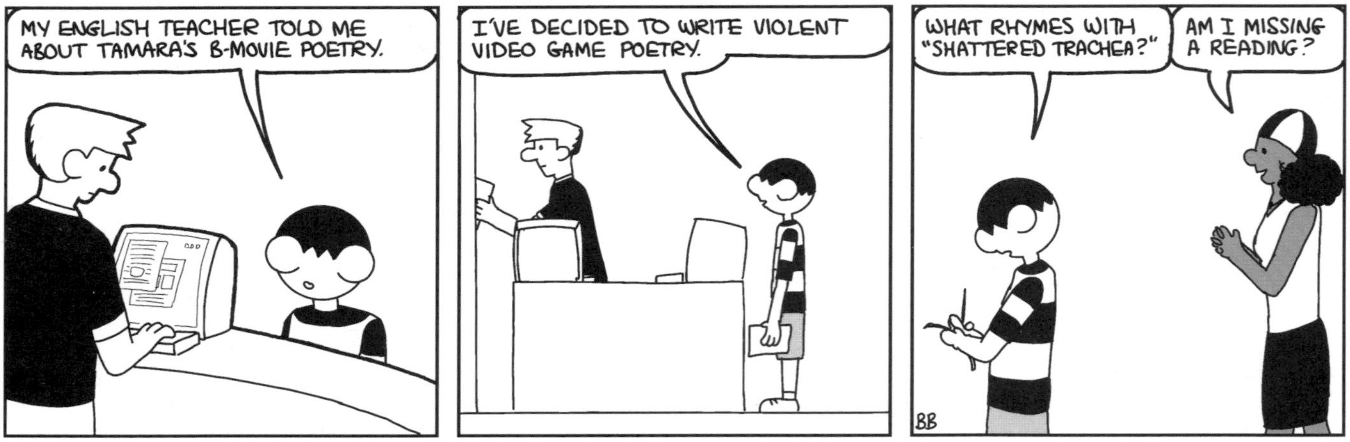
MY ENGLISH TEACHER TOLD ME ABOUT TAMARA'S B-MOVIE POETRY.
I'VE DECIDED TO WRITE VIOLENT VIDEO GAME POETRY.
WHAT RHYMES WITH "SHATTERED TRACHEA?"
AM I MISSING A READING?
BB

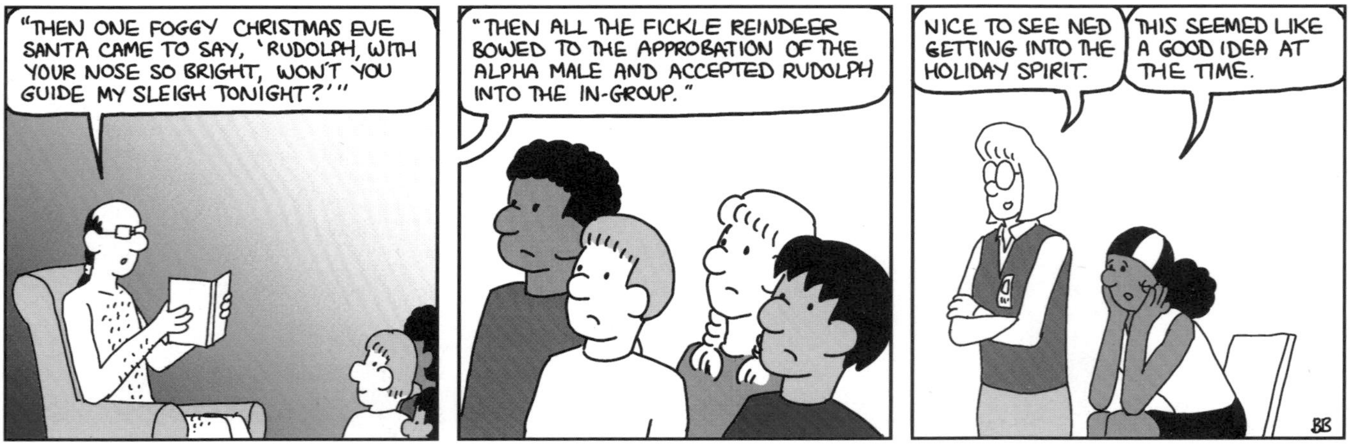
"THEN ONE FOGGY CHRISTMAS EVE SANTA CAME TO SAY, 'RUDOLPH, WITH YOUR NOSE SO BRIGHT, WON'T YOU GUIDE MY SLEIGH TONIGHT?'"
"THEN ALL THE FICKLE REINDEER BOWED TO THE APPROBATION OF THE ALPHA MALE AND ACCEPTED RUDOLPH INTO THE IN-GROUP."
NICE TO SEE NED GETTING INTO THE HOLIDAY SPIRIT.
THIS SEEMED LIKE A GOOD IDEA AT THE TIME.
BB

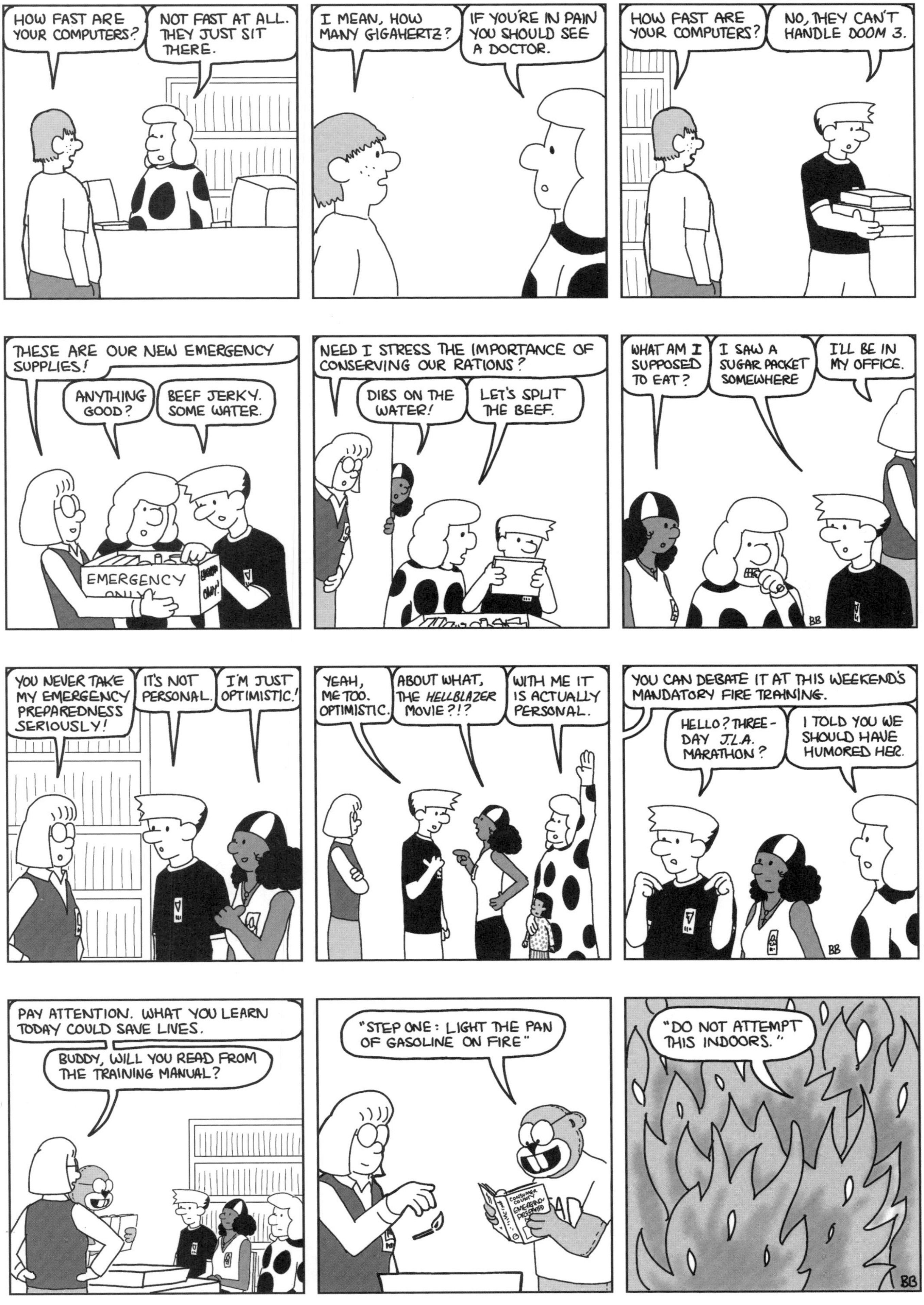
HOW FAST ARE YOUR COMPUTERS?
NOT FAST AT ALL. THEY JUST SIT THERE.
I MEAN, HOW MANY GIGAHERTZ?
IF YOU'RE IN PAIN YOU SHOULD SEE A DOCTOR.
HOW FAST ARE YOUR COMPUTERS?
NO, THEY CAN'T HANDLE DOOM 3.
THESE ARE OUR NEW EMERGENCY SUPPLIES!
ANYTHING GOOD?
BEEF JERKY. SOME WATER.
EMERGENCY ONLY
NEED I STRESS THE IMPORTANCE OF CONSERVING OUR RATIONS?
DIBS ON THE WATER!
LET'S SPLIT THE BEEF.
WHAT AM I SUPPOSED TO EAT?
I SAW A SUGAR PACKET SOMEWHERE
I'LL BE IN MY OFFICE.
BB
YOU NEVER TAKE MY EMERGENCY PREPAREDNESS SERIOUSLY!
IT'S NOT PERSONAL.
I'M JUST OPTIMISTIC!
YEAH, ME TOO. OPTIMISTIC.
ABOUT WHAT, THE HELLBLAZER MOVIE?!?
WITH ME IT IS ACTUALLY PERSONAL.
YOU CAN DEBATE IT AT THIS WEEKEND'S MANDATORY FIRE TRAINING.
HELLO? THREE-DAY J.L.A. MARATHON?
I TOLD YOU WE SHOULD HAVE HUMORED HER.
BB
PAY ATTENTION. WHAT YOU LEARN TODAY COULD SAVE LIVES.
BUDDY, WILL YOU READ FROM THE TRAINING MANUAL?
"STEP ONE: LIGHT THE PAN OF GASOLINE ON FIRE"
CONSUMER COUNTY EMERGENCY PREPAREDNESS
"DO NOT ATTEMPT THIS INDOORS."
BB

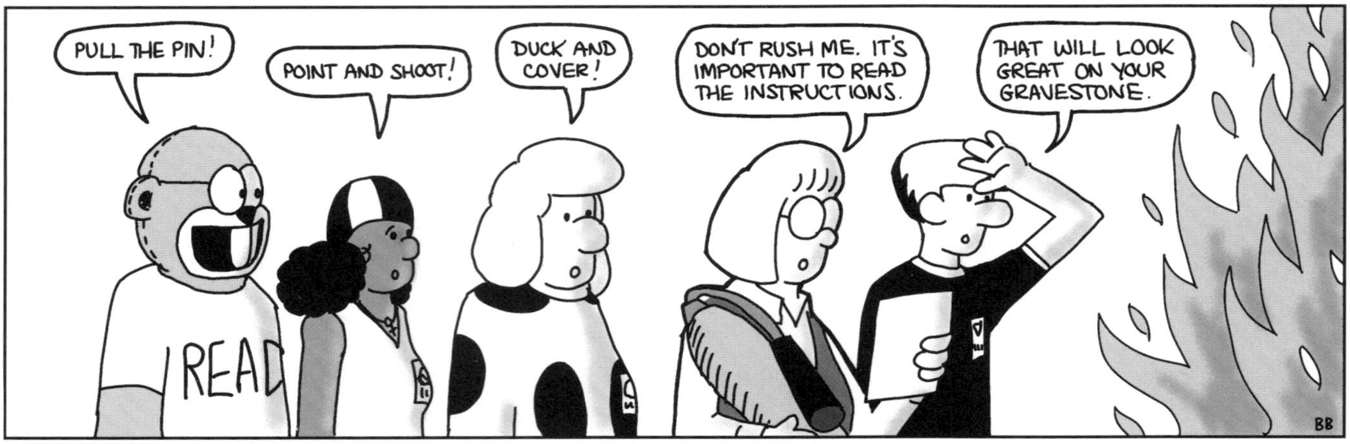
PULL THE PIN!
POINT AND SHOOT!
DUCK AND COVER!
DON'T RUSH ME. IT'S IMPORTANT TO READ THE INSTRUCTIONS.
THAT WILL LOOK GREAT ON YOUR GRAVESTONE.
READ
BB

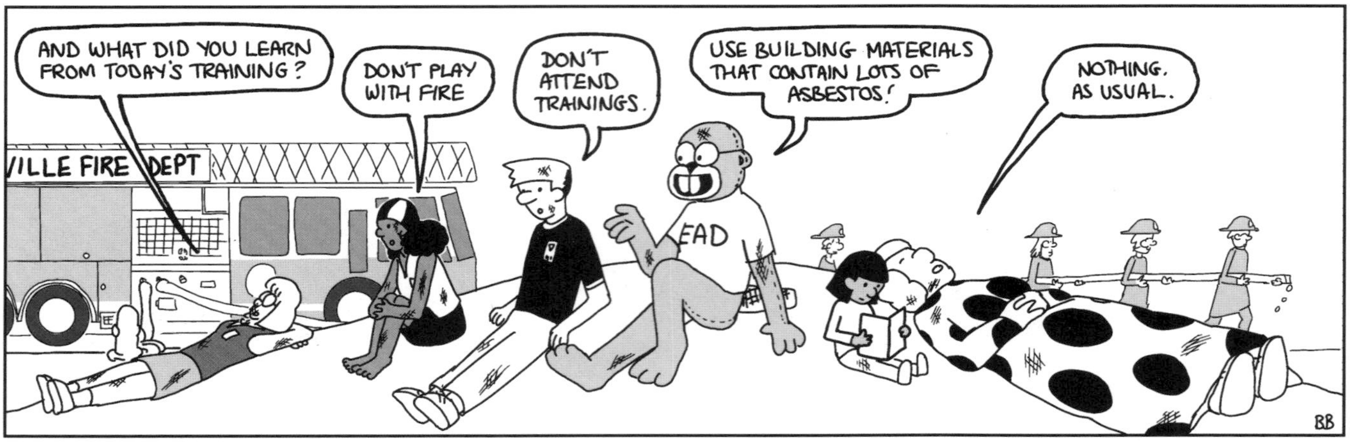
AND WHAT DID YOU LEARN FROM TODAY'S TRAINING?
DON'T PLAY WITH FIRE
DON'T ATTEND TRAININGS.
USE BUILDING MATERIALS THAT CONTAIN LOTS OF ASBESTOS!
NOTHING, AS USUAL.
VILLE FIRE DEPT
EAD
BB

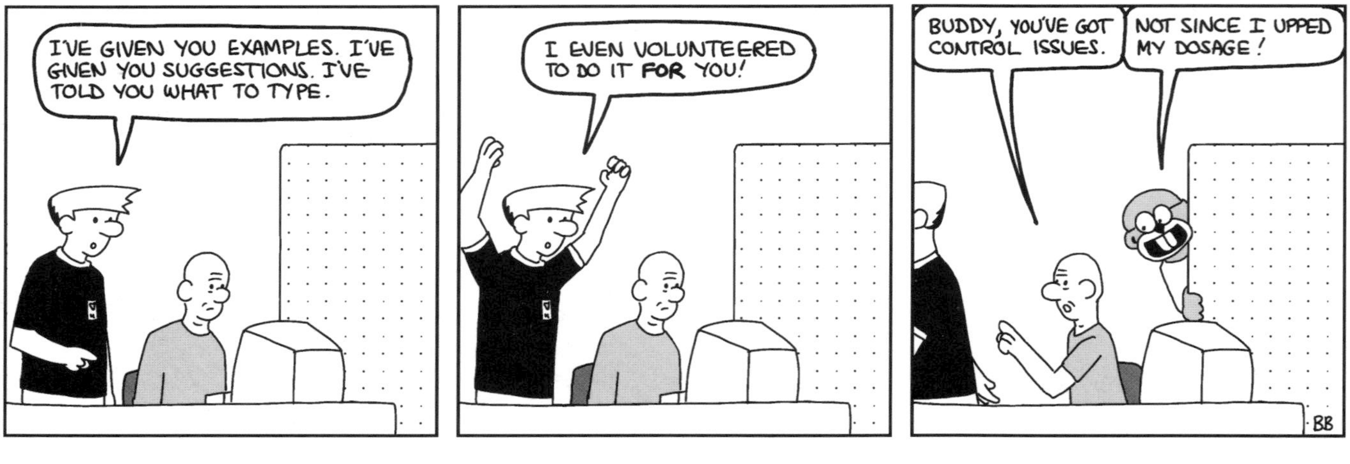
I'VE GIVEN YOU EXAMPLES. I'VE GIVEN YOU SUGGESTIONS. I'VE TOLD YOU WHAT TO TYPE.
I EVEN VOLUNTEERED TO DO IT **FOR** YOU!
BUDDY, YOU'VE GOT CONTROL ISSUES.
NOT SINCE I UPPED MY DOSAGE!
BB

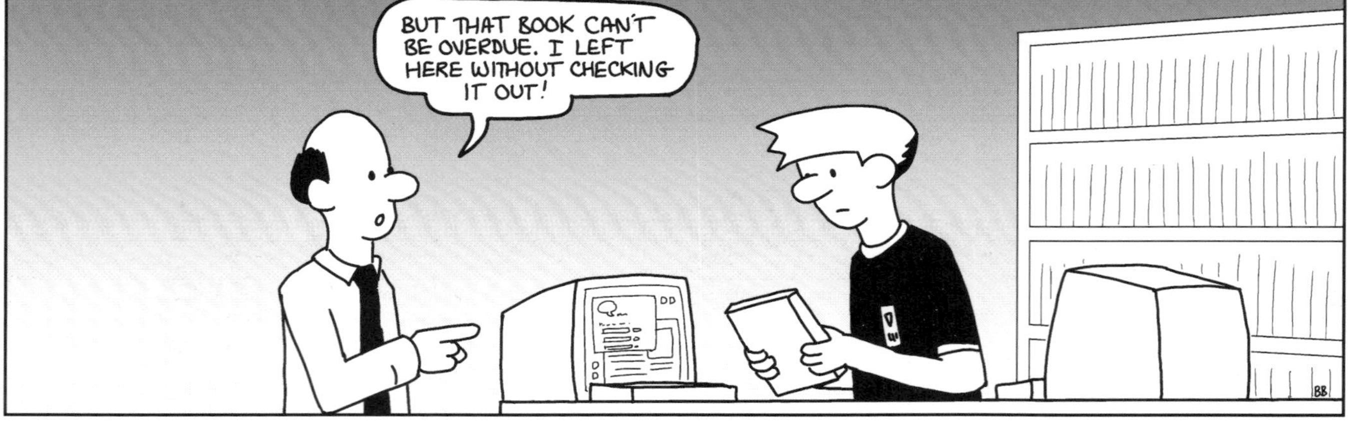
BUT THAT BOOK CAN'T BE OVERDUE. I LEFT HERE WITHOUT CHECKING IT OUT!
BB

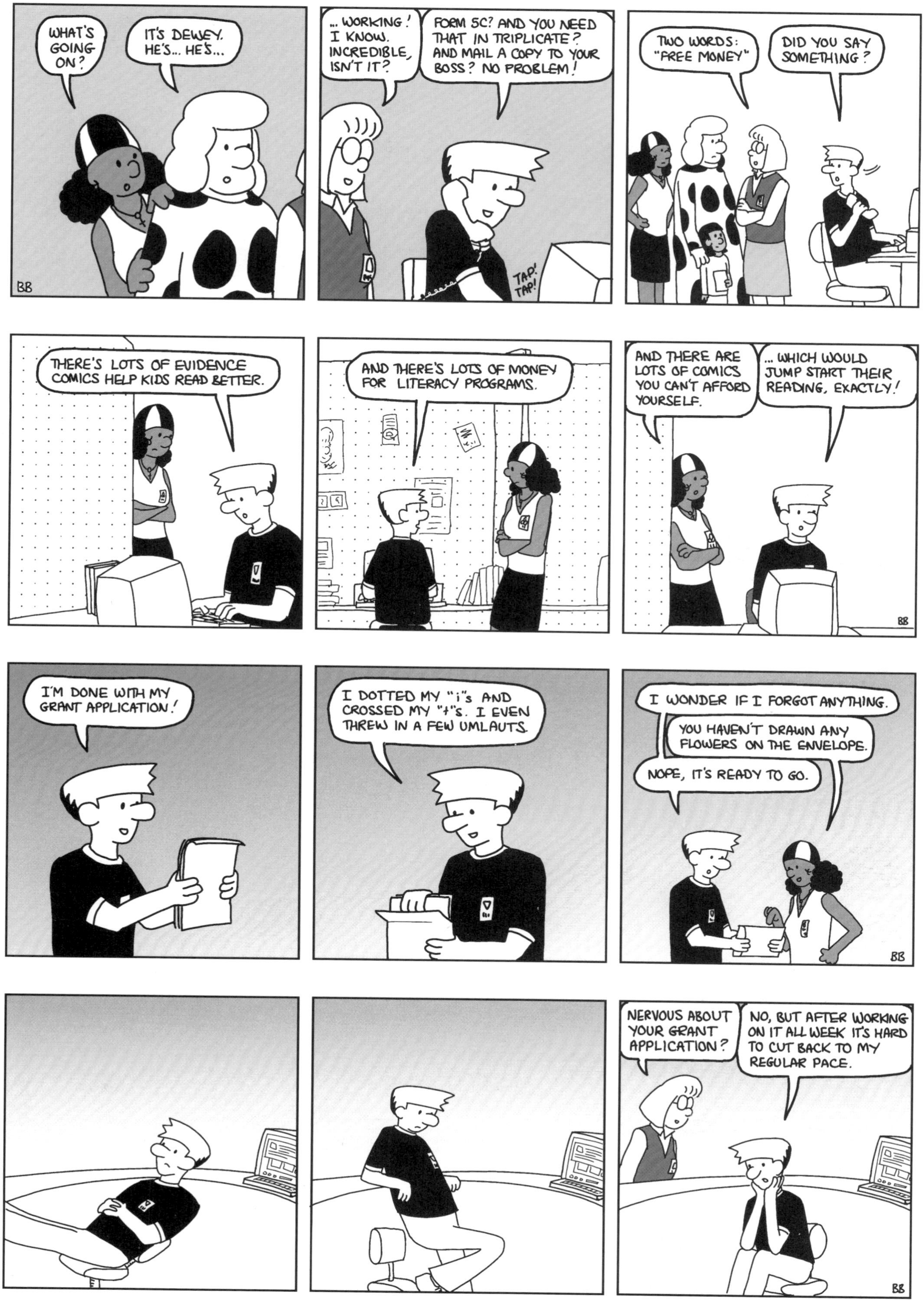
WHAT'S GOING ON?
IT'S DEWEY. HE'S... HE'S...
BB
... WORKING! I KNOW. INCREDIBLE, ISN'T IT?
FORM 5C? AND YOU NEED THAT IN TRIPLICATE? AND MAIL A COPY TO YOUR BOSS? NO PROBLEM!
TAP! TAP!
TWO WORDS: "FREE MONEY"
DID YOU SAY SOMETHING?
THERE'S LOTS OF EVIDENCE COMICS HELP KIDS READ BETTER.
AND THERE'S LOTS OF MONEY FOR LITERACY PROGRAMS.
AND THERE ARE LOTS OF COMICS YOU CAN'T AFFORD YOURSELF.
... WHICH WOULD JUMP START THEIR READING, EXACTLY!
BB
I'M DONE WITH MY GRANT APPLICATION!
I DOTTED MY "i"s AND CROSSED MY "t"s. I EVEN THREW IN A FEW UMLAUTS.
I WONDER IF I FORGOT ANYTHING.
YOU HAVEN'T DRAWN ANY FLOWERS ON THE ENVELOPE.
NOPE, IT'S READY TO GO.
BB
NERVOUS ABOUT YOUR GRANT APPLICATION?
NO, BUT AFTER WORKING ON IT ALL WEEK IT'S HARD TO CUT BACK TO MY REGULAR PACE.
BB

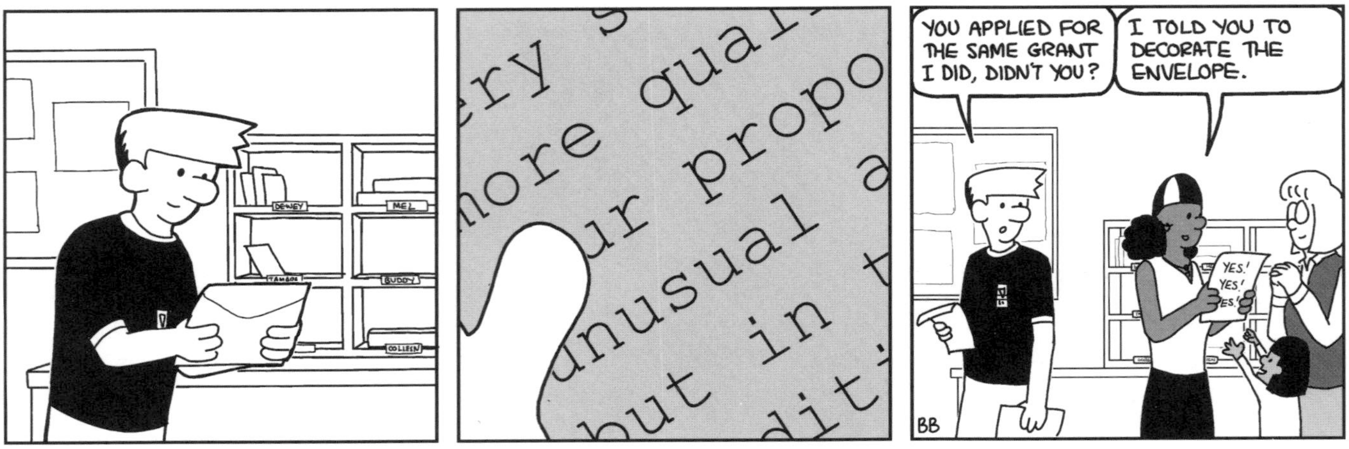
ery s
more qual
ur propo
unusual a
but in t
dit
YOU APPLIED FOR THE SAME GRANT I DID, DIDN'T YOU?
I TOLD YOU TO DECORATE THE ENVELOPE.
YES! YES!

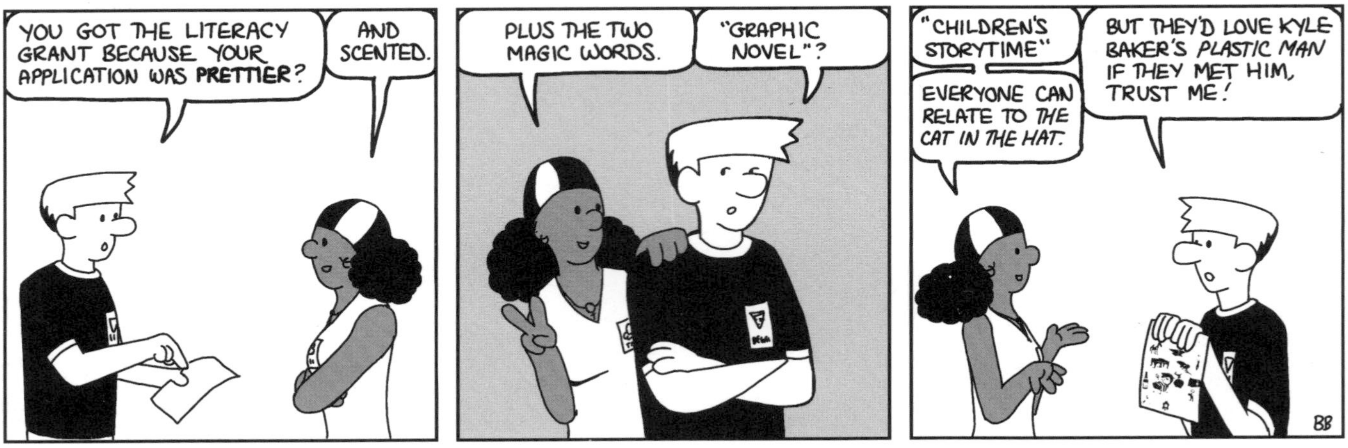
YOU GOT THE LITERACY GRANT BECAUSE YOUR APPLICATION WAS **PRETTIER**?
AND SCENTED.
PLUS THE TWO MAGIC WORDS.
"GRAPHIC NOVEL"?
"CHILDREN'S STORYTIME"
EVERYONE CAN RELATE TO *THE CAT IN THE HAT*.
BUT THEY'D LOVE KYLE BAKER'S *PLASTIC MAN* IF THEY MET HIM, TRUST ME!

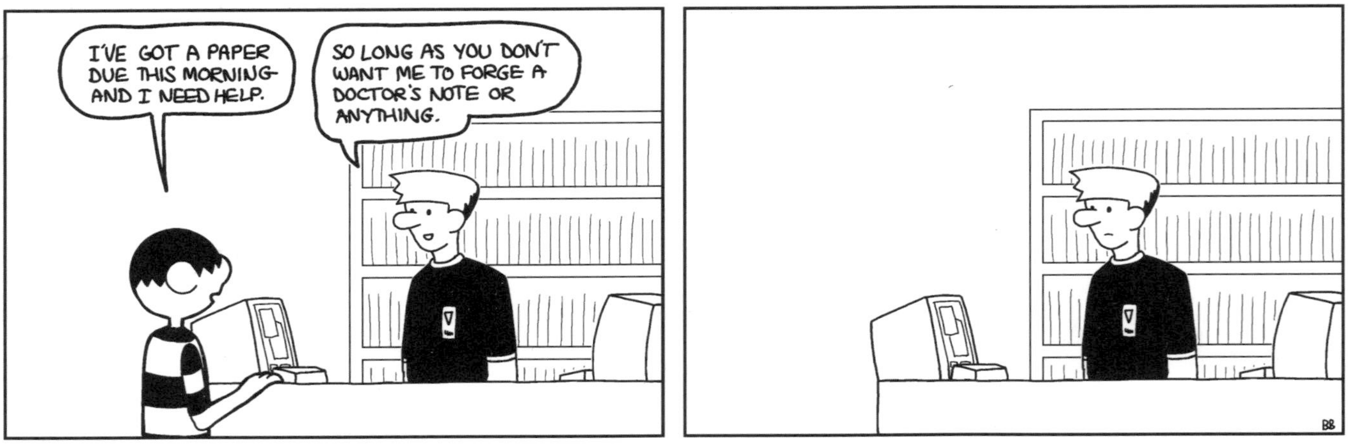
I'VE GOT A PAPER DUE THIS MORNING AND I NEED HELP.
SO LONG AS YOU DON'T WANT ME TO FORGE A DOCTOR'S NOTE OR ANYTHING.

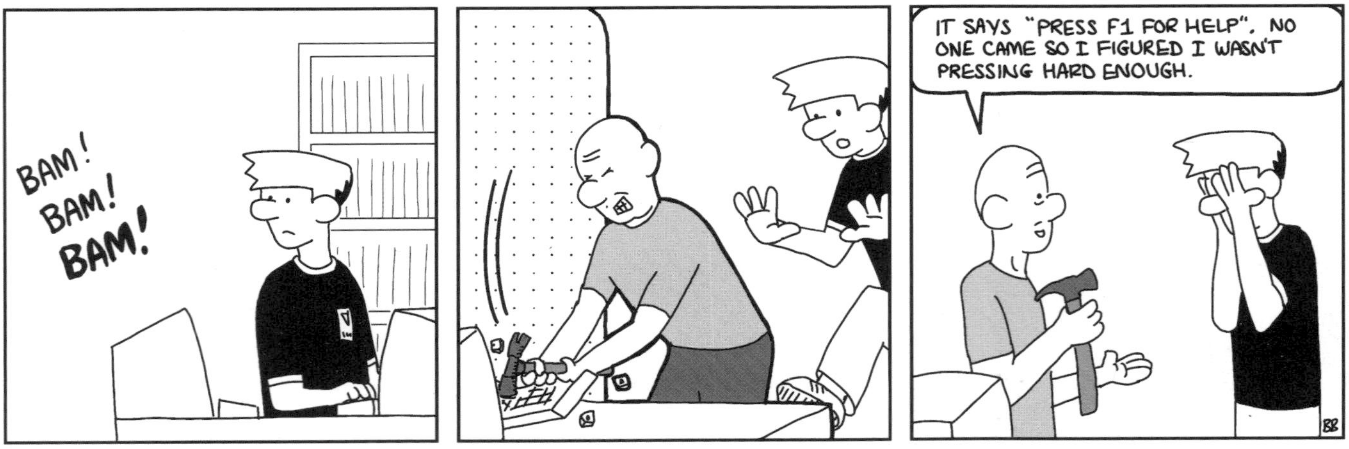
BAM! BAM! BAM!
IT SAYS "PRESS F1 FOR HELP". NO ONE CAME SO I FIGURED I WASN'T PRESSING HARD ENOUGH.

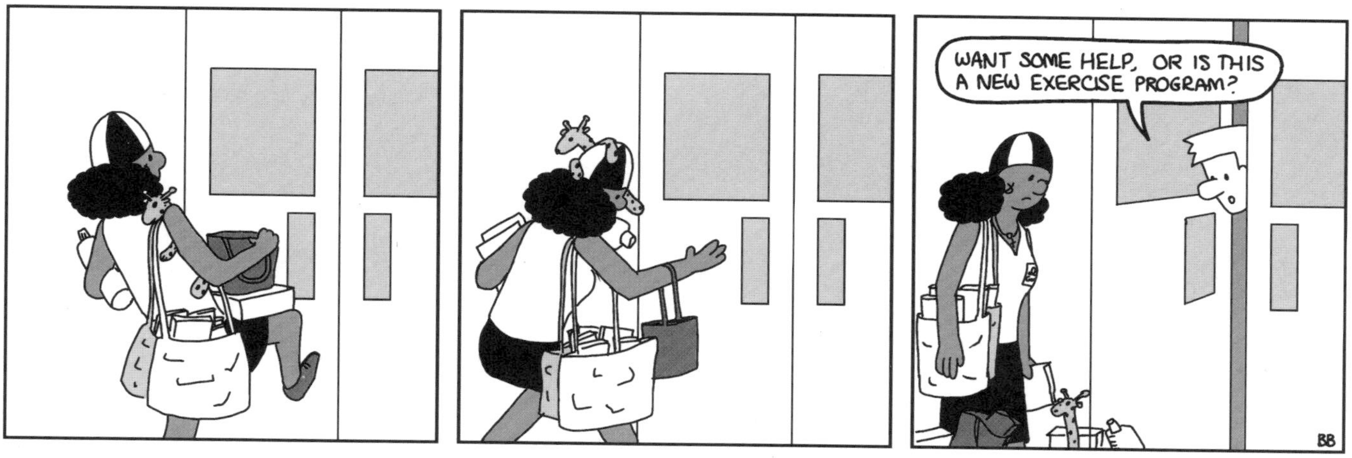
WANT SOME HELP, OR IS THIS A NEW EXERCISE PROGRAM?

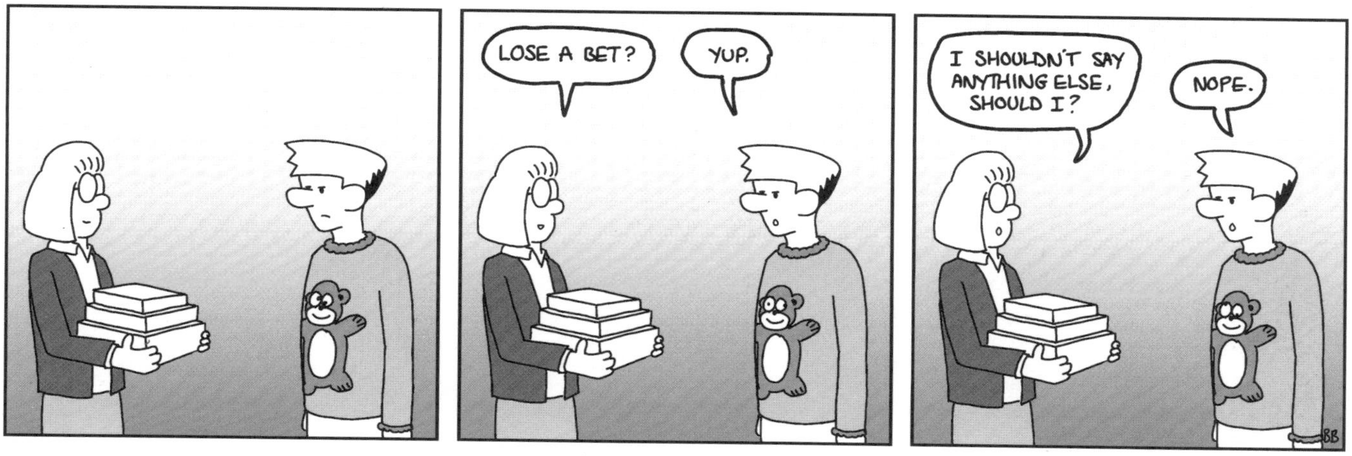
LOSE A BET?
YUP.
I SHOULDN'T SAY ANYTHING ELSE, SHOULD I?
NOPE.

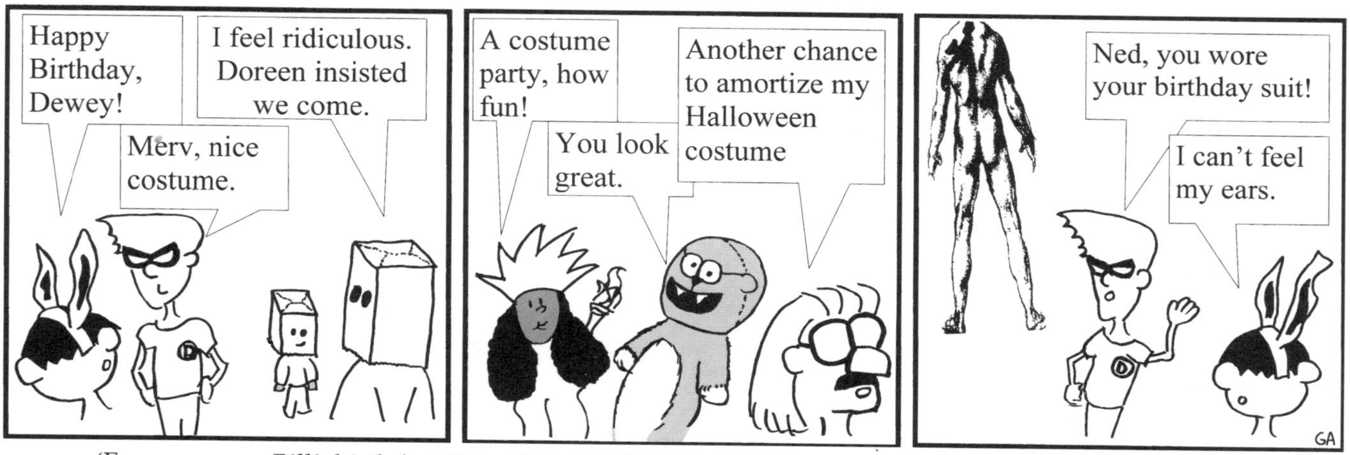
Happy Birthday, Dewey!
I feel ridiculous. Doreen insisted we come.
Merv, nice costume.
A costume party, how fun!
Another chance to amortize my Halloween costume
You look great.
Ned, you wore your birthday suit!
I can't feel my ears.

(Every year on Bill's birthday Gene draws and edits the strip. This year's was particularly surreal.)

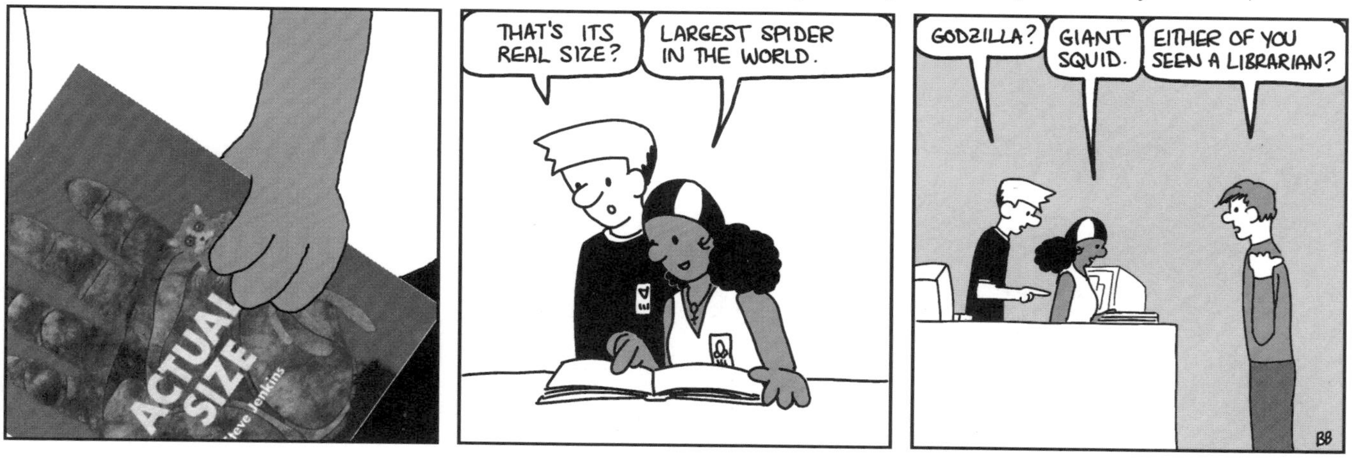
ACTUAL SIZE
THAT'S ITS REAL SIZE?
LARGEST SPIDER IN THE WORLD.
GODZILLA?
GIANT SQUID.
EITHER OF YOU SEEN A LIBRARIAN?

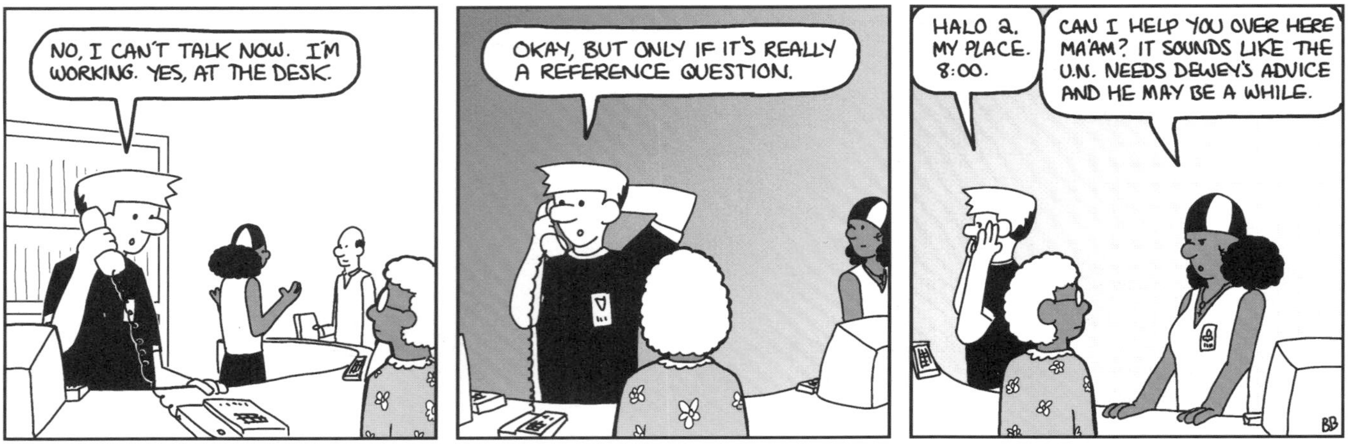
NO, I CAN'T TALK NOW. I'M WORKING. YES, AT THE DESK.
OKAY, BUT ONLY IF IT'S REALLY A REFERENCE QUESTION.
HALO 2. MY PLACE. 8:00.
CAN I HELP YOU OVER HERE MA'AM? IT SOUNDS LIKE THE U.N. NEEDS DEWEY'S ADVICE AND HE MAY BE A WHILE.
BB

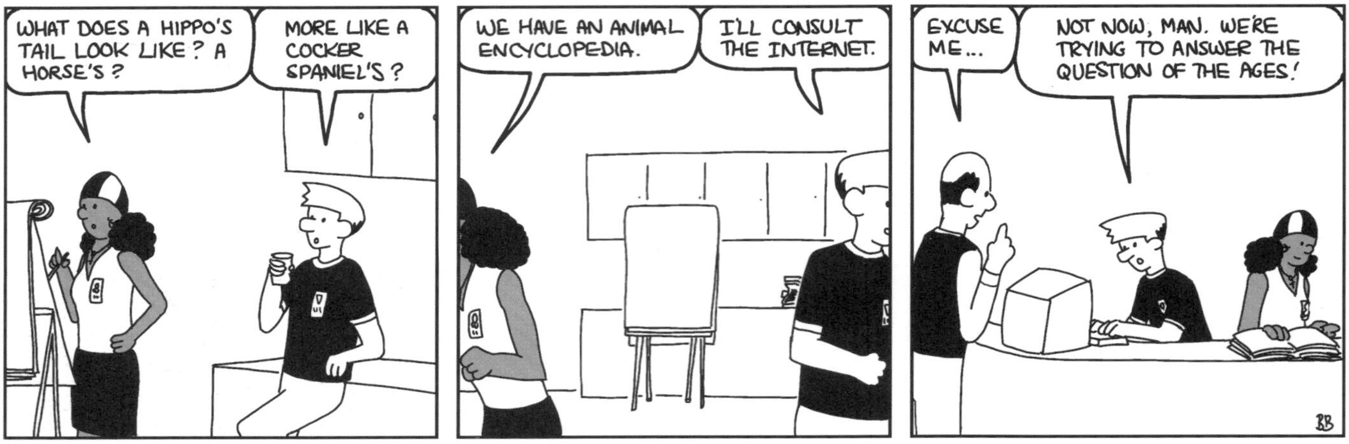
WHAT DOES A HIPPO'S TAIL LOOK LIKE? A HORSE'S?
MORE LIKE A COCKER SPANIEL'S?
WE HAVE AN ANIMAL ENCYCLOPEDIA.
I'LL CONSULT THE INTERNET.
EXCUSE ME...
NOT NOW, MAN. WE'RE TRYING TO ANSWER THE QUESTION OF THE AGES!
BB

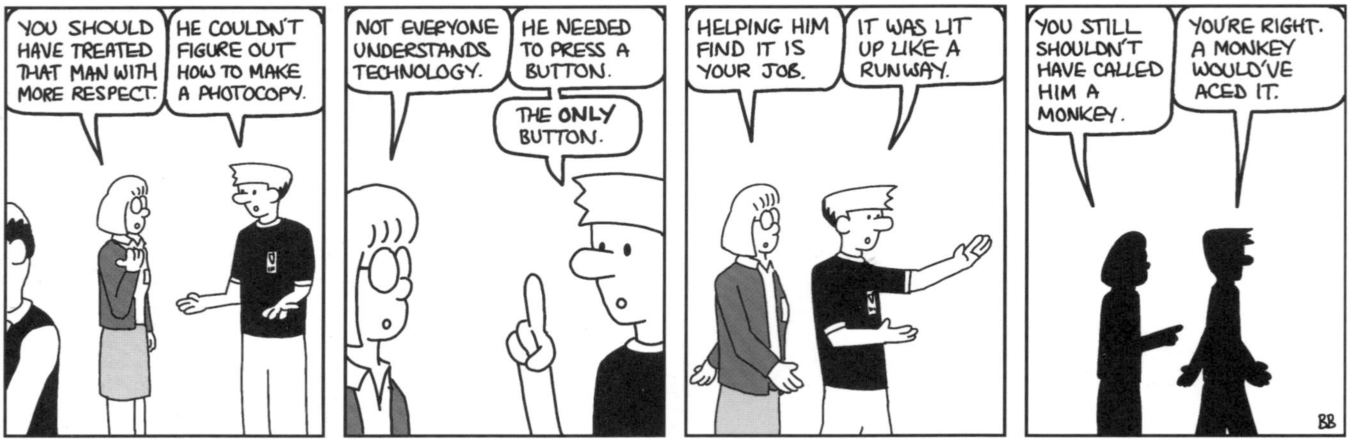
YOU SHOULD HAVE TREATED THAT MAN WITH MORE RESPECT.
HE COULDN'T FIGURE OUT HOW TO MAKE A PHOTOCOPY.
NOT EVERYONE UNDERSTANDS TECHNOLOGY.
HE NEEDED TO PRESS A BUTTON.
THE **ONLY** BUTTON.
HELPING HIM FIND IT IS YOUR JOB.
IT WAS LIT UP LIKE A RUNWAY.
YOU STILL SHOULDN'T HAVE CALLED HIM A MONKEY.
YOU'RE RIGHT. A MONKEY WOULD'VE ACED IT.
BB

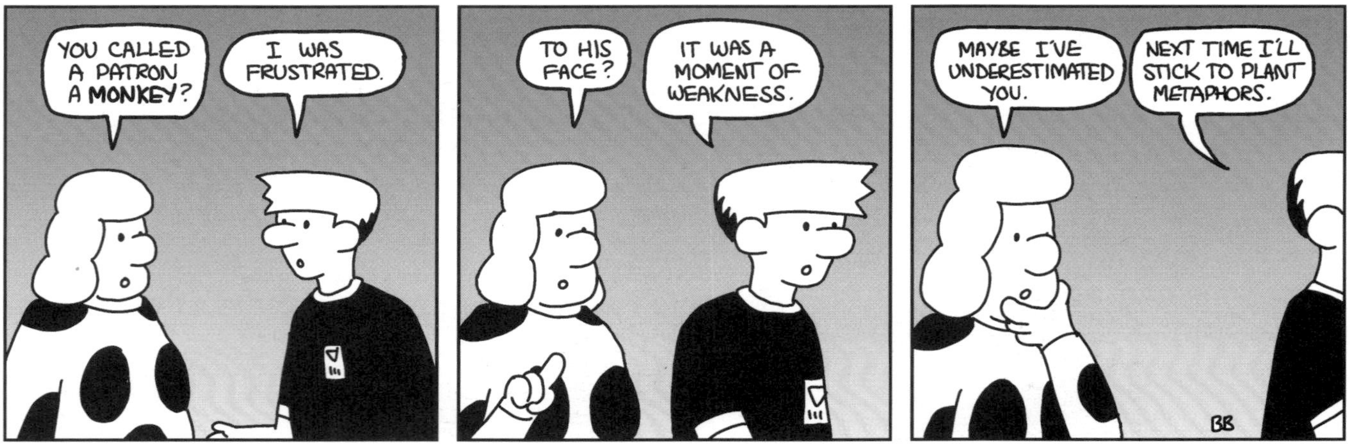
YOU CALLED A PATRON A **MONKEY**?
I WAS FRUSTRATED.
TO HIS FACE?
IT WAS A MOMENT OF WEAKNESS.
MAYBE I'VE UNDERESTIMATED YOU.
NEXT TIME I'LL STICK TO PLANT METAPHORS.
BB

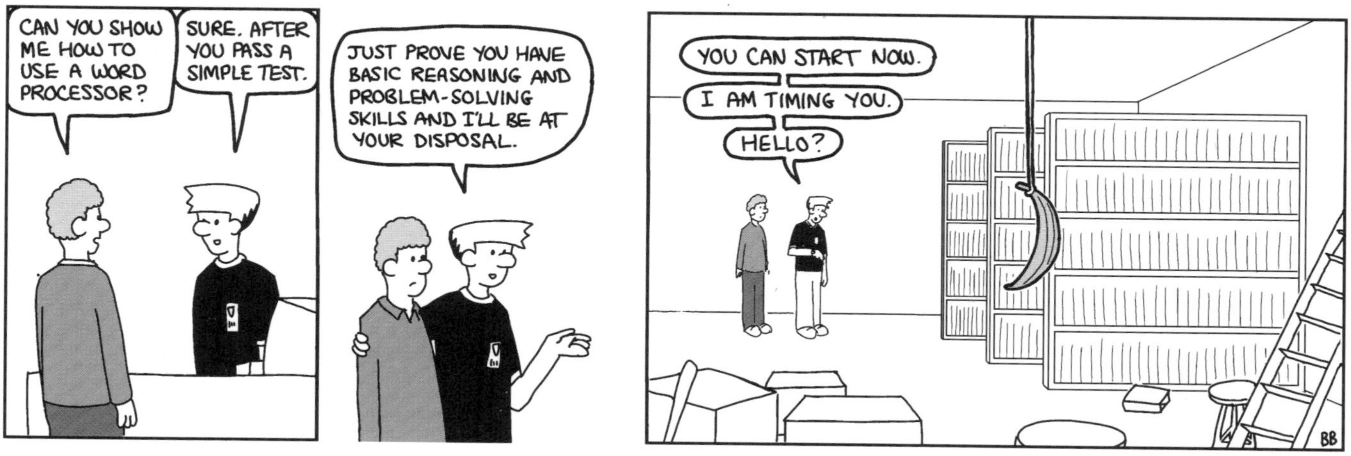
CAN YOU SHOW ME HOW TO USE A WORD PROCESSOR?
SURE. AFTER YOU PASS A SIMPLE TEST.
JUST PROVE YOU HAVE BASIC REASONING AND PROBLEM-SOLVING SKILLS AND I'LL BE AT YOUR DISPOSAL.
YOU CAN START NOW.
I AM TIMING YOU.
HELLO?
BB

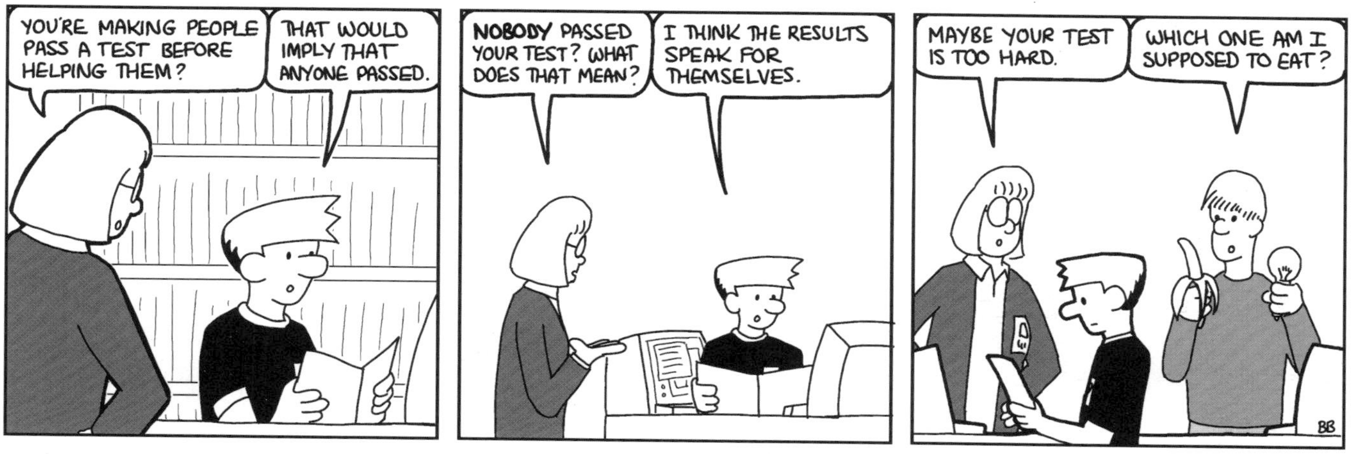
YOU'RE MAKING PEOPLE PASS A TEST BEFORE HELPING THEM?
THAT WOULD IMPLY THAT ANYONE PASSED.
NOBODY PASSED YOUR TEST? WHAT DOES THAT MEAN?
I THINK THE RESULTS SPEAK FOR THEMSELVES.
MAYBE YOUR TEST IS TOO HARD.
WHICH ONE AM I SUPPOSED TO EAT?
BB

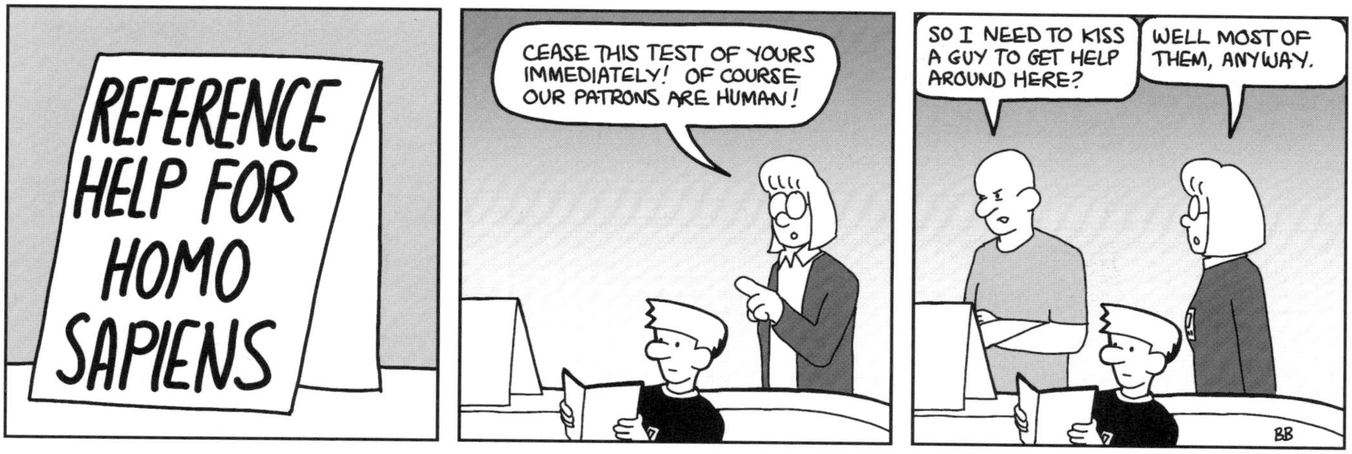
REFERENCE HELP FOR HOMO SAPIENS
CEASE THIS TEST OF YOURS IMMEDIATELY! OF COURSE OUR PATRONS ARE HUMAN!
SO I NEED TO KISS A GUY TO GET HELP AROUND HERE?
WELL MOST OF THEM, ANYWAY.
BB

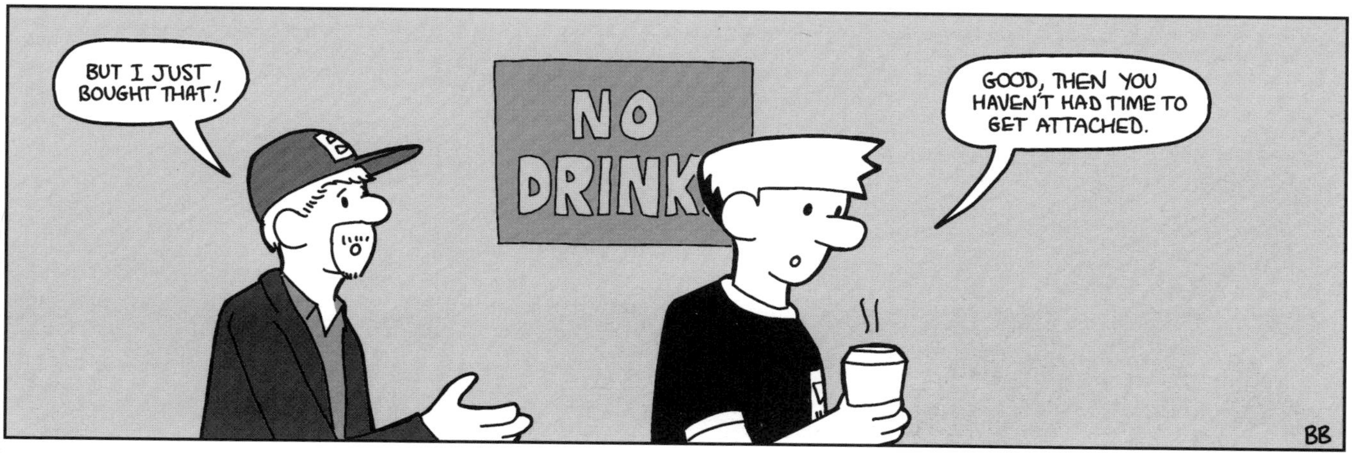
BUT I JUST BOUGHT THAT!
NO DRINK
GOOD, THEN YOU HAVEN'T HAD TIME TO GET ATTACHED.
BB

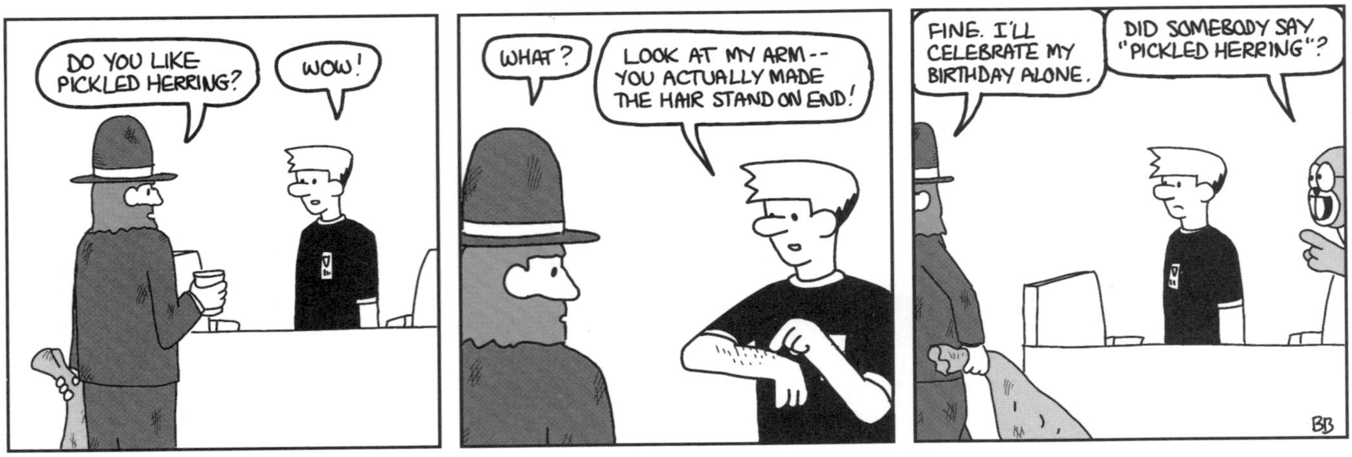
DO YOU LIKE PICKLED HERRING?
WOW!
WHAT?
LOOK AT MY ARM -- YOU ACTUALLY MADE THE HAIR STAND ON END!
FINE. I'LL CELEBRATE MY BIRTHDAY ALONE.
DID SOMEBODY SAY "PICKLED HERRING"?
BB

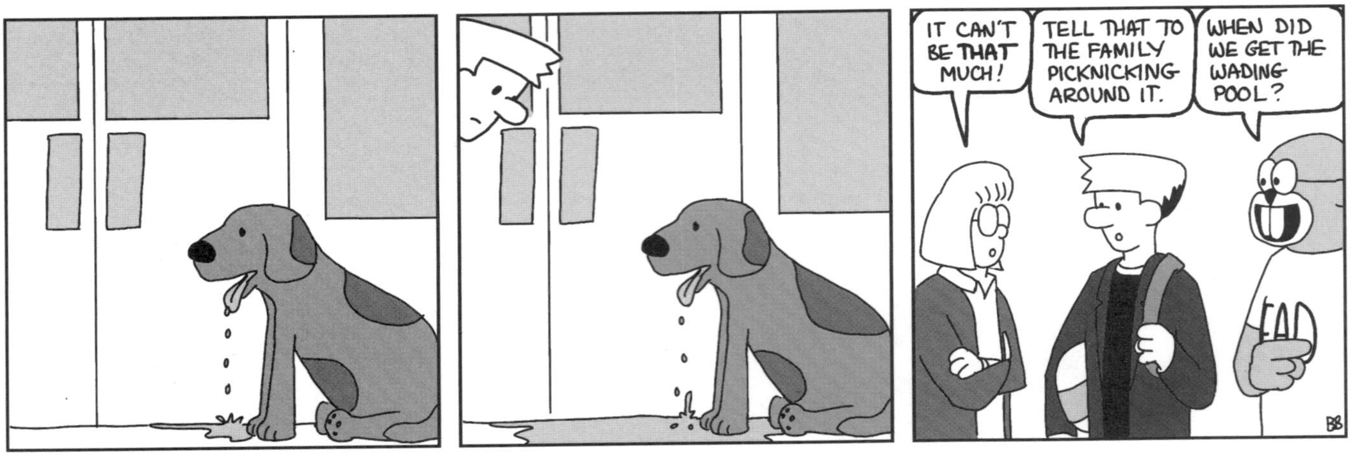
IT CAN'T BE **THAT** MUCH!
TELL THAT TO THE FAMILY PICKNICKING AROUND IT.
WHEN DID WE GET THE WADING POOL?
FAD
BB

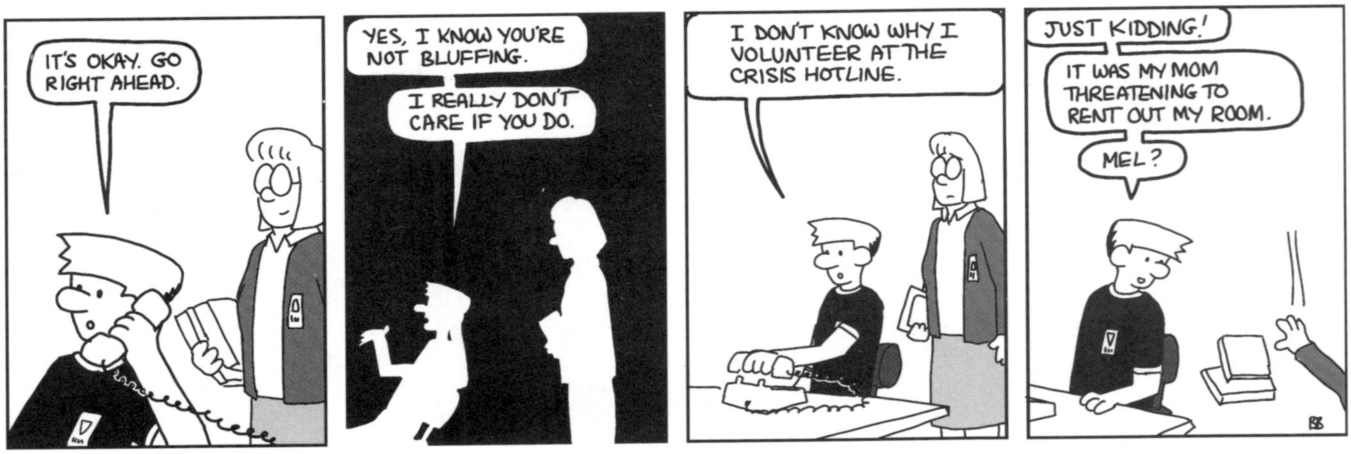
IT'S OKAY. GO RIGHT AHEAD.
YES, I KNOW YOU'RE NOT BLUFFING.
I REALLY DON'T CARE IF YOU DO.
I DON'T KNOW WHY I VOLUNTEER AT THE CRISIS HOTLINE.
JUST KIDDING!
IT WAS MY MOM THREATENING TO RENT OUT MY ROOM.
MEL?
BB

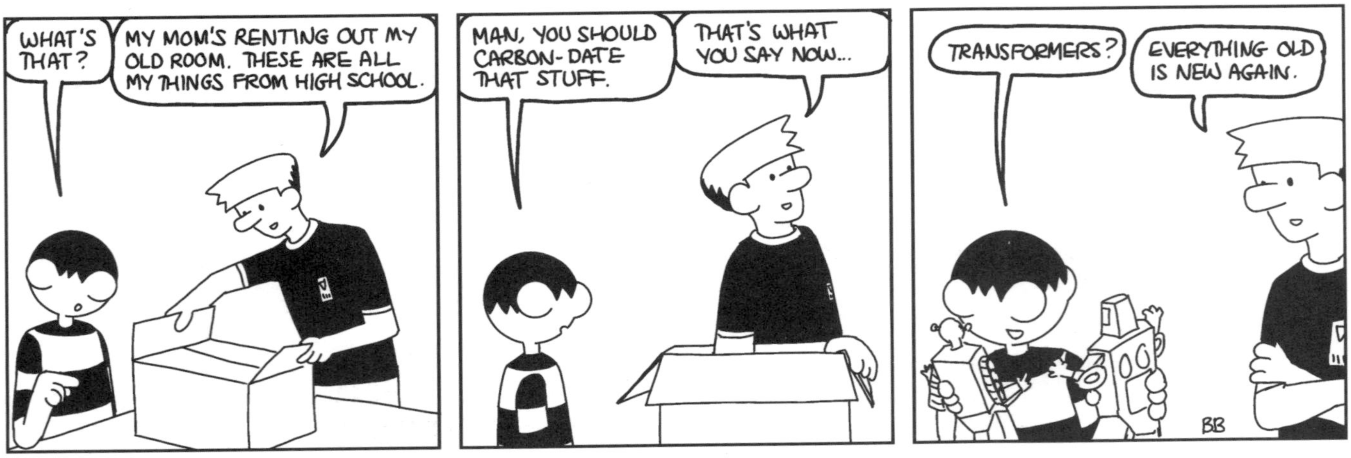
WHAT'S THAT?
MY MOM'S RENTING OUT MY OLD ROOM. THESE ARE ALL MY THINGS FROM HIGH SCHOOL.
MAN, YOU SHOULD CARBON-DATE THAT STUFF.
THAT'S WHAT YOU SAY NOW...
TRANSFORMERS?
EVERYTHING OLD IS NEW AGAIN.
BB

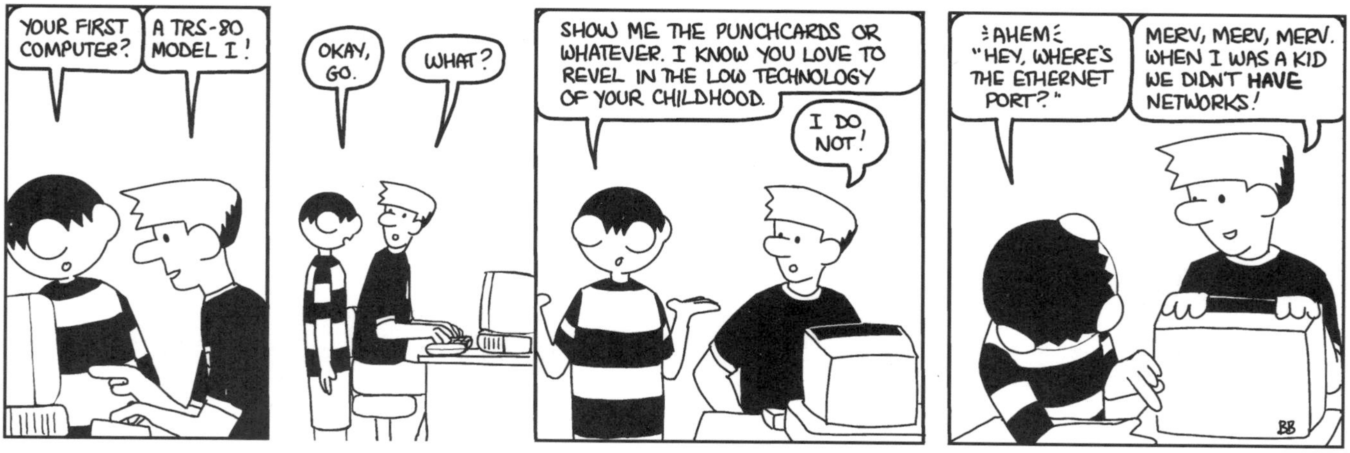
YOUR FIRST COMPUTER?
A TRS-80 MODEL I!
OKAY, GO.
WHAT?
SHOW ME THE PUNCHCARDS OR WHATEVER. I KNOW YOU LOVE TO REVEL IN THE LOW TECHNOLOGY OF YOUR CHILDHOOD.
I DO NOT!
AHEM "HEY, WHERE'S THE ETHERNET PORT?"
MERV, MERV, MERV. WHEN I WAS A KID WE DIDN'T **HAVE** NETWORKS!
BB

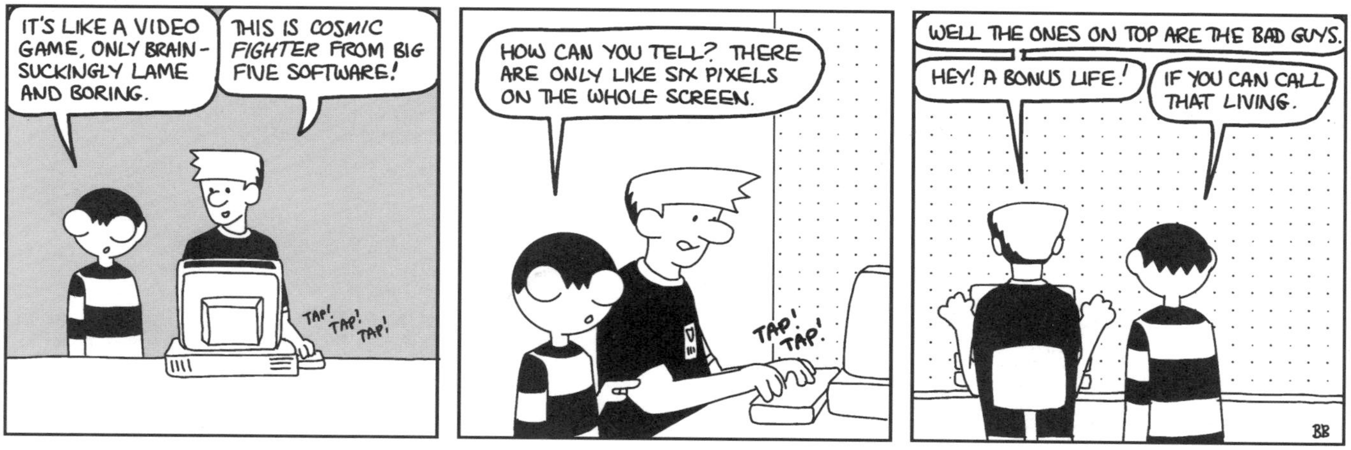
IT'S LIKE A VIDEO GAME, ONLY BRAIN-SUCKINGLY LAME AND BORING.
THIS IS *COSMIC FIGHTER* FROM BIG FIVE SOFTWARE!
TAP! TAP! TAP!
HOW CAN YOU TELL? THERE ARE ONLY LIKE SIX PIXELS ON THE WHOLE SCREEN.
TAP! TAP!
WELL THE ONES ON TOP ARE THE BAD GUYS.
HEY! A BONUS LIFE!
IF YOU CAN CALL THAT LIVING.
BB

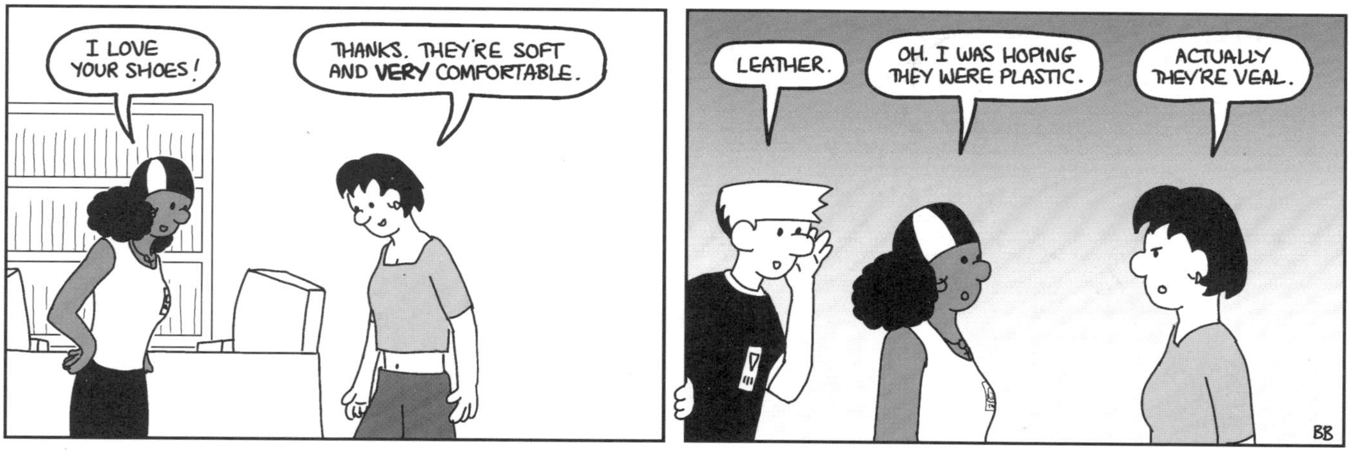
I LOVE YOUR SHOES!
THANKS. THEY'RE SOFT AND **VERY** COMFORTABLE.
LEATHER.
OH. I WAS HOPING THEY WERE PLASTIC.
ACTUALLY THEY'RE VEAL.
BB

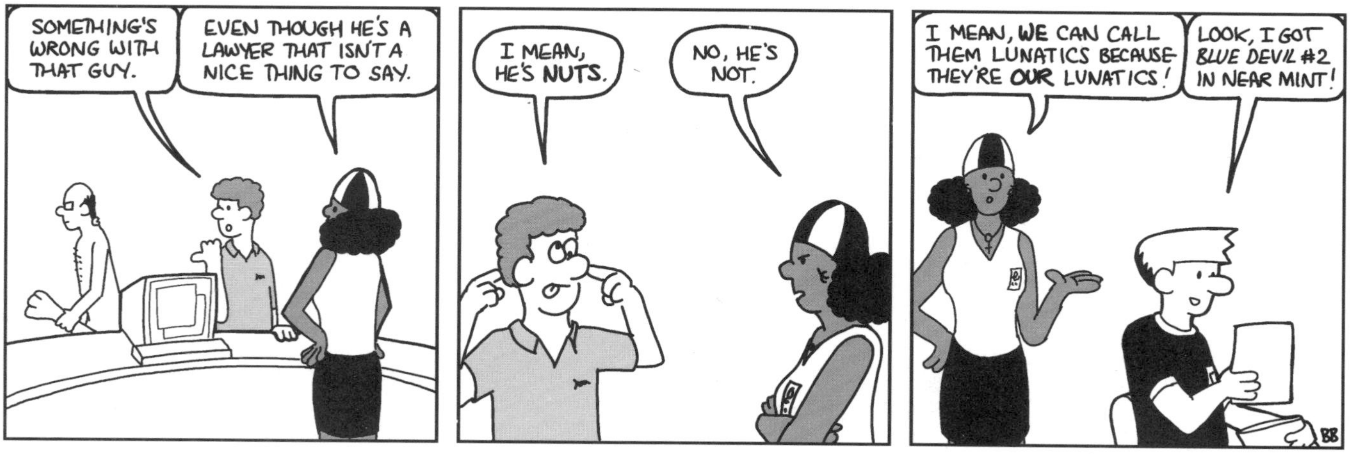
SOMETHING'S WRONG WITH THAT GUY.
EVEN THOUGH HE'S A LAWYER THAT ISN'T A NICE THING TO SAY.
I MEAN, HE'S **NUTS**.
NO, HE'S NOT.
I MEAN, **WE** CAN CALL THEM LUNATICS BECAUSE THEY'RE **OUR** LUNATICS!
LOOK, I GOT *BLUE DEVIL* #2 IN NEAR MINT!
BB

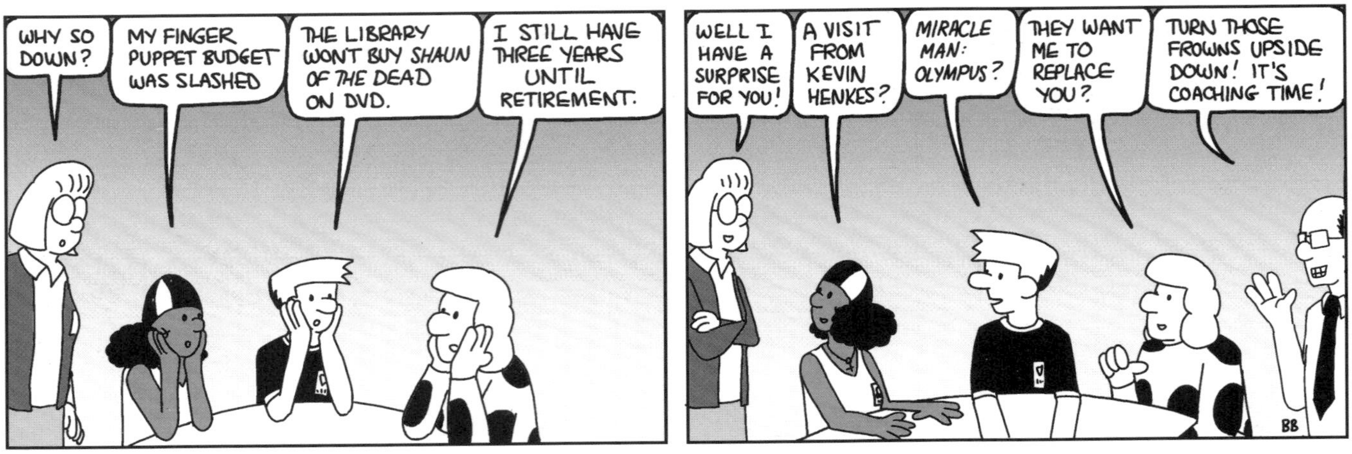
WHY SO DOWN?
MY FINGER PUPPET BUDGET WAS SLASHED
THE LIBRARY WON'T BUY *SHAUN OF THE DEAD* ON DVD.
I STILL HAVE THREE YEARS UNTIL RETIREMENT.
WELL I HAVE A SURPRISE FOR YOU!
A VISIT FROM KEVIN HENKES?
MIRACLE MAN: OLYMPUS?
THEY WANT ME TO REPLACE YOU?
TURN THOSE FROWNS UPSIDE DOWN! IT'S COACHING TIME!
BB

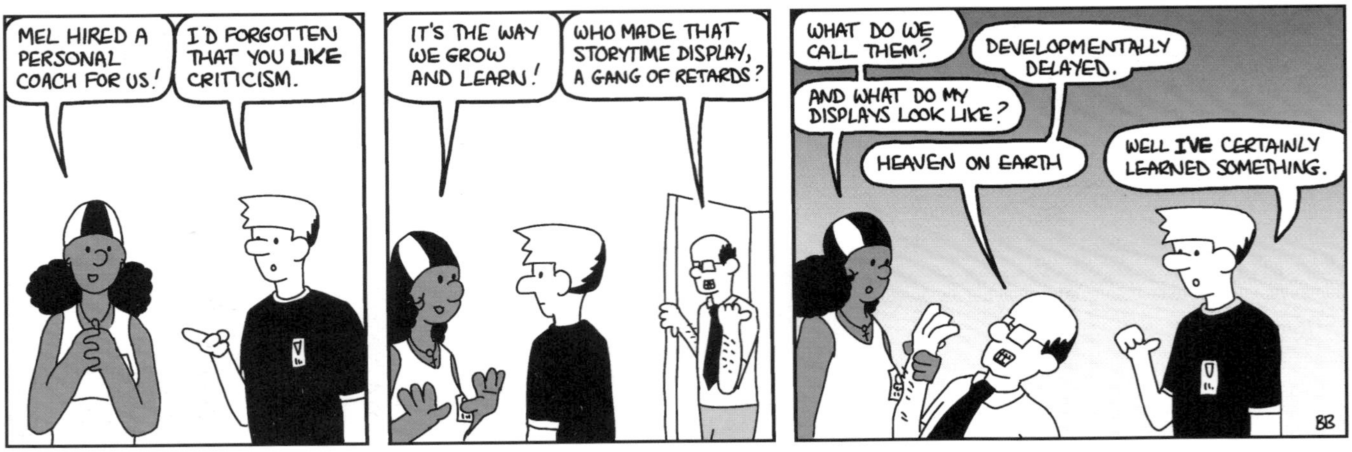
MEL HIRED A PERSONAL COACH FOR US!
I'D FORGOTTEN THAT YOU **LIKE** CRITICISM.
IT'S THE WAY WE GROW AND LEARN!
WHO MADE THAT STORYTIME DISPLAY, A GANG OF RETARDS?
WHAT DO WE CALL THEM?
DEVELOPMENTALLY DELAYED.
AND WHAT DO MY DISPLAYS LOOK LIKE?
HEAVEN ON EARTH
WELL **I'VE** CERTAINLY LEARNED SOMETHING.
BB

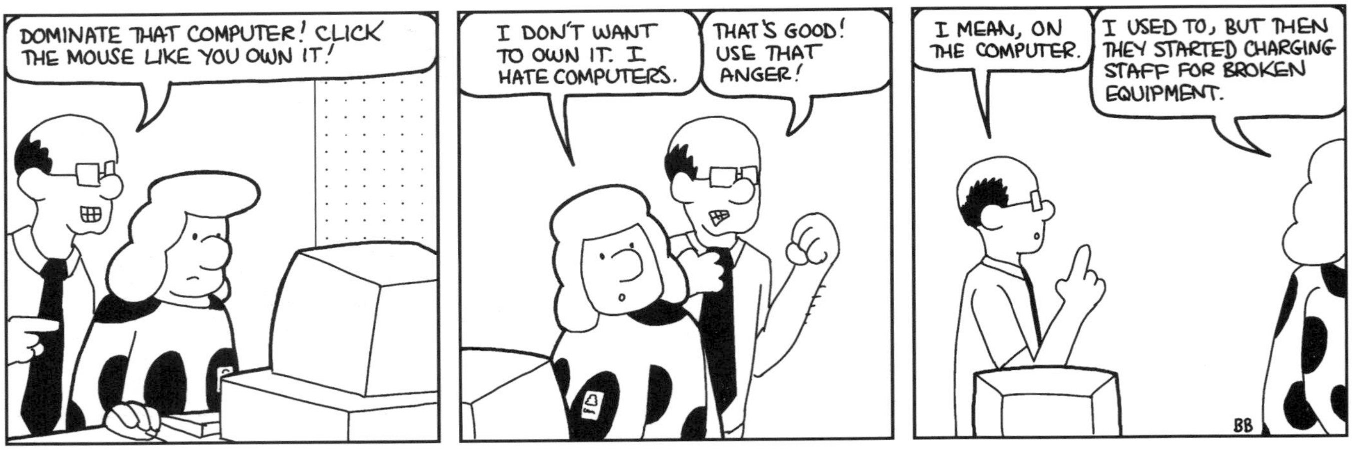
DOMINATE THAT COMPUTER! CLICK THE MOUSE LIKE YOU OWN IT!
I DON'T WANT TO OWN IT. I HATE COMPUTERS.
THAT'S GOOD! USE THAT ANGER!
I MEAN, ON THE COMPUTER.
I USED TO, BUT THEN THEY STARTED CHARGING STAFF FOR BROKEN EQUIPMENT.
BB

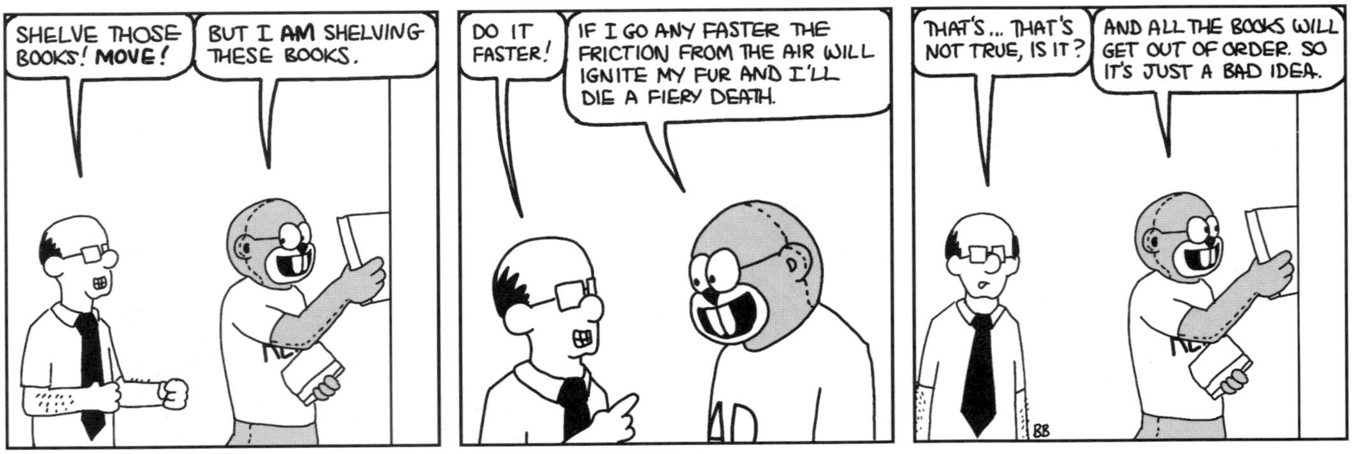
SHELVE THOSE BOOKS! **MOVE**!
BUT I **AM** SHELVING THESE BOOKS.
DO IT FASTER!
IF I GO ANY FASTER THE FRICTION FROM THE AIR WILL IGNITE MY FUR AND I'LL DIE A FIERY DEATH.
THAT'S... THAT'S NOT TRUE, IS IT?
AND ALL THE BOOKS WILL GET OUT OF ORDER. SO IT'S JUST A BAD IDEA.
BB

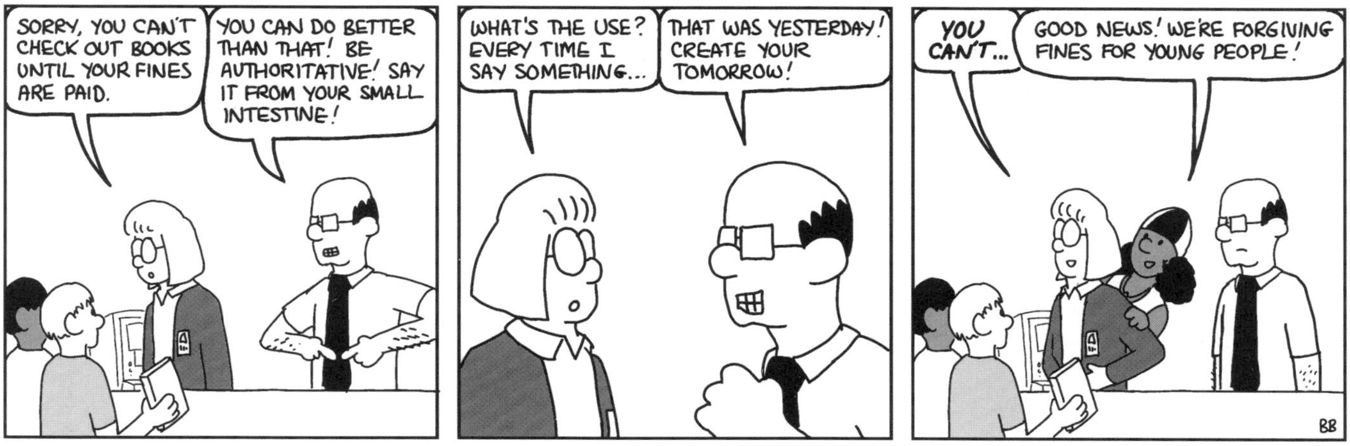
SORRY, YOU CAN'T CHECK OUT BOOKS UNTIL YOUR FINES ARE PAID.
YOU CAN DO BETTER THAN THAT! BE AUTHORITATIVE! SAY IT FROM YOUR SMALL INTESTINE!
WHAT'S THE USE? EVERY TIME I SAY SOMETHING...
THAT WAS YESTERDAY! CREATE YOUR TOMORROW!
YOU CAN'T...
GOOD NEWS! WE'RE FORGIVING FINES FOR YOUNG PEOPLE!
BB

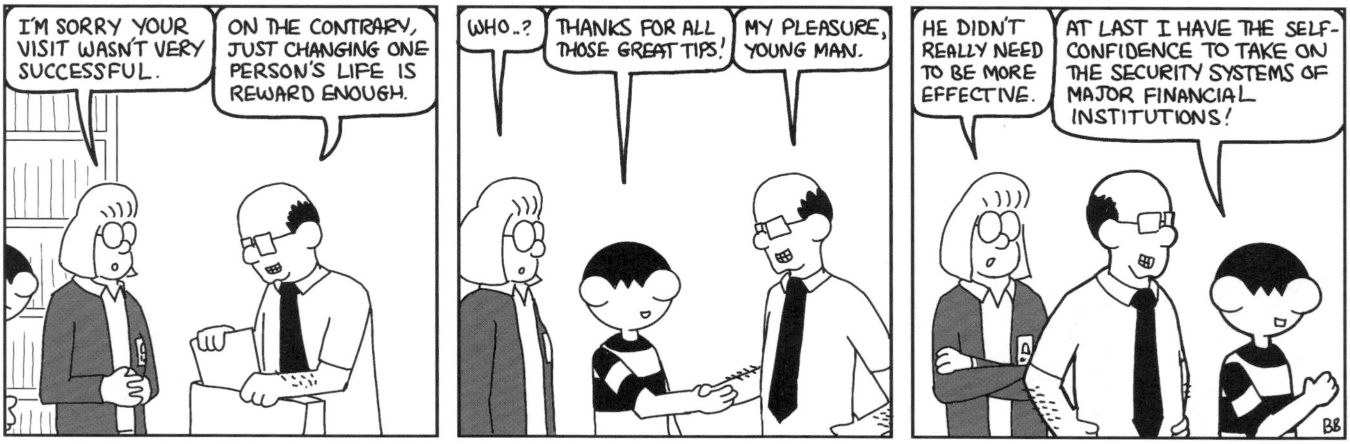
I'M SORRY YOUR VISIT WASN'T VERY SUCCESSFUL.
ON THE CONTRARY, JUST CHANGING ONE PERSON'S LIFE IS REWARD ENOUGH.
WHO..?
THANKS FOR ALL THOSE GREAT TIPS!
MY PLEASURE, YOUNG MAN.
HE DIDN'T REALLY NEED TO BE MORE EFFECTIVE.
AT LAST I HAVE THE SELF-CONFIDENCE TO TAKE ON THE SECURITY SYSTEMS OF MAJOR FINANCIAL INSTITUTIONS!
BB

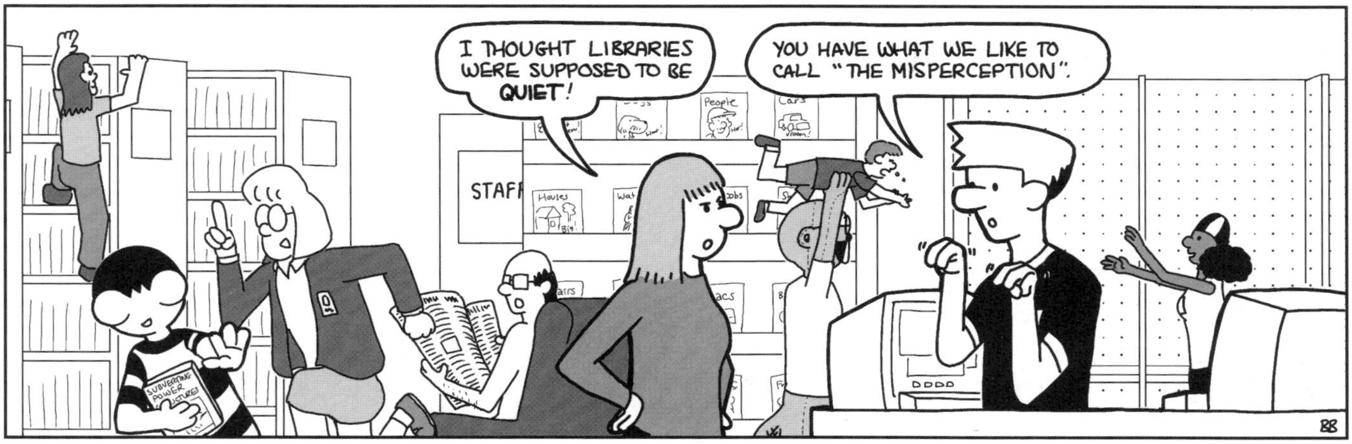
I THOUGHT LIBRARIES WERE SUPPOSED TO BE **QUIET**!
YOU HAVE WHAT WE LIKE TO CALL "THE MISPERCEPTION".
STAFF
BB

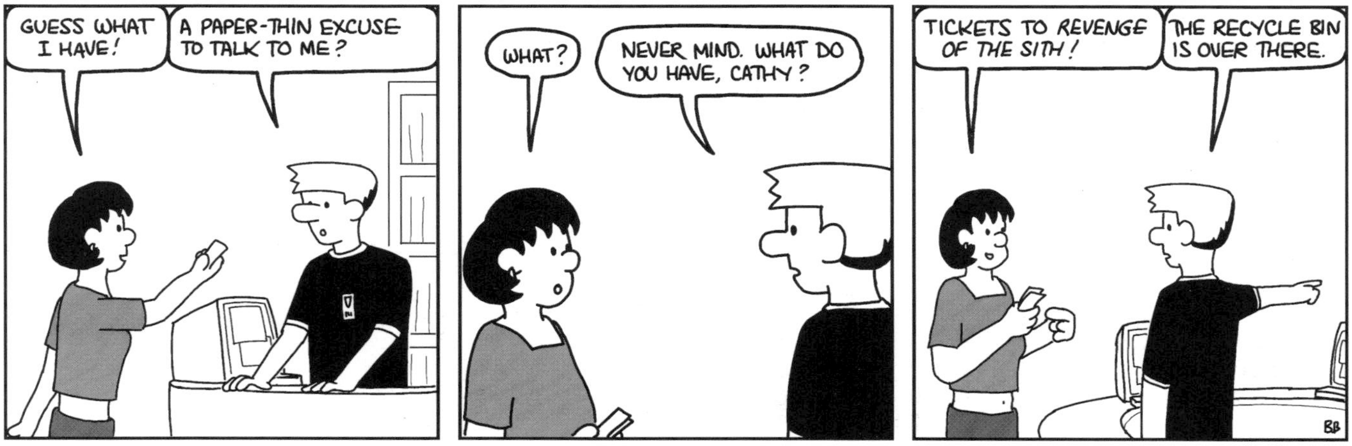
GUESS WHAT I HAVE!
A PAPER-THIN EXCUSE TO TALK TO ME?
WHAT?
NEVER MIND. WHAT DO YOU HAVE, CATHY?
TICKETS TO *REVENGE OF THE SITH*!
THE RECYCLE BIN IS OVER THERE.
BB

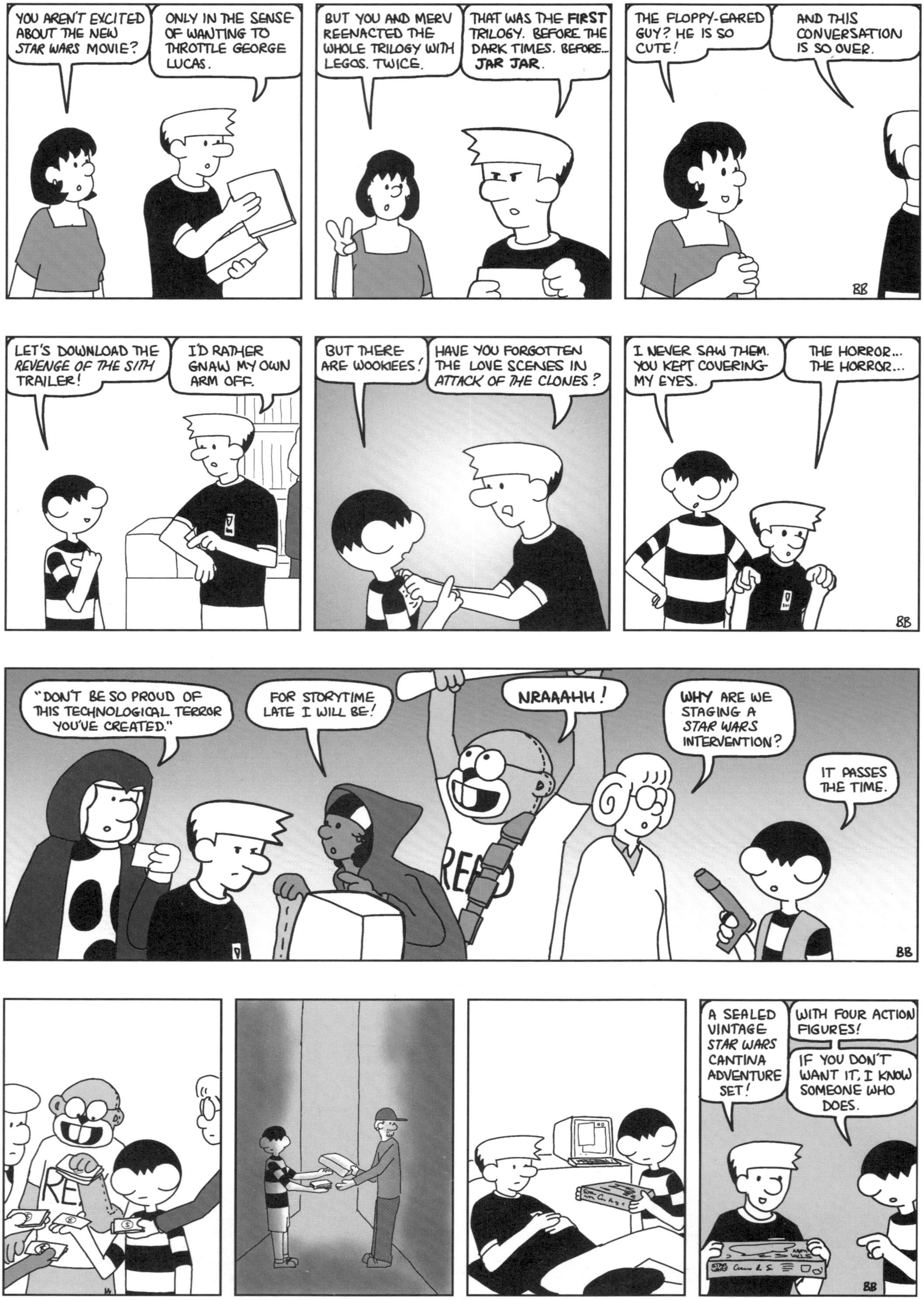
YOU AREN'T EXCITED ABOUT THE NEW STAR WARS MOVIE?
ONLY IN THE SENSE OF WANTING TO THROTTLE GEORGE LUCAS.
BUT YOU AND MERV REENACTED THE WHOLE TRILOGY WITH LEGOS. TWICE.
THAT WAS THE FIRST TRILOGY. BEFORE THE DARK TIMES. BEFORE... JAR JAR.
THE FLOPPY-EARED GUY? HE IS SO CUTE!
AND THIS CONVERSATION IS SO OVER.
BB
LET'S DOWNLOAD THE REVENGE OF THE SITH TRAILER!
I'D RATHER GNAW MY OWN ARM OFF.
BUT THERE ARE WOOKIEES!
HAVE YOU FORGOTTEN THE LOVE SCENES IN ATTACK OF THE CLONES?
I NEVER SAW THEM. YOU KEPT COVERING MY EYES.
THE HORROR... THE HORROR...
BB
"DON'T BE SO PROUD OF THIS TECHNOLOGICAL TERROR YOU'VE CREATED."
FOR STORYTIME LATE I WILL BE!
NRAAAHH!
WHY ARE WE STAGING A STAR WARS INTERVENTION?
IT PASSES THE TIME.
BB
A SEALED VINTAGE STAR WARS CANTINA ADVENTURE SET!
WITH FOUR ACTION FIGURES!
IF YOU DON'T WANT IT, I KNOW SOMEONE WHO DOES.
BB

Panel 1: I HEARD YOU'VE LIGHTENED UP ABOUT EPISODE III. / I CAN'T MISS THE ORIGIN OF DARTH VADER, CAN I?

Panel 2: SO WE'RE ON FOR MAY 19TH? / OKAY, BUT IT'S NOT A DATE. IT'S A SHARED MEDIA EXPERIENCE.

Panel 3: HEY, WHERE'S THE REST? / A "SHARED MEDIA EXPERIENCE" IS WORTH HALF.

LIBRARY TIP #27: DON'T TAKE IT PERSONALLY

Panel 4: THE CATALOG WON'T WORK FOR ME. / IT WON'T WORK FOR ANYBODY. THE SYSTEM'S DOWN.

Panel 5: YOU MUST REALLY HATE ME. / LOOK, MINE'S DOWN TOO.

Panel 6: THIS IS BECAUSE I LOST *THE FIVE PEOPLE YOU MEET IN HEAVEN*, ISN'T IT? / ACTUALLY YOU GOT BONUS POINTS FOR THAT.

Panel 7: I'M SORRY, YOU CAN'T RENEW THEM AGAIN.

Panel 8: YES, THAT IS A LOT OF DVD'S TO WATCH BEFORE TOMORROW.

Panel 9: MAYBE IF YOU HAD A T.V. IN EVERY ROOM? / NO PROBLEM, I'M HERE TO HELP.

Panel 10: THIS WOMAN SAYS YOU TOLD HER HUSBAND TO BUY A T.V. FOR EVERY ROOM IN THEIR HOUSE. / IT WAS A SUGGESTION.

Panel 11: YOU'RE AN AUTHORITY FIGURE! / REALLY? / LOAN ME $200.

Panel 12: DON'T BE SILLY. / SO, NOT THAT MUCH OF AN AUTHORITY FIGURE.

Conference Tips

Unshelved is read by lots of different kinds of people: booksellers, book lovers, comic fans, IT geeks, folks in service jobs of all kinds, and Bill's wife (but not Gene's - she doesn't think it's funny). Still, in the end this is a comic strip set in a library. If we want to go to one place where we are the most likely to encounter fans it's a library convention. We attend quite a few every year, giving talks, signing books, and selling our terribly clever merchandise. Somewhere along the line we established a tradition of providing custom strips for *CogNotes*, the daily newspaper of the American Library Association meetings. Here are the past year's.

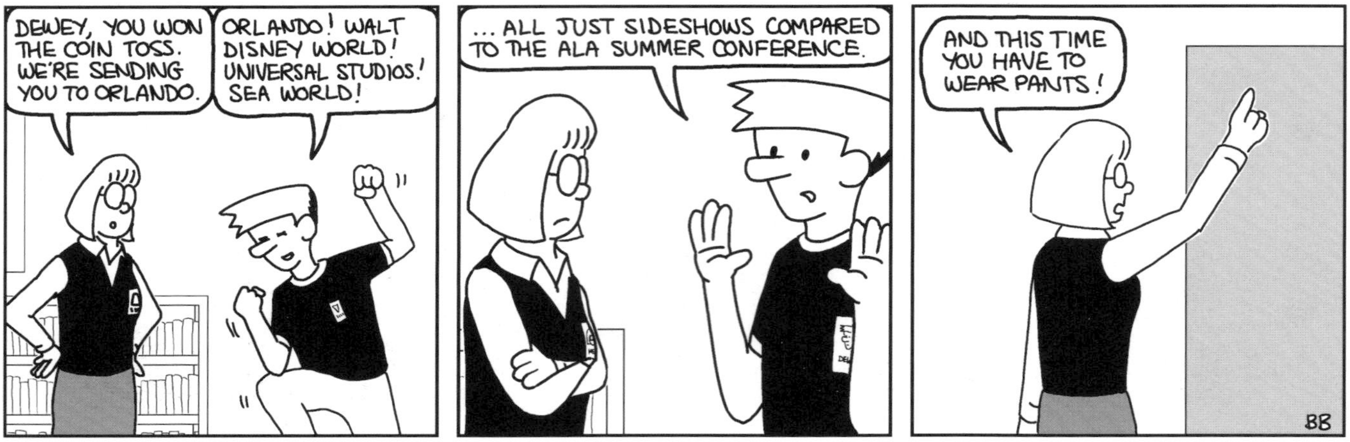
DEWEY, YOU WON THE COIN TOSS. WE'RE SENDING YOU TO ORLANDO.
ORLANDO! WALT DISNEY WORLD! UNIVERSAL STUDIOS! SEA WORLD!
... ALL JUST SIDESHOWS COMPARED TO THE ALA SUMMER CONFERENCE.
AND THIS TIME YOU HAVE TO WEAR PANTS!
BB

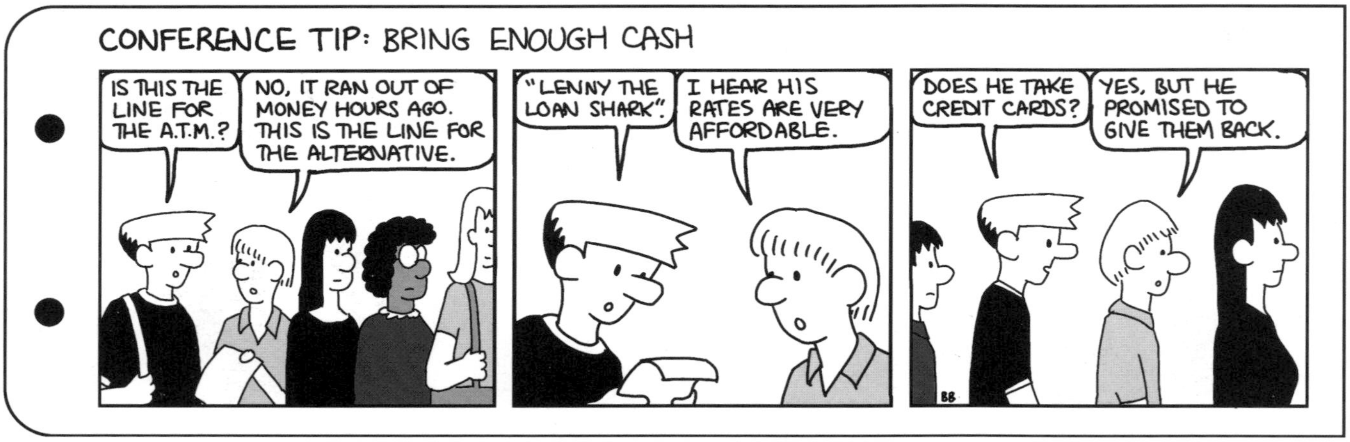
CONFERENCE TIP: BRING ENOUGH CASH
IS THIS THE LINE FOR THE A.T.M.?
NO, IT RAN OUT OF MONEY HOURS AGO. THIS IS THE LINE FOR THE ALTERNATIVE.
"LENNY THE LOAN SHARK".
I HEAR HIS RATES ARE VERY AFFORDABLE.
DOES HE TAKE CREDIT CARDS?
YES, BUT HE PROMISED TO GIVE THEM BACK.
BB

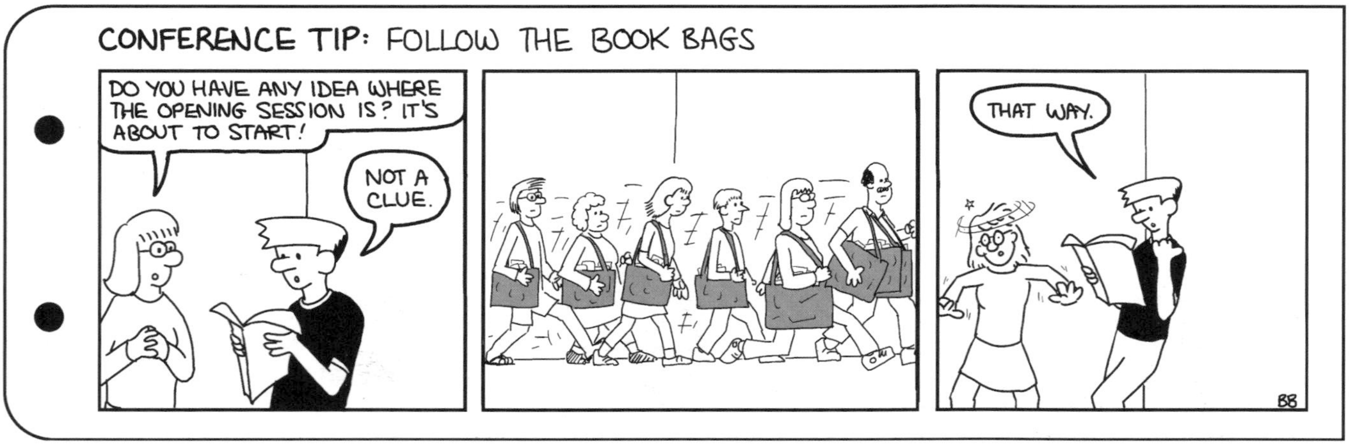
CONFERENCE TIP: FOLLOW THE BOOK BAGS
DO YOU HAVE ANY IDEA WHERE THE OPENING SESSION IS? IT'S ABOUT TO START!
NOT A CLUE.
THAT WAY.
BB

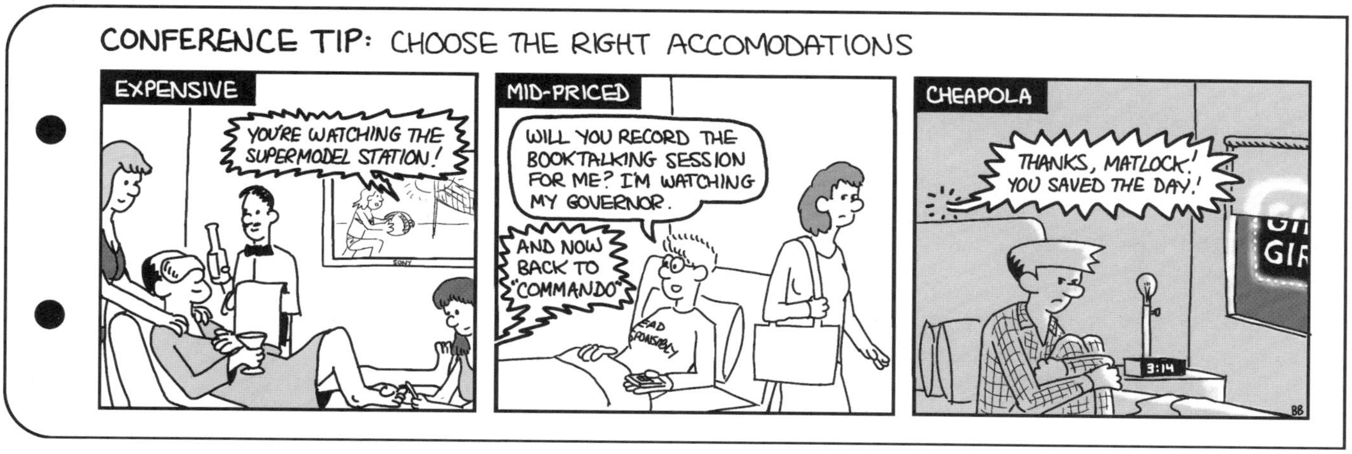
CONFERENCE TIP: CHOOSE THE RIGHT ACCOMODATIONS
EXPENSIVE
YOU'RE WATCHING THE SUPERMODEL STATION!
MID-PRICED
WILL YOU RECORD THE BOOKTALKING SESSION FOR ME? I'M WATCHING MY GOVERNOR.
AND NOW BACK TO "COMMANDO"
CHEAPOLA
THANKS, MATLOCK! YOU SAVED THE DAY!
3:14

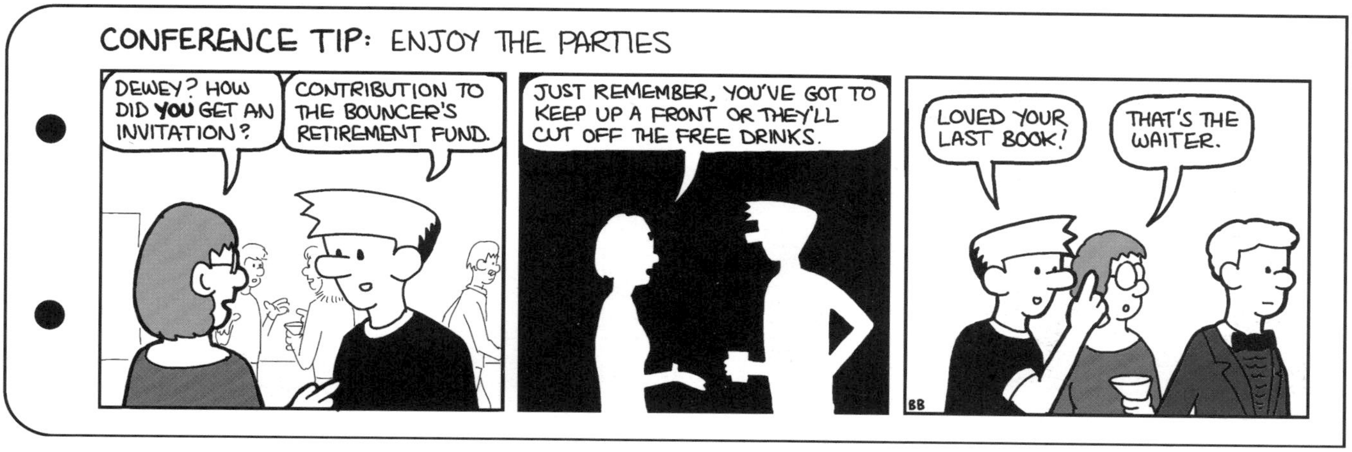
CONFERENCE TIP: ENJOY THE PARTIES
DEWEY? HOW DID YOU GET AN INVITATION?
CONTRIBUTION TO THE BOUNCER'S RETIREMENT FUND.
JUST REMEMBER, YOU'VE GOT TO KEEP UP A FRONT OR THEY'LL CUT OFF THE FREE DRINKS.
LOVED YOUR LAST BOOK!
THAT'S THE WAITER.

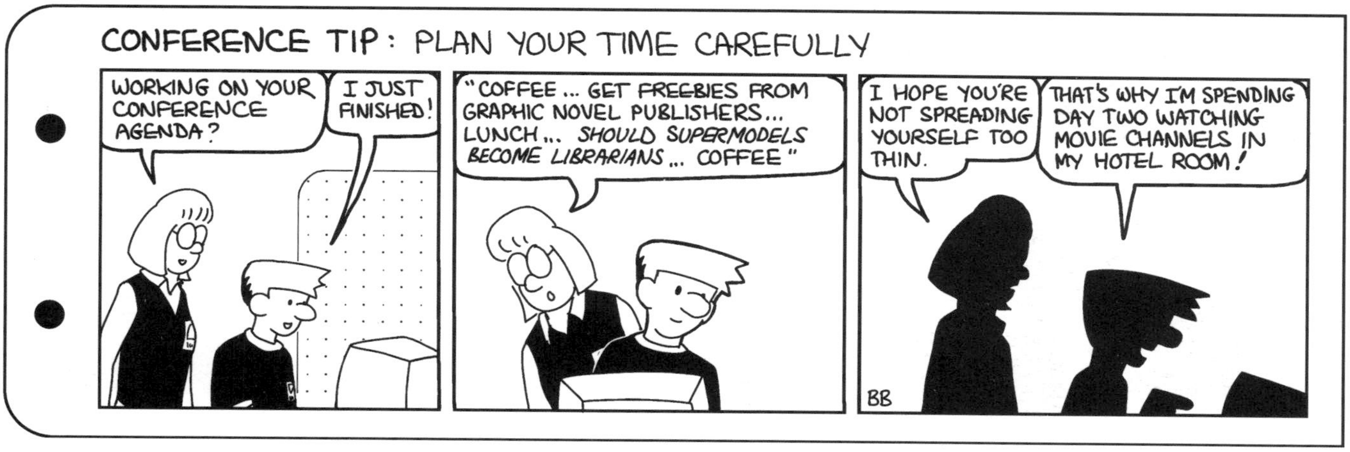
CONFERENCE TIP: PLAN YOUR TIME CAREFULLY
WORKING ON YOUR CONFERENCE AGENDA?
I JUST FINISHED!
"COFFEE ... GET FREEBIES FROM GRAPHIC NOVEL PUBLISHERS... LUNCH... SHOULD SUPERMODELS BECOME LIBRARIANS... COFFEE"
I HOPE YOU'RE NOT SPREADING YOURSELF TOO THIN.
THAT'S WHY I'M SPENDING DAY TWO WATCHING MOVIE CHANNELS IN MY HOTEL ROOM!

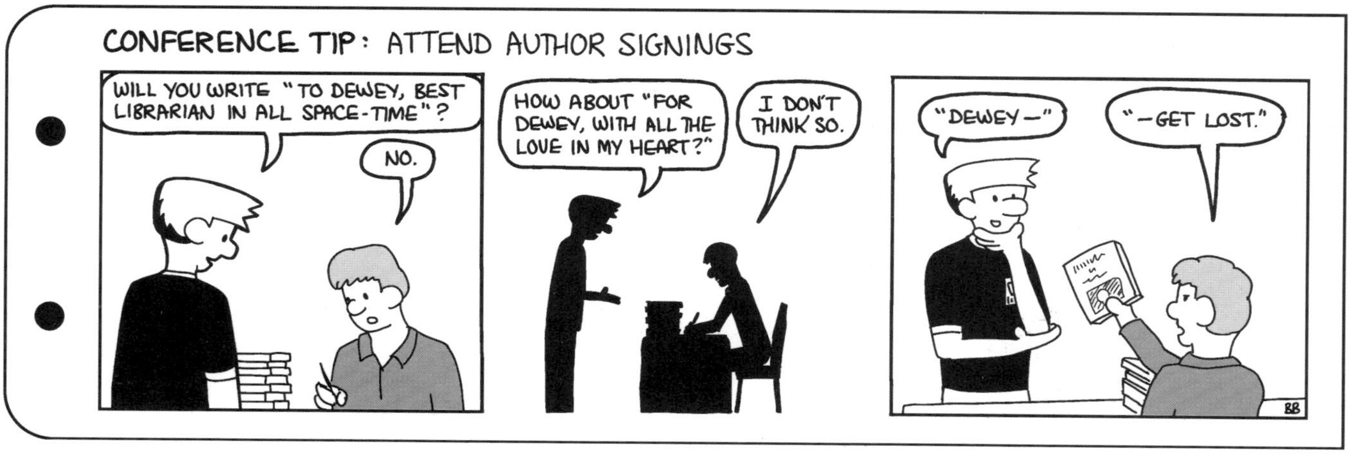
CONFERENCE TIP: ATTEND AUTHOR SIGNINGS
WILL YOU WRITE "TO DEWEY, BEST LIBRARIAN IN ALL SPACE-TIME"?
NO.
HOW ABOUT "FOR DEWEY, WITH ALL THE LOVE IN MY HEART?"
I DON'T THINK SO.
"DEWEY —"
"— GET LOST."

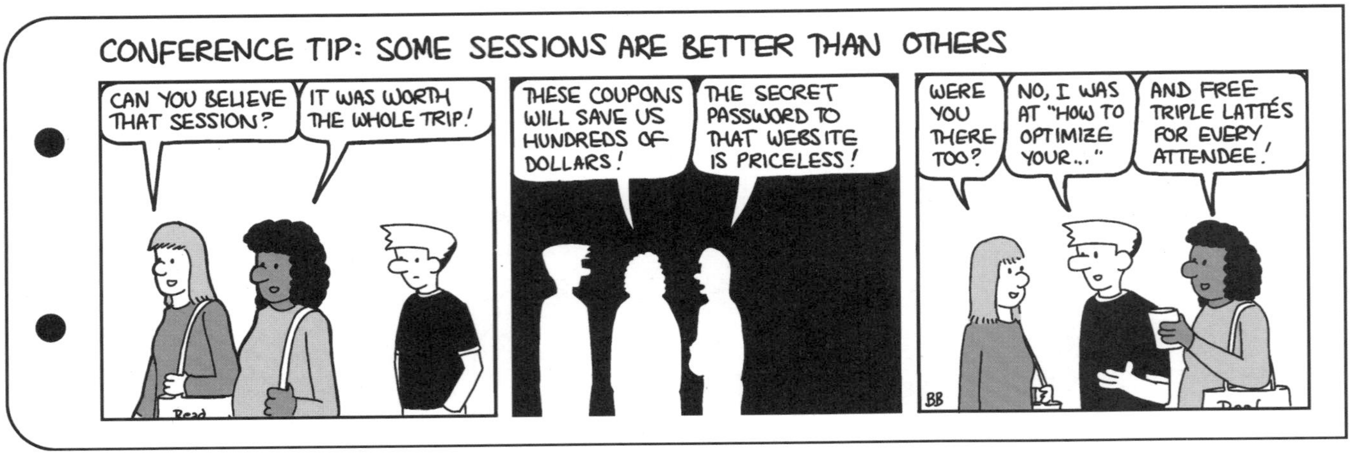
CONFERENCE TIP: SOME SESSIONS ARE BETTER THAN OTHERS
CAN YOU BELIEVE THAT SESSION?
IT WAS WORTH THE WHOLE TRIP!
THESE COUPONS WILL SAVE US HUNDREDS OF DOLLARS!
THE SECRET PASSWORD TO THAT WEBSITE IS PRICELESS!
WERE YOU THERE TOO?
NO, I WAS AT "HOW TO OPTIMIZE YOUR..."
AND FREE TRIPLE LATTÉS FOR EVERY ATTENDEE!
BB

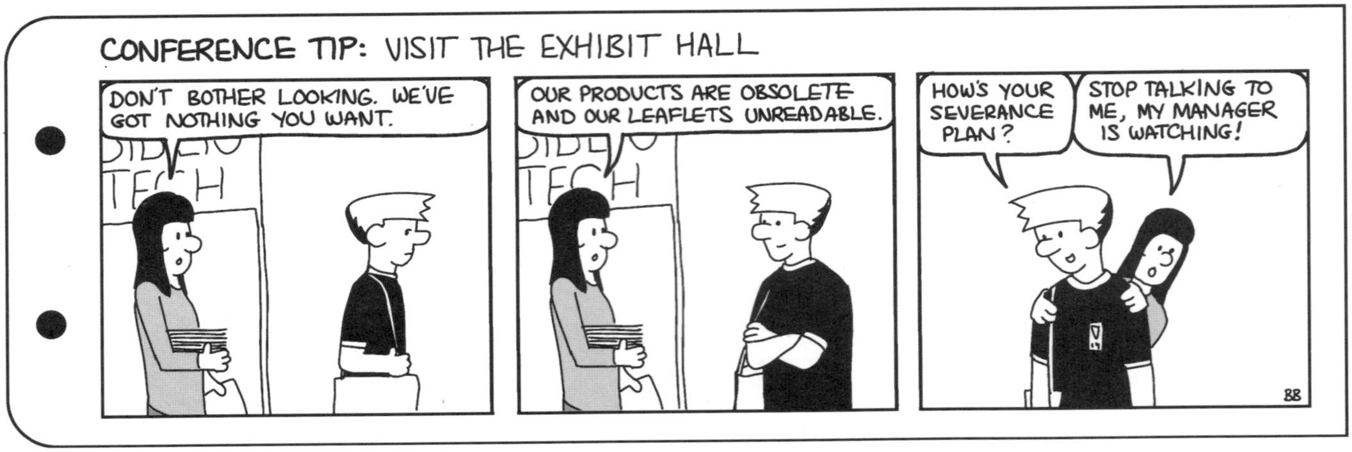
CONFERENCE TIP: VISIT THE EXHIBIT HALL
DON'T BOTHER LOOKING. WE'VE GOT NOTHING YOU WANT.
OUR PRODUCTS ARE OBSOLETE AND OUR LEAFLETS UNREADABLE.
HOW'S YOUR SEVERANCE PLAN?
STOP TALKING TO ME, MY MANAGER IS WATCHING!
BB

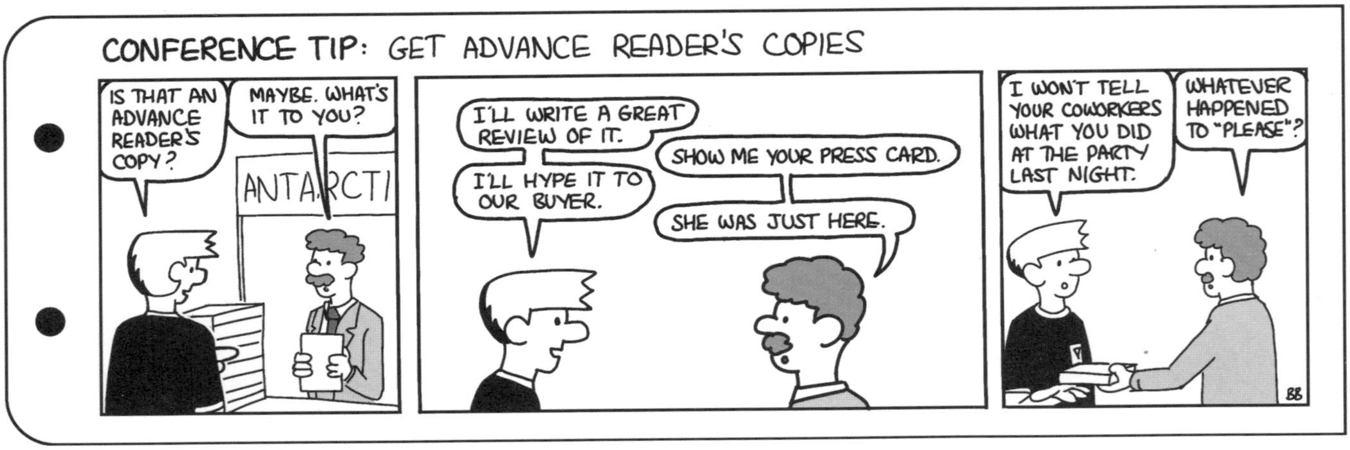
CONFERENCE TIP: GET ADVANCE READER'S COPIES
IS THAT AN ADVANCE READER'S COPY?
MAYBE. WHAT'S IT TO YOU?
ANTARCTI
I'LL WRITE A GREAT REVIEW OF IT.
SHOW ME YOUR PRESS CARD.
I'LL HYPE IT TO OUR BUYER.
SHE WAS JUST HERE.
I WON'T TELL YOUR COWORKERS WHAT YOU DID AT THE PARTY LAST NIGHT.
WHATEVER HAPPENED TO "PLEASE"?
BB